The construction of deeds and statutes

Charles Edwin Odgers

THE CONSTRUCTION

OF

DEEDS AND STATUTES

BY

SIR CHARLES E. ODGERS, M.A., B.C.L.,

OF THE MIDDLE TEMPLE, BARRISTER-AT-LAW, LATE PUISNE
JUDGE OF THE HIGH COURT OF JUDICATURE AT MADRAS

LONDON:

SWEET & MAXWELL, LIMITED,

2 & 3 CHANCERY LANE, W.C.2

TORONTO:	AUSTRALIA:
THE CARSWELL COMPANY, LIMITED	LAW BOOK CO. OF AUSTRALASIA, (PTY), LIMITED

1939

(Printed in England)

PRINTED IN GREAT BRITAIN BY
THE EASTERN PRESS, LTD , LONDON AND READING

PREFACE.

THIS book is intended for students and others beginning the study of the interpretation of Deeds and Statutes. It makes no claim to originality and the debt I owe to the standard works of Norton, Maxwell and Craies will be at once apparent. It is felt that these well-known embodiments of the law on the subject are somewhat formidable to students and this book is an attempt to state concisely the leading principles contained therein. This has involved a method of selection and compression with all the chances of omission of important matters and faults of expression to which it is liable. It is hoped, however, that, so far as it goes, the work is accurate and comprehensible. Trained as I have been in a deep respect for Judicial authority, the quotations from judgments and the cases quoted are perhaps too numerous. I felt, however, that the selection of cases—very numerous on every point in this subject—might remain in case at any time it was thought that the book needed expansion or any points further elucidation. If so, I believe the cases referred to will supply these needs.

I have prepared the Index with some completeness in order that it may form a summary of the contents of the book. This may be a help to students.

I have pleasure in acknowledging the generous help I have received from my friend and former colleague, Professor Harold Potter of King's College, London. He has not only kindly read most of the book in proof and advised me on numerous points from his greater experience as a writer of legal text-books, but has guided me through the pitfalls of conveyancing — always a terror to a common lawyer like myself — in so far as this subject comes within the purview of the book. I also owe a special debt of gratitude to Professor John Willis of the Dalhousie Law School, N.S, who has generously allowed me to use the substance of a very suggestive article of his in the Canadian Bar Review entitled "Statute Interpretation in a Nutshell". This forms the basis of the last section of the book—"Methods of Construction".

I should like to add my thanks to my wife who has helped me in the irksome and monotonous task of preparing and checking the Table of Cases and to all concerned with the production of the book for their signal success in interpreting what I know to be an almost illegible script.

C. E. O.

1 BRICK COURT,
   TEMPLE
     March 14, 1939.

(v)

TABLE OF CONTENTS

TABLE OF CASES

A.

TABLE OF CASES.

THE CONSTRUCTION OF DEEDS AND STATUTES

PART I

DEEDS AND OTHER INSTRUMENTS

I.—The Nature of a Deed

In this book it is proposed to set out the main general principles adopted by the Courts in construing and interpreting deeds (including other instruments) and statutes The large number of cases extending over centuries bear witness to the fact that this duty of construction is an everyday occurrence in our Courts, and it is therefore important that those who desire to practice the law should have studied the outlines of the subject.

Definition of a deed.—All deeds are documents, but not all documents are deeds For instance, a legend chalked on a brick wall, or a writing tattooed on a sailor's back may be documents but they are not deeds. A deed is, therefore, a particular kind of document. It must be a *writing* and a writing on *paper* or its like, *e.g.*, vellum or parchment Any instrument under seal is a deed if made between private persons (Odgers, *Common Law*, Vol II, p. 13). It must be *signed, sealed* and *delivered*. It must either (*a*) effect the transference of an interest, right or property, or (*b*) create an obligation binding on some person, or (*c*) confirm some act whereby an interest, right or property has already passed.

"Writing" includes print "A charter of feoffment is a deed; so is a gift or grant; power of attorney; a release or disclaimer. I would go further and say that any instrument delivered as a deed and which either itself passes an interest in property or is in affirmance or confirmation of something whereby an interest or property passes is a deed. . . . I by no means say that I have enumerated all the possible kinds of deeds, there may be others "[1]

By the common law, signing was not essential to a deed, as long as it was sealed and delivered. All people can now either write their names or make their mark, so by section 73 of the Law of Property Act, 1925, the executant must either sign or place his mark on the deed, and sealing alone is not sufficient. Many documents under seal are not deeds, e.g., a diploma of a degree or a certificate of having passed an examination Bovill, C.J., said in the case cited[2]: " Many documents under seal are not deeds, for instance, an award, though sealed. Again, a will is often under seal. So is a certificate of magistrates, a certificate of admission to the College of Physicians or to other learned bodies. So is a share certificate. Yet it can hardly be said that all these are deeds. The probate of a will is very similar, it is given under the seal, formerly of the Ordinary, now of the Court of Probate. It is a certificate of the will having been proved and administration granted; but I never heard it suggested that it is a deed."

Deed, when required.[3]—A deed, as opposed to an instrument in writing or document (including books, maps, plans, drawings and photographs[4]), was required by the common law in all cases in which writing was necessary,

---

[1] *Per* Bovill, C J , in *R* v. *Morton* (1873), L R 2 C. C R 22, at p 29 He omitted contracts under seal. A memorandum of association is not a deed, though it may have the effect of a deed *Re Whitley Partners, Ltd* (1886), 32 Ch D. 337.

[2] *S C* , at p. 27

[3] See generally, Littleton's Tenures.

[4] Evidence Act, 1938, s 6 (1)

for in olden days it was only by a man's seal that his writing could be evidenced and accordingly the seal of the executant of the writing was essential. So by the common law, conveyances of incorporeal hereditaments, all releases, conditions in defeasance of freeholds, and powers of attorney had to be made by deed. There are also very many statutes requiring deeds for various transactions. A few may be cited: bargain and sale; conveyances of corporeal hereditaments; disentailing assurances; dispositions of married women under the Fines and Recoveries Act, 1833; assignments of chattel interests; under the Conveyancing Act, 1881, under the Law of Property Act, 1925 (ss. 52, 53); alienations of contingent or future interests; appointment of new trustees; leases under the Settled Land Acts; transfers of shares; transfers of British ships (Merchant Shipping Act, 1894), and many more of less importance. Equity follows the law as to formalities, but, as we shall see, was never hampered by notions of the sanctity of a deed, and in fact never insisted on deeds for matters purely within its jurisdiction, though equity was often affected by statutes requiring writing, *e g* , for the creation of a trust of lands, or the assignment of a trust, required by the Statute of Frauds. All conveyances of land or of any interest therein must be by deed, subject to certain exceptions, the most important of which are surrenders by operation of law or which the law does not require to be evidenced by writing, leases or tenancies or other assurances not required by law to be in writing, and conveyances taking effect by operation of law (Law of Property Act, 1925, s. 52 (1) (2)).

Deeds when void or voidable.—The plea is *non est factum*—it has not been done—by the person sought to be charged owing to some mistake on his own part or to some misrepresentation by the other party. It applies not only to deeds but to other written contracts.[5] If there has been

---

[5] *Foster* v. *Mackinnon* (1869), L. R 4 C. P. 704, 711 Cf. *Westminster Bank* v *Wilson*, [1938] 3 All E R. 652

a fraudulent misrepresentation as to the nature of the
document, the executant may avoid it notwithstanding that
rights under it have been acquired by an innocent third party
and that, at least in the case of a negotiable instrument, he
was himself guilty of negligence in signing it.[6] If, however,
the executant knows the nature of the document as apart from
its contents, he cannot rely on the plea as regards third
parties, though the document may be voidable as between
the immediate parties thereto.[7] As Mellish, L J., said [8]:
"When a man knows that he is conveying or doing something with his estate, but does not ask what is the precise
effect of the deed, because he is told it is a mere form, and
has such confidence in his solicitor as to execute the deed in
ignorance, then a deed so executed, although it may be
voidable on the ground of fraud, is not a void deed."

Lunatics —Formerly the deed of a lunatic was not voidable
by himself, but is now voidable by his committee or heir, or
by himself if the other party knew of his lunacy or such
facts about the alleged lunatic that he must be taken to have
known of it [9] A deed poll by a lunatic so found by inquisition of her property during a lucid interval is void, while
the inquisition is in force,[10] and so is a charge given by a
man whose estate is the subject of a receivership order under
the Lunacy Act, 1890.[11]

Signing.—This, as stated above, was not essential, though
very usual, till 1925. Before that date a document was

---

[6] *Carlisle and Cumberland Banking Co v Bragg*, [1911] 1 K. B 489;
Bank of Ireland v *McManamy*, [1916] 2 Ir. R. 161

[7] *National Provincial Bank* v. *Jackson* (1886), 33 Ch D 1, 10; *Howatson*
v *Webb*, [1908] 1 Ch 1; *Blay* v *Pollard*, [1930] 1 K B 628 Cf *Chitty*,
Contracts (19th ed), 359

[8] In *Hunter* v *Walters* (1871), L R 7 Ch 75, at p. 88.

[9] *Molton* v *Camroux* (1848), 2 Ex 487; (1849), 4 Ex. 17, *Imperial
Loan Co* v. *Stone*, [1892] 1 Q B. 599; *York Glass Co , Ltd* v *Jubb*
(1925), 42 T. L R. 1

[10] *Re Walker*, [1905] 1 Ch 160

[11] *Re Marshall*, [1920] 1 Ch. 284

sometimes required to be "under hand and seal" as in the
execution of a power, so that signing was essential, though
the deed, as such, was valid without it. See now Law of
Property Act, 1925, s. 73. For the admissibility of a statement in a "document" as evidence under the Evidence Act,
1938,[12] the document must have been written, made or
produced, or signed or initialed by the person deemed to
have made the statement, or otherwise recognised by him in
writing as one for the accuracy of which he is responsible.

Sealing.—An ancient essential of a deed. Before writing
became a general accomplishment, a man signified his assent
to a document by impressing it with his seal. "No writing
without a seal can be a deed", says Sheppard, Touchstone
(56). Any seal, however, will do; it need not necessarily
be that of the executant, he may use a borrowed one "To
constitute a sealing neither wax nor wafer nor a piece of
paper nor even an impression is necessary."[13] As long as
some act is done with the intention of sealing, that is sufficient.
In one case[14] where a transfer of shares contained no impression but only a place for a seal, though the attestation clause
stated that it had been "signed, sealed and delivered",
North, J., refused to assume that the document had been
sealed, but the document was inoperative for another reason.
Nowadays a wafer with a design on it is frequently used.
It is a question of fact as to whether a deed was or was not
sealed by a particular person.[15]

This indulgence in the matter of sealing does not extend
to companies, building societies or industrial and provident
societies. Their deeds must be executed in accordance with
their articles of association and be sealed with a formal
engraved seal Where a seal had never been affixed and an

---

[12] 1 & 2 Geo 6, c 28, s 1 (4).
[13] *R v Inhabitants of St Paul, Covent Garden* (1845), 7 Q B 232,
per Bovill, C J.
[14] *Re Balkis Consolidated, Ltd* (1888), 36 W R 392
[15] *National Provincial Bank* v. *Jackson, supra*

attesting witness was not called, the Court held that it could not presume sealing.[16]

Delivery.—This is an essential element in a deed, which takes effect not from its date but from delivery. "After a deed is written and sealed, if it be not delivered, all the rest is to no purpose" (Termes de la Ley). "Where a contract is to be by deed, there must be delivery to perfect it." [17] Delivery signified the handing over of something, for instance, land, or an intangible interest in it, which could not be actually transferred by hand as a chattel could be

The ordinary form of words used is " I deliver this as my act and deed ", but there need be no words. Any act of the party which shows that he intended to deliver the deed as an instrument binding on him is enough He must make it his deed [18] and recognise it as presently binding on him.

Delivery is none the less complete and effective because the grantor retains the deed in his own possession, so that it was early recognised that the deed need not be physically delivered to the other party to the deed. "The efficacy of a deed depends on its being sealed and delivered by the maker of it, not on his ceasing to retain possession of it." [19] "Was it essential that the deed should be given out of the defendant's possession in order to its perfect delivery as an operative instrument? I know of no such necessity in law or good sense." [20]

Corporations —It has been much discussed as to whether delivery of deeds by corporations is essential or whether the sealing in that case is equivalent to delivery [21] The better

---

[16] *Re Smith* (1892), 67 L T 64 Cf *Re Sandilands* (1871), 6 C P. 411.
[17] *Per* Martin, B., in *Xenos* v. *Wickham* (1863), 14 C. B (N.S) 435, at p 473.
[18] *Tupper* v. *Foulkes* (1861), 9 C. B. (N s) 797; *Xenos* v *Wickham* (1867), L. R. 2 H L. 296, at p. 302; *Re Seymour*, [1913] 1 Ch 475.
[19] *Xenos* v *Wickham, supra, per* Lord Cranworth, at p 323.
[20] *Ibid , per* Pigott, B , at p 309
[21] See the discussion of the cases in Norton (2nd ed), pp. 11-13.

opinion seems to be that though sealing *prima facie* imports delivery, yet if it be intended otherwise it is not so.[22] In the case of debentures it was said by Cotton, L.J., that they must be delivered before they can be binding on the company. "The fact of their being dated and sealed does not show that they were delivered."[23] The old law required delivery to be made by a corporation at a corporate meeting, but in modern times it has long been the practice for directors of joint stock and trading companies to execute deeds on behalf of their companies without calling a meeting of the company, which would include the shareholders, for otherwise the business of these companies could not be carried on. The authority for this is the statutory force given to the articles of association of joint stock companies by the Companies Act, 1929, ss. 8, 20.

Escrow.—This is a limitation or condition on the delivery, and therefore on the effect, of a deed. The delivery is made subject to a condition or the happening of some event; in fact, the document is not an operative deed if it has such a contingency attached to it until such time as the contingency is resolved, *i.e.*, the condition is fulfilled or the event takes place. "The maker may so deliver it as to suspend or qualify its binding effect. He may declare that it shall have no effect until a certain time has arrived or till some condition has been performed, but when the time has arrived or the condition has been performed, the delivery becomes absolute and the maker of the deed is absolutely bound by it, whether he has parted with the possession or not. Until the specified time has arrived, or the condition has been performed, the instrument is not a deed. It is a mere escrow."[24] Sheppard (Touch. 59) mentions two forms of escrow: (*a*) where the

[22] *Mayor, etc., of Merchants of the Staple of England* v. *Governor and Co of Bank of England* (1887), 21 Q B D 160, at p. 165

[23] *Mowatt* v *Castle Steel and Iron Works Co* (1886), 34 Ch D 58

[24] *Per* Lord Cranworth in *Xenos* v *Wickham, supra*, at p 323; *Macedo* v *Stroud*, [1922] 2 A. C. 330, 337 (P C)

deed is delivered to a third party to be delivered to the grantee on the fulfilment of the condition, thus necessitating a second delivery by the third party to the grantee, and (*b*) where the deed is delivered to the grantee directly but made subject to a condition; in this case there is, of course, no necessity for a second delivery and the deed takes effect as soon as the condition is fulfilled or the event happens. Sheppard is of opinion that the latter may not be a safe procedure and suggests that the first is the only effective way to constitute an escrow, declaring also that apt words must be used, *i.e.*, the instrument must be distinctly delivered to the third party as an escrow. The modern law is that no express words are necessary: "It was not necessary that any express words should be used at the time. The conclusion was to be drawn from all the circumstances." [25] "It is quite settled that it is not necessary in delivering an instrument as an escrow to say that it is delivered as an escrow." [26] Evidence is admissible " to show the character in which and the terms upon which the deed was so delivered ".[27]

It is a question of intention, and " though it is in form an absolute delivery if it can be reasonably inferred (from the evidence) that it was delivered not to take effect as a deed till a certain condition was performed, it will nevertheless operate as an escrow ".[28] Evidence is admissible of circumstances either before or simultaneous with the delivery of the instrument, but not subsequent to the delivery; evidence as to the circumstances at the time of the delivery are, of course, relevant evidence.[29] If a grantee is in possession of

[25] *Per* Abbott, C J., in *Murray* v *Earl of Stair* (1823), 2 B & C 82, at p 88

[26] *Per* Lord Sugden, L C , in *Nash* v *Flynn* (1844), 1 Jo & Lat. 162, at p 175 see also *Watkins* v. *Nash* (1875), L R. 20 Eq. 262, at p 266.

[27] *Per* Lindley, L J., in *London Freehold and Leasehold Property Co.* v. *Suffield*, [1897] 2 Ch 608, at p. 621

[28] *Per* Parke, B , in *Bowker* v *Burdekin* (1843), 11 M & W. 128, at p 147, *Governors, etc , of Foundling Hospital* v. *Crane*, [1911] 2 K. B 367.

[29] *Davis* v *Jones* (1856), 17 C B. 625, at p. 634

a deed which had been delivered to a third person as an escrow (see *supra*) it is cogent *prima facie* evidence that the matter on which the delivery was made contingent has been performed or fulfilled.[30] When once the condition has been fulfilled no further delivery is necessary and the deed takes effect automatically. An escrow cannot be delivered to take effect at the death of the grantor, for that is necessarily testamentary and is in fact a will, which is governed by other considerations.[31] As to the first of Sheppard's propositions—that the deed was to be delivered to a stranger—this is no longer the law, and a conveyance may be held to be an escrow till the purchase-money is paid without any delivery to a third party As stated above, it is a question of the intention with which the deed was delivered.

Attestation.—This is not necessary to the validity of a deed, but in practice is invariably adopted and in some cases attestation is required by law. The commonest examples are wills, bills of sale, conveyances to charitable uses under the Mortmain Act; marriage registers; powers of attorney to transfer, and receive dividends on, colonial stock; and all agreements, alterations of agreements, releases and indentures of apprenticeship executed under the Merchant Shipping Act, 1894.[32] The witness must sign as a witness and for the purpose of attesting the execution and consequently a party to a deed cannot be a witness The meaning of attestation is " that one or more persons are present at the time of the execution *for that purpose* (*i.e* , for the purpose of attesting the execution) and that as evidence thereof they sign the attestation clause, stating such execution ".[33] Directors in whose presence the seal of a corporation is affixed to a document are not strictly witnesses to the deed, they attest the

---

[30] *Hare* v *Horton* (1833), 5 B & Ad 715
[31] *Governors, etc , of Foundling Hospital* v *Crane, supra*
[32] For a complete list see Taylor, *Evidence* (12th ed), 1840, 1841.
[33] *Per* Lord Romilly, M R , in *Wickham* v *Marquis of Bath* (1865), L. R. 1 Eq 17, at p 24

sealing only as part of that operation. Section 74 of the Law of Property Act, 1925, provides as follows: (1) That in favour of a purchaser a deed is duly executed by a corporation if the seal is affixed in the presence of and attested by the clerk or other official and a member of the governing body. (2) The governing body of a company may appoint a general or special agent to execute any agreement not under seal in relation to any matter within the powers of the corporation. (3) Where an agent is to execute a deed he will be authorised by a power of attorney or some statutory or other power. He may execute by signing the name of the corporation in the presence of at least one witness and affixing his own seal. These provisions are without prejudice to any other mode of execution authorised by law or practice or the articles or other instrument constituting the corporation. In *Re British Games, Ltd*, a contract signed by a director and the secretary of a company was held to have been duly executed in accordance with section 29 of the Companies Act, 1929, although no seal was affixed.[34] It is important to note that " it is well-known law that an agent cannot execute a deed or do any part of the execution which makes it a deed, unless he is appointed under seal ".[35] As to execution under powers of attorney, see further sections 123, 124, 126 and 127 of the Law of Property Act, 1925, and section 25 of the Trustee Act, 1925

Indentures and Deeds Poll.—The difference between these two kinds of deeds is no longer of importance. Formerly indentures were deeds with serrated or indented edges so that each party had a similar deed and they were supposed to fit together as a sort of tally " All the parts of a deed indented in judgment of law do make up but one deed " (Shep. Touch. 52). Therefore they applied only where there were at least

---

[34] [1938] Ch. 240 See also Companies Act, 1929, s. 29; Table A, art 71; Table C, art. 33
[35] *Per* Bowen, L.J , in *Powell* v. *London and Provincial Bank*, [1893] 2 Ch. 555, at p 563.

two parties to a deed, whereas a deed poll, *i.e* , with a shaven
or straight edge, applied to a unilateral deed   Even to-day
we hear of people changing their names by "deed poll".
By section 57 of the Law of Property Act, 1925, any deed,
whether an indenture or not, may be simply described as a
deed, mortgage, charge, trust deed and so on according to the
transaction intended to be effected—all technical words as to
description of a deed are thus rendered unnecessary.   Another
distinction followed on that between deeds poll and indentures.
Under the former, the person with whom the covenant was
made could always sue on it, though he was, of course, no
party to the deed (*i.e.*, joined as an executant of it), whereas
in the case of an indenture or a deed *inter partes,* the old
rule was that nobody not a party could sue. If, for instance,
A covenanted with B to convey land to C, C not being a
party could not sue   This is analogous to the rule in the
law of contract—that a person not a party to the contract
cannot sue, though the contract may have been made for his
benefit.   However, the old rule has gone as far as deeds are
concerned.   The Real Property Act of 1845, s. 5, made an
exception in the case of indentures executed after October 1,
1845, by enacting that an immediate estate or interest in *any
tenements or hereditaments* and the benefit of any condition
or covenant respecting such may be taken, although the taker
thereof be not named as a party to the indenture. So in 1908
Farwell, L.J., said in *Forster* v. *Elvet Colliery Co.*[36]: "The
old rule of law that no one can sue on a covenant in an
indenture who is not mentioned as a party to it (*Berkeley*
v *Hardy* (1826), 5 B & C. 355) still holds good, except so
far as it has been altered by the Real Property Act, 1845,
s. 5." Now all distinction is abolished, and by section 56 (1)
of the Law of Property Act, 1925, "A person may take
an immediate or other interest in land or other property, or
the benefit of any condition, right of entry, covenant or

---

[36] [1908] 1 K. B. 629.

agreement over or respecting land or other property, although he may not be named as a party to the conveyance or other instrument ''.

Writing required as opposed to a deed.—(1) No interest in land can be created or disposed of except by writing signed by the person creating or conveying the same or his agent authorised in writing or by will or by operation of law.

(2) A declaration of trust must be proved by writing signed by some person able to declare such trust or by his will.

(3) A disposition of an equitable interest or trust must be in writing signed by the person disposing of the same or his agent authorised in writing or by will.[37]

Parol.—All interests in land created by parol are to have effect as interests at will only, except leases in possession for a term not exceeding three years at the best rent that can reasonably be obtained without taking a fine.

II.—ALTERATIONS AND ERASURES

An instrument may come before the Court for construction with all the requisite essentials of a deed indicated above, but with obvious interlineations or erasures or other alterations in it. How should the Court deal with these?

Presumptions.—The presumption is in the case of deeds that these were made prior to execution. In the case of a will the presumption is that they were made after execution In either case the presumption may be displaced by evidence.

In the case of documents not under seal, the party relying on the document must show when the alterations were made,

---

[37] Law of Property Act, 1925, s. 53.

unless it is obvious that they were made before the document was signed. It also lies upon him to explain the alterations.[1] The rules as to the effect of alterations in deeds apply also to documents under hand only—as those not under seal are called. The presumption in the case of deeds is supposed to rest on the principle that " a deed cannot be altered after it is executed, without fraud or wrong, and the presumption is against fraud or wrong ".[2] However, this seems to apply equally to the case of documents under hand only, and it is doubtful if this is the real ground of the rule, though there is no doubt that the rule exists " And this is consistent with good sense, for every deed expresses the mind of the parties at the time of its execution; and so, to alter it afterwards, would be fraudulent and in many cases highly criminal." [3]

Sometimes a common printed form is used with additions and alterations made in writing. In case of doubt as to the meaning of the document it appears that the written words should be given more weight than the printed, " inasmuch as the written words are the immediate language and terms selected by the parties themselves for the expression of their meaning ",[4] whereas the printed matter is common form applying not only to the case of the particular party or parties using it, but to numerous others.

Effect of alterations.—It was held in *Pigot's Case* [5] that all alterations in a deed made after execution rendered it void, no matter whether the alterations were material or not. " The strictness of the rule on this subject as laid down in

---

[1] *Henman* v. *Dickenson* (1828), 5 Bing 183, *Knight* v *Clements* (1838), 8 Ad. & El 215; *Cariss* v *Tattersall* (1841), 2 Man & G 890, *Clifford* v *Parker* (1841), 2 Man & G 909

[2] *Per* Lord Campbell, C J , in *Doe* v *Catomore* (1851), 16 Q B. 745

[3] *Per* Lord Cranworth, V -C , in *Simmons* v *Rudall* (1851), 1 Sim (N s) 115, at p 136 As to interlined words in a holograph will, cf *In the goods of Benn*, [1938] Ir. R 313

[4] *Per* Lord Ellenborough, C J , in *Robertson* v *French* (1803), 4 East 130, at p 136. See *infra*, p 43

[5] (1615), 11 Rep 266.

Pigot's Case can only be explained on the principle that a party who has the custody of an instrument made for his benefit is bound to preserve it in its original state. . . . The party who may suffer has no right to complain, since there cannot be any alteration except through fraud or laches on his part " [6] In this case the alteration was the affixing of the seal by some person unknown. It was said that under the rule in *Pigot's Case* even the act of a stranger will invalidate the deed.

Mr. Norton (p. 35) is of opinion that the rule as expressed is too wide and states that no case can be found where the effect of a deed operating at the moment of its execution has been nullified by having been altered after execution; *e.g.*, a conveyance takes effect to pass the property in the land at the moment the conveyance is duly executed, and no alteration made thereafter will have the effect of avoiding the conveyance and revesting the property conveyed.[7] The same principle has been applied to the cancellation of a deed after execution [8]

The point is made clear by Lord Abinger, C.B., in *Davidson* v. *Cooper*,[9] in the Court of Exchequer: "The moment after their execution the deeds become valueless, so far as they relate to the passing of the estate, except as affording evidence of the fact that they were executed. If the effect of the execution of such deeds was to create a title to the land in question, that title cannot be affected by the subsequent alteration of the deeds: and the rule in *Pigot's Case* would not be applicable " The learned Chief Baron went on to say that if the party is proceeding, not to recover the land already conveyed, but on covenants in the deed, any

[6] *Per* Lord Denman, C J , in *Davidson* v *Cooper* (1844), 13 M. & W. 343, at p 352

[7] Holroyd, J., in *Doe* v *Bingham* (1821), 4 B. & Ald 672, 677.

[8] *Bolton* v *Bishop of Carlisle* (1793), 2 Hy Bl. 259, at p 263; *Magennis* v *MacCullogh* (1714-25), Gilb Eq Rep 235, *Roe* v. *Archbishop of York* (1805), 6 East 86; *Doe* v *Thomas* (1829), 9 B & C. 288.

[9] (1843), 11 M & W 778.

material alteration (he adds, even by a stranger) after its execution would defeat the right of the party suing. An altered deed even in a material part is not void *ab initio*; it ceases to have any new operation or to give a cause of action on any pending obligation which would have arisen if it had remained in its original state.[10]

An altered deed may even be given in evidence to prove a right or title produced by its execution or any collateral fact,[11] and this is so even if it is tendered in evidence by the person responsible for the alteration.

What is a material alteration?—This is a question of law.[12] No general principle can be stated, except that it must be an alteration in some essential part of the deed or document, as, for instance, the erasure of the numbers on Bank of England notes[13] "Any alteration seems to me material which would affect the business effect of the instrument, if used for any business purpose."[14]

The principle of *Pigot's Case (supra)* was applied to negotiable instruments by *Master* v *Miller*,[15] and a promissory note was held to have been materially altered by causing an additional maker to sign as a joint and several maker,[16] and an unauthorised alteration of a general acceptance by the addition of a place of payment was held to discharge the acceptor even against a *bona fide* holder without notice.[17] On the other hand, the insertion of the Christian name of the attorney in a power of attorney is immaterial[18] Where the

[10] *Per* Lord Campbell, C J , in *Agricultural Cattle Insurance Co.* v *Fitzgerald* (1851), 16 Q. B 432, at p 440
[11] *Ibid , Earl of Falmouth* v *Roberts* (1842), 9 M & W. 469, *Pattinson* v. *Luckley* (1875), L R 10 Exch 330
[12] *Vance* v. *Lowther* (1876), 1 Ex D 176
[13] *Suffell* v. *Bank of England* (1882), 9 Q. B D. 555, at pp. 562-8, 572-4. Cf. Bills of Exchange Act, 1882, s 64, and Chalmers (10th ed), p 256
[14] *Per* Brett, L J., *loc cit*
[15] (1793), 5 T R 367
[16] *Gardner* v *Walsh* (1855), 5 E & B. 83
[17] *Burchfield* v *Moore* (1854), 3 E & B 683, 686
[18] *Eagleton* v. *Gutteridge* (1843), 11 M & W 465, 468

description of the shares and their numbers were filled in after sealing by the company, and the shares were registered, the transaction was held not to have been thereby invalidated by the transfer deed having been thus executed in an incomplete form.[19]

An immaterial alteration has no effect either on the deed or on the rights of any of the parties. In an immaterial alteration is included anything which would have been implied in the deed before the alteration was made.[20] For example, in a bond conditioned for the payment of £100 by six equal instalments " until the full sum of *one pounds* was paid "—and a stranger inserted the word " hundred " between " one " and " pounds "—it was held an immaterial alteration.[21] The insertion of the names of two creditors in a registered deed of arrangement to which before registration the requisite number of creditors had subscribed, was an immaterial alteration [22] The Christian names of a mortgagee were altered after execution [23]; after execution the date and consideration for a transfer deed were filled in [24]—both these were held to be immaterial. So where the date was filled in and the year altered after all but one of the executants had signed, this was held not to affect the validity of the deed, and *Pigot's Case* must be taken to apply only to material alterations since the decision in *Aldous* v. *Cornwell* (1868), L. R. 3 Q. B. 573.[25]

A material alteration has certain effects as follows:—

(1) A material alteration made by or with the consent of a party to the deed debars that party from any remedy on

[19] *Re Barned's Banking Co.* (1867), 3 Ch App. 105, 115
[20] *Sanderson* v *Symons* (1819), 1 Brod & B 426; *Aldous* v *Cornwell* (1868), L R. 3 Q. B 573; *Crediton (Bishop)* v. *Exeter (Bishop)*, [1905] 2 Ch. 455.
[21] *Waugh* v *Bussell* (1814), 5 Taunt. 707
[22] *Wood* v. *Slack* (1868), L R 3 Q B 379
[23] *Re Howgate and Osborn's Contract*, [1902] 1 Ch 451
[24] *Roots* v. *Williamson* (1888), 38 Ch D 485, at p 492
[25] *Crediton (Bishop)* v *Exeter (Bishop)*, [1905] 2 Ch 455.

the deed against any other party who did not consent to the alteration. . This rule has been applied to alterations in a bond [26]; policies of insurance [27]; a charterparty [28]; a creditors' deed [29]; bought and sold notes [30]; Bank of England notes [31], and many others. One surety of four in a joint and several bond of suretyship, and whose liability was £50, signed last and added to his signature " £25 only ". The alteration was *bona fide* and was accepted by the obligee, but was held a material alteration. The consequence was that the other three sureties were discharged, and as the fourth had only executed a joint and several bond he was not bound by it, as he was entitled to say that that was not the contract he had entered into [32] The rule is therefore equally applicable to deeds and to instruments under hand [33]

(2) A material alteration made with the consent of all parties for the purpose of carrying out their intention at the time of execution does not prevent the person making the alteration from enforcing the deed [34] So a space left in a trust deed for the benefit of creditors for the insertion of one of the principal debts when ascertained, and filled up when this was known and with the consent of the creditor was upheld [35] In *Rudd* v. *Bowles* [36] the dates of leases were inserted by agreement of the parties after execution, and it was held that the leases were not rendered void thereby, but the grantor was estopped from denying that the leases were

---

[26] Bro. Ab Faits, pl 7; (1572), Keilw 162, pl 2, 164, pl. 7

[27] *Fairlie* v *Christie* (1817), 7 Taunt 416, *Forshaw* v *Chabert* (1821), 3 Brod & B. 158; *Langhorn* v *Cadogan* (1812), 4 Taunt 330

[28] *Crookewit* v. *Fletcher* (1857), 1 H & N 893

[29] *Fazakerly* v *M'Knight* (1856), 6 El & B 795, *Sellin* v *Price* (1867), L. R 2 Ex. 189

[30] *Mollett* v. *Wackerbarth* (1847), 5 C B 181

[31] *Suffell* v. *Bank of England* (1882), 9 Q B D 555

[32] *Ellesmere Brewery Co* v *Cooper*, [1896] 1 Q. B 75

[33] *Master* v. *Miller* (1791), 4 T. R 320, (1793), 5 T R. 367, *Byrom* v *Thompson* (1839), 11 A & E. 31

[34] Cf *French* v. *Patton* (1808), 9 East 351, at p 354

[35] *Hudson* v *Revett* (1829), 5 Bing 368.

[36] [1912] 2 Ch 60 Cf also *Adsetts* v *Hives* (1863), 33 Beav 52

executed on the dates inserted with his consent. If the
alteration is made not for the purpose of carrying out the
intention of the parties at the time of execution but for
effectuating something that has occurred to them since that
date, the old deed has gone and no party can enforce any
of the obligations contained in the deed as it originally stood.[37]
This rule applies equally to instruments under hand only.[38]

Blank transfers.—It is a common practice on the Stock
Exchange for a seller of shares to sign an instrument of
transfer (which may or may not be required to be a deed)
in blank, *i.e.*, with the name of the transferee omitted, and
this may go on from hand to hand through several transactions. Will this be effective as a deed if the blank is
ultimately filled up with the consent of all parties? In the
cases cited above, it was pointed out that the alteration made
with this consent must be for the purpose of carrying out an
arrangement or contract already arrived at before execution;
but A may sign a blank transfer with no idea of the identity
of the ultimate purchaser, Z, the person whose name will
finally be inserted in the blank space. As Lord Lindley says
in his work on companies: "A *deed* executed to ——, *i.e.*,
to nobody, is altogether inoperative as a deed"; consequently
the property in shares, if only transferable by deed, remains
in the seller, and "the holder of the deed acquires no other
title to the shares than a right to have them properly transferred or to have the transferor declared a trustee for them ".[39]
Therefore such a deed of transfer in blank is as a deed invalid
in law as well as in equity, and the shares remain the property
of the transferor.[40] This applies even though the transferor

---

37 *French* v *Patton* (1808), 9 East 351.
38 *Bates* v *Grabham* (1703), Salk. 444, *Kershaw* v *Cox* (1800), 3 Esp 246;
Byrom v. *Thompson* (1839), 11 A. & E 31
39 Bk. III (6th ed), p 654, Buckley, Companies (11th ed), pp 679—682
40 *Tayler* v *G I P. Ry.* (1859), 4 De G. & J 559, *Swan* v. *North
British Australasian Co* (1862), 7 H & N. 603, (1863), 2 H & C. 175,
Powell v *London and Provincial Bank*, [1893] 1 Ch 610; 2 Ch 555

subsequently acknowledges the deed as ultimately completed, as a mere acknowledgment does not amount to a redelivery. If a redelivery took place after the blanks were filled up, it would be the deed of the transferor.[41]

On the same principle, if there is a complete contract in all essentials before execution, the fact that a blank is left in the deed for a further and better description of the property concerned, the parties being in ignorance of the full description when they executed the deed, will not invalidate it and the deed will pass the property. This must be carefully distinguished from a case where there is no complete contract before execution and the description is wholly lacking, so that in fact the deed passes nothing at the time of execution. This may be illustrated by the case of *Re Barned's Banking Co.*[42] A deed of transfer of shares was executed. It contained no description of the shares, but this with the numbers was afterwards filled in. The intention at the time of execution was proved to be that all the shares held in the company described by the transferor should be transferred to the transferee who would accept them. The deed of transfer was therefore not invalidated by the additions made subsequent to execution. Where, however, there was no duty to be performed by the transferee named in a deed (to which a schedule was recited as attached thereto but which in fact was not so attached) without the schedule, it was held that without the schedule it was not the deed of the transferee and his plea of *non est factum* prevailed.[43] A blank transfer, though void as a deed, may be good as an instrument under hand, as the transferor must be taken to have authorised the transferees to complete the transaction by such additions to the document as will enable them to have the shares legally

[41] *Société Générale de Paris* v. *Tramways Union Co., Ltd* (1884), 14 Q B D 424, 11 App Cas 20 (*sub nom Société Générale de Paris* v *Walker* (1885))

[42] (1867), L R. 3 Ch. 105, 115, *supra*, p 16

[43] *Weeks* v *Maillardet* (1811), 14 East 568

[44] *Re Indo-China Steam Navigation Co*, [1917] 2 Ch 100, at pp. 105, 106.

vested in themselves or their nominees.[44] In practice, therefore, the transfer is thus executed in blank and becomes a legal transfer when registered in the company's books The legal interest in the stock or shares transferred in short becomes vested on registration. When shares are sold there is an implied contract to indemnify the purchasers against all calls on the shares, and this is so whether or not the transfer was in blank, as the obligation arises from the actual contract of sale and not from the particular mode of its performance.[45]

Alterations by a stranger, i.e. a person not a party to or claiming through a party to a deed, have no effect,[46] although it is said that if the deed were in the custody of the person seeking to enforce it at the time of the alteration he will be unable to enforce it, presumably on the ground of laches or estoppel.[47] Nor will cancellation by accident or mistake affect the deed or the rights of any person entitled thereunder. In some of the old cases, seals were found to have been torn off.[48] As Lord Ellenborough said in *Henfree* v. *Bromley* [46]: " I can no more consider this [act of stranger] as avoiding the instrument than if it had been obliterated or cancelled by accident." So also with unintentional cancellation : " If the absence of intention to cancel be shown, the thing is not cancelled." [49] If a bond is several, the cancellation by the obligees of the seal of one of the obligors discharges him alone [50]; if the bond is joint and several, such cancellation would discharge all.[47]

---

[45] *Spencer* v. *Ashworth, Partington & Co*, [1925] 1 K. B 589.

[46] Sugd Pow. (8th ed), 603, *Henfree* v. *Bromley* (1805), 6 East 309, *Hutchins* v. *Scott* (1837), 2 M & W 809, at p. 814

[47] *Bayly* v *Garford* (1641), March 125

[48] *Anon.* (1625), Latch 226, *Clerke* v *Heath* (1669), 1 Mod 11; *Master* v *Miller* (1791), 4 T. R 420, at p. 439.

[49] *Per* Maule, J , in *Bamberger* v *The Commercial Credit* (1855), 15 C. B. 676, at p. 693.

[50] *Collins* v *Prosser* (1823), 1 B & C 682.

III.—GENERAL RULES OF INTERPRETATION

The foregoing remarks have been directed to the state of
the document when presented to the Court for interpretation
or construction.   We have seen what the nature of the
document presented to the Court is; what the essentials of a
deed are; when it is void or voidable; when a deed is required,
or writing under hand will suffice.   It is, of course, obvious
that we are only concerned with written documents, whether
deeds or not, and have nothing to do with parol transactions.
We also considered the *state* of the document when it comes
before the Court—is it a deed that has once been sealed but
the seals have disappeared, or does the document appear with
alterations, erasures or interlineations upon its face?   If so,
what is the effect of this?   This has been considered in the
previous sections   We now have a document which is either
a deed or a writing under hand only; we have had all preliminary questions as to its character and validity disposed of.
It is now placed before the Court for interpretation.   What
does it mean?   It must be noticed that this is not necessarily
the same as " what did the parties intend when they executed
the document? "   They are presumed to have intended to
say that which they have in fact said, so their words as they
stand must be construed.   The question is, *not* what did the
parties intend to say?—that is precluded by the presumption
that they have said what they intended to say.   The question
to be solved is, what have they said?   What meaning is to
be attached to the expressions they have used?   To a layman,
the easiest way to answer this question might seem to be to
call the parties before the Court and ask them what they
meant.   In that case, the parties would not only usurp the
function of the Court, but would probably hold hardly
unanimous opinions as to what was meant by the words used
We shall notice the limited scope allowed to oral evidence
in these matters; that direct evidence is inadmissible to
construe the language of a document is beyond question.

Rule 1.—The meaning of the document or of a particular part of it is therefore to be sought for in the document itself. In other words, the intention of the parties as expressed in the words they have used must be discovered, if possible. In the large majority of cases this causes no difficulty, but the reports show a very large number of cases going back many centuries where the expressions used by the parties to documents have caused difficulty of interpretation; *i.e*, of determining what the parties meant or their intention when they used certain words or made use of particular expressions From these cases certain rules have been formulated and have been acted upon by the Courts, many of them for very many years past Lord Wensleydale [1] gives a warning of the distinction indicated above when he said " the question is not what the parties to a deed may have intended to do by entering into that deed, but what is the meaning of the words used in that deed: a most important distinction in all cases of construction and the disregard of which often leads to erroneous conclusions ". So in a very old case it was said: " The Court cannot understand the true intent of the indenture but only by the words of the indenture." [2] " I am disposed to follow the rule of construction which was laid down by Lord Denman and Baron Parke . They said that in construing instruments you must have regard, not to the presumed intention of the parties, but to the meaning of the words which they have used." [3] " One must consider the meaning of the words used, not what one may guess to be the intention of the parties ", said Jessel, M.R., [4] which plainly shows that however much one may suspect that the parties intended one thing, yet if their words plainly import another, the latter is the true construction, as the " Court deals with a deed according to

[1] In *Monypenny* v *Monypenny* (1861), 9 H L C. 114, at p. 146.
[2] *Kidder* v. *West* (1684), 3 Lev. 167
[3] *Per* Brett, L J , in *Ex p. Chick, re Meredith* (1879), 11 Ch. D. 731, at p 739.
[4] In *Smith* v *Lucas* (1881), 18 Ch D 531, at p. 542, *Clayton* v *Glengall* (1841), 1 Dr. & W 1, 14, 17.

the clear intention of the parties appearing in the four corners of the deed itself." [5]

Certain statutory rules of construction exist; for instance, by section 58 of the Law of Property Act, 1925, an instrument expressed to be supplemental to a previous instrument shall, as far as may be, be read and have effect as if the supplemental instrument contained a full recital of the previous instrument By section 61, after January 1, 1926, in all deeds, contracts, wills, orders and other instruments, " month " means calendar month, " person " includes a corporation, the singular includes the plural and *vice versa,* and the masculine includes the feminine and *vice versa.*

A rule of law naturally prevails over any judicial rule of construction. [6] As Pearson, J., said [7]: " I conceive that all deeds are to be construed not only strictly according to their words, but so far as possible, without infringing any rule of law, in such a way as to effectuate the intention of the parties."

The Court must not by supplying intention substitute its own ideas of what the parties meant. "The deed may be drawn inartificially, from ignorance or inadvertence or other causes; but still, if there is enough clearly to convey information as to its real meaning, the object is attained The mind is with certainty discovered, and being known, must be the guide, or the act and deed would not be the act and deed of the party, but of the Court " [8] And more recently Jessel, M.R [9]· " I have always thought and still think that it is of the utmost importance as regards contracts between adults—persons not under disability or at arm's length—that the Courts of law should maintain the performance of the

---

[5] *Per* Romilly, M.R , in *Beaumont* v *Marquis of Salisbury* (1854), 19 Beav 198, at p. 206

[6] *S. C.*

[7] *Hilbers* v *Parkinson* (1883), 25 Ch D 200, at p 203

[8] *Per* Plumer, M R., in *Cholmondeley* v *Clinton* (1820), 2 J & W 1, at p. 92.

[9] *Wallis* v. *Smith* (1882), 21 Ch D 243, at p 266.

contracts according to the intention of the parties; that they should not overrule any clearly expressed intention on the ground that the Judges know the business of the people better than the people know it themselves."

Rule II —The intention may prevail over the words used.
Ordinarily, parties use apt words to express their intention; but often they do not. We have seen that the most essential thing is to collect the intention of the parties from the expressions they have used in the deed itself. What if the intention so collected will not square with the words used? The answer is that the intention prevails This clearly appears from a passage in a judgment of Lord Cottenham[10]: "If the provisions are clearly expressed and there is nothing to enable the Court to put upon them a construction different from what the words import, no doubt the words must prevail: but if the provisions and expressions be contradictory and if there be grounds, appearing from the face of the instrument, affording proof of the real intention of the parties, then that intention will prevail against the obvious and ordinary meaning of the words. If the parties have themselves furnished a key to the meaning of the words used, it is not material by what expression they convey their intention."

"Another maxim is 'that such a construction should be made of the words in a deed, as is most agreeable to the intention of the grantor, the words are not the principal things in a deed, but the intent and design of the grantor'."[11]

The law is anxious to save a deed if possible. This is sometimes expressed in the maxim *ut res magis valeat quam pereat.* If by any reasonable construction the intention of the parties can be arrived at and that intention carried out consistently with the rules of law, the Court will take that course. So anxiously is this intention sought, that if words are capable of more than one construction, the con-

10 *Lloyd* v *Lloyd* (1837), 2 My. & Cr. 192, at p. 202.
11 *Per* Willes, C J., in *Smith* v *Packhurst* (1742), 3 Atk 135, at p 136

struction to be adopted in interpreting the document is to be that which is in accordance with the intention: " a deed shall never be void, where the words may be applied to any intent to make it good ", as was said in 1555.[12]   Also it follows from this that if a deed cannot take effect in the manner expressed by the parties owing to some rule of law, it will be construed if possible to carry the intention into effect in some other way This is perhaps analogous to the *cy-près* doctrine in trusts— " A deed that is intended and made to one purpose may enure to another, for if it will not take effect in that way it is intended it may take effect in another way: provided it may have that effect consistently with the intention of the parties." [13]   So rather more recently by Lord Mansfield, C.J., in *Goodtitle d. Edwards* v *Bailey* [14]: " The rules laid down in respect of the construction of deeds are founded in law, reason and common sense, that they shall operate according to the intention of the parties, if by law they may; and if they cannot operate in one form, they shall operate in that which by law will effectuate the intention "

Many of the authorities on this head are cases turning on the old methods of conveyancing which have been abolished by section 51 of the Law of Property Act, 1925.   For example, deeds of feoffment without livery have been construed as covenants by the feoffor to stand seised   In one old case [15] a conveyance made in consideration of an intended marriage was so construed, it being held invalid as a bargain and sale because there was no pecuniary consideration; as a release because there was no lease for a year; as a confirmation because neither of the grantees was in possession; as a feoffment, because there was no livery   Other cases have been held to operate as grants at common law; as releases of land; as confirmations or as bargain and sale.   The cases are collected in

---

[12] By Staunford, J , in *Throckmerton* v. *Tracey* (1555), 1 Plowd 145, at p. 160
[13] Shep. Touch 82, *Chester* v *Willan* (1669), 2 Wms. Saund. 96a (notes)
[14] (1777), 2 Cowp 597, at p 600.
[15] *Doe* v *Salkeld* (1755), Willes 674

Norton (pp. 54—61). The modern cases under this head are concerned chiefly with Powers and Leases. Some may very shortly be referred to in order to show the meaning of the rule. For instance, a covenant not to exercise a power may operate as a release of the power,[16] or the donee of the power may covenant that he will not by exercising the power reduce the share of any particular object below a certain amount [17]; though a covenant to exercise a testamentary power in a particular way is void,[18] the last case being distinguished in that there the benefits flowed from the trusts in default of appointment declared by the donor of the power and not from the bargain for the exercise of the power So in the case of statutory powers, a lease granted by a tenant by the curtesy could operate under the Settled Land Act, 1882, to convey the land, the tenant being a tenant for life under the provisions of that Act [19] In the same way the will of a testator was held not to authorise the trustees of the will to lease unopened mines. This could, however, be effected by section 11 of the Settled Land Act, 1882 [20] A grantor who "licensed" to another "all that tract of land", etc., was held not to have merely licensed but to have demised the land as a lease.[21] So a covenant may be held to run with the land though the parties may have expressed themselves as though the covenant were merely personal to the covenantees [22] A tenancy agreement for over three years not under seal was void as a lease under the Real Property Act of 1845, but it was held that as it was regarded as a lease in equity it must be treated as though it were a lease under seal [23]

Although it was stated above that this anxiety of the Courts

---

[16] *Scrope* v *Offley* (1740), 1 Br P C 276 For the opposite case, cf. *Nottidge* v *Dering*, [1910] 1 Ch 297.

[17] *Re Evered*, [1910] 2 Ch 147

[18] *Re Cooke*, [1922] 1 Ch 292

[19] *Mogridge* v. *Clapp*, [1892] 3 Ch 382

[20] *Re Daniels*, [1912] 2 Ch 90.

[21] *Glenwood* v *Phillips*, [1904] A C 405

[22] *Manchester Brewery Co* v *Coombs*, [1901] 2 Ch 608

[23] *Rickett* v *Green*, [1910] 1 K B 253

to save the deed if possible by carrying out the intention of the parties, in spite of the expressions they may have used to convey their meaning, was somewhat analogous to the equitable doctrine of *cy-près* where a general charitable intention must of course be discerned, it must be borne in mind that by way of exception to this rule, as equity will not help a volunteer, a voluntary settlement where no completed transfer has been effected cannot be upheld as a declaration of trust.[24]

If a deed may be read in two ways, one lawful and the other unlawful, the Court will read it in the lawful way[25] in accordance with the policy stated above

Rule III.—Words are to be taken in their literal meaning Thus in 1803[26] it was said of a policy of insurance: "It is to be construed according to its sense and meaning as collected in the first place from the terms used in it, which terms are themselves to be understood in their plain, ordinary and popular sense unless they have generally in respect of the subject-matter, as by the known usage of trade or the like, acquired a peculiar sense different from the popular sense of the same words or unless the context evidently pointed out that they must in the particular instance and in order to effectuate the immediate intention of the parties to that contract be understood in some other and peculiar sense" So Jessel, M.R.[27]: "The grammatical and ordinary sense of the words is to be adhered to, unless that would lead to some absurdity, or some repugnance or inconsistency with the rest of the instrument, in which case the grammatical or ordinary sense of the words may be modified, so as to avoid that absurdity and inconsistency, but no

[24] *Milroy* v *Lord* (1862), 4 De G. & J 264, at p 274, *Richards* v *Delbridge* (1874), L R 18 Eq 11, *Macedo* v *Stroud*, [1922] 2 A C 330, at p. 338.
[25] Co Litt 42 a
[26] *Per* Lord Ellenborough, C J , in *Robertson* v. *French* (1803), 4 East 130, at p 135
[27] In *Re Levy, ex p Walton* (1881), 17 Ch D 746, at p 751

further. And in *Beard* v. *Moira Colliery Co.*[28] it was said " in the construction of deeds, ordinary words should be given their plain and ordinary meaning ": Thus it is not neces- sarily the etymological or dictionary sense which is to be applied, but the sense in which the words are used by the majority of people—the popular sense—which *prima facie* would be the meaning intended by the parties at the time of the execution of the instrument. That would be one meaning of the expression " literal sense "; a second would be the meaning attached to the words by the parties, having regard to the circumstances, *e.g.*, that they are both engaged in a certain trade where certain words do not bear the popular meaning. There may be yet a third " literal " meaning, *viz.*, that which it can be shown that the parties were in the habit of applying to particular words It was said above that the intention of the parties must be discovered and if possible effectuated, no matter what words or expressions they had employed to show their intention. So now we come to the methods by which the meaning of the words used is to be discovered; always bearing in mind that, in the first place, the clues to that meaning—the evidence of their intention—is to be sought for in the document itself, and not outside it.

Rule IV.—Literal meaning depends on the circumstances of the parties. So Lord Halsbury, L.C.,[29] expressed the " modern view " to be, " which is I think in accordance with reason and common sense, that whatever the instrument, it must receive a construction according to the plain meaning of the words and sentences therein contained ". For the purpose of proving what the literal meaning of the words used is, according to the senses in which the expression " literal meaning " is explained above, extrinsic evidence is admissible, not to construe the deed, but to translate for the Court the terms used by the parties. Take, for instance, a deed in a foreign

---

28 *Per* Swinfen Eady, L J., [1915] 1 Ch. 257, at p 268
29 *Leader* v. *Duffey* (1888), 13 App Cas 294, at p 301

language, it cannot be doubted that the Court may receive evidence of the proper meaning of that language.[30] So with a deed in English, the terms and expressions used may be translated for the Court by giving evidence to show who the parties to the instrument are, the circumstances under which the document was executed, and the meaning which the parties were in the habit of affixing to the expressions they employed. "I am not offering declarations of what the party said she meant, I am not construing a legal instrument by the acts of the parties or by their understanding upon it, but, by showing the circumstances and situation of the party and the estates and interest she had at the time, I am enabling the House to judge what, in legal construction, was her meaning." [31]

Lord Blackburn,[32] said: "In construing a document in all cases the object is to see what is the intention expressed by the words used. But from the imperfection of language it is impossible to know what that intention is without inquiring further and seeing what the circumstances were in reference to which the words were used and what was the object appearing from those circumstances which the person using them had in view, for the meaning of words varies according to the circumstances in respect of which they were used."

The *locus classicus* on this subject is the judgments in *Shore* v. *Wilson*,[33] and the following quotations are taken from those judgments.

Coleridge, J.[34]: " Where language is used in a deed which

---

[30] See *per* Parke, B., in *Shore* v *Wilson* (1842), 9 Cl. & F. 355, at p. 555

[31] *Per* Lord Eldon, L C , in *Smith* v *Doe* (1821), 2 Brod. & Bing 473, at p 550.

[32] In *River Wear Commissioners* v *Adamson* (1877), 2 App Cas. 743, quoted by Halsbury, L C , in *Butterley* v *New Hucknall Colliery*, [1910] A. C 381.

[33] (1842), 9 Cl. & F. 355. This case was concerned with the interpretation of Lady Hewley's trusts for "poor and godly preachers of Christ's holy gospel " in which the opinions of the Judges were taken

[34] S C., pp 525, 527, *The N S P C. C* v *Scottish N. S P C C* , [1915] A. C. 207 " What a man has said ought to be acted upon unless it

in its primary meaning is unambiguous and in which that meaning is not excluded by the context, and is sensible with regard to the extrinsic circumstances in which the writer was placed at the time of writing, such primary meaning must be taken conclusively to be that in which the writer used it; such meaning in that case conclusively states the writer's intention and no evidence is receivable to show that in fact the writer used it in any other sense or had any other intention. . . . This rule thus explained implies that it is not allowable in the case supposed to adduce any evidence, however strong, to prove an unexpressed intention varying from that which the words used impart. This may be open no doubt to the remark that, though we profess to be exploring the intention of the writer, we may be led in many cases to decide contrary to what can scarcely be doubted to have been the intention, rejecting evidence which may be most satis-factory in the particular instance to prove it The answer is, that interpreters have to deal with the written expression of the writer's intention and Courts of law to carry into effect what he has written, not what it may be surmised, on however probable grounds, that he intended only to have written." So also Parke, B., in the same case [35] : " No extrinsic evidence of the intention of the party to the deed, from his declarations, whether at the time of his executing the instrument or before or after that time, is admissible, the duty of the Court being to declare the meaning of what is written in the instrument, not of what was intended to have been written." Likewise Tindal, C.J. [36] : " In no case what-ever is it permitted to explain the language of a deed by evidence of the private views, the secret intentions, or the known principles of the party to the instrument, whether religious, political or otherwise, any more than by the express

---

is clearly proved that he meant something different from what he has said "
(*per* Lord Loreburn, at p 212)
  [35] *S C*, p. 555.
  [36] *S C.*, p. 565

parol declarations made by the party himself, which are universally excluded, for the admitting of such evidence would let in all the uncertainty before adverted to."

Rule V.—When is extrinsic evidence admissible to translate the language? "Where any doubt arises upon the true meaning or sense of the words themselves, or any difficulty as to their application under the surrounding circumstances, the sense and meaning of the language may be investigated and ascertained by evidence *dehors* the instrument itself; for both reason and common sense agree that by no other means can the language of the instrument be made to speak the real mind of the party." [37]

(a) Where the document is written in a foreign language, evidence may be given to prove its meaning.[38]

(b) "If the language be technical or scientific and it is used in a matter relating to the art or science to which it belongs, its technical or scientific must be considered its primary meaning" [39] "This description of evidence is admissible in order to enable the Court to understand the meaning of the words contained in the instrument itself, and without reference to the extrinsic facts on which this instrument is intended to operate." [40] Frequent examples of this occur in patent cases, where expert witnesses are called to inform the Court as to the meaning of the expressions used in the specifications under consideration.

So with regard to Lady Hewley's trusts, discussed at great length in *Shore* v. *Wilson* (*supra*), evidence was admitted as to the meaning of " poor and godly preachers of Christ's holy gospel ", and what denominational sects were included therein. So the word " provision " in collocation with " merchant " or " dealer " was proved by extrinsic evidence

---

[37] *S. C*, *per* Tindal, C.J., at p. 565
[38] See *supra*, p 29
[39] *S. C.*, *per* Coleridge, J, at p 525, *per* Tindal, C J, at p 555, *per* Jessel, M.R, *Taylor* v *Corporation of St. Helens* (1877), 6 Ch D 264, 270
[40] *S. C.*, *per* Parke, B, at p. 555

to have acquired a technical meaning in the trade.[41]   In
Rowett, Leakey & Co. v. *Scottish Provident Institution* [42]
the question was as to the meaning of the expression " *bona
fide* onerous holders " in a Scottish policy of insurance. This
is a meaningless term in English law, but evidence by an
eminent Scots lawyer [43] was admitted to show that the
expression meant " persons who by transmission have acquired
a right to a document for valuable consideration ".   " If it
is a word which is of a technical or scientific character then
it must be construed according to that which is its primary
meaning, namely, its technical or scientific meaning. But
before you can give evidence of the secondary meaning of a
word, you must satisfy the Court from the instrument itself
or from the circumstances of the case that the word ought
to be construed not in its popular or primary signification
but according to its secondary intention." [44]   " In accordance
with this rule, evidence in *Lovell and Christmas* v. *Wall*
(*supra*) was disallowed as to the meaning of the word
" merchant " by itself, there being nothing either in the
instrument itself or from the circumstances of the case to
show that it ought to be construed in a secondary sense,
i e., in any other than its common and popular sense.

    (*c*) The same remarks apply to trade usages and terms.
" The meaning of a particular word may be shown by parol
evidence to be different in some particular place, trade or
business from its proper and ordinary acceptation." [45]
Evidence of mercantile usages is admitted in order to expound
and arrive at the meaning of a mercantile contract [46]   " This
is but an application of the well-known rule that the interpretation of contracts must be governed by the intention of

---

[41] *Lovell and Christmas, Ltd.* v *Wall* (1911), 103 L. T. 588; *Holt & Co.*
v *Collyer* (1881), 16 Ch. D. 718, at p 720.
[42] [1927] 1 Ch. 55
[43] Mr. Macmillan   I believe, Mr H. P. Macmillan, now Lord Macmillan
[44] *Per* Fry, J , in *Holt & Co.* v *Collyer, supra*
[45] *Mallan* v *May* (1844), 13 M & W. 511, at p 517.
[46] *Browne* v *Byrne* (1854), 3 E & B. 703, 715

the parties. And from the nature of the case, the peculiar meaning of the terms used can be discovered only by means of parol evidence." [47] In *Spartali* v. *Benecke* it is laid down that in mercantile contracts evidence is admissible (1) to prove that the words in the particular trade to which the contract refers are used in a peculiar sense and different from the sense they ordinarily bear; (2) to prove usage in order to annex incidents to the contract upon which the contract is silent—both rules being subject to the qualification that the peculiar sense or meaning which it is proposed by the evidence to attach to the words of the contract must not vary or contradict either expressly or by implication the terms of the written instrument. [48] So the custom sought to be proved must not be inconsistent with the written contract. [49] It is important to remember that in these cases extrinsic evidence is admitted solely for the purpose of explaining the meaning of words used in the contract. Platt, B., said this was "translating the contract", [50] and Lord Cairns, L.C., said the purpose of such evidence was "to supply, as it were, a mercantile dictionary in which you are to find the mercantile meaning of the words which are used" (*Bowes* v *Shand* (1877), 2 App. Cas 455, at p. 465). See also *per* Lord Cranworth in *Att.-Gen.* v. *Clapham* (1855), 4 De G M & G. 591, at p. 627. Where the words of the contract have reference to a particular profession such as the stage, a written contract to act for three years was interpreted according to the proved uniform usage of the profession to mean that the plaintiff was only entitled to salary during the theatrical season in those three years. [50] So in a covenant to insure leasehold property, the question was whether the covenant required an unqualified policy to be taken out or only the

---

[47] *Per* Cockburn, C J , in *Myers* v. *Sarl* (1860), 3 El & El 306, at p 315
[48] (1850), 10 C. B. 212, 222, *per* Wilde, C J
[49] *Miller, Gibb & Co* v *Smith & Tyrer*, [1917] 2 K B. 141, *Re an Arbitration between L. Sutro & Co. and Heilbut, Symons & Co.*, [1917] 2 K B 344, at p 366
[50] *Grant* v *Maddox* (1846), 15 M. & W. 737.

one usually issued by the companies designated in the covenant, as the lessee refused to insure against damage by aircraft. Evidence was admitted to show that the company named and other insurance companies had never insured against such risks and that their policies always excepted these.[51] Note that the admissibility of parol evidence in cases of this kind does not depend on any ambiguity in the expression to be construed; the question merely is " whether or not the expression has, with reference to the subject-matter of the contract, acquired a peculiar meaning ".[52] Nor are the judgment or opinions of the witnesses relevant, the character of the evidence admissible for this purpose being the fact of a general usage prevailing in a particular trade.[53]

(d) Sometimes parol evidence will be admitted to explain terms used in ancient documents where by lapse of time and change of manners the words have acquired in the present age a different meaning from that which they bore when originally employed.[54]

(e) Evidence of circumstances — i.e., to identify the persons and objects to which the expressions used in the instrument were applied. The instrument must be construed with reference to the facts, and in order to determine what passes by it and who takes an interest under it evidence is admitted of " every material fact which will enable the Court to identify the person or thing mentioned in the instrument and to place the Court, whose province it is to declare the meaning of the words of the instrument, as near as may be in the position of the parties to it ".[55] So in the case of wills, it is commonly said to be the duty of the Court to put itself as far

---

[51] Upjohn v Hitchens, [1918] 2 K B. 48

[52] Per Hill, J , in Myers v. Sarl (1860), 3 El & El 306, at p 318, per Blackburn, J , S C, p 319

[53] Lewis v Marshall (1844), 7 Mans & Gr 729, 745

[54] Per Tindal, C J., in Shore v Wilson, supra, at p 565; per Lord Campbell, Drummond v Att -Gen for Ireland (1849), 2 H L C. 837, at p. 863; see infra, p 82

[55] Per Parke, B , in Shore v. Wilson, supra, at p 555; London Financial Association v. Kelk (1884), 26 Ch D 107, 134.

as possible " in the testator's arm-chair ". As Lord Wensley-dale said,[56] " the will must be in writing and the only question is what is the meaning of the words used in that writing. To ascertain which every part of it must be considered with the help of those surrounding circumstances which are admissible in evidence to explain the words, and put the Court as nearly as possible in the situation of the writer of the instrument ". Hence the voluminous evidence admitted in *Shore* v. *Wilson* as to the state of religious parties at the time the deeds were executed So Kay, J., in *Hart* v. *Hart*[57]: " I agree that here the Court must not shut its eyes or blindfold itself, but must try to put itself, in order to understand this agreement, in the position as near as it can of the parties making the agreement. That is the rule, as I understand, on the construction of every deed or document, whether it be an agreement, a deed or a will: the Court has a right to know, and is bound to know, all the material facts which were known to the parties at the time when the agreement, deed, will or whatever it may be was entered into or made. That is legitimate in all cases for the purpose of construing a written instrument." It is on this principle that evidence was admitted in such cases as *Raffles* v. *Wichelhaus*[58] to show that the parties were not *ad idem* as to the identity of a particular ship, or *Behn* v. *Burness*[59] as to whether a particular expression was intended as a condition or a warranty. As Jessel, M.R , said in *Tucker* v. *Linger*,[60] " considering the peculiarity of the wording, considering the position of the parties, and the nature of the custom, it seems to me that the word ' minerals ' was not intended to be used in such a sense as to cover those flints to which the custom related, though it might include flints

---

[56] *Grey* v. *Pearson* (1857), 6 H L C 61, at p 106 Cf the same learned lord in *Roddy* v *Fitzgerald* (1858), 6 H. L. C 823, at p 876
[57] (1881), 18 Ch. D. 670, at p 692
[58] (1864), 2 H. & C 906
[59] (1862), 1 B & S 877; 3 B & S 751
[60] (1882), 21 Ch D 18, at p. 36.

not got according to the custom ". Evidence may not be given where the meaning of a word has been defined by Act of Parliament—as " acre ", " quarter ", " pound ", " bushel ", notwithstanding local customs to the contrary. For example, certain words are defined by the Law of Property Act, 1925, s. 61, as pointed out at p. 23 (*supra*). And there are many other examples in statutes.

Rule VI.—Technical legal terms will have their legal meaning. Technical legal terms, or words of well-known legal import, used by lawyers, especially conveyancers, will have their technical legal import, " though the testator uses inconsistent terms or gives repugnant or impossible directions ".[61] So Lord Sterndale, M.R., quoting *Lewin on Trusts* (12th ed., p 125), thought that strict legal language having been used, it must receive its legal meaning, and pointed out the advantage of adhering to the recognised meaning of words of conveyancing if the settlor chose to use them. They have a recognised conveyancing meaning, and if used the settlor must be taken to have used them in that meaning.[62] Lord Buckmaster[63] observed that the words " restoration " and " confirmation " have been used for many years by learned conveyancers " whose preciseness of language has often been the subject of undeserved reproach " and that it was impossible to assume that the words meant the opposite of what they said. As Judges are generally the only authorities for the meaning of legal terms, it is obvious that only the opinions of Judges are of weight in this connection. " We are bound to have regard to any rules of construction which have been established by the Courts, and subject to that we are bound to construe the will as trained legal minds would do."[64] So the opinions in text-books of living writers are not receivable in evidence, though Judges often either quote passages

---

61 *Per* Lord Wensleydale in *Roddy* v *Fitzgerald* (1858), 6 H. L C. 823
62 *Re Bostock's Settlement*, [1921] 2 Ch 469, at pp 480, 481.
63 *Parr* v. *Att -Gen* , [1926] A C. 239, at p. 266.
64 *Per* Cotton, L J., in *Ralph* v *Carrick* (1879), 11 Ch. D. 873, at p. 878.

from these or refer to them as containing either the right or the wrong statement of the law on the particular point under discussion. "These problems must now be determined by the rules of law applicable to the interpretation of statutes. They cannot be resolved by reliance upon the opinions of writers of text-books, however able, who are yet living, or of those who have been closely and devotedly identified with the passage of this legislation through Parliament." [65] And Sargant, L.J., in the same case,[66] thought such expressions of opinion "no authority on the construction and effect of recent legislation; at the most they can only be adopted by counsel as embodying their argument or by the Court as representing its ultimate view". At the same time the recognised practice of conveyancers carries weight with the Court. Lord Eldon said [67]: "I am not sorry to have this opportunity of stating my opinion that great weight should be given to that practice." Lord Justice James [68] thought the settled practice of conveyancers was to be looked upon as part of the common law. And more recently,[69] Byrne, J., said: "For the exposition of our very complicated real property law, it is proper in the absence of judicial authority to resort to text-books which have been recognised by the Courts as representing the views and practice of conveyancers of repute." The learned Judge proceeded to quote from the works of Challis, Lewis, Sanders and others.

It must be again emphasised that the extrinsic evidence referred to above as admissible is admitted simply and solely for the purpose of translating the words and expressions of the document for the Court—it is in no sense direct evidence of what the executant intended to effect apart from the meaning of the words and expressions he has used. The

[65] Per Lord Hanworth, M.R , in Re Ryder and Steadman's Contract, [1927] 2 Ch. 62, at p 74.
[66] S C , at p 84
[67] Howard v. Ducane (1823), 1 T & R. 81, at p 87
[68] Re Ford and Hill (1879), 10 Ch. D 365, at p 370
[69] Hollis Hospital and Hague's Contract, [1899] 2 Ch 540, at p. 551.

rule set out *supra* (p. 22) is still maintained in full, *i.e.*, that the intention is to be sought for within the four corners of the instrument itself. That is to say, the intrinsic evidence furnished by the deed itself is the primary means of interpretation.

Rule VII.—Therefore the deed is to be construed as a whole. It was said in a very old case: "Every part of the deed ought to be compared with the other and one entire sense ought to be made thereof." [70] So Lord Ellenborough, C.J., in *Barton* v. *Fitzgerald*,[71] said: "It is a true rule of construction that the sense and meaning of the parties in any particular part of an instrument may be collected *ex antecedentibus et consequentibus* (*i.e.*, from what goes before and from what follows); every part of it may be brought into action in order to collect from the whole one uniform and consistent sense, if that may be done." This is collecting the general intention from the instrument as a whole and inferring that intention from the general frame of the deed. So Lord Davey in *N. E. Ry.* v. *Hastings*, [1900] A. C 260, 269, quoting Lord Watson in *Chamber Colliery Co* v *Twyerould* (1893), [1915] 1 Ch. 265 n. : " The deed must be read as a whole in order to ascertain the true meaning of its several clauses and that the words of each clause should be so interpreted as to bring them into harmony with the other provisions of the deed if that interpretation does no violence to the meaning of which they are naturally susceptible." The intention must be inferred not from the force of a single expression, if it militates against the collected general intention, but at the same time, as it is the rule that "ordinary words ought to be given their plain and ordinary meaning", the Court cannot disregard that meaning or deviate from the force of any particular expression unless it finds from other parts of the deed some expression

---

[70] *Per* Staunford, J , in *Throckmerton* v. *Tracey* (1555), 1 Plow. 145, at p. 161

[71] (1812), 15 East 530, at p 541

which shows that the author could not have had the intention which the expression used and in its literal form would imply.[72] So Lord Cottenham in *Lloyd* v. *Lloyd*[73]: "If the provisions are clearly expressed and there is nothing to enable the Court to put upon them a construction different from that which the words import, no doubt the words must prevail; but if the provisions and expressions be contradictory, and if there be grounds appearing upon the face of the instrument affording proof of the real intention of the parties, then that intention will prevail against the obvious and ordinary meaning of the words If the parties have themselves furnished a key to the meaning of the words used, it is not material by what expression they convey their intention." For instance, "son" has the definite legal meaning of a legitimate son, but it may well appear from the instrument that the author was speaking of an illegitimate son, *e.g.*, if he had no legitimate son "The proper mode of construing any written instrument is to give effect to every part of it, if this be possible, and not to strike out or nullify one clause in a deed, unless it be impossible to reconcile it with another and more express clause in the same deed "[74] In that case, one clause of the articles of association of a company limited the borrowing powers of the directors to a certain sum unless authorised by a "general meeting". By another clause of the articles a "special meeting" (defined as an "extra-ordinary special general meeting") might authorise the directors to borrow such sums as it thought fit. Sir John Romilly held that the directors might be authorised to borrow beyond the limit in the former clause by either a general or a special meeting of the company; thus harmonising the two clauses.

This does not mean that the same expression necessarily

---

[72] Cf. *per* Leach, V.-C, in *Hume* v. *Rundell* (1824), 2 S & S 174, 177.
[73] (1837), 2 My & Cr 192, at p 202.
[74] *Per* Sir John Romilly, M.R, in *Re Strand Music Hall Co., Ltd* (1865), 35 Beav. 153, at p. 159.

bears the same meaning in all parts of the instrument. In
Watson v. *Haggitt* [75] the question arose as to the meaning
of " net profits " in a deed of partnership. By one clause of
the deed, one of the partners, who subsequently died, was to
receive a certain proportion of the net profits. By another
clause, on the death of a partner, his representatives were to
receive one-third of the annual net profits. The question was
whether the salaries of the partners were to be deducted in
order to arrive at the " annual net profits " The Privy
Council held that the expression " net profits " was used in
the two clauses in different meanings and that there was no
rule of general application that the same meaning ought to
be given to an expression in every part of a document in
which it appears.

Again, the word " month " meant in law a lunar month
except in a mortgage [76] and some other instances. But if
the context showed that the parties intended a calendar
month, effect was given to that intention; the presumption
being that " month " meant lunar month [77] The presumption
is now by the Law of Property Act, 1925, s. 61, the other
way; so, unless the context otherwise requires, in all deeds,
contracts, wills, orders and other instruments executed, made
or coming into operation after January 1, 1926, " month "
means calendar month. Apart from this Act, other statutory
provisions had been enacted in favour of the calendar month,
e.g., in a contract for the sale of goods [78]; in the case of
cheques, bills of exchange and promissory notes [79]; also in all
statutes passed after 1850 " unless a contrary intention
appears " [80]

Transaction contained in more than one document.—This

---

[75] [1928] A. C 127.

[76] *Schiller* v. *Petersen & Co.*, [1924] 1 Ch 394; see p. 87, *infra*

[77] *Simpson* v *Margitson* (1847), 11 Q B 23, 31; *Bruner* v *Moore*,
[1904] 1 Ch 305; *Phipps & Co.* v. *Rogers*, [1925] 1 K B. 14

[78] Sale of Goods Act, 1893, s 10 (2)

[79] Bills of Exchange Act, 1882, s. 14 (4)

[80] Interpretation Act, 1889, s. 3.

is of very frequent occurrence, whether in deeds or in contracts, where the agreement is often to be gathered from correspondence passing between the parties. As to deeds the rule is that all the deeds relevant to the transaction are to be read together. This was so from early times—"notwithstanding divers assurances be in different times and all but to perfect one assurance and by construction of law they shall all be said to be made at one and the same time; otherwise you may shake all assurances".[81] So a lease and release were treated as one deed [82]; a fine and recovery and deed " to lead the uses " were one [83]; "and the deed and the fine and recovery may well be taken as several parts of one and the same conveyance ".[84]

The deeds need not be executed simultaneously, so long as the Court, having regard to the circumstances, comes to the conclusion that the series of deeds represents a single transaction between the same parties. If this is so, the series will be treated as one deed "and of course one deed between the same parties may be read to show the meaning of a sentence and be equally read, although not contained in one deed, but in several parchments, if all the parchments together in the view of the Court make up one document for this purpose ".[85] So the articles of association of a company may be read to explain the memorandum [86] So where there was a manifest error in the lease, the duration of the term differing in the *habendum* and *reddendum*, the counterpart may be looked at and the two, lease and counterpart, construed together.[87] Lord Justice Moulton, in a judgment which was approved on appeal to the House of Lords, said : " Where

---

[81] *Per* Mountague, C.J., in *Havergil* v *Hare* (1617), 3 Buls 250, at p. 256
[82] *Per* North, C J., in *Barker* v *Keat* (1677), 2 Mod 249, at p 252
[83] *Per* Holt, C J., *Mountague* v *Bath* (1693), 2 Rep in Ch 417, at p 434.
[84] *Per* Trevor, C.J , in *Abbot* v *Burton* (1708), 11 Mod 181, at p 184.
[85] *Per* Jessel, M.R , in *Smith* v *Chadwick* (1882), 20 Ch D 27, at p 62
[86] *Per* Chitty, J , *Re Capital Fire Insurance Association* (1882), 21 Ch D. 209.
[87] *Burchell* v *Clark* (1876), 1 C P. D 602; 2 C. P D. 88; *Matthews* v *Smallwood*, [1910] 1 Ch 777

several deeds form part of one transaction and are contemporaneously executed they have the same effect for all purposes such as are relevant to this case as if they were one deed. Each is executed on the faith of all the others being executed also and is intended to speak only as part of the one transaction, and if one is seeking to make equities apply to the parties they must be equities arising out of the transaction as a whole " [88]

Although the learned Lord Justice spoke of deeds " contemporaneously executed ", there is no doubt that this is not essential. Jessel, M.R., in the case cited *supra*, said the deeds might be executed " at the same moment, a very common case, or within so short an interval that having regard to the nature of the transaction " the Court regards the transaction as a single one   So four deeds bearing date on four consecutive days were held to be necessarily connected together to form one transaction.[89] In *Whitbread* v. *Smith* [90] three deeds on three consecutive dates were held to form one transaction under the circumstances of the case.

The same applies in the case of a written contract.   A company issued a prospectus inviting applications for deposit notes on certain terms.   The plaintiff wrote applying for a deposit note in terms of the prospectus.   The company sent the plaintiff a letter of allotment and subsequently a deposit note which, however, omitted one of the terms contained in the prospectus.   It was held that all these four transactions were incorporated one in another by reference and therefore constituted only one transaction and must be construed together [91]   The well-known case of *Boydell* v. *Drummond* [92] does not run contrary to this rule, but was decided on the requirements of the Statute of Frauds alone.   So Russell, J.,

---

[88] *Manks* v *Whiteley*, [1912] 1 Ch 735, at p 754, [1914] A C. 132 (*sub nom. Whiteley* v *Delaney*)

[89] *Ford* v *Stuart* (1852), 15 Beav. 493

[90] (1854), 3 De G. M & G 727, *Selwyn* v *Selwyn* (1761), 2 Burr 1131.

[91] *Jacobs* v *Batavia Trust, Ltd*, [1924] 2 Ch. 329

[92] (1809), 11 East 142.

said [93] " the incorporation of the terms is merely a shorthand method of expressing and creating rights and liabilities as between B and C by reference to the language of some other document. The document which contains the reference is to be read as if the wording of the document referred to were repeated therein so as to create rights and liabilities as between the parties thereto ".

Moreover, the Court will presume that where there are several deeds forming one transaction, they were executed in such order as will effect the manifest intention of the parties. Fry, J., in a case where the priority of the sealing of debentures was important, said: " When two deeds are executed on the same day the Court must inquire which was in fact executed first, but that if there is anything in the deeds themselves to show an intention either that they shall take effect *pari passu* or even that the later deed shall take effect in priority to the earlier, in that case the Court will presume that the deeds were executed in such order as to give effect to the manifest intention of the parties." [94]

There are similar examples from cases on bills of sale, where the form and matter have been laid down by the Bills of Sale Act, 1882. A bill of sale is executed and a contemporaneous or subsequent mortgage or condition is executed or agreed to and not inserted in the bill of sale, and questions have arisen as to how far these are valid. Their effect on the bill of sale is often to invalidate it. The question seems to be whether the subsequent transaction was a defeasance, and if inserted in the bill of sale would have rendered it void under the Act. [95]

Documents partly printed.—Contracts and other documents are often contained in a printed form with either blanks filled

---

[93] *Aktieselskabet* v *Harding*, [1928] 2 K B 371, 393

[94] *Gartside* v *Silkstone and Dodworth Coal and Iron Co* (1882), 21 Ch D 762

[95] *Edwards* v *Marcus*, [1894] 1 Q B 587, *Smith* v *Whiteman* [1902], 2 K. B 437, *Hall* v *Whiteman*, [1912] 1 K B. 683, *Stott* v *Shaw*, [1928] W. N 14

in with written words or with some of the printed words deleted with or without written words substituted These sometimes cause difficulties in construction Lord Ellenborough said in *Robertson* v. *French*,[96] a case relating to an insurance policy contained partly in a printed form: " The greater part of the printed language of them [forms] being invariable and uniform has acquired from use and practice a known and definite meaning, but the written words are entitled to have a greater effect attributed to them than the printed words inasmuch as the written words were the immediate language and terms selected by the parties themselves for the expression of their meaning and the printed words are a general formality adapted equally to their case and to that of all other contracting parties upon similar occasions and subjects."

In *Baumvoll Manufactur von Scheibler* v. *Gilchrist & Co.*[97] Lord Esher said in the Court of Appeal: " We have a right to look at what is written into the printed form and what is struck out. There are stipulations in the charterparty which ought to have been struck out if the parties had been careful . . taken with the rest of the stipulations they must be treated as inefficient and must be disregarded. . ." And Lord Herschell in the same case in the House of Lords said: " This is a document which was not specially prepared for this purpose; a good deal of it is in print, altered in writing to suit the particular arrangement; but some of the provisions that have been left standing were undoubtedly not specifically inserted with a view to this agreement but have been left standing it may be more or less from oversight. . . . To infer from the presence of such a proviso in the charterparty that the parties must have had it in contemplation that such a liability would be imposed inasmuch as otherwise they would not have provided for an indemnity against it, appears to me to be straining the effect of a printed provision in a document of this sort much beyond the extent to which it is legitimate

---

[96] (1803), 4 East 130, at p. 135
[97] [1892] 1 Q B. 253, [1893] A C 8, 15.

to do so.'' In *Glynn* v. *Margetson*,[98] there was a wide deviation clause printed in a bill of lading for carrying oranges from Malaga to Liverpool The ship left Malaga for a port not on the way to Liverpool at all and in consequence of the delay the cargo of oranges was damaged. The House of Lords held that the printed clause must not be construed to defeat the main object and intent of the contract, which was to carry the oranges from Malaga to Liverpool and that therefore the liberty to deviate must be restricted to ports which were in the course of that voyage.

These instances are, of course, only further examples of the anxiety of our Courts to give effect to the intentions of the parties and to save the deed or contract if it can be done. Many other examples might be given A few are added. It was found that the signature to a letter from the borrower was a condition of obtaining an advance. The Court supplied the signature.[99] A bill of sale was executed to secure an advance of £70 and interest. Principal and interest were to be repaid by monthly instalments of '' seven '' on a certain day each month. The Court held the bill of sale valid and inserted '' pounds '' or '' £ '' after or before the word '' seven ''.[1]

Variations made in deed by the Court.—There are some additional rules adopted by our Courts to give effect to the intention of the parties. To that end the Court will supply words (as above), reject words or transpose them.

The duty of the Court in this respect is summed up by Chief Baron Kelly[2]: '' The result of all the authorities is that when a Court of law can clearly collect from the language within the four corners of the deed or instrument in writing

---

[98] [1893] A C. 351
[99] *Hall* v *Whiteman*, [1912] 1 K B 683
[1] *Mourmand* v *Le Clair*, [1903] 2 K B. 216; *Coles* v *Hulme* (1828), 8 B & C. 568
[2] In *Gwyn* v. *Neath Canal Co* (1865), L R 3 Ex. 209, at p 215

the real intention of the parties, they are bound to give effect to it by supplying anything necessarily to be inferred from the terms used and by rejecting as superfluous whatever is repugnant to the intention so discerned." So repugnant words will be rejected. In a lease granted to two jointly and severally, the word " severally " was rejected.[3] A bond was conditioned for payment " of lawful money which shall be in the year 1599 in and upon the 13th October next ensuing the date hereof ". The last three words were rejected.[4] So another bond was conditioned if the obligor did *not* pay. The " not " was rejected.[5] Where the only possible estate in the events which happened was a tail general, the word " male " in " tail male " was struck out [6] A separation deed provided that the expenses in respect of certain estates should be paid by the husband up to a certain date and afterwards should be paid by the wife and that the husband should be indemnified therefrom *and from all the present debts and liabilities* of the husband. The words in italics were disregarded as they made the clause inconsistent and repugnant.[7] Four persons covenanted with A that they their successors and assigns would pay certain sums, then followed a proviso that nothing in the deed should extend to any personal covenant of or obligation to the four persons or in anywise personally affect any of them. The Court held that the covenant was personal and the proviso repugnant and must be struck out. Had the proviso only restricted but not destroyed the personal liability it would have been good.[8]

So words may be supplied. The name of the grantor,[9]

---

3 *Slingsby's Case* (1588), 5 Rep 18b
4 *Sharplus* v. *Hankinson* (1597), Cro Eliz. 420
5 *Anon*, cited by Buller, J, in *Bache* v *Proctor* (1780), Doug 382, at p. 384
6 *Re Alexander's Settlement*, [1910] 2 Ch 225
7 *Wilson* v. *Wilson* (1847), 15 Sim 487.
8 *Furnivall* v *Coombes* (1843), 5 Man. & Gr 736. Cf. *Forbes* v. *Git*, [1922] 1 A C 256, at p 259
9 *Lord Say and Seal's Case* (1711), 10 Mod 41, at p. 45

the obligor,[10] the grantee,[11] "heirs",[12] and "heirs of the body",[13] or "of the body",[14] where the intention manifestly was to create successive estates tail So the word "assigns"[15] has been inserted, and "without issue".[16] "Pounds" has often been inserted (see p. 45). A post-nuptial settlement settled certain stock on the wife for life and after her death in trust for every child of the marriage who being a son or sons should attain twenty-one. If there were only one such child, the whole should be held in trust for such only child and *his* or *her* executors, etc. The maintenance clause also spoke of "*his* or *her* maintenance". The Court inserted the words "or being a daughter or daughters shall attain twenty-one" in the trusts for children.[17] So where a settlement recited that it was the desire of the settlor to benefit certain persons "all the children present and future of the marriage of A and B", and the trust was worded "in trust for such of the grandchildren as being male shall have attained the age of twenty-one or being female shall have married under that age". The Court held that the settlement should be given effect to considered as a whole, and that the provision for female children should be taken to read "or being female shall have attained the age of twenty-one years or shall have married under that age".[18] The obvious missing words were thus supplied. In a will there was a devise of real estate to a class of persons "or their issue". The words were held to be words of limitation and not of substitution—so the word "or" was taken as equivalent to the word "and".[19] (See *infra*, p. 255)

---

[10] *Dobson* v *Keys* (1610), Cro. Jac. 261
[11] Co Litt. 7a; *Butler* v *Dodton* (1579), Cary's Rep in Ch 86
[12] *Vernon* v. *Gatacre* (1566), Dy 253 a
[13] *Galley* v. *Barrington* (1824), 2 Bing 387.
[14] *Wall* v. *Wright* (1837), 1 Dr & Wal 1
[15] *Roe* v. *Hayley* (1810), 12 East 464
[16] *Kentish* v *Newman* (1713), 1 P Wms 234.
[17] *Re Daniel's Settlement Trusts* (1875), 1 Ch D 375
[18] In *Re Hargreaves' Trusts*, *Leach* v *Leach*, [1937] 3 All E R 545
[19] In *Re Hayden*, [1931] 2 Ch 333, distinguishing *Re Whitehead*, [1920] 1 Ch 198, where the same words were used but not applied to a class.

Words will also be transposed if necessary. " Words shall be transposed to support the intent of the parties."[20] "The law is not nice in grants, and therefore it doth often transpose words contrary to their order to bring them to the intent of the parties."[21] For instance, in a marriage settlement the words " such younger child or children " were made to include both sons and daughters by transposing the clause creating the power to make provision " for such younger children " and that containing the limitation to the daughters.[22] Punctuation may be inserted or disregarded. It is usual in formal documents to have no punctuation except full stops. " It is from the words and from the context, not from the punctuation, that the sense must be collected."[23] So the words " for her separate use during her coverture " were read as in parenthesis, so as to give the *cestui que trust* a life interest by implication.[24] In the old days there was much bad spelling and bad grammar both in the Latin and the English of documents, but so long as the " intent of the parties doth plainly appear "[25] neither vitiated a deed, unless the variation was so marked that the defence of *non est factum* was open to the defendant. Many instances of mistakes in the Latin of documents will be found in Norton.[26] Where the allegation is that the document is illegible, it appears that that is a question for the Judge and not for the jury; if the Court cannot decipher it, experts may be called.[27]

This may be summed up in Sir John Romilly's words in *Beaumont* v. *Salisbury*[28]: " If the Court sees an intention clearly and distinctly established by it [the deed] it has no

---

20 Comyns' Digest, art " Parols ", A. 21.
21 *Per* Willes, L C.J , in *Parkhurst* v *Smith* (1742), Willes 327, at p 332. Cf. *Magrath* v *M'Geaney*, [1938] Ir. R 309
22 *Fenton* v. *Fenton* (1837), 1 Dr. & Wal. 66.
23 *Per* Grant, M R , in *Sanford* v *Raikes* (1816), 1 Mer. 646. See *infra*, p 209.
24 *Tunstall* v. *Trappes* (1829), 3 Sim 286, at p. 312
25 *Per* Willes, L C J , in *Parkhurst* v. *Smith*, *supra*.
26 2nd ed , pp 103—105.
27 *Remon* v *Hayward* (1835), 2 Ad & El. 666.
28 (1854), 19 Beav 198, at p. 200.

difficulty in carrying that into effect, subject, of course, to any rules of law that may be applicable to it, but only qualified to that extent " In that case the words " to them and their heirs " were held obviously intended to take effect as an estate *pur autre vie.*

So where a deed of partnership provided that the capital of a deceased partner as at the last balance should be paid out to his representatives by instalments " with interest thereon from the date of the last balance " it was held that " thereon " referred not to the last antecedent instalment, but to the balance of capital for the time being remaining unpaid.[29] In *Anglo-Newfoundland Development Co.* v. *Newfoundland Pine and Pulp Co.*,[30] the construction of sub-leases to cut timber came before the Privy Council. The grant was " to the licensees and their assigns " with reservations to the licensors and their assigns " for the purpose of cutting such timber as the licensors may require ". The licensors claimed to have this last clause read as if the words " and their assigns " had been inserted after the word " licensors ". Their Lordships declined to do so, holding that the reservation was restricted to the personal requirements of the licensors, as otherwise they would be enabled to derogate from their own grant A clause in a deed founding and endowing a college provided that at no time was a woman to be appointed a governor. A later clause allowed a majority of three-quarters of the governors after the death of the founder and twenty years from the date of the original deed to revoke or alter the regulations The Court held that it was competent by this majority to revoke the rules as to enable a woman to be appointed a governor. This was not a fundamental principle which could not be altered [31] Debentures secured by a trust deed were issued by a company. The debentures contained a condition that nothing " herein "

---

[29] *Ewing* v *Ewing* (1882), 8 App Cas 822
[30] (1913), 83 L J P. C. 50
[31] *Re Holloway's Trusts* (1909), 26 T. L. R. 62.

contained should prevent the company from effecting specific mortgages on after-acquired property. Some seven years later the plaintiff took a mortgage from the company with notice of the debentures and the trust deed. It was held that the company had no power to create a mortgage in priority to the trust deed; that the security created by the trust deed and the debentures was cumulative and that the former was not controlled or qualified by the proviso in the latter; that " herein " meant " in this debenture " or " by this debenture ".[32] Of course, sometimes the Court finds it impossible to harmonise the various expressions in a document and when this is so a repugnancy occurs and the repugnant clause will be disregarded or struck out. For instance, in *Watling* v. *Lewis*[33] there was a covenant to pay and to indemnify the plaintiff from all claims in respect of a certain sum of money with an added proviso " not so as to create any personal liability on them (the defendants) or either of them ". The proviso was clearly repugnant to the covenant as its effect would be to destroy the personal liability of the defendants, which liability was, of course, the whole object of the covenant. It was therefore rejected. The old rule was stated to be that if two parts or clauses of a deed be repugnant, the first shall be received and the latter rejected.[34] This seems to be a mere rule of thumb, totally unscientific and only to be resorted to when all else fails. It did happen in the last case cited above that the repugnancy was in the later clause and this no doubt often happens, but the rejection of the repugnant clause or proviso is not based on the fact that it comes after the other, but that its rejection is necessary to effectuate the real intention of the parties. As Wilde, C J., said[35]: " As the different parts of the deed are inconsistent with each other, the question is, to which part effect ought

---

32 *Wilson* v. *Kelland*, [1910] 2 Ch 306
33 [1911] 1 Ch 414
34 Shep Touch. 88
35 In *Walker* v *Giles* (1848), 6 C. B 662, at p. 702.

to be given. There is no doubt that, applying the approved rules of construction to this instrument, effect ought to be given to that part which is calculated to carry into effect the real intention, and that part which would defeat it should be rejected." In *Forbes* v. *Git* [36] the Privy Council had before it two clauses of a building contract, the question being whether the effect of the first clause was destroyed or only qualified by the later clause. Lord Wrenbury said: " If in a deed the earlier clause is followed by a later clause which destroys altogether the obligation created by the earlier clause, the later clause is to be rejected as repugnant and the earlier clause prevails. . . . But if the later clause does not destroy but only qualifies the earlier, then the two are to be read together and effect is to be given to the intention of the parties as disclosed by the deed as a whole "

Occasionally, the question is determined by statute. The Bills of Exchange Act, 1882, s. 9 (2), provides that where there is a discrepancy between words and figures in a negotiable instrument, the amount denoted by the words is the amount payable. In a recent case of a legacy, stated in words and figures which did not agree—" the sum of one hundred pounds (£500) "—Simonds, J., rejected the rule in negotiable instruments and adopted Coke's rule (Co Litt. 112-6) with regard to wills that the last words are the effective ones. [37]

IV.—AMBIGUITIES AND EQUIVOCATIONS

An ambiguity is defined as " an expression capable of more than one meaning ", and ambiguities in deeds and documents are classed as patent or latent. A total blank, for example, is sometimes called a patent ambiguity, for it is apparent on the face of the deed. But this seems to be inaccurate for the phrase " I leave £100 to —— ", though apparent on the

[36] [1922] 1 A. C. 256.
[37] *Re Hammond, Hammond* v *Treherne*, [1938] W. N 236

face of the document, simply means nothing at all   It is hardly a patent ambiguity for it is not capable of *any* meaning, far less of more than one. So "a complete blank cannot be filled up by parol testimony, however strong".[1] Thus a true patent ambiguity will exhibit on the face of the deed an uncertainty or inconsistency: "I leave £100 to A or B", "I leave my horse to one of the sons of C", "I bequeath £500 to my granddaughter ——".   To a person reading these documents, and knowing nothing of the circumstances, there is clearly an ambiguity; whereas in a latent ambiguity the sense *seems* perfectly clear on a perusal of the document. It is not until further facts are disclosed that the ambiguity appears: "I leave £100 to my nephew John William Jones." It *looks* quite clear and the intention plain, until it appears that the testator had no nephew called John William, but one called Frederick Arthur Jones, or he may have had two nephews each called John William Jones.   It is thus discovered that there are several persons to whom the description adopted by the testator may apply. Where this happens, an *equivocation* is said to arise—that is to say, an equivocation arises where the description employed seems to be applicable to more than one, it being clear that only one was intended. An inaccurate description is one which does not exactly fit any person or thing or class of persons or things. A description may be equivocal without being inaccurate: A leaves to D "my house at E", where A has two houses at E and it is uncertain which he means to give D, but it is not an inaccurate description of A's house at E, or a description may be inaccurate without being equivocal as, *e.g.*, "I leave my shares in the Reigate Drapers Company to F"—whereas the only shares the testator had were in the Reigate Dyers Company

It is commonly said that no evidence is admissible to explain a patent ambiguity. The rule is derived from Bacon,

[1] *Per* Lord Hannen in *In the Goods of De Rosaz* (1877), 2 P. D 66

who said [2] that "*ambiguitas patens* is never holpen by averment", *i.e.*, evidence. The reason given by Bacon is that
if evidence were admitted it would "make all deeds hollow"
and would in fact nullify the requirements of the law as to
transactions for which deeds are necessary, for the deed
would practically be displaced by the extrinsic evidence As
Phipson [3] points out, this has become embedded in our law
of evidence, whereas it had in its origin application only to
pleading upon instruments under seal.

Any of the evidence previously set out [4] as admissible to
interpret a document may be brought to bear on the interpretation of a patent ambiguity. For instance, "I leave
£100 to A or B", may refer to a single person whom the
testator knew by either name So extrinsic evidence may be
given of the circumstances surrounding the testator at the
time he made his will; of the literal meaning of the words
he used; the intrinsic evidence, if any, afforded by the deed
itself What may *not* be given is direct evidence of the
testator's intention—and it is most probably this that is meant
when it is said that no extrinsic evidence may be given to
explain a patent ambiguity. As in *Saunderson* v. *Piper*,[5]
where Tindal, C.J., said: "Where there is a doubt on the
face of the instrument the law admits no extrinsic evidence
to explain it" The learned Chief Justice meant direct
evidence of intention and the case quoted involved a variation
in the figures and words in a bill of exchange.

To take a few examples of the kind of evidence admitted
in cases of patent ambiguity: In *Kell* v. *Charmer* [6] a will ran
as follows: "I give and bequeath to my son William the sum
of i.x.x. To my son Robert Charles the sum of o.x x."
Evidence was called to show that the testator was a jeweller
and these signs were private marks of prices used in his

---

[2] Elem Rules, 23; Bac Law Tracts (ed 1737), p 99
[3] Manual of Evidence (5th ed), p 285.
[4] Pp 28-36, *supra*
[5] (1839), 5 Bing. N C 425, at p 431
[6] (1856), 23 Beav 195

trade and meant £100 and £200 respectively—an example of the translation of the terms used in a document which we saw [7] was permissible. A voting paper for the election of an alderman began " I, the undersigned A B " and ended with the signature " C D ". Evidence was admitted that the town clerk had inserted A B's name in order that the voting paper might be used by. him, but that by mistake he had handed it to C D who had signed it. The evidence was held admissible and the vote valid.[8] A testator left " to my grandnephew Robert O. £100 ". There was no such grand-nephew, but he had four of other names. Another document in the testator's writing was admitted in evidence to show that he thought a grandnephew, who was the brother of Alfred O., was called Robert, whereas his real name was Richard. Instructions to his solicitor for his will were also admitted, not as evidence of the deceased's testamentary intentions but to show that the testator was under a mistake as to the name of Richard O.[9] So in the case of a *partial*, but not a total, blank: " Percival —— of Brighton, Esq., the father." Evidence was admitted that the testator knew two persons called Percival Boxall, father and son, both living at Brighton.[10] If all the admissible evidence fails to elucidate the patent ambiguity, and the intention of the parties cannot be ascertained, the document or the part of it containing the ambiguity will be void for uncertainty.

In a latent ambiguity or equivocation the difficulty is not discovered till evidence as to the literal meaning of the words used and as to the circumstances of the parties at the time the document was executed, in fact all the evidence admissible to resolve a patent ambiguity, is exhausted. The ambiguity still remains. " £100 to my granddaughter ——." The testator has only one. A patent ambiguity is resolved by

---

[7] Pp 32-34, *supra*
[8] *Summers* v *Moorhouse* (1884), 13 Q B D 388.
[9] *Re Ofner*, [1909] 1 Ch. 60
[10] *In the Goods of De Rosaz* (1877), 2 P D. 66

extrinsic evidence of circumstances; or possibly by intrinsic evidence in the will itself, as, for example, if in another part of the will the testator leaves a watch " to my granddaughter Rose, to whom I have already left £100 ". But suppose the testator is discovered to have three granddaughters, a latent ambiguity arises which the evidence so far admissible will probably fail to solve, unless there is some intrinsic evidence such as that just cited. When it has so failed, but only then, an entirely new category of evidence is admissible, *viz.*, evidence of intention, or evidence of what must have been in the mind of the party or parties when the document was executed. It tends to prove intention as an independent fact—independent, that is, of the words used in the document—and will be directed as to whom or what the party had in mind when he made that particular provision. It cannot be too strongly emphasised that this is an entirely different class of evidence from that admissible in the case of patent ambiguities. The evidence is " in support of " the express words and therefore not an infringement of the rule [11] against adding to or varying a written document by oral evidence. That such evidence is admissible was laid down centuries ago, *e.g., Lord Cheyney's Case* (1591),[12] where direct evidence was held admissible as to which son was intended to take under his father's will; or where a father and son bore the same name.[13] Sir James Wigram [14] says with regard to wills : " Notwithstanding the rule of law, which makes a will void for uncertainty, where the words, aided by evidence of the material facts of the case, are insufficient to determine the testator's meaning—Courts of law, in certain special cases, admit extrinsic evidence of *intention* to make certain the *person* or *thing* intended, where the description in the will is insufficient for the purpose." Lord Dunedin applied the

---

[11] See *infra*, p. 70
[12] 5 Rep 68, at p 68b
[13] *Haliwel* v *Courtney* (1496), Y B 12 Hen 7
[14] Extrinsic Evid , Prop VII

following test as a definition of an ambiguity [15]: "Would the description standing as it does, supposing there had been no competitor who had the exact name, have fitted the second competitor? If that is so, I think the question of ambiguity arises." There was in fact no ambiguity in that case as the testator had accurately described the English society and inaccurately described the Scottish Society which tried to show that the testator must have meant something different from what he had said.[16] To give some examples of cases where a latent ambiguity was held to render direct evidence of intention admissible: "83 Cambridge Road to my great-nephew, Frederick Johnson." Earlier in her will the testatrix gave another house "to my great-nephew Richard Johnson". She had a niece, Elizabeth Johnson, who had three sons, Robert William, Joseph Francomb (known as "Frank") and Richard Johnson. Extrinsic evidence was admitted to show that Joseph Francomb was the person to take 83 Cambridge Road.[17] A. made provision for "my nephew Arthur Murphy".[18] There were three nephews called Arthur Murphy; two were legitimate sons of brothers, and one was the illegitimate son of a sister who had married a legitimate niece. The Court laid down five propositions: (i) If there had been only the two legitimate nephews, it would have been impossible on the evidence before the Court to tell which was intended and the result would have been an intestacy (ii) As against one legitimate claimant evidence could not be admitted in favour of the illegitimate claimant,[19] but the Court was entitled to look at the evidence as to the family. (iii) If from that evidence it appeared

---

[15] *National Society for the Prevention of Cruelty to Children* v. *Scottish Society for the Prevention of Cruelty to Children*, [1915] A C 207, at p 214

[16] Cf *Re Raven*, [1915] 1 Ch 673, where, although there was no society of exactly the name used by the testator, no extrinsic evidence was admitted as to intention as the description adopted did not apply indifferently to more than one society—hence no latent ambiguity.

[17] *Re Ray*, [1916] 1 Ch 461

[18] *Re Jackson, Beattie* v. *Murphy*, [1933] Ch 237.

[19] See *infra*, p 156

that the testatrix did not intend either of the legitimate nephews but did intend to describe the illegitimate nephew, the Court could not disregard such evidence (iv) To avoid the ambiguity the Court was entitled to consider the claims of the illegitimate nephew. (v) On the evidence the person who had married a niece and so was in a sense a nephew was clearly intended and he took a share in the residuary estate. A will contained the following bequest: " To my nephew, Clifford Rich, the infant child of my late niece Annie Gertrude Rich £1,000 " There was no such nephew, but a great-nephew called Kenneth Higham Rich. The Court of Appeal pointed out that in the case of *James* v *Smith* [20] there was an interpretation clause in the will, whereby great-nieces were referred to as nieces. In the case before it,[21] Lawrence, L.J , said: " A mere misdescription in one part of the will does not necessarily imply that the same misdescription will be applied in other parts of the will, though it is no doubt some, but by no means conclusive, indication when a testatrix calls a great-nephew a nephew that she means that word to be applied in the same sense in other parts of her will " " What is really meant by saying that the testator has made his own dictionary is that on the construction of the particular will as a whole, the testator has shown an intention that a certain expression should bear a certain meaning That is not a principle, it is merely construing the will according to the true meaning of the language employed by the testator to express his intention The governing canon of construction is that the Court's function is to ascertain from the expressed words of the will, what is the true intent of the testator " So in *Re Hubback*,[22] " to my granddaughter —— ". The latent ambiguity appeared when it was found that the testatrix had three granddaughters.

[20] (1844), 14 Sim 214

[21] *Re Ridge* (1933), 149 L T 266, at pp 269, 270   Cf *Re Green*, [1914] 1 Ch 134

[22] [1905] P. 129; *Re Waller* (1899), 80 L T 701, *Re Jeffery*, [1914] 1 Ch 375

Extrinsic evidence was admitted to explain the latent ambiguity and to establish the intention of the testatrix. In a case [23] unconnected with a will a railway engineer was to receive an extra commission " on the estimate of £35,000 in the event of being able to reduce the *total cost of the works* below £30,000 "; the dispute was as to the meaning of the words in italics and evidence was held to be admissible to show what items of cost the estimate related to and that the words meant " the cost to the owner of the completed railway ", *i.e.*, to include cost of works and land, under the rule that where the words are susceptible of more than one meaning, extrinsic evidence is admissible to show what were the facts which the negotiating parties had in mind, in other words, their intention.

Evidence of user.—This means that in the case of an ambiguity, judicial notice will be taken of the way in which the parties themselves have interpreted their rights and duties under the document (see *infra*, p. 80) In *Leprairie* v. *Compagnie de Jésus*,[24] Lord Cave said: " In view of the ambiguity of the grant, it is permissible to take note of the manner in which it was construed at or about the time of its execution, and accordingly reference may be made to certain agreements. . . ." In *Doe* v. *Rias*,[25] Tindal, C.J., in a case of a modern document, said. " We are to look at the words of the instrument and to the acts of the parties to ascertain what their intention was; if the words of the instrument be ambiguous, we may call in the aid of the acts done under it as a clue to the intention of the parties." And in *Chapman* v *Bluck*[26] Park, J ; said: " The intention of the parties may be collected from the

---

23 *Bank of New Zealand* v. *Simpson*, [1900] A. C 182. Cf. *Macdonald* v. *Longbottom* (1859), 1 E & E. 977 (" Your wool "), *Smith* v *Thompson* (1849), 8 C. B (o s) 44 (" money remitted for business purposes ")

  24 [1921] A C 314, at p 323

  25 (1832), 8 Bing 178, at p. 186

  26 (1838), 4 Bing N. C 187, at p. 195

language of the instrument and may be elucidated by the conduct they have pursued."

In a more recent case [27] the question arose as to whether the land intended to be conveyed was that described by the boundaries in the certificate issued by the Government or the area marked on the plan, which disagreed. The parties had always treated the latter as the true area conveyed. It was held by the Privy Council that evidence of user may be given in order to show the sense in which the parties used the language employed, and that this rule applies to both modern and ancient documents and whether the ambiguity be patent or latent.

Election. — This is another method of resolving an ambiguity, *viz*, by the election or choice of one of the parties, and there is much learning in the old books and cases on this subject.[28] Which of the parties had the option depended on whether the property had passed or not. "If I give to a man my cow or my horse, he can take either at his election; but if I promise to give him a cow or horse at a future time, it is in my election to give him which I choose" [29] "If I give you one of my horses, although that be uncertain, yet by your election that may be made a good gift." [30] Apart from leases and tenancy agreements, the subject has occurred in two or three modern cases, though in one (*Savill* v. *Bethell*) it seems to have been doubted in the Court of Appeal whether an uncertainty could be made good by election. Thus, in *South Eastern Ry.* v. *Associated Portland Cement Co , Ltd.*,[31] the vendor was held to have the election as to where the tunnel was to be made within the limits of the strip designated

[27] *Watcham* v *East Africa Protectorate*, [1919] A C 533 Cf *Att. Gen* v. *Drummond* (1842), 1 Dr & War. 353; *Van Diemen's Land Co.* v. *Table Cape Marine Board*, [1906] A C 92
[28] Co Litt 145; 1 Roll Ab 725
[29] (1506), Y B. 21 Hen VII, 1813
[30] *Mervyn* v *Lyds* (1554), Dy 90 a, at p. 91 a
[31] [1910] 1 Ch. 12 See *infra*, p 134.

in the grant. In *Savill Bros., Ltd.* v. *Bethell,*[32] there was an
exception in favour of the vendor in a grant of a piece of
land not less than 40 feet wide, undefined by boundaries or by
colour on the plan. The piece was held to be not effectually
excepted, for as the conveyance operated at common law it
was void as an estate *in futuro*; or if it operated under the
Statute of Uses it offended the rule against perpetuities, as the
election by the vendor might not be made within the time
allowed by that rule. Stirling, L J., speaking of election,
said [33]: "If then by a deed there had been a grant of a plot·
of land to be ascertained by election it follows that till that
election nothing passed, and if the deed granted certain
specified lands, with the exception of a plot to be ascertained
by election, it seems to us that the deed would at once pass
the whole, but subject to the exception, which could only be
ascertained to take effect when the election was made."

A lease or tenancy agreement very often contains a clause
allowing either the lessee or the lessor or both the option
of breaking the lease at certain periods. A lease for twenty-
one years terminable at seven or fourteen years is very
common; the option generally being with the lessee to elect.
"For a term of two years certain from 24th June 1909
and thereafter from year to year until either party shall give
the other three calendar months' notice to terminate the
tenancy hereby created" was held to be a tenancy for three
years at least, determinable by notice expiring at the end
of the third or any other year [34] "Tenancy to continue from
year to year until determined by three calendar months' notice
which may be given on either side and at any time" Notice
before the end of the first year was held invalid.[35] A tenancy
began on May 1, 1895; rent was payable quarterly on May 1,
August 1, November 1 and February 1 in each year, "subject

[32] [1902] 2 Ch 523   See *infra*, pp 132, 134
[33] S C , p 539.
[34] *Re Searle*, [1912] 1 Ch 610
[35] *Mayo* v. *Joyce*, [1920] 1 K B 824.

to three months' notice on either side at any time ". The lessor gave the lessee on January 24, 1901, notice to quit on April 25, 1901 The notice was good.[36] A grantee from the King is said to have no right of election [37]

Inaccuracy.—The difference between an inaccuracy and an ambiguity has been already pointed out, as, for example, in the *Society for the Prevention of Cruelty to Children Case* [38] Suppose a testator or any other maker of a document says in one place " my house in London " and in another " my house in Piccadilly ". At first sight it looks like a patent ambiguity, but in fact it is an inaccuracy; the writer has adopted a general vague description in the first case and a particular description in the other, always assuming, of course, that he is referring to one and the same house This will in many instances be only possible to establish by extrinsic evidence as to the meaning of "my house " in each clause or by intrinsic evidence in the document itself It is possible that this fact has caused inaccuracies to be sometimes classed as ambiguities. So the particular or definite description is preferred to the general and vague, if there is no necessary inconsistency between the two For instance, a testatrix devised the real estate to which she had become entitled under her father's will " namely, the residence known as Orford House in the parish of Oakley " In addition to this, she had inherited under her father's will a freehold house in London, but there was no evidence that she knew that this had formed part of the property passing under her father's will. The word " namely " was held to amount not to a merely imperfect enumeration of the property intended to be devised, but to form the leading description and therefore to exclude the London property [39] In the case of a life assurance policy, the assured agreed that if *any statement in his written*

[36] *Soames* v *Nicholson*, [1902] 1 K B 157
[37] *Sir Walter Hungerford's Case* (1585), 1 Leon 30, *Brand* v *Todd* (1618), Noy 29
[38] *Supra*, p 56   [39] *Re Brocket, Dawes* v *Miller*, [1908] 1 Ch 185

declaration were untrue, the policy should be void, the assured then went on to declare that all the particulars furnished by him were correct and true and that " if it shall hereafter appear that *any fraudulent concealment or designedly untrue statement* be contained therein ", then the policy was to be void. (The generality of the first clause and the particularity of the second have been emphasised by italics.) The Court held that the policy could only be avoided for fraud, *i.e.*, a wilfully false statement,[40] Blackburn, J., observing : " In all deeds and instruments the language used by one party is to be construed in the sense in which it would be reasonably understood by the other." [41]

Uncertainty.—If the description as a whole or any part of it fails to ascertain the object of the writer or the parties, no meaning can be extracted and the document or the clause must be rejected for uncertainty, as, *e.g*, a conveyance of " all those trees that could reasonably be spared " [42]; an agreement to retire from business " so far as the law allows ".[43] It must be remembered in dealing with a matter of this sort that there is no rule that the same meaning ought to be attached to an expression in every part of a document in which it appears.[44] Part of the description may apply and part may not; if so, the latter will be rejected. Sometimes the description as a whole applies to no single object, but part of it applies to one, and part of it to another, object   As in *Doe* v. *Hiscocks*,[45] where the devise was to " John Hiscocks the eldest son of John Hiscocks ". John Hiscocks had two sons, Simon, his eldest, and John, his second son, but his eldest son by a second marriage. Evidence of the circumstances of the family may be given, and in fact all the evidence admissible in the

---

[40] *Fowkes* v *Manchester and London Life Assurance and Loan Association* (1863), 3 B & S 917.
[41] *S. C*, p 929
[42] *Mervyn* v. *Lyds* (1554), Dy. 90 a
[43] *Davies* v. *Davies* (1887), 36 Ch D. 359.
[44] *Watson* v *Haggitt*, [1928] A C. 127.
[45] (1839), 5 M. & W. 363.

case of a patent ambiguity, but not direct evidence of the testator's intention. In *Re Knox*,[46] a will contained a bequest to "the Newcastle-upon-Tyne Nursing Home" There was no such home correctly answering the description. A lapse was prevented by the general charitable intention, which emerged from other bequests in the will, and the Court applied the *cy-près* doctrine.

V.—SOME MISCELLANEOUS RULES

I —The expression of what is implied has no operation. This is a rendering of the Latin *expressio eorum quæ tacite insunt nihil operatur.* In other words the law takes its course and no notice is taken of the words used by the maker of the document; *e.g.*, if rent be reserved in a lease to the lessor during his life and after his death to his assigns,[1] the addition of assigns is implied by law; or a clause in a lease providing for demand and distress, the same being required by law[2]; the words are unnecessary So again, in *Cardigan* v. *Armitage*,[3] "assigns" was unnecessarily used in a reservation clause in a conveyance but omitted in another clause, and Bailey, J., asked[4]: "Because a useless word is inserted in one clause, is it necessary to insert it in every other where it is intended to have the same effect?" This case is an illustration of another rule of construction of which there are many instances in the cases

II.—Generally speaking, an expressed grant of a right or liberty does not restrict the implications of the law. In the case just cited the vendor reserved all coals in the lands conveyed, the vendor, his heirs and *assigns* to have liberty, during the time the vendor and his *heirs* should continue

---

[46] [1937] Ch. 109
[1] *Sury* v *Cole* (1627), Latch 44 and 225.
[2] *Doe* v. *Alexander* (1814), 2 M & S. 525, at p 532
[3] (1823), 2 B. & C 197
[4] At p 214 The case also illustrates a rule as to exceptions. Cf *infra*, p 132

owners of certain land, to sink and dig pits, and get coals. The heirs of the vendor assigned to a purchaser: it was held that the property in the coals passed to him and he was entitled to dig pits. The express liberty, *viz.*, to sink and dig pits, was not restrictive of that which would be implied by law, whereby the purchaser would be entitled to get the coals as an incidental right to his estate in fee, and, as incidental to his right to get the coals, to do all things necessary thereto.

Bailey, J., quoted *Hodgson* v. *Field*,[5] where there was liberty to make a sough (or drain) to a colliery and to make two sough pits in given parts to carry up the tail of the sough. The pits were made but a new pit was necessary to repair the sough. The grantee made it and had an action of trespass brought against him. It was held that the right of repair to the sough was incidental or implied in the grant of it, and this right was not restricted by the liberty to make the two sough pits. Again, a sum payable to a wife under a separation deed is not terminated by the death of the husband before the wife. It was held that there was no " contrary intention " expressed in the deed to exonerate the husband's estate as required by section 80 of the Law of Property Act, 1925.[5a]

The reverse question has occurred recently in two cases involving the common law right of support, the point being whether this was by implication displaced by the words of the reservation or exception. If the language is plain, the plain construction must be adopted. " It is therefore a question in each case of the proper construction of the instrument of severance, and unless the power to let down the surface be found there expressly or by necessary implication, the common law right of the surface owner will prevail." [6] For instance, where in a conveyance all mines

5 (1806), 7 East 615
5a *Kirk* v *Eustace*, [1937] A C 491
6 *Per* Swinfen Eady, L J , in *Beard* v. *Moira Colliery Co* , [1915] 1 Ch 257, at p 264, *Davies* v *Powell Duffryn Steam Coal Co* , [1917] 1 Ch 488,

and minerals were excepted and power reserved to the grantor
to enter and sink pits and shafts " in as full and ample
a manner to all intents and purposes as if these presents
and the partition and division " of the said lands had not
been done or made, it was held that the common law right
of support in the grantee was displaced and that the
vendors had the right to let down the surface   In the recent
case of *Waring* v. *Foden* and *Waring* v. *Booth Crushed
Gravel Co.*, it was said that in a reservation to a conveyance
the words must be interpreted according to the apparent
intention of the parties and local custom and so on—in fact in
accordance with the ordinary rules for the construction of
documents—and that this rule is applicable to conveyances
between private persons [7] So where a vendor excepted timber
out of a grant made by him and reserved it to himself, as
also liberty to cut and remove it.   In the particulars of sale
a certain date was fixed for the removal of the timber   When
he attempted to remove the timber after that date, the
defendants refused to allow him to do so, alleging that the
timber no longer belonged to him.   The Court of Appeal held
that the limited liberty to remove by the fixed date did not
qualify the absolute nature of the exception, which was
expressed in unambiguous terms.[8]

III.—Expressed stipulations will oust the implication of
any provision to the same effect: *Expressum facit cessare
tacitum.*   The rule is simply this : So long as the writer or the
parties avoid express stipulations, the law will attach any
implications which it allows to the provisions of the document,
but if the writer or the parties condescend to particular stipulations, the law assumes that they have stated all the provisions
they intended to include and have therefore intended to exclude

[1918] A C 555   Cf per Lord Halsbury in *New Sharlston Collieries Co* v
Earl of Westmoreland, [1904] 2 Ch 443 n , at p. 446 n , quoting *Chamber
Colliery Co* v *Twyerould* (1893), reported [1915] 1 Ch 265 n

[7] [1932] 1 Ch 276
[8] *Ellis* v. *Noakes* [1932] 2 Ch 98 n

the provisions which the law would imply. "The presumption is that having expressed some, they have expressed all the conditions by which they intend to be bound by that instrument." [9] So where an iron foundry and two dwelling-houses with their appurtenances were conveyed together with the fixtures in the dwelling-houses, it was held that the fixtures in the iron foundry did not pass. [10] A mortgage by a trustee covenanted for payment out of moneys which should come into his hands as trustee. The question arose as to whether a parol personal covenant to pay could be implied, there being an express covenant under seal with regard to payment. "The rule of law, as well as of reason and good sense, is '*expressum facit cessare tacitum*', and where there is an express covenant that the defendant shall out of the moneys which shall come into his hands and the personal estate of his testator (which was not included in the mortgage security) pay the sum advanced, we think it impossible to conclude that at the same time he made himself absolutely liable for the payment of it *simpliciter*." [11] So the covenants implied by the word " demise " are qualified by an express qualified covenant, *e.g.*, for quiet enjoyment.

IV.—A somewhat similar rule is expressed by the Latin maxim *Expressio unius est exclusio alterius*—that is to say, that the expression of one person or thing implies the exclusion of other persons or things of the same class but which are not mentioned. Suppose one man says to another: "We are looking forward to seeing you on Tuesday, bring the family with you; my wife wants to meet your mother" Does " the family " include everybody living in the other man's-house or only his wife and children with the expressed addition of his mother. Is his father or his sister-in-law not invited? This maxim as well as its " twin " (set out *supra*, p. 65)

9 *Per* Lord Denman, C J , *Aspdin* v. *Austin* (1844), 5 Q. B. 671, at p. 684.
10 *Hare* v. *Horton* (1833), 5 B. & Ad 715
11 *Mathew* v. *Blackmore* (1857), 1 H & N. 762, at p. 771.

must be applied with great caution. In *Lowe* v. *Dorling* [12] Farwell, L.J., said : " The generality of the maxim ' *expressum facit cessare tacitum* ' which was relied on, renders caution necessary in its application. It is not enough that the express and the tacit are merely incongruous; it must be clear that they cannot reasonably be intended to co-exist." In *Colquhoun* v. *Brooks* [13] Wills, J., said : " I may observe that the method of construction *expressio unius exceptio alterius* is one that certainly requires to be watched. The failure to make the *expressio* complete very often arises from accident, very often from the fact that it never struck the draughtsman that the thing supposed to be excluded needed specific mention of any kind." In *Mills* v. *United Counties Bank, Ltd.,* [14] a deed of assignment of an equity of redemption provided for an express and limited indemnity : it was held that the fuller indemnity, *i.e.,* that against a personal liability to repay, was thereby excluded. On the other hand, in *Gregg* v. *Richards* [15] the plaintiff took a conveyance of a house and land and a grant to her of a way four feet wide and forming part of a larger roadway running to the back of plaintiff's house. The right of access for vehicles had been enjoyed with the house conveyed; the conveyance passed the house " with the benefit of all such easements and privileges in the nature of easements which are now subsisting in respect of the property hereby conveyed ". It was held that the plaintiff was entitled to use the whole width of the roadway for the access of vehicles

V.—Words are to be construed against the person or party who uses them, provided this construction works no wrong This means that if two possible meanings remain after all admissible evidence to arrive at the true meaning has been employed, then that meaning will be adopted which is most

[12] [1906] 2 K B. 773, at p 785
[13] (1887), 19 Q B D. 400, at p 406   This statement was approved in the Court of Appeal (21 Q B D 52, at p. 65, *per* Lopes, L J)
[14] [1911] 1 Ch. 669; [1912] 1 Ch 231.
[15] [1926] Ch. 521

against the person using the words or expressions which have
given rise to the difficulty in construction, subject to this, that
the construction thus adopted must not work a wrong. Coke
explains this by an illustration—a tenant for life makes a
lease generally, this must be construed as a lease for his own
life, i e., the life of the lessor; for if it were for the life of
the lessee, "it should be a wrong to him in the reversion,"
or the reversioner. "It is a maxime in law", says Coke,[16]
"that every man's grant shall be taken by construction of law
most forcible against himself." "For in the common law
the grant of every common person is taken most strongly
against himself, and most favourably towards the grantee."[17]
"Every deed shall be taken more strongly against the grantor
and more beneficially for the grantee."[18] "Therefore it
standing so indifferent (or doubtful) we ought to construe
it most strongly against the grantor."[19] And many more
instances in the old reports.

In more modern times Abinger, C B., said in *Stephens*
v. *Frost*[20]: "If there is any difference between a deed
and a will where the instrument admits of two constructions, the deed is to be taken the more strongly against the
grantor" And Lord Romilly, M.R., said in *Johnson* v.
Edgware, etc., Ry[21]: "In the first place it is to be observed
that all deeds are to be construed most strongly against the
grantor"; and Lord Selborne, L C.; "It is well settled that
the words of a deed, executed for valuable consideration, ought
to be construed as far as they properly may in favour of the
grantee"[22] In spite of this body of judicial opinion,
Jessel, M R., discounted the rule in *Taylor* v. *Corporation
of St. Helens.*[23] He said: "I do not see how, according to

16 Co Litt 183 a, b.
17 *Per* Weston, J , in *Willion* v *Berkley* (1562), Plow 223, at p 243
18 *Justice Windham's Case* (1589), 5 Rep. 7, at p 7b.
19 *Manchester College* v *Trafford* (1679), 2 Show 31
20 (1837), 2 Y. & C. Ex. 297, at p 309
21 (1866), 35 Beav. 480, at p 484
22 *Neill* v *Duke of Devonshire* (1882), 8 App Cas 135, at p. 149.
23 (1877), 6 Ch D 264, at p 270.

the now established rules of construction, as settled by the House of Lords, in the well-known case of *Grey* v *Pearson*,[24] followed by *Roddy* v. *Fitzgerald*[25] and *Abbott* v. *Middleton*,[26] that maxim can be considered as having any force at the present day The rule is to find out the meaning of the instrument according to the ordinary and proper rules of construction. If we can thus find out its meaning, we do not want the maxim. If, on the other hand, we cannot find out its meaning, then the instrument is void for uncertainty, and in that case it may be said that the instrument is construed in favour of the grantor, for the grant is annulled." It may be noted that the cases cited by Sir George Jessel turned on the construction of wills and that *Neill* v *Duke of Devonshire* in the House of Lords and in which Lord Selborne spoke of the rule as " well settled " was decided after *Taylor* v. *Corporation of St. Helens*. It seems, therefore, that the rule still exists and that some effect will be given to it in a case of ambiguity, but it will only be applied in the last resort and where all other rules of construction fail.[27]

The same rule is applied to the construction of exceptions in a grant, as in *Savill Bros., Ltd.* v. *Bethell*, where Stirling, L.J., said[28]: " It is a settled rule of construction that where there is a grant and an exception out of it, the exception is to be taken as inserted for the benefit of the grantor and to be construed in favour of the grantee. If then the grant be clear, but the exception be so framed as to be bad for uncertainty, it appears to us that on this principle the grant is operative and the exception fails."

In *Willion* v *Berkley* (*supra*, p. 68) Weston, J , said: " The King's grant is taken most strongly against the grantee,

---

[24] (1857), 6 H. L C 61.
[25] (1858), 6 H. L C. 823
[26] (1858), 7 H L C 68
[27] *Lindus* v *Melrose* (1858), 3 H. & N 177, 182, 2 Bl Com 380; Bac. Max., reg 3
[28] [1902] 2 Ch 523, at p 537, cf p 60, *supra* Cf *per* Holroyd, J., in *Bullen* v. *Denning* (1826), 5 B & C 842, at p 850

although the thing which he grants came to the King by purchase or descent." This is in distinction to the grants of "every common person" referred to in the extract from his judgment above, and the last clause is inserted to show that not only Crown lands are included. We saw previously that there is no election against the King.[29]

VI.—PAROL EVIDENCE AND WRITTEN DOCUMENTS

It is a familiar rule of law that no parol evidence is admissible to add to, contradict, vary or alter the terms of a deed or any written instrument, for the rule applies as well to deeds as to contracts in writing. As it stands this is not a rule of interpretation but of law, and means that the interpretation of the document must be found in the document itself with the addition, if necessary, of such evidence as we have previously seen is admissible for explaining or translating the words and expressions used therein. Whether this rule of law can be said to be maintained inviolate in the face of what follows may at the present day be questioned; that it exists and is well-recognised is undoubted. Thus Lord Thurlow in 1781: "The rule is perfectly clear that where a deed is in writing, it will admit of no contract that is not part of the deed. Whether it adds to, or deducts from, the contract, it is impossible to introduce it on parol evidence."[1] Park, J., in 1821,[2] said: "I have never heard the general rule contradicted, that parol or extrinsic evidence cannot be admitted to contradict, vary or add to the terms of a deed." And Cozens-Hardy, M.R., in 1914[3]: "It is perfectly clear that when you have a conveyance which expresses the final concluded deliberations of the contract between the parties you cannot affect or alter that by reference to the antecedent

29 *Supra*, p. 61.
1 *Lord Irnham* v *Child* (1781), 1 Br. C C. 92, at p 93
2 *Smith* v *Doe* (1821), 2 Brod & Bing 473, at p. 541.
3 *Millbourn* v. *Lyons*, [1914] 2 Ch. 231, at p. 240.

contract." The Master of the Rolls quoted Brett, L.J., in *Leggott* v. *Barrett* [4]: " I entirely agree with my Lord that where there is a preliminary contract in words which is afterwards reduced to writing, or where there is a preliminary contract in writing which is afterwards reduced into a deed, the rights of the parties are governed in the first case entirely by the writing and in the second case entirely by the deed, and if there be any difference between the words and the written document in the first case and between the written agreement and the deed in the other case, the rights of the parties are entirely governed by the superior document and the governing part of that document " So in the same case [5] James, L.J., said : " It is very important according to my view of the law of contract both at common law and at equity that if the parties have made an executory contract which is to be carried out by a deed afterwards executed, the real completed contract is to be found in the deed and that you have no right whatever to look at the contract, although it is recited in the deed, except for the purpose of construing the deed itself." So the drafts of a deed cannot be admitted either to alter its language or to help in its interpretation. [6] As debentures contain the whole contract between the company and the debenture-holders, the prospectus cannot be imported to interpret the contract [7] In *Mercantile Bank of Sydney* v. *Taylor* [8] it was held that the legal effect of a release could not be modified by evidence of verbal negotiations to show an agreement to reserve rights against the sureties, all previous communications having been superseded by the agreement and that these could not be referred to either for adding a term to the agreement or for altering its ordinary legal construction.

---

[4] (1880), 15 Ch. D 306, at p 311.
[5] S. C., at p 309
[6] *National Bank of Australasia* v *Falkingham*, [1902] A. C. 585, at p 591
[7] *Re Chicago and North-Western Granaries Co., Ltd*, [1898] 1 Ch 263
[8] [1893] A C 317 Cf *Re Tewkesbury Gas Co*, [1911] 2 Ch 279, and contrast *Jacobs* v. *Batavia and General Plantations Trust, Ltd*, [1924] 1 Ch 287, *infra*, p 74

It ought, perhaps, to be added that by the common law a deed could not be varied or discharged save by another deed, and not by a writing under hand only or by word of mouth,[9] but by the rules of equity contracts under seal could be discharged by parol[10] and that rule now prevails.[11]

The Statute of Frauds.—Some difficulty has arisen with contracts for which a memorandum in writing is required by the Statute of Frauds. In *Goss* v. *Lord Nugent*,[12] Lord Denman referred to the inadmissibility of verbal evidence as to what passed between the parties so as in any way to vary or qualify the written contract. There the inadmissible evidence referred to an alleged verbal waiver of a defect in title on a sale of land. In *Noble* v. *Ward*,[13] on the other hand, there was a written contract for the sale of goods of over £10 in value, and an alleged verbal agreement to extend the contract time for delivery. It was held that the original contract was unaffected by the parol variation. Sir John Salmond says[14]: " The combined result of *Goss* v. *Nugent* and *Noble* v. *Ward* is that a subsequent parol variation of a written contract under the Statute of Frauds or the Sale of Goods Act is inoperative either to enable the contract to be enforced in its altered form or to prevent it from being enforced in its original form. The variation operates neither by way of contract nor by way of rescission."

But though a contract under the Statute of Frauds cannot be *varied* by a parol agreement, it can be rescinded by that method, though the rescinding contract would itself be unenforceable under the Statute of Frauds.[15] A limit of time

---

9 *Kaye* v *Waghorn* (1809), 1 Taunt 428
10 *Webb* v *Hewitt* (1857), 3 Kay & J 438
11 15 & 16 Geo 5, c 49, s 44, *Steeds* v *Steeds* (1889), 22 Q B D 537; *Berry* v *Berry*, [1929] 2 K. B 316
12 (1833), 5 B & Ad. 64, at pp. 64 65
13 (1867), L R 2 Ex 135
14 Salmond and Winfield, Law of Contracts, p 325
15 *Morris* v *Baron*, [1918] A. C. 1

for the acceptance of an offer or for the delivery of goods may be extended by parol, and this is not a parol variation of a written contract (*Levey & Co.* v. *Goldberg*, [1922] 1 K B 688), or, if not extended, the actual acceptance, though out of time, may be treated as a valid acceptance and a memorandum in writing is unnecessary.[16] The postponement of delivery is a mere forbearance (*Bessler, Waechter and Glover & Co* v *S. Derwent Coal Co.*, [1938] 1 K. B. 408). The Statute of Frauds will, however, not be allowed to be pleaded if to do so would be to protect a fraud. "The principle of the Court is that the Statute of Frauds was not made to cover fraud."[17]

Extrinsic evidence when admissible.—Apart from the Statute of Frauds, "it is competent to the parties, at any time before the breach of it [*i.e*, their written contract], by a new contract not in writing, either altogether to waive, dissolve or annul the former agreements, or in any manner to add to or subtract from or vary or qualify the terms of it, and thus to make a new contract which is to be proved partly by the written agreement and partly by the subsequent verbal terms engrafted on what will be thus left of the written agreement"[18] So that extrinsic evidence may be given to show that the writing is not the agreement come to by the parties or is not the whole of it, *e g*., where bought and sold notes did not contain the real contract (which was not in writing) between the parties.[19] In the case cited Bramwell, B., said[20]: "Where the parties to an agreement have professed to set down their agreement in writing, they

---

[16] *Bruner* v *Moore*, [1904] 1 Ch 305; *Morrell* v *Studd and Millington*, [1913] 2 Ch 648; *Hartley* v *Hyams*, [1920] 3 K. B 475

[17] *Per* Turner, L J, in *Lincoln* v *Wright* (1859), 4 De G & J 22, *Haigh* v *Kaye* (1872), L R 7 Ch 469, *Re Duke of Marlborough*, [1894] 2 Ch 133, at pp 142, 145

[18] *Per* Lord Denman, C J, in *Goss* v *Lord Nugent* (1833), 5 B & Ad 58, at p 64

[19] *Rogers* v *Hadley* (1863), 2 H & C 227.

[20] *S C*, p 249 Cf *Rose and Frank Co* v *Crompton*, [1925] A C 445

cannot add to it or subtract from it or vary it in any way by parol evidence; otherwise they would defeat that which was their primary intention in committing it to writing. But where at the time when a document which is apparently an agreement was signed the parties expressly stated that they did not intend it to be the record of any agreement between them, though this is a conclusion of fact which the jury should adopt with extreme reluctance, the parties would not in such a case be bound by the document." Evidence was also admissible where it related to circumstances under which the plaintiff's name was appended to a document which was no part of the agreement, but was placed before him for signature after the agreement was concluded.[21] The document may, therefore, be proved not to be the contract between the parties, but to have been executed for some other or subsidiary purpose, as in *Jervis* v *Berridge*,[22] where a document purported to be a transfer of a contract for the purchase of land, and was held to be a " mere piece of machinery . . . subsidiary to and for the purposes of the verbal and only real agreement ". In other words, the document did not form part of a contract partly in writing and partly verbal, but was in fact not the real contract between the parties at all The action was to restrain the defendant from using the written document in a manner inconsistent with the real agreement and was not one to enforce the verbal agreement. So evidence can be admitted to show that the contract is contained in several deeds or documents of which the deed or document sued on is only one and that the contract must be construed from the whole series. Of course, the document produced may itself bear evidence that it is only one of a series, which series constitutes a single document for the purpose of construing the contract This happened in *Jacobs* v. *Batavia and General Plantations Trust, Ltd.*[23] And under

---

21 *Bank of Australasia* v *Palmer*, [1897] A. C 540.
22 (1873), L R 8 Ch 351, 359—360
23 [1924] 1 Ch. 287 Cf p 42, *supra*

the Statute of Frauds, although no extrinsic evidence may be given to connect writings in order to satisfy the requirements of the statute (cf. *Boydell* v. *Drummond, supra,* p. 42), if the writings contain in themselves evidence of connection, that may be sufficient to constitute the requisite memorandum, and parol evidence to identify references in various documents has frequently been admitted.[24]

Evidence of collateral agreement.—Although evidence may not be given with the object of adding to a written contract, still evidence of a collateral agreement may be given and the parol agreement and the writing must be construed together as forming one contract. This in effect in many instances adds to the written agreement, but it must not contradict or be inconsistent with the written document. As Bowen, L.J , said in *Palmer* v. *Johnson*[25]: "Suppose the parties should make a parol contract, with the intention that it should afterwards be reduced into writing, and that that which is reduced into writing should be the only contract, then, of course, one cannot go beyond it; but if they intend, as they might, that there should be something outside such contract, they might agree that that should exist, notwithstanding that it was not in the contract which was put into writing. In the same way, when one is dealing with a deed by which the property has been conveyed, one must see if it covers the whole ground of the preliminary contract." So Lord Watson in *Barton* v. *Bank of New South Wales*[26]: "Where there is simply a conveyance and nothing more, the terms on which the conveyance is made not being apparent from the deed itself, collateral evidence may easily be admitted to supply the considerations for which the parties interchanged such a deed " So where a tenant agreed to become so on condition

[24] *Oliver* v. *Hunting* (1890), 44 Ch D. 205, *Filby* v *Hounsell,* [1896] 2 Ch 737, *Pearce* v. *Gardner,* [1897] 1 Q B 688, *Stokes* v *Whicher,* [1920] 1 Ch. 411.

[25] (1884), 13 Q B D 351, at p 357.

[26] (1890), 15 App. Cas 379

that the landlord would keep down rabbits [27] or repair and furnish [28]; or a verbal warranty by the landlord that the drains were in order, [29] or that a bill of sale should be suspended till the grantee had exhausted certain other securities for his loan. [30] So, too, the cases where the written agreement is subject to a verbal condition that it should not bind until certain conditions had been fulfilled, as in *Pym* v. *Campbell*, [31] where Erle, J., said . " Evidence to vary the terms of an agreement in writing is not admissible, but evidence to show that there was not an agreement at all is admissible."

It is probable that the type of case illustrated by *Taylor* v. *Caldwell* [32] comes under this head. The parties contract on some unexpressed basis, *e.g.*, that the subject-matter of the contract shall be in existence when the time comes for performance. If that basis is destroyed, the contract comes to an end or is " frustrated " The " bottom has dropped out of it " and neither party is bound. The " coronation cases ", illustrated by *Krell* v. *Henry*, [33] are of this kind and the many cases arising out of war emergency regulations and so on. [34] Evidence of a collateral agreement which would contradict the written terms will not be admitted, as where a tenant covenanted in the lease to pay rent quarterly in advance Before the lease was executed, the parties verbally agreed that the lessee should pay his rent each quarter by a bill at three months. This mode of payment was tendered and refused by the lessor, who sued for the rent. The Court

---

27 *Morgan* v *Griffith* (1871), L R 6 Ex. 70
28 *Angell* v *Duke* (1875), L R 10 Q B 174, *Erskine* v *Adeane* (1873), L R 8 Ch 756
29 *De Lassalle* v *Guildford*, [1901] 2 K. B. 215
30 *Heseltine* v *Simmons*, [1892] 2 Q B 547, 555
31 (1856), 6 E & B 370, at p 374; *Pattle* v *Hornibrook*, [1897] 1 Ch. 25.
32 (1863), 3 B & S 826
33 [1903] 2 K B 740
34 *Tamplin S S Co* v *Anglo-Mexican Petroleum Products Co.*, [1915] 3 K B 668, *Marshall* v *Glanvill*, [1917] 2 K B 87, *Metropolitan Water Board* v *Dick, Kerr & Co , Ltd.*, [1918] A C 119.

construed the covenant as meaning a payment in cash; payment by bill was not payment in cash and as the collateral agreement contradicted the written contract, evidence of it could not be admitted [35] But where the collateral agreement is itself in writing it is immaterial if it adds to or varies the terms of the document to which it is collateral. It is receivable in evidence and the Court must construe the two documents together.[36]

Implied terms.—Reference has been made in a previous section (p 31) to the rule which allows extrinsic evidence whereby the peculiar meaning of the words used may be discovered to the Court, *i.e* , evidence to translate the words and expressions in a document, just as we saw was the case with foreign or technical and scientific terms. To this end it was said that evidence of trade usages and terms was admissible. We now pass to a rule which is somewhat similar and is therefore often confused with the rule already considered. The rule is this: that certain *unexpressed* terms may be annexed to a written contract if not inconsistent with or repugnant to the written terms. In considering the former rule we were concerned with construing the *expressed* terms of the document and saw that-evidence of custom and usage might be given to explain those expressed terms The rule to be now illustrated is solely concerned with matters on which the writing is silent; *i.e.*, implied additional terms. So Parke, B ,[37] said: " The custom of trade, which is a matter of evidence, may be used to annex incidents to all written contracts, commercial or agricultural and others, which do not by their terms exclude it, upon the presumption that the parties have contracted with reference to such usage, if it is applicable." And Lord Campbell [38] explained the principle on which such

---

[35] *Henderson* v. *Arthur*, [1907] 1 K B 10
[36] *Jacobs* v *Batavia and General Plantations, Ltd* , [1924] 1 Ch 287
[37] *Gibson* v *Small* (1853), 4 H L C 353, at p 397
[38] *Humfrey* v *Dale* (1857), 7 El & Bl. 266, 274

evidence is admitted as being that the parties had not set down the whole of the terms of the contract in the writing, but only such as were to be defined by the specific agreement, leaving it to be understood that all the usual and invariable incidents of uniform usage were to be implied. He quotes as a repugnant example the case of *Yates* v. *Pym*,[39] where the warranty was for " prime singed bacon ", adding " that is to say, slightly tainted ". As a modern instance of repugnancy and of the custom being, therefore, inadmissible, *Westacott* v. *Hahn*[40] may be quoted. There the lessee's covenant to repair contained the words " being allowed all necessary materials for the purpose (to be previously approved in writing by the lessors) and carting such materials free of cost a distance not exceeding five miles from the farm ". Evidence of a custom for the lessee to repair with lessor's materials and to provide cartage was held inadmissible as it would be inconsistent with the terms of the lease. Again, a contract [41] to ship rubber from the East to New York " direct and/or indirect " was alleged to have been duly executed by shipping goods to the American Pacific seaboard and across to New York by train. Evidence of such a practice, said to have been general during the Great War, was disallowed as being contrary to the contract

A custom of the London Corn Exchange that a buyer of barley by sample is not entitled to reject for difference or variation unless the same were excessive or unreasonable was held a good custom.[42] So where the contract was for the sale of " best oil " which was to arrive by a certain ship, " wet, dirty and inferior oil, if any, at a fair allowance ". The oil arrived and contained only one-fifth of " best oil ". It was held that a usage might be proved that the contract was satis-

---

39 (1816), 6 Taunt. 446
40 [1918] 1 K B 495
41 *Re an Arbitration between L Sutro & Co and Heilbut, Symons & Co*, [1917] 2 K B 348
42 *Re Arbitration between Walker & others and Shaw, Son & Co.*, [1904] 2 K B. 152

fied if the oil delivered contained a substantial portion of " best oil " [43] As custom in this sense is not necessarily either ancient or universal, Sir Frederick Pollock thinks that " usage is the more appropriate term ".[44] Where a broker has purchased as such but without disclosing the name of his principal, he is in some cases liable by usage as the purchaser.[45] This, as Sir Frederick Pollock points out, is a strong instance of the rule under discussion as it in effect adds not only new terms but a new party to the contract. Where, however, the terms of the contract clearly indicate that the undisclosed principal is the only party to the contract, evidence of a custom. that the broker alone is liable is inadmissible.[46]

The principle is applied not only to contracts of all kinds, whether under seal or not, but to leases, as, e.g., to the customary right of the tenant to enter after the expiry of his lease and to take way-going crops.[47] Here again, if the custom be repugnant to the express terms of the lease, evidence of it will not be admitted, e.g , where the custom was for the outgoing tenant to leave the manure for the landlord and to be paid for it; the lease, however, contained a stipulation that the tenant should leave the manure for the landlord but said nothing about payment.[48]

It should be added, for the sake of completeness, that, although it is not a rule of interpretation, evidence may always be given to show that a deed or contract is not binding either on the ground of incapacity of one or all the parties to it, or by reason of fraud or duress or mistake, or, again, that the consideration is unlawful or that to enforce the bargain would be contrary to public policy, or to stifle a

[43] *Lucas* v *Bristow* (1858), El B & El. 907.
[44] Contract, (10th ed), pp 250, 251.
[45] *Humphery* v *Dale* (1858), El. B. & El 1004; *Pike* v. *Ongley* (1887), 18 Q. B D 708
[46] *Miller, Gibb & Co.* v *Smith and Tyrer*, [1917] 2 K B 141
[47] See *Wigglesworth* v *Dallison* (1779), 1 Doug 201, *Dashwood* v *Magniac*, [1891] 3 Ch 306, and 1 Sm L C (13th ed), 597
[48] *Roberts* v. *Barker* (1833), 1 Cr & M 808.

prosecution or as a reward for indemnity. Or again, that
in the case of a deed it was delivered as an escrow or subject
to a condition (see p. 7, *supra*), or in the case of a contract
under hand that it was conditional on some event which has
not been fulfilled.[49]

User to explain or construe deed.—Is the fact that the
parties have interpreted their contract in a certain way and
have been in the habit of acting upon it in accordance with
that interpretation any admissible guide to the construction
of the document? The answer in the case of a plain and
unambiguous contract is " No ". For instance, a subsequent
will of one of the parties was held inadmissible to aid the
construction of a settlement.[50] So in leases. In *Wynn* v.
Conway Corporation,[51] where the plaintiffs had been lessees
for ninety years under the same form of lease renewed
every eleven years, there was a lease for twenty-one years
with a covenant for renewal for twenty-one years after the
expiry of the first eleven years, " and so often as every
eleven years of the said term shall expire (the lessor) will
grant and demise such new lease upon surrender of the old
lease as aforesaid " This was held to entitle the lessee to a
perpetual right of renewal at the end of every successive period
of eleven years. But conversely in *Sherwood* v. *Tucker*.[52]
There a three years' tenancy agreement terminated on
December 25, 1917, and there was an option to the tenant to
purchase " during the three years hereby provided for ".
There were subsequently two informal endorsed extensions
each for three years The Court held that it was not intended
to extend the lease with all its provisions and that the option
did not extend beyond the first three years, as the words " We

   49 *Collins* v *Blantern* (1769), 2 Wils 347, 1 Sm L C. (13th ed.), 406;
Pym v *Campbell* (1856), 6 E & B 370, *Pattle* v *Hornibrook*, [1897] 1 Ch 25.
   50 *Doran* v. *Ross* (1789), 1 Ves. Jr 57, 59
   51 [1914] 2 Ch 705.
   52 [1924] 2 Ch 440 Cf. *Woodall* v. *Clifton*, [1905] 2 Ch 257, *per*
Romer, L J , at p 279

agree that this lease be extended " did not include the option. " The intention of the parties must be collected from the language of the instrument and may be elucidated by the conduct they have pursued " [53], e.g., to show on what terms the plaintiff was let into possession [54] or to test the accuracy of secondary evidence of a deed.[55] A curious example occurs in *North Eastern Ry* v. *Lord Hastings*,[56] where the parties had for many years interpreted a lease granted in 1854 in a sense different from that which it plainly bore. The parties had assumed that no rent was payable on coal not carried over Lord Hastings' land, whereas the true and plain construction was that the railway company was in fact liable to pay on all coal conveyed over any part of that particular line of railway, whether it passed over Lord Hastings' land or not The lease was unambiguous and the actings of the parties clearly contrary to its terms It is obvious that their mistake ought not to affect the construction of the lease and that no amount of user could prevail over the plain meaning of the words. Where, however, the document is ambiguous, evidence of user under it to show the sense in which the parties used the language employed is admissible and also acts of user before the grant These lead up to and explain what was afterwards granted and are cogent evidence of what was intended to pass by the grant. " When the obvious intention is to give a title to what has been so taken and retained before the actual grant, it is manifest that what has been so taken and retained is cogent evidence of what is granted." [57] In cases of partnership, evidence is admissible to prove a departure either by express or implied consent of the partners from the provisions of the partnership deed The evidence is not admitted to

---

[53] *Per* Park, J , in *Chapman* v *Bluck* (1838), 4 Bing N C 187, at p 195
[54] *S C.*, p 196.
[55] *Sadler* v *Biggs* (1853), 4 H L Cas. 435
[56] [1900] A C 260, 269 Cf *Clifton* v *Walmesley* (1794), 5 T R 564
[57] See p 58, *supra*, and the cases there cited *Van Diemen's Land Co.* v. *Table Cape Marine Board*, [1906] A C 92, at p 98, *per* Lord Halsbury; *Watcham* v. *East Africa Protectorate*, [1919] A C 533

C D S.   G

construe the written agreement but to prove that the partners
have agreed to abandon certain of the written provisions and to
substitute others either by express words or by conduct [58] As
Lord Langdale, M R., said in *England* v. *Curling* [59]. " With
respect to a partnership agreement, it is to be observed that, all
parties being competent to act as they please, they may put an
end to or vary it at any moment; a partnership agreement is
therefore open to variation from day to day and the terms of
such variations may not only be evidenced in writing, but also
by the conduct of the parties in relation to the agreement and
to their mode of conducting their business "

VII —User under Ancient Documents

In the case of very ancient documents, there may be great
difficulty in deciding on the meaning of the words employed,
and in that case evidence of usage is admissible to show
what was the meaning attached to the document soon after
its execution by those interested in its interpretation.   There
is a probability that at least some of these persons would have
insisted on a proper interpretation of the instrument, and if
a certain interpretation has been adopted and acquiesced
in for a long period of years this affords a probability of its
correctness.   This is what is called " contemporaneous interpretation " or " *contemporanea expositio* ", which Coke says
is a very strong factor in the law.   " In the construction of
ancient grants and deeds, there is no better way of construing
them than by usage · *contemporanea expositio* is the best way
to go by." [1]   " In construing such an instrument (*i.e* ,- an
ancient document) you may look to the usage to see in what

---

[58] See Partnership Act, 1890, s. 19.
[59] (1844), 8 Beav 129, at p 133. Cf. *Const* v *Harris* (1824), Turn & R
496, at p 523, *per* Lord Eldon.
[1] *Per* Lord Hardwicke, L C., in *Att.-Gen* v *Parker* (1747), 3 Atk. 576,
at p 577.

sense the words were used at that time."[2] "Contemporaneous usage is, indeed, a strong ground for the interpretation of doubtful words and expressions"[3] And in the same case in the Irish Court of Appeal Sugden, L.C., said: "One of the most settled rules for the construction of ambiguities in ancient documents is, that you may resort to contemporaneous usage to ascertain the meaning of the deed; tell me what you have done under such a deed and I will tell you what that deed means"[4] As we saw (*supra*, p. 58) the principle is equally applicable to a modern instrument.[5] Usage means not the common usage of mankind but usage under the instrument, and "when such acts have been done by persons purporting to act under the document, they afford the best possible evidence as to the interpretation which those persons placed upon it"[6]

Lord Halsbury, in *Van Diemen's Land Co* v *Table Cape Marine Board*,[7] thought that contemporaneous exposition was not confined to usage under the deed. Any circumstances tending to show the intentions of the parties whether before or after execution of the deed may be relevant. From what has been said it will be obvious that although usage is cogent with regard to what was taken to be the true interpretation of the document where the document is doubtful or ambiguous, no evidence of usage can override the words of the document where these are plain and clear. (Cf. *North Eastern Ry.* v. *Lord Hastings*, p 81, *supra*.) "Suppose the words of the charter are doubtful, the usage in this case is of great force; not that usage can overturn the clear words of a charter; but if they are doubtful, the usage under the charter will tend to explain the meaning of them."[8] So in *Chad* v *Tilsed*[9]

---

[2] *Per* Lord Campbell in *Drummond* v *Att -Gen* (1849), 2 H L C 837, at p. 863
[3] *S C*, *per* Lord Cottenham, at p. 861
[4] *Att -Gen.* v *Drummond* (1842), 1 Dr & War 353, at p 368
[5] *Watcham* v *East Africa Protectorate*, [1919] A C 533
[6] Norton on Deeds, p. 156   [7] [1906] A C 92, at p 98
[8] *Per* Lord Mansfield, C J , in *R* v *Varlo* (1775), 1 Cowp 248, at p 250
[9] (1821), 2 Brod & Bing 403, at p 406

Dallas, C.J., said · " In the case of a grant, no usage, however long, can countervail the clear words of the instrument, for what is done under usurpation cannot constitute a legal usage; but it is equally clear, that when a grant of remote antiquity contains general words, the best exposition of such a grant is long usage under it." Even evidence of modern usage is admissible. If usage has persisted up to the time of living memory, the presumption, if there is nothing to the contrary, is that the usage had continued beyond that time, just as in a case of prescription.[10] " As with respect to ancient deeds the state of the subject at their date can seldom, if ever, be proved by direct evidence, modern usage and enjoyment for a number of years is evidence to raise a presumption that the same course was adopted from an earlier period and so to prove contemporaneous usage and enjoyment at the date of the deed." [11] " It is not to be disputed ", said Bacon, V.-C., in *Earl de la Warr* v *Miles*,[12] " that when the necessity of the case requires it, evidence of more recent usage and custom may be adduced for the purpose of explaining old or obsolete, or even imperfect expressions to be found in ancient documents." But here again the evidence will not be admitted to vary or contradict the terms of the document if they are clear. " The necessity " (*i.e.*, for admitting evidence of usage) " must be apparent—the ambiguity must be found to be existing " [13] So ancient grants of manors were taken, on evidence of usage of such long standing that it might be assumed to be contemporaneous with the grant itself, to include the seashore between high and low water mark, and modern acts of ownership were admitted in evidence to show that these grants included such land [14] A right of nomination

---

10 Cf. *per* Lord Selborne, L C , in *Neill* v, *Devonshire (Duke of)* (1882), 8 App Cas 135, at p 156

11 *Per* Lord Wensleydale in *Waterpark* v. *Fennell* (1859), 7 H L C 650, at p 684

12 (1880), 17 Ch D 535, at p 573

13 S C

14 *Beaufort (Duke of)* v *Swansea (Mayor of)* (1849), 3 Ex 413, 425 *per* Parke, B.

of a schoolmaster given to " the vicar and his successors and the churchwardens for the time being " was held on evidence of usage to have been validly exercised by the vicar and a majority of the churchwardens [15] The examples already given (p. 80, *supra*) are applicable here, and there are many cases collected from the reports in Norton [16]

When does a document become ancient? In the law of evidence a document formerly thirty, now, by section 4 of the Evidence Act, 1938, twenty, years old is accounted " ancient ", but it does not follow that this rule would be applied here. In fact it certainly would not be applied, and a document of not more than thirty or twenty years old would not be regarded as ancient for the purpose of the admission of the evidence of user above referred to. This seems clear from the words of Lord Davey in *North Eastern Ry* v. *Hastings* [17]: " I have formed my opinion on what is to be found within the four corners of the instrument to be construed without adverting to the fact that the actings of the parties for forty-three years before the commencement of the action have been inconsistent with the views taken by your Lordships. I do not think that I could properly advise your Lordships to hold that the actings of the parties during that period, which does not exceed the limits of living memory, is evidence, upon which you can act without other grounds for doing so, of a lost agreement varying that of 1854 or, which is the same thing in another form, adopt the construction acted on by the parties as *contemporanea expositio.*" The same opinion has been applied to the case of " modern statutes ". It would therefore seem that in order to be " ancient " under this rule and so to let in evidence of *contemporanea expositio*, the document must have been executed before the time of living memory.

---

[15] *Withnell* v *Gartham* (1795), 6 T R 388.
[16] Pp 158—162
[17] [1900] A C 260, 268 see *supra*, p 81

VIII.—RULES AS TO TIME AND DATE

The reformed calendar was adopted by statute in the reign of George II in 1752.[1] This is the Gregorian calendar (1582) with corrections. The year now begins on January 1. So in deeds where feast days are mentioned, *e.g.*, as the commencement of a lease, those days mean the days in the reformed calendar and not those in the unreformed. Thus April 6 was old Lady Day and October 11 old Michaelmas Day; Martinmas was on November 23 instead of November 11 as it is to-day. Generally, in old leases the construction would be according to the modern dates, and no extrinsic evidence will be admitted to show that they relate to the old dates of the feasts; but in parol lettings evidence has been admitted to show a custom of the country to let with reference to the old dates.[2] This is of little importance to-day. We shall proceed to explain the ordinary references to time as used in deeds and written contracts.

Year—A period of twelve calendar months calculated either from January 1 or some other named day and consisting of 365 days in an ordinary year, and 366 days in a leap year. The ecclesiastical year, however, still begins on March 25, and the official revenue year ends on March 31 in each year. The intercalary day in leap years is theoretically attached to the preceding day, so that they together form only one day; thus a hiring on October 13, 1807, to serve till October 11, 1808, was held not to be a service for a year even though the year 1808 was a leap year.[3] A *quarter* consists of ninety-one days and a *half-year* is 182 days, a *full year*, however, being 365 days.[4] There are four "quarter days" in our

---

[1] By statute 24 Geo 2, c 23
[2] *Furley* v *Wood* (1794), 1 Esp 198; *Doe* v *Benson* (1821), 4 B & Ald. 588
[3] *R.* v *Inhabitants of Worminghall* (1817), 6 M. & S 350.
[4] *Anon.* (1575), 3 Dyer 345a, pl. 5.

calendar, *viz.*, March 25 (Lady Day) June 24 (Midsummer Day), September 29 (Michaelmas Day), and December 25 (Christmas Day). Sometimes a year is computed at actually less than 365 days A hiring from Whitsuntide in one year to Whitsuntide in the next will be a contract for one year, though, Whitsuntide being a movable feast, the period may contain fewer than 365 days.[5] So in *Grant* v. *Maddox* an agreement to act for three years meant three seasons or parts of those years when the theatre was open [6]

In cases where the Apportionment Act, 1870, does not apply, if a payment is to be made " in each year " or " per annum ", the sum is not apportionable and is only payable in respect of a complete year If the payment is " at the rate of " so much a year, it is apportionable and payable in respect of a portion of a year   " Shall be entitled to receive by way of remuneration in each year £5,000 " was held not to give remuneration at the rate of £5,000 a year.[7] So " £100 per annum " gave nothing for a broken part of a year, though " if the words had been at the rate of £100, I suppose there can be no question that the sum would have been apportionable ".[8] Any question of apportionment is now generally avoided by using the words " at the rate of ". In the definition of " term of years " in the Law of Property Act, 1925,[9] the expression is *inter alia* to include a term for less than a year or for a year or years and a fraction of a year, and from year to year

Month.—This always meant a lunar month of twenty-eight days, unless the context showed the contrary, or the circumstances of the case or a custom to the contrary displaced this presumption. " It is also clear that ' months ' denote at

---

[5] *R* v *Inhabitants of Newstead* (1769), Burr S C 669
[6] (1846), 15 M. & W. 737.
[7] *Per* Cozens-Hardy, J , in *Salton* v *New Beeston Cycle Co* , [1899] 1 Ch 775, at p 779
[8] *Per* Wright, J , in *Re Central de Kaap Gold Mines* (1899), 69 L J Ch 18
[9] S. 205 (1) (xxvii)

law lunar months unless there is admissible evidence of an intention in the parties using the word to denote 'calendar' months'": *per* Denman, C.J.[10] Apart from this, it meant a calendar month in ecclesiastical documents, mercantile documents (at least in the City of London), mortgages, statutes since 1850 (13 & 14 Vict. c. 21, s. 4) "unless a contrary intention appears" (Interpretation Act, 1889, s. 3), and the Rules and Orders of Court. Blackstone says[11]: "A month in law is a lunar month or twenty-eight days unless otherwise expressed; not only because it is always a uniform period, but because it falls naturally into a quarterly division by weeks Therefore a lease for 'twelve months' is only for forty-eight weeks, but if it be for a 'twelvemonth' in the singular number, it is good for the whole year." This was criticised by Atkin, L J , in *Phipps* v. *Rogers* (*infra*), where he said: "The reason seems inadequate. The result is to adopt a meaning which is nearly always contrary to the intention of the parties. The rule is fortunately almost destroyed by exceptions It does not apply to mercantile documents or to statutes or to mortgages or to cases where the context requires the meaning of calendar months. It never did apply to ecclesiastical law. In the residue of cases, however, it clearly does apply as it is established by a series of authorities which we cannot overrule" In many old ecclesiastical cases "month" has been held to mean calendar month.[12] As to mortgages, there is a pronouncement by Sir Ernest Pollock, M R , in *Schiller* v. *Petersen & Co*[13]: "There is a rule whereby in mortgage transactions the word 'month' is to be taken to mean calendar month." But in a contract for or connected with the sale of land "month"

---

10 *Simpson* v *Margitson* (1847), 11 Q B 23, 31, *Bruner* v *Moore*, [1904] 1 Ch 305, *Morrell* v. *Studd and Millington*, [1913] 2 Ch 648; *Helsham-Jones* v. *Hennen* (1914), 84 L J Ch 569

11 Com , Bk. II (8th ed), 141

12 *E g , Catesby's Case* (1607), 6 Rep 61b, *Sharp* v *Hubbard* (1675), 2 Mod. 58, *Burton* v *Woodward* (1692), 4 Mod. 95

13 [1924] 1 Ch 394, at p 417

means *prima facie* a lunar month unless from the context or surrounding circumstances it appears that the parties intended the contrary.[14] So in tenancy agreements, the Court of Appeal has held that the relationship of landlord and tenant has never been held to come within the statutory exceptions and that "three months" in a tenancy agreement, in the absence of evidence of a contrary intention, means three lunar months.[15] But where the holding was held to be from three months to three months, calendar months must have been intended.[16] So where the tenancy was "for the term of six months from the 1st of January next, and so on from six months to six months until one of the said parties shall give to the other of them six months' notice in writing to determine the tenancy, at and under the rent of £13 for every six months, the first payment to be made on the 1st day of July, 1830", it was plain that calendar months were intended.[17]

"The law in all cases, not mercantile contracts in the City of London, as to the meaning of the word 'month' meant lunar month. In all mercantile transactions in the City of London a month means a calendar month."[17] It is sometimes said that in *all* mercantile contracts "month" means calendar month, but this was doubted by Farwell, J, in *Bruner* v *Moore (supra)*, who thought that this did not apply to all mercantile contracts, and in that case, where the parties were aliens temporarily residing in London, an option to purchase "during the period of six months" was held to refer to lunar months. However, in a case concerning the sale of wine "at twelve months' credit", Pollock, C.B., said: "In commercial matters a 'month' always means a calendar month. In bills of exchange, promissory notes, invoices, times of credit and everything else relating to commercial

---

[14] Dart, V. & P (7th ed.), p 505
[15] *Phipps & Co* v *Rogers*, [1925] 1 K B 14
[16] *Per* Lord Ellenborough in *Kemp* v *Derrett* (1814), 3 Camp 510.
[17] *Per* Erle, C J , in *Turner* v *Barlow* (1863), 3 F. & F. 946, at p 949

matters, it is so and I know of no instance to the contrary." [18]
Further, with regard to the sale of goods " a month " *prima
facie* means a calendar month,[19] and in bills of exchange,
cheques and promissory notes the same presumption prevails.[20]

The presumption is now statutory that in all deeds,
contracts, wills and other instruments coming into force after
January 1, 1926, " month " means calendar month unless
the context otherwise requires.[21]

A calendar month ends on the day of the next following
month having the same number as that on which computation
began, *e.g.*, March 30 to April 30; but if the next month has
no day of the same number, the calendar month ends on the
last day of the next month, January 30 to February 28 or
29 (in leap year).

Day.—A day is a period of twenty-four hours—from
midnight to midnight. Generally speaking, a day is
indivisible—it is considered in law as the minimum in the
time scale. " For regularly the law maketh no fraction of
a day." [22] So a tenancy granted " from March 25 " commenced at midnight on March 25.[23] In reckoning age, a man
born on January 17, 1870, will attain full age on January 16,
1891.

In a modern case [24] the question arose as to whether a
legatee under a will had attained the requisite age of twenty-
five at the time of his death. He was born on July 22, 1891,
and died on July 21, 1916 It was held that he had attained
twenty-five years of age at the date of his death. So where
a tenancy agreement was for one year commencing on

18 *Hart* v *Middleton* (1845), 2 Car & Kir 9, at p 10; *Titus* v. *The
Lady Preston* (1726), 1 Str 652
19 Sale of Goods Act, 1893, s. 10 (2)
20 Bills of Exchange Act, 1882, s. 14 (4)
21 Law of Property Act, 1925, s 61
22 Co 3 Inst 53
23 *Meggeson* v. *Groves*, [1917] 1 Ch 158
24 *Re Shurey*, [1918] 1 Ch 266, cf *Anon* (1704), 1 Salk 44, *Toder* v.
Sansam (1775), 1 Bro P. C. 468.

September 30 inst., and the tenant went out of possession on the succeeding September 29 in the afternoon, the tenant was held to have occupied for a complete year.[25] So in charter-parties—*e.g.*, where demurrage was chargeable at a specified rate " per day or part of a day " if the goods were not unloaded and removed within forty-eight hours of the notice which the defendant received on a Saturday. He unloaded up to 1 p.m. on the Saturday, all Monday, and finished on Tuesday. The defendant was held liable for demurrage for the Tuesday.[26] So in " weather working days "—over half a day was reckoned as a whole day,[27] and where a fraction of a day was required to complete a discharge, the charterer was held entitled to the whole of that day.[28]

But " the law will distinguish fractions of a day where it is necessary . . . for the purposes of the decision to show which of two events first happened "; *e.g*, where the interests of third parties may be concerned [29] Where the Act 30 Vict. c. 5 provided that a dog licence should commence on the day it was granted and a man took out a licence at 1.10 p.m. on October 21, it was held he might be convicted of keeping a dog without a licence by proving that he had so kept the dog at 12 40 p.m on that day.[30]

Although, generally speaking, in computing lapse of time a day, as stated above, is to be taken to be a calendar day, still if the contract or plain intention requires, any period of twenty-four hours may be taken—*e.g.*, a motor car insurance policy generally begins at noon on one day and ends at noon on another day. So an insurance policy on a ship was for " thirty days in port after arrival ". She arrived at 11.30 a.m. on August 2, 1902, and stayed till September 1,

[25] *R* v *St Mary, Warwick* (1853), 1 El & Bl 816
[26] *L & Y. Ry.* v *Swan*, [1916] 1 K B 263
[27] *Branckelow S.S. Co* v *Lamport and Holt*, [1897] 1 Q B 570
[28] *Houlder* v *Weir*, [1905] 2 K B 267
[29] *Thomas* v *Desanges* (1819), 2 B. & Ald 586.
[30] *Campbell* v *Strangeways* (1877), 3 C P. D 105 Cf *Clarke* v. *Bradlaugh* (1881), 7 Q B D 151

1902, and was totally lost at 4 30 p.m. on that day. The Court of Appeal (affirming the judgment below) held that "thirty days" here meant thirty consecutive periods of twenty-four hours each, and that the first period had begun to run at 11.30 a m. on August 2, 1902, and that therefore the policy had ceased to cover the risk.[31] In charterparties days and running days are consecutive and inclusive of Sundays and holidays or days when work is prevented by weather, unless there is some agreement or custom to the contrary. And in *Nielsen* v. *Wait*[32] it was said that "running days" and "days" are the same and include not only working days but *every* day, Sundays and holidays also

"Working days" mean days on which it is lawful or customary to work as well as days on which work is actually done.

"*From*".—The rule, illustrated by many cases from the seventeenth century onwards, is that the day of the date, or the date of a deed or any fixed day, is to be *excluded* in the computation; e.g., "from to-day for seven days" would exclude to-day (Monday) but include the following Monday. So the day of doing the act was excluded[33] In 1904 Mathew, L.J , said[34]: "The rule is now well-established that where a particular time is given, from a certain date, within which an act is to be done, the day of the date is to be excluded." In that case the powers of a company given by a special Act were to cease after three years from the passing of the Act. The Act received the Royal Assent on August 9, 1899, and on August 9, 1902, the company purported to do something under the authority of their special Act. It was

31 *Cornfoot* v. *Royal Exchange Assurance Co* , [1903] 2 K B. 363, [1904] 1 K B 40 Cf. *Mercantile Marine Insurance Co.* v *Titherington* (1864), 5 B & S 765.

32 *Per* Esher, M R (1885), 16 Q B. D. 67, at p 72.

33 *Lester* v. *Garland* (1808), 15 Ves 248; *Webb* v. *Fairmaner* (1838), 3 M & W. 473, 476, *Radcliffe* v *Bartholomew*, [1892] 1 Q. B. 161.

34 In *Goldsmiths' Co.* v. *West Metropolitan Ry* , [1904] 1 K. B. 1, at p 5

held that the day of the passing of the Act was to be excluded in computing the period of three years. So under the Prevention of Cruelty to Animals Act, 1849 (12 & 13 Vict. c. 92), s. 13, a complaint must be made "within one month after the cause of complaint shall arise". On June 30, 1891, a complaint was lodged for alleged cruelty on May 30, 1891. The day of the alleged offence was held to be excluded.[35] And with regard to leases Denman, C.J , said in *Ackland* v. *Lutley*[36] : "The general understanding is that terms of years last during the whole anniversary of the day from which they are granted."

On the other hand, it is said that the former strict rule now gives way to intention,[37] and Warrington, J , in *English* v. *Cliff*[38] thought there was no absolute rule with regard to the inclusion or exclusion of the day on which a particular event takes place: "I have to determine the meaning of this particular deed." So in respect of a further lease *from* March 25, 1920, rent must be taken to have been increased *since* March 25, 1920, under the Rent Restriction Acts.[39]

"*On*".—If a period of time begins on a fixed day, that day is *included*. So where a tenancy agreement stated that the tenancy was commencing *on* May 19, 1890, with an apportioned part of the rent to be paid up to June 24, 1890 at once and thenceforth regularly on the usual quarter days; the tenancy was held to have begun on May 19 and not on June 24.[40] Ordinarily where a tenant comes in between quarter days and pays a proportionate rent up to the next quarter day, his tenancy commences from this latter date unless there is something in the agreement to the contrary [41]

---

[35] *Radcliffe* v *Bartholomew, supra, South Staffordshire Tramways Co* v *Sickness and Accident Assurance Association,* [1891] 1 Q B 402
[36] (1839), 9 Ad & E 879, at p 894
[37] *Pugh* v *Duke of Leeds* (1777), Cowp. 714.
[38] [1914] 2 Ch 376
[39] *Brakspear & Sons* v *Barton,* [1924] 2 K B 88, *Raikes* v *Ogle,* [1921] 1 K B. 576
[40] *Sidebotham* v *Holland,* [1895] 1 Q B 378
[41] *Doe* v *Johnson* (1806), 6 Esp 10

In the former case cited the tenancy ended on May 18 following, and Lord Justice Lindley said [42]: "In considering the validity of a notice to quit given in time and expiring on the anniversary of the commencement of a tenancy, I can find no distinction ever drawn between tenancies commencing 'at' a particular time or 'on' a particular day and 'from' the same day. 'At', 'on', 'from' and 'on and from' are for this purpose equivalent expressions." A notice to quit on May 18 would be good, and so would a notice to quit on May 19 as being the anniversary of the commencement of the term.

"From the doing of an act or the happening of an event." —The day on which the act is done or the event happens is *included* Up to 1793 this rule was universally observed, but now the "rational mode of computation is to have regard in each case to the purpose for which the computation is to be made".[43] An umpire was to make his award "within five calendar months". He was appointed on June 29 and made his award on November 29 The award was in time.[44] An agreement was made on October 5 for the sale of goods to be paid for in two months. The writ was issued on December 5. It was held that the parties must be taken to have intended calendar and not lunar months and that the day of the contract must be excluded; "the party is to have two entire calendar months in which to make payment exclusively of the day of sale". The writ was therefore premature.[45] However, the presumption is excluded if it would work hardship. A debtor commits an act of bankruptcy if his goods are seized and held by the sheriff for twenty-one days It was held that the day on which the sheriff seizes the goods is not to be counted as one of the

42 *Sidebotham* v *Holland*, [1895] 1 Q. B 378, at p 384
43 *Per* Lord Esher, M R , in *Re North, ex p. Hasluck*, [1895] 2 Q B 264, at p 269
44 *Re Higham and Jessop* (1840), 9 D. P. C 203
45 *Webb* v. *Fairmaner* (1838), 3 M & W. 473

twenty-one days [46] Where two provisional orders were confirmed by statutes passed on the same day and the question arose which of the two first came into operation, it was found that one order came into operation *on the day of* the passing and that the other took effect *from and after* the passing of the statute Consequently it was held that the former was the first to come into operation.[47] Sometimes words are inserted with the object of counteracting the operation of the rule, "clear days"—so many days "at least"—"a month or more"—"not less than"

A contract to serve for a year from the next day to the date on which the contract is made is not within the Statute of Frauds as the last day of the service will be the anniversary of the day on which the contract is made [48]

"Till" *"Until"*.—These are ambiguous expressions and may be either inclusive or exclusive. "Till the first day of Hilary Term" was held to include the first day and an award made on that day was good.[49] The defendant obtained an order giving him "till Tuesday next" to plead. The Judge said he meant "till" to include the Tuesday so that the plaintiff could not properly sign judgment on that day.[50] On the other hand, a stay of execution was granted "until May 1 next" and on that day execution was issued, and it was held rightly so "I think the word 'until' does not mean 'after'; I do not think that this differs from the case of an attachment not issuing until such a day "[51] In a fire policy goods were covered "from the 14th day of February 1868 until 14th day of August 1868", and the Court held that they were protected during the whole of August 14,

[46] Bankruptcy Act, 1914, s 1 (1) (e) *Re North, ex p. Hasluck, supra*
[47] *Sheffield Corporation* v *Sheffield Electric Light Co*, [1898] 1 Ch 203
[48] *Smith* v *Gold Coast and Ashanti Explorers*, [1903] 1 K B. 285, 538 (C. A.), overruling an opinion to the contrary in *Dollar* v *Parkington* (1901), 84 L T. 470 Cf Pollock, Contract (10th ed), p. 159
[49] *Knox* v. *Simmonds* (1791), 3 Bro C. C 358.
[50] *Per* Patteson, J, in *Dakins* v *Wagner* (1835), 3 Dowl 535, 536
[51] *Rogers* v *Davis* (1845), 8 Ir L R 399, at p 400

1868 [52] There seem to be no very modern cases where the question has arisen

As already stated (p. 6, *supra*) a deed takes effect from the date of its delivery, the presumption being that the date of delivery is the day of the date of the deed. "All deeds do take effect from, and therefore have relation to, the time not of their date but of their delivery; and this is always presumed to be the time of their date unless the contrary do appear." [53]

In a contract where no time is fixed for performance and a party undertakes to do something which depends entirely on himself, the law implies an engagement that it shall be executed within a reasonable time having regard to all the circumstances of the case. [54] This implied engagement is that where an act is to be done in which both parties are to concur, each shall use reasonable diligence in performing his part. [55] Where a contract is to be performed "directly", this does not mean within a reasonable time, but "speedily" or "as soon as possible", [56] and "forthwith" means "without any delay or loss of time". [57] It perhaps should be added that expressions as to time in instruments having operation in Great Britain are to be taken to intend Greenwich mean time, or in the summer-time period, summer time; but this provision as to summer time does not apply to verbal contracts. [58] Evidence is admissible to prove the true date of a deed, that is, the time of its delivery. In ancient times a

---

[52] *Isaacs* v. *Royal Insurance Co* (1870), L R 5 Exch 296

[53] Shep Touch 72

[54] Per Lord Blackburn in *Postlethwaite* v *Freeland* (1880), 5 App Cas 599; *Carlton S S Co* v *Castle Mail Packet Co*, [1898] A C 486, *Barque Quilpué Ltd* v *Brown*, [1904] 2 K B. 464

[55] *Ford* v *Cotesworth* (1868), L. R 4 Q B 127; (1870), L R 5 Q. B 544

[56] *Duncan* v *Topham* (1849), 8 C B 225, *Verlest* v. *Motor Union Insurance Co*, [1925] 2 K B. 137

[57] *Roberts* v *Brett* (1865), 11 H. L. C 337, *Hudson* v *Hill* (1874), 43 L J C P 273

[58] Statutes Definition of Time Act, 1880, Summer Time Act, 1922, Summer Time Act, 1925

deed frequently bore no date: "He that doth plead such a deed without any date, or with such an impossible date, must set forth the time when it was delivered and support the averment by proof."[59] And again, in an ancient case[60] it was said: "The date of a deed is not of the substance of a deed; for if it hath no date, or hath a false or impossible date, as the 30th day of February, yet the deed is good." In such a case, if a reference to its date occurs in the deed, the reference will be taken to be to the date of delivery, otherwise the word "date" occurring in a deed means the day of the date and not that of the delivery.[61] "When a written document contains no date, parol evidence is admissible to show when it was written and from what date it was intended to operate".[62]

In a contract for the payment of money, a lower rate of interest was chargeable for "punctual payment". A payment due on August 1, 1918, was tendered and refused on August 7, 1918. The House of Lords held that this was not "punctual".[63]

IX.—Names and Misdescriptions

Evidence may be given to correct any mistake or imperfect description of any party to a deed or contract. In any formal document persons are usually described by their baptismal (or Christian) name and their surname. This last name may be, and frequently is, changed, and for this no Act of Parliament, royal licence, deed poll, advertisement or any other formality is necessary; a new surname may be assumed by reputation merely and this may be proved by

[59] Shep. Touch 55.
[60] *Goddard's Case* (1584), 2 Rep 4, 6.
[61] *Per* Bailey, J., in *Styles* v *Wardle* (1825), 4 B & C. 908, at p 911.
[62] *Per* Astbury, J., in *Morrell* v *Studd and Millington*, [1913] 2 Ch 648, at p. 658.
[63] *Maclaine* v *Gatty*, [1921] 1 A. C. 376

evidence.[1] As Sir William Scott said [2]: "Yet there may be cases where names acquired by use and habit may be taken by repute as the true Christian and surname of the parties."

On marriage a woman acquires a name which becomes her actual name and can only be changed by reputation. A commoner married a peer, divorced him and married another commoner. An attempt was made by her former husband to restrain her from using the title; but the House of Lords held that she could not be so restrained though she had ceased to have any legal right to it.[3] Generally speaking, every man is by the law of England free to call himself by what name he chooses or by different names for different purposes, so long as he does not use this liberty as a means of fraud or as interfering with the substantive rights of his fellow citizens. And this extends to commercial transactions as well as to the other affairs of life: " It is clear that individuals may carry on business under any name or style they may choose to adopt " (per Erle, C.J., in *Maugham* v. *Sharpe* (1864), 17 C. B. (N.S.) 443, at p. 462).[4] And referring to this case Lord Halsbury [5] said it was a good illustration of " a very familiar principle of law, that where you are dealing with a grantee, you may describe that grantee in any way which is capable of ascertainment afterwards: you are not bound to give him a particular name; you are not bound to give his Christian name or his surname; you may describe him by any description by which the parties to the instrument think it right to describe him ". So where four persons carried on business in partnership under the name of " Wm. Wray " and a conveyance was taken by one of them, with the consent of the others, signing Wm. Wray on the conveyance, it was held that the legal estate passed to the four as joint tenants.[6]

---

1 *Re Croxon*, [1904] 1 Ch 252
2 In *Frankland* v. *Nicholson* (1805), 3 M. & S. 259n., at p 260
3 *Cowley* v. *Cowley*, [1900] P 305; [1901] A. C 450.
4 Pollock, Digest of Law of Partnership (5th ed), p 21.
5 In *Simmons* v. *Woodward*, [1892] A. C. 100, at p 105.
6 *Wray* v. *Wray*, [1905] 2 Ch. 349.

So a class capable of being ascertained may be made parties by the name of that class, *e.g.*, "the several persons whose names are affixed, creditors of S. G. on behalf of themselves and all and every other of the creditors of S. G.".[7] The meaning of "class" has given rise to much discussion, particularly in the case of wills. Lord Davey, in *Kingsbury* v. *Walter*,[7a] referred to the cases, and said: "*Prima facie* a class gift is a gift to a class consisting of persons who are included and comprehended under some general description and bear a certain relationship to the testator" But it may be none the less a class because some of the individuals of the class are named, as "to C and all other my nephews and nieces" There may also be a "composite class", as a gift to "the children of A and the children of B".

A corporation has a fixed name, *i.e.*, that by which it was incorporated This, of course, is its correct designation, like "The Chancellor, Masters and Scholars of the University of Oxford"; but a bequest to the "University of Oxford" would, of course, be good; and any name sufficient to identify the corporation intended will suffice As a party may be described by any name sufficient to identify him, a mere false description of him in a deed does not vitiate the deed, if it is clear that a definite party is intended. So in *Cloak* v. *Hammond*[8] a legacy was left to "my cousin Harriet Cloak"; there was no such cousin, but a married cousin Harriet Crane whose maiden name was Cloak; there was also a cousin T. Cloak whose wife's name was Harriet. Extrinsic evidence was held admissible to show the testatrix's knowledge of and intimacy with the Cloak family and it was said "'cousin' might be understood in the popular sense of the wife of a cousin" The limits of this freedom to use any

[7] *Isaacs* v *Green* (1867), L. R. 2 Ex. 352; *McLaren* v. *Baxter* (1867), L R. 2 C. P. 559.
[7a] [1901] A C. 187, at p. 192. Cf. article "Class" in Encyclopædia of the Laws of England (3rd ed.).
[8] (1887), 34 Ch D. 253.

name one chooses is well illustrated by the case in the **Privy
Council** of *Fung Ping Shan* v. *Tong Shun* [9] where it is said:
" There can be no doubt that parol evidence as to the identity
of a party to a deed is always admissible, but in considering
such evidence it is.of paramount importance to bear in mind
the indicia of identity afforded by the deed itself. A person
who signs, seals and delivers a deed of covenant cannot avoid
liability under the deed by signing a name which he represents as, but which is not in fact, his own, nor can he saddle
such liability on the person whose name he uses, unless he
is the duly constituted agent of such person."

X.—Recitals

We have now completed a short general survey of the
common difficulties which occur in the interpretation of deeds
and other written documents. It is beyond the scope of this
book to consider the numerous and often very intricate
difficulties in construing technical words and expressions of
conveyancing, resulting trusts, perpetuities, contingent
remainders, uses, limitations, and many other topics. In some
of these, expressions have obtained a special meaning recognised by the Courts and used by conveyancers for very many
years. These matters belong to the special learning of real
property and conveyancing. All that it is proposed to do in
the following pages of this part of the book relating to Deeds
is to give some general rules of interpretation for matters
which are to be found in most deeds and in some contracts.
It is most common in deeds, for example, to find Recitals.
These are a narrative of what has led up to the necessity or
desirability of executing a deed; they may also be found in
contracts drawn up with formality Hence the familiar
opening " Whereas " the parties are desirous of or have

---

9 [1918] A C. 403, at p. 406.

agreed on some particular course of action, etc. Or the
recitals may detail a long history of title designed to show
that, *e.g.*, the grantor is entitled to make the disposition he
is about to make by the deed, or the recitals may be, in the
words of Lord Halsbury, " a preliminary statement of what
the maker of the deed intended should be the effect and
purpose of the whole deed when made ". The recitals must
of course be carefully distinguished from the operative part
of the deed—the words that actually effect the transfer of the
property or the interest or declare the parties bound by some
agreement. In 1693 Lord Holt declared that " the reciting
part of a deed is not at all a necessary part either in law
or equity. . . . it hath no effect or operation." [1] Though
not a necessary part of a deed, recitals are very commonly
employed, and our purpose is to inquire shortly how and when
these recitals may be invoked to help in the interpretation
of the operative part of the deed.

Relation of Recitals to Operative Part

(i) *Where operative part unambiguous.*—The first rule is—
that " it is impossible by a recital to cut down the plain effect
of the operative part of a deed ".[2] " The rule is that a
recital does not control the operative part of a deed where the
operative part is clear." [3] The words here to be emphasised
are *plain* and *clear*. So in *Inland Revenue Commissioners
v. Raphael* [4] Lord Warrington of Clyffe said the appeal
involved the consideration of whether the words in the
operative part of a deed are capable as a matter of construction
of being construed and modified so as to give effect to the
intention of the settlor as declared by the recitals. He quoted
Lord Halsbury as saying [5]: " I never in my life heard of the
language of a deed which contained a perfectly unambiguous

[1] *Bath and Mountague's Case* (1693), 3 Ca Ch 55, at p 101
[2] *Per* Romilly, M.R., in *Holliday* v. *Overton* (1852), 14 Beav. 467, at p 470.
[3] *Per* Jessel, M R , in *Dawes* v. *Tredwell* (1881), 18 Ch D 354, at p. 358.
[4] [1935] A. C. 96, at p. 135
[5] In *Mackenzie* v *Duke of Devonshire*, [1896] A C 400, at p 405.

provision being twisted from the natural, ordinary meaning of the words by a preliminary statement of what the maker of the deed intended should be the effect and purpose of the whole deed when made " In that case, Lord Davey is also quoted as saying [6]: " I take it to be a settled principle of law that the operative words of a deed which are expressed in clear and unambiguous language are not to be controlled, cut down or qualified by a recital or narrative of intention." And Lord Warrington himself said: " The fact is that the narrative and operative parts of a deed perform quite different functions, and intention in reference to the narrative and the same word in reference to the operative parts respectively bear quite different significations. As appearing in the narrative part it means ' purpose '. In considering the intention of the operative part the word means ' significance ' or ' import '—' The way in which anything is to be understood ' (Oxford English Dictionary) supported by the illustration: ' The intention of the passage was sufficiently clear ' " Where the words in the operative part are " susceptible of two constructions the context may properly be referred to for the purpose of determining which of the two constructions is the right meaning ".[7] And Lord Blackburn said [8]: " I take the canon of construction to be that where the description of the premises assigned is clear and unambiguous, effect must be given to it by the Court, even though convinced from other parts of the deed that it was not what the parties meant to say." To cite one or two examples. The recital in a bond was to the effect that the parties had agreed that a bond should be executed for £500; as a matter of fact the bond was taken in a penal sum of £1,000. The penalty could not be reduced to £500.[9] The respondent and others gave a joint and several guarantee to a bank to secure the overdraft of a certain customer up to £2,500. Subsequently these same

[6] *S. C.*, p. 408.
[7] *Per* Lord Watson in *Orr* v. *Mitchell*, [1893] A. C 238, at p 254
[8] In *Lee* v *Alexander* (1883), 8 App. Cas 862, at p 869
[9] *Ingleby* v. *Swift* (1833), 10 Bing. 84

persons gave a joint and several bond to the bank in which
a desire for further advances over and above the amount
of £2,500 was recited. The bond secured the repayment
of *all* moneys due to the bank from that customer. The
guarantee was found to be invalid and the respondents contended that all the bank could recover was moneys advanced
by it to the customer in excess of £2,500. The Privy Council
found that the bond clearly secured the repayment of *all*
moneys due to the bank and this operative part could not
be controlled by a recital which was not plainly inconsistent
therewith.[10] The title of a seller depended on the construction of a certain will The seller agreed to sell by a deed
which recited the will in full and the purchase money was
paid. After the death of the seller, her children claiming
under the will sued the purchaser for the return of the
purchase money and the purchaser in turn sued the representatives of the seller under her covenant for title contained
in the deed of sale It was contended that the covenant for
title must be read subject to the terms of the recited will
and to the doubt raised thereby. The Court held the purchaser
entitled to recover from the representatives of the seller on the
ground that defects in a title expressed to be conveyed are
not to be excluded on the ground that they were recited or
otherwise made known to the purchaser. The covenant for
title was quite plain and unambiguous and the construction
and effect of a covenant cannot be controlled by extrinsic
evidence of notice or intention.[11] In *Dawes* v. *Tredwell* [12]
Jessel, M.R., said: " If the covenant is clear, it cannot be
controlled by the recital "

(ii) *Where operative part ambiguous.*—The reader will
have gathered from the insistence in all these extracts
from the judgments of eminent Judges on the epithets
" plain ", " clear ", " unambiguous " and so on that

10 *Australian Joint Stock Bank* v *Bailey*, [1899] A. C 396
11 *Page* v. *Midland Ry.* [1894] 1 Ch 11.
12 (1881), 18 Ch. D 354, at p. 359.

a different rule is followed if the operative part of a deed is found not to be plain, clear or unambiguous. And this is the fact. The function of the Court being, as was said at the beginning (p. 22, *supra*), to discover the intention of the parties from the words and expressions used by them, " if the operative part of a deed be doubtfully expressed, there the recital may safely be referred to as a key to the intention of the parties ".[13]

In *Ex p. Dawes, re Moon*,[14] Lord Esher, M.R., enunciated three rules applicable to this matter The first is: If the operative part is ambiguous, the recitals govern the construction. For example, a separation deed recited that the husband agreed to pay his wife five shillings a week during her life so long as she remained chaste, the operative covenant by the husband was simply to pay the said sum to the wife Here the covenant was ambiguous in that it did not say whether the sum was to be paid during the husband's life or the wife's. The recital could therefore be called in to aid the construction and this made it clear that the life of the wife was intended.[15] Lord Herschell said in *Orr* v. *Mitchell*[16]: " But where language is employed which may appropriately be used for different purposes or which has a wider or more restricted sense, I think it is perfectly legitimate to look to other parts of the deed to see how it was intended to be used in the disposition clause or whether it has there such wider or more restricted sense." And Lord Macnaghten, in the same case (at p. 254), said: " Where those words [in the operative part] are susceptible of two constructions the context may properly be referred to for determining which of the two constructions is the true meaning. . . . The rule applies though one of the two meanings is the more obvious one and

13 *Per* Leach, M.R., in *Bailey* v *Lloyd* (1829), 5 Russ. 330, at p 344
14 (1886), 17 Q B D 275, at p 286; *Eastwood* v. *Ashton*, [1915] A. C. 900, *per* Lord Parker at p 910
15 *Crouch* v *Crouch*, [1912] 1 K. B. 378; *Hesse* v *Albert* (1828), 3 Man. & Ry 406; *Kirk* v. *Eustace*, [1937] A C 491
16 [1893] A C 238, at p 253

would necessarily be preferred if no light could be derived from the rest of the deed. For the purpose of construing the dispositive or operative clause the whole of the instrument may be referred to, though the introductory narrative of recitals leading up to the clause are perhaps more likely to furnish the key to its true construction than the subsidiary clauses of the deed." So a marriage settlement recited an agreement by the husband and wife to settle any personal estate which might come to the wife or to the husband "*during their joint lives*". The husband died and the wife subsequently became entitled to a fund in Court. It was held that the covenant to settle property during her life being ambiguous, the recital might be referred to in order to explain it, and it then became clear that it was intended that the wife's covenant should only be operative during coverture.[17] In *Richmond* v. *Savill*,[18] on negotiations with his tenant for the surrender of a lease, the landlord agreed that if the tenant would pay rent up to a certain future day the landlord would "release him"—not saying from what. It was held that the release must be read as limited to the matters within the contemplation of the parties at the time when the release was given and did not release the tenant from liability for past breaches of his covenant to repair. A marriage settlement recited an agreement to settle property and that the husband would enter into a covenant to settle any future property of the wife. The covenant was to settle any estate which should come to or devolve upon the wife. A contingent reversionary interest of the wife did not fall into possession till after her death. By reference to the recital it was held that this property was not within the covenant.[19] So in the case in which Lord Esher set forth his rules, *Ex p. Dawes* (*supra*), a composition deed contained a recital by the debtor

[17] *Re Coghlan*, [1894] 3 Ch. 76. Cf. *per* Hall, V.-C., in *Re Campbell's Policies* (1877), 6 Ch. D. 686, at p. 690.

[18] [1926] 2 K. B. 530.

[19] *Re Michell's Trusts* (1878), 9 Ch. D. 5.

of an agreement to assign all the property set forth in the schedule; the operative part purported to assign all the property set forth in the schedule and all other the estate, if any, the property of the debtor. The question was whether a certain life interest of the debtor not included in the schedule passed by the deed—it was held that it did not. So in releases " the general words of a release are limited always to that thing or those things which were specially in the contemplation of the parties at the time when the release was given ".[20] And as Farwell, L.J., said in *Cloutte* v. *Storey*[21]: " It is not in accordance with principle or authority to construe deeds of compromise of ascertained specific questions so as to deprive any party thereto of any right not then in dispute and not in contemplation of any of the parties to such deed ".[21]

The second of Lord Esher's rules (*supra*) is as follows: " If the recitals are ambiguous and the operative part is clear, the operative part must prevail." This rule has been practically already illustrated by such cases as *Australian Joint Stock Bank* v. *Bailey* (*supra*, p 103) and stands to reason. As we saw, recitals are not a necessary part of a deed at all; if they are ambiguous, they are of no account in aiding construction. As in *Page* v. *Midland Ry.* (*supra*, p. 103) a defect or possible defect appearing in a recital cannot affect an absolute covenant for title in the operative part. A recital may be quite general and indefinite, as a recited agreement to settle " all my property ", whereas the operative part settled only a single house at L. out of the property of the covenantor.

The third rule is that if both the recitals and the operative part are clear but inconsistent with each other, the operative part is to be preferred. This may be a case of misrecital, in which case the operation of the deed will not be affected if the

---

[20] *Per* Lord Westbury in *L. & S. W. Ry.* v. *Blackmore* (1870), L. R. 4 H L. 610, at p. 623.
[21] [1911] 1 Ch. 18, at p. 34

intention is clear. A misrecital of a lease in a grant of the reversion was held not to invalidate the grant in an old case [22]

Recital as estoppel —Any recital, though inaccurate in fact, may operate by way of estoppel   In order to have this effect, the recital must be precise and not general, it must be " certain to every intent ".[23]   " A general recital will not operate as an estoppel, but the recital of a particular fact will have that effect." [24]   So it must be clear, precise and unambiguous. It must also be a statement of a material fact, and will take effect, if at all, only as between the parties to the deed. As Baron Parke put it: " If a distinct statement of a particular fact is made in the recital of a bond or other instrument under seal, and a contract is made with reference to that recital, it is unquestionably true that as between the parties to that instrument and in an action upon it, it is not competent for the party bound to deny the recital." [25] This does not, however, apply to an action not founded on the deed but wholly collateral to it; nor are recitals representations of fact on which a stranger to the deed is entitled to act without inquiry. As, for example, in *Trinidad Asphalte Co.* v. *Coryat*,[26] there was an erroneous recital of the defendants' predecessors' title   The plaintiff purchaser had notice that the defendants obtained possession of the land under a deed which purported to convey to them an equitable title. The Court held that he (plaintiff) must convey the legal estate, for the erroneous recitals in the deed as to the derivation of the equitable title did not estop the defendants nor vitiate the constructive notice to the plaintiff of the defendants' equity when he bought the legal estate, on the ground that

---

[22] *Withes* v. *Casson* (1614), Hob. 128
[23] *Per* Lord Tenterden, C J , in *Right* v *Bucknell* (1831), 2 B & Ad. 278, at p 281.
[24] *Per* Lord Lyndhurst, L C , in *Bensley* v. *Burdon* (1830), 8 L J (o s) Ch. 85, at p 87
[25] *Carpenter* v. *Buller* (1841), 8 M & W. 209, at p 212.
[26] [1896] A. C. 587.

recitals in a deed are not representations of fact on which a stranger to the deed is entitled to act without inquiry. The plaintiff was found to have had notice, and had no right to treat the recital as indisputable. The erroneous recital of the earlier title did not preclude a grantee from showing what interest really passed by the grant. So where a married woman executed a deed ‘poll reciting that an event had occurred which had the effect of determining her life interest in certain property, and purporting to release her interest in it to her husband. On the faith of this a creditor of the husband made favourable arrangements with him; the wife continuing to receive the income of the property. The Court held that she could not by her own act get rid of the protection afforded by the restraint on anticipation in the original settlement and that she was entitled to receive the income. She was therefore not estopped.[27] On the other hand, where there was a recital that a wife and her heirs were entitled to a right of way across a certain plot of land and that she had agreed that she would join in the conveyance in order to release the land conveyed from the right of way, and the operative part stated that " she hereby releases the piece of land conveyed from the right of way ", but the defendant took a conveyance of the house and right of way without notice of the release, it was held that the recital was precise and estopped the defendant, who claimed through the wife, from denying that the right of way had been released.[28] But where the conveyance did not contain any distinct averment that the defendants were seised of the estate when they executed, they will not be estopped from denying that they were seised. " It would be dangerous ", said Bowen, L J., " to extract a proposition by inference from the statement in a deed and hold the party estopped from denying it; estoppel can only arise from a clear, definite statement."[29] A recital may be

---

[27] *Lady Bateman* v *Faber*, [1898] 1 Ch. 144   Contrast *Re Wimperis*, [1914] 1 Ch 502.

[28] *Poulton* v. *Moore*, [1915] 1 K B 400

[29] *Onward Building Society* v. *Smithson*, [1893] 1 Ch. 1.

true but inaccurate, as where it stated what the then interest of the party was, but omitted reference to the fact that the interest was defeasible by the exercise of a power of appointment. It was held to create no estoppel as the recital could have a meaning given to it in strict accordance with the facts, and need not be construed as a statement of what was not true at the time.[30]

It is said that there can be no estoppel by reason of recitals if the truth appears by the same instrument.[31] But this apparently will not apply when in a mortgage transaction the parties have agreed that the relationship of landlord and tenant should be established between them, on the well-known ground that a tenant is estopped from disputing his landlord's title. In a case of this kind, the mortgagor was held estopped from denying that the defendants were his landlords or that they had the legal reversion though the fact that the mortgagor had only the equitable reversion appeared on the face of the deed.[32] In a similar case a receiver was appointed with all the powers of a lessor and the mortgagor attorned tenant to him, the latter was estopped, although it was apparent that the receiver did not possess the legal reversion.[33]

Who is estopped.—To whom does estoppel by recitals apply? Are the recitals to be taken to be those of all the parties or of some or one only? It is a question of construction on the whole deed. The law on this point is concisely put by Patteson, J., in *Stroughill* v. *Buck*[34]: "When a recital is intended to be a statement which all the parties to a deed have mutually agreed to admit as true, it is an estoppel upon all But when it is intended to be the state-

[30] *Lovett* v. *Lovett*, [1898] 1 Ch 82
[31] *Per* Lord Tenterden, C J , in *Right* v. *Bucknell*, *supra*
[32] *Morton* v. *Woods* (1868), L R 3 Q B 658
[33] *Dancer* v. *Hastings* (1826), 12 Moore 34, *Jolly* v. *Arbuthnot* (1859), 4 De G. & J 224
[34] (1850), 14 Q B. 781, at p. 787.

ment of one party only, the estoppel is confined to that party, and the intention is to be gathered from construing the instrument " In *Young* v. *Raincock* [34a] Coltman, J., said: "Where it can be collected from the deed, that the parties to it have agreed upon a certain admitted state of facts as the basis on which they contract, the statement of the facts, though but in the way of recital, shall estop the parties to aver the contrary." These cases were approved by the House of Lords in *Greer* v. *Kettle*,[34b] where Lord Maugham pointed out that for over two hundred years a recital in a deed was not considered to be so direct an affirmation as to amount to an estoppel [34c] This theory was not displaced till 1834.[34d] It was a rule of common law and " it is at least equally clear that in equity a party to a deed could not set up an estoppel in reliance on a deed in relation to which there is an equitable right of rescission or in reliance on an untrue statement or untrue recital induced by his own misrepresentation, whether innocent or otherwise, to the other party ". The learned Lord compared this with a receipt clause in a deed which does not act as an estoppel if the money has not in fact been paid.[34e] In *Greer* v. *Kettle* the recital was a statement of matters within the knowledge of one party only, and the other party was held not to be estopped.

Recital as a covenant.—If it appears to have been the intention of the parties, a recital may sometimes create a covenant. "Where words of recital or reference manifested a clear intention that the parties should do certain acts, the Courts have from these inferred a covenant to do such acts" (*per* Lord Denman, C J., in *Aspdin* v. *Austin*

34a (1849), 7 C. B. 310, at p. 338.
34b [1938] A C. 156, 168 See the same learned lord as to estoppel by deed generally, S. C , p. 171.
34c Co Litt. 352
34d By *Lainson* v. *Tremere* (1834), 1 A & E. 792, and *Bowman* v *Taylor* (1834), 2 A. & E. 278
34e See p 115, *infra*, and *per* Lord Romilly, M R , in *Brooke* v *Haymes* (1868), L R 6 Eq 25

(1844), 5 Q. B. 671, at p. 683). For instance, a recital of an intention to create restrictive covenants on the part of the vendors who execute the deed and made as an inducement to purchasers may operate as a formal covenant contained in the operative portion of the deed.[35] So an ante-nuptial settlement recited an agreement between the intended wife and husband to settle the wife's property held in trust. The wife was an infant. It was held that although the covenant was not binding on her, the agreement operated to bind the husband and the trustees[36] A recital in a separation deed that the husband and wife had agreed to live apart implied a covenant by the wife to live apart.[37] But a recited agreement will not operate as a covenant where there is an express covenant to be found in the witnessing or operative part[38] An admission of a debt by an instrument under seal generally amounts to a covenant to pay it,[39] and a recital in an instrument capable of operating as the execution of a power may amount to an execution of the power.[40] On a requisition of title the question was whether a purchaser was entitled to inquire how the trust arose, when the recital was that one of the parties to a partition deed held freeholds as trustee partly for himself and partly for the other party to the deed The purchaser was held not entitled to inquire, and Cozens-Hardy, M.R., remarked : " I do not entertain any doubt that a recital that the owner of a legal estate is trustee for A B under a will or under a deed, affects a purchaser with notice of the contents of the deed or of the will. But that doctrine has no bearing upon a case where there is nothing more than a statement that he holds on trust for A B. Such a statement is an admission against interest by the owner of the legal estate." [41]

[35] *Mackenzie* v *Childers* (1889), 43 Ch D 265
[36] *Buckland* v. *Buckland*, [1900] 2 Ch. 534.
[37] *Re Weston*, [1900] 2 Ch. 164.
[38] *Per* Jessel, M R., in *Dawes* v *Tredwell* (1881), 18 Ch D 354, at p 359
[39] *Per* Malins, V -C., in *Jackson* v. *N E Ry* (1877), 7 Ch. D 573, at p 583
[40] *Re Sugden*, [1917] 2 Ch 92, at p 98
[41] *Re Chafer and Randall's Contract*, [1916] 2 Ch 8, at p. 18.

XI.—OPERATIVE PART—PREMISES

Consideration.—After the recitals, the operative part of a deed begins, generally by the words " Now this deed witnesseth ", etc. That portion of the operative part before the *habendum* is called the *Premises.* Certain clauses in these Premises are now considered. Among these clauses it is usual in a deed to set out the consideration for it, and this is commonly done in written contracts also. We saw previously (p. 79, *supra*) that extrinsic evidence may be given to show that a deed or contract is not binding as having been made for an illegal consideration. A contract under seal does not as such require consideration and will be enforceable against a party deriving no advantage from it.[1] In a recent case,[2] a deed had been executed by one party but not by the other. It was held that the execution of the deed bound the first party, but as he only executed on the faith that the other party would execute also, the failure of the latter to do so rendered the deed inoperative even to bind the first party. It was in effect a written offer of a contract, which offer had been refused. It has been suggested that a total failure of the consideration upon which the contract under seal was founded might afford a good defence to an action on the deed.[2a] Specific performance will generally be refused to a contract under seal but entirely without consideration.[3] And a voluntary assignment of an expectancy even under seal will not be enforced by a Court of Equity.[4] " It is settled that an agreement to do an act that is illegal or immoral or

---

[1] Plowd 308; *Morley* v. *Boothby* (1825), 3 Bing 107; *Pratt* v. *Barker* (1828), 1 Sim. 1.

[2] *Westminster Bank* v *Wilson*, [1938] 3 All E R 652

[2a] *Pitman* v. *Woodbury* (1845), 3 Ex. 4, *Rose* v *Poulton* (1831), 2 B. & Ad. 822; *Bunn* v *Guy* (1803), 4 East 190.

[3] *Wycherley* v *Wycherley* (1763), 2 Eden 177, *Groves* v. *Groves* (1829), 3 Y & J 163; *Kekewich* v. *Manning* (1851), 1 De G M & G. 176, 188, *Hoblyn* v. *Hoblyn* (1889), 41 Ch D 200.

[4] *Meek* v. *Kettlewell* (1842), 1 Hare 464, *Re Ellenborough, Towry-Law* v. *Burne*, [1903] 1 Ch 697

contrary to public policy or to do any act for a consideration that is illegal, immoral or contrary to public policy, is unlawful and therefore void.''[5]   As to immoral consideration, the rules are fully laid down in *Ayerst* v. *Jenkins*[6] The contract, whether under seal or not, is under these circumstances unenforceable.   In the case of a conveyance, it is probably operative to pass the property conveyed, though it might be set aside and a reconveyance ordered.   As an instance of this: a secretary of a building society made default.   His father gave a written undertaking to the society to make good the default and executed two promissory notes to the society, the consideration being the forbearance of the society to prosecute and the object of the transaction to prevent such prosecution.   The Court held it to be an implied term in the arrangement that there should be no prosecution and the agreement was therefore founded on an illegal consideration and the promissory notes ought to be set aside.[7] So Equity refused to enforce an agreement by a father to make an equitable mortgage of his property in order to save his son from a prosecution for forgery.[8]

Suppose no consideration is expressed or it is expressed inaccurately or only in part, is extrinsic evidence admissible to supply the deficiency? It used to be said that if no consideration was stated in a contract under hand no evidence was admissible to show a consideration,[9] and in the case of a deed Lord Hardwicke held[10] that '' where any consideration is mentioned as of love and affection only, if it is not said also

---

[5] *Alexander* v. *Rayson*, [1936] 1 K. B 169, at p 182; *Berg* v *Sadler*, [1937] 2 K. B. 158.

[6] (1873), L R 16 Eq 275, at p. 282, *per* Lord Selborne, L C   On the whole subject, cf *Chitty, Contracts* (19th ed), Chap XII   As to public policy, see *per* Lord Atkin in *Fender* v *Mildmay*, [1938] A. C 1, at pp 10—16

[7] *Jones* v *Merionethshire Permanent Benefit Building Society*, [1891] 2 Ch 587   Cf. *Collins* v *Blantern* (1767), 2 Wils. 341.

[8] *Williams* v. *Bayley* (1866), L R 1 H L. 200   Cf the meaning of '' pressure '' in such cases, *per* Lord Cranworth, L C , at pp 209—211.

[9] *Per* Best, C J , *Morley* v *Boothby* (1825), 3 Bing 107, 112

[10] *Peacock* v *Monk* (1748), 1 Ves Sen 128.

C D S.

8

and for other considerations, you cannot enter into proof of any other : the reason is because it would be contrary to the deed ". Accordingly he held evidence only admissible where no consideration is mentioned   On the other hand, nearly a century afterwards Lord Lyndhurst thought that evidence might be given provided it did not contradict the deed [11] : " The settled rule of law is that you may go out of the deed to prove a consideration that stands well with that stated on the face of the deed, but you cannot be allowed to prove a consideration inconsistent with it." *Leifchild's Case* [12] decided that evidence of a consideration not mentioned in the deed may be given provided it is not inconsistent with the consideration expressed and that the expression of a nominal consideration is not inconsistent with the fact that money or money's worth was the real consideration.   An additional consideration may also be proved provided it do not contradict the stated consideration.[13] " The rule is that where there is one consideration stated in the deed, you may prove any other consideration which existed, not in contradiction to the instrument, and it is not in contradiction to the instrument to prove a larger consideration than that which it stated." [14]

Evidence may as a general rule be given to show that a deed voluntary in form was in truth for valuable consideration.   " The Statute of Frauds excludes such evidence in the case of a post-nuptial settlement unless there is a signed agreement or note or memorandum.   A settlement in no way referring to the parol contract cannot be a note or memorandum thereof nor can the marriage be regarded as a part performance sufficient to take the case out of the statute." [15]

[11] *Clifford* v *Turrell* (1845), 9 Jur. 633.
[12] (1865), L R. 1 Eq. 231.
[13] *Frith* v. *Frith*, [1906] A C. 254, *Townend* v. *Toker* (1866), L. R. 1 Ch 466
[14] *Per* Knight-Bruce, V.-C., in *Clifford* v. *Turrell* (1841), 1 Y. & C C C 138, at p. 149.
[15] *Per* Cozens-Hardy, L.J , in *Re Holland, Gregg* v. *Holland*, [1902] 2 Ch 360, at p 388. Cf *Pott* v. *Todhunter* (1845), 2 Coll. 76; *Gale* v. *Williamson* (1841), 8 M. & W. 405

In the case cited the post-nuptial settlement was made with a memorandum of a recited ante-nuptial agreement in consideration of marriage (within section 4 of the Statute of Frauds) to the effect that the husband would settle a certain fund when it fell into possession, his own life interest therein to be made determinable on his bankruptcy. The settlement was held good as against the trustee in bankruptcy, the recital of the parol agreement being held sufficient to satisfy the Statute for the purpose of proof of the agreement. Where there is no question of proof but only what was the position at the time when the transaction alleged to be an act of bankruptcy took place and a finding that at that time there was no memorandum, see *Re Davies, ex p. Miles* [16] Where the only consideration stated is " natural love and affection " evidence may be given of another consideration such as payment of money [17] or marriage.[18] And where this consideration is united with " divers other good causes and considerations ", or words to that effect, valuable consideration may be proved [18] But the converse of this does not hold good. Where a deed is expressed to be for valuable consideration and this is displaced by evidence, the party concerned cannot fall back on a consideration of natural love and affection, and probably the same holds good where fraud is alleged. In a case where an uncle, ill and imbecile, purported to grant a lease to his nephew for valuable consideration, Lord Redesdale said: " But where an agreement purported in the body of it to be for valuable consideration, it could never, though obtained by a relation, be supported on the ground of natural love and affection, for if it could, every agreement made with a relation must be supported, however inadequate the consideration."[19]

Receipt clause.—In a deed a receipt for consideration

---

[16] [1921] 3 K. B 628
[17] *Attwell* v *Harris* (1619), 2 Roll. Rep. 91; *Tanner* v. *Byne* (1827), 1 Sim. 160
[18] *Pott* v *Todhunter, supra, Thompson* v *Webster* (1852), 4 Drew. 628; *Bayspoole* v *Collins* (1871), L R 6 Ch 228.
[19] *Willan* v *Willan* (1814), 2 Dow 274, at p. 282

money or securities in the body of it shall be a sufficient discharge for the same to the person paying or delivering the same without any further receipt being indorsed on the deed. This was the practice prior to the Conveyancing Act, 1881.[20] Prior to the operation of the Supreme Court of Judicature Act, 1873 (*i.e.*, November 1, 1875) a receipt clause in the body of the deed was conclusive at law that the money had been paid.

Even at law this did not apply in all cases, as, for instance, where a cheque given for the purchase-money had been dishonoured.[21]   But in equity as between the parties to a deed a receipt whether in the body of the deed or indorsed thereon was not conclusive and the vendor was allowed to prove that the purchase-money had not been paid.[22] And this is now also the rule at law. It is obvious that when a deed containing a receipt clause gets into the hands of third parties different considerations prevail. For instance, when a deed recited the consideration and acknowledged receipt of the purchase-money, evidence was tendered to show that no consideration was in fact given, that the vendor remained in possession and that no beneficial interest was intended for the alleged grantee. The object of the evidence was to show that the transaction was a "make-believe with no word of truth in the operative provisions". Their Lordships of the Judicial Committee held[23] that with regard to a third party, a mortgagee, the evidence was inadmissible to contradict the plain terms of the deed and the decision in *Rimmer* v. *Webster*[24] was applied and quoted. "If a man acknowledges that he has received the whole of the purchase-money from the person to whom he transfers the property 'he voluntarily arms the purchaser with the means of dealing

20 S 54 See now Law of Property Act, 1925, s. 68.
21 *Deverell* v *Whitmarsh* (1841), 5 Jur. 963
22 *Deverell* v *Whitmarsh, supra*; *Hawkins* v *Gardiner* (1854), 2 Sm. & G. 441, *Wilson* v *Keating* (1859), 27 Beav 121
23 *Tsang Chuen* v. *Li Po Kwai*, [1932] A C 715. The vendor was also held estopped by having registered a memorial as required by the colonial law Cf. *Re King's Settlement*, [1931] 2 Ch. 294, 299
24 [1902] 2 Ch. 163, 173.

with the estate as the absolute legal and equitable owner, free from every shadow of incumbrance or adverse equity' and he cannot be heard to say that he has not in fact received such purchase-money." "There is no reason", said Fry, L.J.,[25] "for giving a receipt till the money is actually received, unless it be to enable the person taking the receipt to produce faith by it." Now section 67 of the Law of Property Act, 1925, provides that a receipt for consideration money or securities in the body of a deed shall be a sufficient discharge for the same to the person paying or delivering the same, without any further receipt for the same being indorsed on the deed This applies to all deeds executed after 1881. And by section 68, which similarly applies, a receipt for consideration money or other consideration in the body of a deed or indorsed thereon shall, in favour of a subsequent purchaser [26] not having notice that the money or other consideration thereby acknowledged to be received was not in fact paid or given, wholly or in part, be sufficient evidence of the payment or giving of the whole amount thereof. The section is re-enacted from section 55 of the Conveyancing Act, 1881. So in *Bateman* v. *Hunt*,[27] a sub-mortgagee, through whom the plaintiffs claimed, had no notice actual or constructive that the amount specified in the mortgage deed had not been paid, and the plaintiffs were held to be entitled to rely on the acknowledgment contained in the deed and therefore to have a better equity than the defendants, the mortgagors. Where the receipt of the mortgage money was acknowledged in the deed but in fact no money passed, the Court held that the plaintiff, knowing the money was never paid, was nevertheless estopped by his own receipt, on the faith of which a sub-mortgagee had made an advance, from saying as against the sub-mortgagee that he, the plaintiff,

[25] In *Bickerton* v *Walker* (1885), 31 Ch. D 151, at p. 159, where the Lord Justice points out the importance of an indorsed receipt.
[26] For the definition of "purchaser", cf L. P Act, 1925, s 205 (1) (xxi).
[27] [1904] 2 K. B. 530.

had not received the money so acknowledged to have been received by him.[28] The receipt may be in any form so long as the words are express; for instance, a mortgage was transferred in consideration " of £—— paid " by A to B without a definite receipt clause; the words were held sufficient to raise an estoppel against the transferor " from asserting his equitable title against a person to whom the transferee has disposed of his property for value ".[29] The third party must, of course, have relied on the receipt in order to establish his prevailing equity. Owing to the fraud of a solicitor, a building society endorsed a statutory receipt on a mortgage to itself, but the money was never paid. The mortgage deed was suppressed, but the solicitor obtained possession of the title deeds and deposited them with a bank to secure a loan to himself, the bank not having relied on the receipt in the mortgage was postponed to the rights of the society, who was entitled to show that it had never been paid off and that the statutory receipt and mortgage had been delivered as an escrow, the legal estate still remaining with the society.[30] There was no question of estoppel here. This case was distinguished in *Capell* v. *Winter*,[31] where beneficiaries under a trust for sale were defrauded by one of themselves who purported to convey part of the trust property to one who had lent money to himself. The other beneficiaries were not parties to the deed and were held not estopped by the receipt clause in the conveyance.

XII —Operative Part—Parcels

Descriptions.—The property comprised in a deed, generally called " the parcels ", may be described either generally, *i.e.*,

---

[28] *Powell* v. *Browne*, [1907] W. N. 228   Cf. *French* v. *Hope* (1887), 56 L J. Ch. 363.

[29] *Rimmer* v   *Webster*, *supra*   A receipt clause may be statutory. Cf schedule to Bills of Exchange Act, 1882, and *Burchell* v. *Thompson*, [1920] 2 K B 80.

[30] *Lloyds Bank, Ltd* v *Bullock*, [1896] 2 Ch 192

[31] [1907] 2 Ch 376.

by a name that fits every member of that class, as "a house", or specifically to point out which particular member or members of the class mentioned is intended. A thing may be described by more than one general name; *i.e.*, as belonging to more than one class: *e.g.*, a brown horse out of those at present in A's stables at B. If a single thing satisfies all the descriptions—if there is only one brown horse in A's stables at B—there is no difficulty; if there is more than one brown horse there, an equivocation (see *supra*, p. 54) arises. Usually, a special description is added to the general—"The house called Horton", "my house situate in the parish of Bowdon"—where the owner has more than one house. If the object is sufficiently defined by the general description, no special description is required and if employed is useless; but where, as is usual, the general description indicates more than one thing, the special description indicates which of those things is meant, and the special description restricts the general. Often the description or part of it is inaccurate "My house situate in the parish of Bowdon now in the occupation of A." It is in fact occupied by B, it is clear that this part of the description is wrong and may be rejected if the writer has only one house at Bowdon. Sometimes, however, a general and accurate description is followed by words which properly apply to only some of the parcels, and a question may arise as to whether those words are to be construed as restrictive of the general description or whether they are to be rejected altogether.

Often collective or group names are used, as "an estate", "a farm", "issue"—one description superadded may denote the particular group intended, as "A's estate", "B's issue"—and some further description may show that only some members of the particularised group are intended, as "A's estate in the county of Herts", "B's male issue", or the further description may merely be a further designation of the particular group, as "B's male issue by his wife C", where B has only married once

So we get certain recognised rules for the interpretation of deeds containing descriptions of the " parcels ".

(1) When the descriptions are all general, or a collective and a general description, only those parcels pass which satisfy *all* the descriptions or, in other words, if the parcels are described as belonging to more than one class, only those will pass which are members of each class—*e.g.*, " my farm, part of my inheritance from my father ".

(2) Where the description is general or collective and also special, only those parcels will pass which satisfy *both* descriptions (subject to the next rule). Bacon [1] lays down : " But if I have some land wherein all these demonstrations are true and some wherein part of them are true and part false, then shall they be intended words of true limitation to pass only those lands wherein all those circumstances are true." The question often is whether the special description can be disregarded as a *falsa demonstratio* (see next rule) or whether it acts as a restriction on the prior general description " The rule means that if it stand doubtful upon the words, whether they import a false reference or demonstration, or whether they be words of restraint that limit the generality of the former words, the law will never intend error or falsehood." [2] An excellent example is to be found in the case of *Re Brocket*.[3] The testatrix devised " the real estate to which I under the codicil to the will of my late father " had become entitled, " namely the residence known as Orford House in the parish of Oakley in the said county of Essex ", and lands and hereditaments " in the same county " to her sister for life with remainders over She then disposed of the residue. The testatrix had also become entitled under the codicil to her father's will to a freehold house in London, and the question was, did this pass under the general or group description " the real estate to which ", etc., or did

[1] Law Tracts, Rule 13
[2] *Per* Alderson, B , in *Morrell* v. *Fisher* (1849), 4 Ex. 591, at p 604.
[3] [1908] 1 Ch. 185.

the special description "namely the residence known as ", etc., qualify and limit the general words? Joyce, J., held that the latter rule was to be applied, so that the house in London did not pass by the general devise but fell into the residue. He said[4]. " It is quite clear to my mind that if there be a conveyance of real estate described in general terms followed by a definite and specific enumeration of particulars, as by schedule with or without plan, which enumeration omits something which might otherwise have been covered by the general description, then, generally speaking, the designation by schedule and plan would not be read as an imperfect enumeration to be disregarded as *falsa demonstratio*, but as restrictive of the prior general description "

As further examples. A demise of " all that messuage, etc., on the south side of Speenham land, called the ' Old Fighting Cocks ', now or late in the occupation of J ' "; these last words were held essential and not mere words of demonstration, the critical question in the case being whether the soil of a gateway passed by the demise, it not having been proved as ever having been in the exclusive occupation of J [5] So an assignment of household goods and furniture has been held in some cases to be limited to those described in the schedule though the general words were wider,[6] and in others not to be so restricted, depending on the circumstances of each case.[7] A lease of a piece of land " lying near to the said cottage containing, etc., lately used as garden ground " did not pass a particular piece of waste land unless it could be shown to have been used as garden ground.[8]

(3) The third rule, referred to above by anticipation, is that where there is both a general or group and a special

[4] *S. C.*, at p 196
[5] *Dyne* v *Nutley* (1853), 14 C B 122, 127
[6] *Wood* v *Rowcliffe* (1851), 6 Exch 407, *Re Craig* (1869), Ir R 4 Eq 158
[7] *Baker* v *Richardson* (1858), 6 W R 663; *Cort* v *Sagar* (1858), 3 H & N 370 Cf. *Griffiths* v *Penson* (1863), 1 N. R 330
[8] *Kingsmill* v. *Millard* (1855), 11 Exch 313 Further examples will be found in Norton, pp 234—239

description or descriptions and nothing exists which satisfies all the descriptions, but something exists which satisfies one or more of them and this thing is described with sufficient certainty, the unsatisfied description or descriptions may be disregarded and rejected.

Falsa demonstratio —The rule is known as *falsa demonstratio non nocet*—a false description does no harm, or does not vitiate the deed. As Lord Sumner pointed out [9] the Latin maxim is deficient and he would add to it "*cum de corpore constat*"—when the thing is described with certainty. "A false description of a person or thing will not vitiate a gift in a deed or will if it be sufficiently clear what person or thing was really meant," [10] or, as Baron Parke put it in *Llewellyn* v. *Earl of Jersey*,[11] "As soon as there is an adequate and sufficient definition, with convenient certainty, of what was intended to pass by a deed, any subsequent erroneous addition will not vitiate it." A bequest of "all my stock or shares in the Great Eastern Railway" after that railway had been amalgamated with the London and North Eastern Railway and the stock owned by the testator had formerly been Great Eastern Railway stock was treated as a *falsa demonstratio* [12]

Baron Alderson said in *Morrell* v. *Fisher* [13]: "One of the rules of construction is '*falsa demonstratio non nocet*'" and adopted the definition of Baron Parke. A false description may be in a name [14]; or a bill of sale may include "all goods, fixtures, etc., in or about the messuage . . . the chief articles whereof are particularly enumerated and described in a certain schedule hereunto annexed". The schedule was not annexed and the deed was held to be operative without

---

[9] In *Eastwood* v *Ashton*, [1915] A C. 900, at p 914
[10] *Per* Joyce, J., in *Re Brocket* (*supra*), at p 194
[11] (1843), 11 M & W 183, at p. 189 Cf. *Eastwood* v. *Ashton*, *supra*.
[12] *Re Anderson* (1928), 44 T. L. R 295.
[13] (1849), 4 Exch. 591, at p. 604
[14] *Simmons* v. *Woodward*, [1892] A. C. 105.

it.[15] Where rooms on the second floor of Nos. 13 and 14 Old Bond Street were demised " together with free ingress and egress through the staircase and passages of No. 13 ", and there was no staircase in No. 13, but there was one in No. 14, the Court held that the doctrine did not apply but it was a case of common mistake and the demise must be rectified. It was, however, strongly urged in argument that the doctrine can only apply when it occurs at the end of a sentence or where the false part of the description *follows* the true part. This was rejected by the Judges of the Court of Appeal.[16] " Where a description of the parcels is partly true and partly false, if the true part describes the subject with sufficient legal certainty, the untrue part will be rejected as *falsa demonstratio* and will not vitiate the grant or devise. It does not matter in what order the true and untrue parts come " In *Cloak* v. *Hammond* [17] a testatrix left property to " my cousin Harriet Cloak "; there was no such cousin, but there was a married cousin Harriet Crane whose maiden name was Cloak, and also a cousin T. Cloak whose wife's name was Harriet. Extrinsic evidence was admitted to show testatrix's knowledge of and intimacy with the Cloak family, and it was held that " cousin " might be understood in the popular sense of " wife of a cousin ". In *Hardwick* v. *Hardwick* [18] there was a devise of " all my share and interest in the lands known by the name of D situate in the parish of K, now in the occupation of E ". The lands known as D included two small closes in the parish of L, but were only accessible from lands which were in the parish of K There was also one close formerly in the same occupation as the other land, but at the date of the will and the death of the testatrix occupied by M. It was held to be a case of *falsa demonstratio* and that the three closes passed, and Lord Selborne said [19]: " It is perfectly certain that if

---

[15] *Dyer* v *Green* (1847), 1 Ex. Ch 71
[16] *Cowen* v. *Truefitt, Ltd.*, [1899] 2 Ch. 309, 311, 313.
[17] (1887), 34 Ch. D. 253
[18] (1873), 16 Eq. 168.
[19] S C , at p 175

all the terms of description fit some particular property, you cannot enlarge them by extrinsic evidence so as to exclude [? 'include' was intended] anything which any part of those terms does not accurately fit. On the other hand, I apprehend that if the words of description when examined do not fit with accuracy, and if there must be some modification of some part of them in order to place a reasonable construction on the will, then the whole thing must be looked at fairly to see what are the leading words of description and what is the subordinate matter and for this purpose evidence of extrinsic facts may be regarded " So in a land certificate issued by the Crown there was a variance between the stated acreage and the area as described by boundaries Evidence was given of user inconsistent with the area intended to be granted being that included in the boundaries, so as to establish that that description was a *falsa demonstratio*.[20] And in *Horne* v. *Struben*[21] a grant of land was made with certain specified boundaries " as will further appear by the diagram framed by the surveyor ". The diagram was repugnant to the grant and the latter was held to prevail as the right of the grantee must be expressed in his title and when so expressed is not limited by the diagram. So in *Llewellyn* v. *Earl of Jersey* (*supra*) where a conveyance was made with reference to a schedule in which the piece of land in question was described as containing 34 perches; it was identified as No. 153b and stated to be " a small piece " marked on the plan annexed to the deed. In the plan No. 153b contained only 27 perches. It was held that the description in the plan must prevail, the acreage being rejected as *falsa demonstratio*, and Baron Parke said[22]: " The portion conveyed is perfectly described and can be precisely ascertained, and no difficulty arises except from the subsequent statement that it contains 34 perches. That, however, becomes merely a false descrip-

---

[20] *Watcham* v *East Africa Protectorate*, [1919] A. C. 533.
[21] [1902] A. C. 454
[22] (1843), 11 M. & W. 183, at p 199

tion of that which is conveyed with convenient certainty
before . . . It is a mere *falsa demonstratio* and does not
affect that which is already sufficiently conveyed."

Of maps and plans.—Many deeds contain maps or plans
and the question often arises as to the operation of these if the
description in the deed does not accurately correspond with
that in the map or plan. To begin with, if the plan is incorporated by reference into the deed, it becomes part of the deed
and must be construed together with the deed itself It is not,
of course, sufficient merely to annex a plan to the conveyance.[1]
A vendor conveyed to a purchaser property described as
" Bank Hey Farm " with particulars of acreage, etc., " all
which said premises are more particularly described in the plan
endorsed on these presents and are delineated and coloured
red in such plan ". The plan showed a strip of land which
formerly formed part of Bank Hey Farm, but which had at
the date of the conveyance been in the possession of adjoining
owners who had acquired by limitation a title adverse to the
vendor. Held, that the description with reference to the plan
must prevail and the strip was included in the conveyance.[2]
Where the conveyance was full and accurate as to the parcels
which were " described in the annexed map ", and the map
was found to contain several acres which formed no part of
the estate conveyed but part of one of a somewhat similar
name, the first description was held to prevail and nothing
passed which was not part of the estate accurately described
in the conveyance.[3] Where a draft conveyance described the
property by reference to a plan, which was a copy of that
attached to the particulars of sale, the vendor was not allowed
to insert in his conveyance the words " by way of elucidation
and not of warranty " in order to qualify the reference to the

[1] *Re Otway's Estate* (1862), 13 Ir. Ch Rep 222.
[2] *Eastwood* v. *Ashton,* [1915] A C 900.
[3] *Roe* v *Lidwell* (1860), 11 Ir. C L. Rep 320, *Horne* v. *Struben, supra.*

plan, the Court observing that the description of the property in the draft conveyance was insufficient without reference to the plan, and Farwell, J , said: "I am not aware of any decision which shows that a plan on a conveyance amounts to a warranty that the plan is correct."[4] A conveyance contained as part of the description exact dimensions of the property conveyed, " bounded on the west by the seashore ", and referred to a plan. The Court construed "seashore" as meaning "foreshore" and held that this was not an example of the rule that when you have in the words of description a sufficiently certain definition of what is conveyed, inaccuracy of dimensions or of plans as delineated will not vitiate the effect of what is there sufficiently defined (*i.e., falsa demonstratio*[5]), as here the dimensions were part and parcel of the description itself.[6] So where a plan indorsed on a deed showed a four-foot wide way to the property conveyed, which was part of a wider roadway used for vehicles, and the *habendum* was to hold "with the benefit of all easements and privileges, etc.", the purchaser was held to be entitled to the wider way.[7] A map or plan which is drawn on a scale too small to ascertain the boundaries or acreage, or not drawn to scale at all, will not control the description in any case.[8] Nor will it do so if it has been made for a different purpose. Where old maps of a district were produced in order to show the non-existence of a right of way at their date, they were not admitted in evidence though they did not mark the way.[9]

According to the practice of conveyancers, plans may be incorporated by reference in a verbal description, with or without words such as "by way of identification only". Where these additional words are included, the plan cannot

---

[4] *Re Sparrow and James' Contract*, [1910] 2 Ch. 60

[5] Cf *Dublin and Kingstown Ry* v *Bradford* (1857), 7 Ir C. L. Rep. 57.

[6] *Mellor* v *Walmesley*, [1905] 2 Ch 164

[7] *Gregg* v *Richards*, [1926] Ch 521

[8] *Taylor* v. *Parry* (1840), 1 Man & Gr. 604; *Fox* v. *Clarke* (1874), L. R. 9 Q B 565, at pp. 570, 571

[9] *Stoney* v. *Eastbourne R C.*, [1927] 1 Ch. 367.

be taken to define the boundaries of the property conveyed but its operation is limited to the situation of the property.

The " ejusdem generis " rule.—The rule, meaning " of the same kind ", applies where there is a particular description of property, sufficient to identify what was intended, followed by some general or " omnibus " description. This will be confined to objects of the same class or kind as the former, it being assumed that the general words were only intended to guard against some accidental omission in the objects of the kind mentioned and were not intended to extend to objects of a wholly different kind. A few examples will make the meaning of this clear. A ship was to be relieved from liability for not delivering cargo at a certain port or ports if it was in the opinion of the master unsafe to do so " in consequence of war, disturbance or any other cause " The question arose whether a port inaccessible in the opinion of the master through ice was within the exception. It was held not to be so : " any other cause " must be construed to apply to causes *ejusdem generis* or similar to " war or disturbance " [1] " It is a general rule of construction that where a particular class is spoken of, and general words follow, the class first mentioned is to be taken as the most comprehensive, and the general words treated as referring to matters *ejusdem generis* with such class." [2] The rule is based on the principle *noscitur a socus.*

A power of attorney empowered the grantee " where necessary in connection with any purchases made on my behalf as aforesaid or in connection with my said business to make, draw, sign, accept and endorse any bills of exchange or promissory notes which should be requisite or proper in the premises " and to sign plaintiff's name or trading name to any cheques on his banking account in London. The agent borrowed ostensibly for the business and accepted bills for

---

[1] *Tillmanns & Co* v *S S Knutsford Co.*, [1908] 2 K. B. 385; *Re Richard-sons & Samuel*, [1898] 1 Q B. 261; *Thorman* v *Dowgate Steamship Co*, [1910] 1 K B. 410.

[2] *Per* Pollock, C B , in *Lyndon v. Standbridge* (1857), 2 H. & N. 45, at p. 51.

the amount in his own name " *per pro* " and misapplied the amount.   The question was whether the power of attorney conferred on the agent the power to borrow.   It was held it did not, as the general words must be construed, and therefore qualified, by the preceding context [3]   In *Lambourn* v. *McLellan* [4] there was a covenant in a lease to deliver up at the end of the lease " doors, locks, keys, wainscots, hearths, stoves and all other erections, buildings, improvements, fixtures and things which are now or which at any time during the said term shall be fixed, fastened or belong to " the demised premises   The lessee had erected for the purposes of his trade certain machines fastened to the floor by nails and screws.   Machinery was not mentioned in the enumeration, and the question was whether the tenant could remove his trade fixtures.   It was held that the general words (" and all other ", etc.) must be applied only to things *ejusdem generis* with those previously described, that is to say, what are known as landlord's fixtures.

But it may be asked: Are the general words never to have any operative effect of their own; are they always to be confined to the kind of objects already specified?   We have been told that words are to be given their plain, ordinary meaning [5]   Why not apply that rule here?   The answer is that the rule of *ejusdem generis* depends on the *assumed* intention of the writer, *e.g.*, if A leaves " my plate, furniture, pictures and all other of my property or effects in my house at X to B ", the law assumes that he does not mean B to have the title deeds or bonds which happen to be in his safe; it is assumed that what B was to take was what is known as " household effects ".   In *Anderson* v. *Anderson* [6] Lord Esher, M.R., rejected " the supposed rule that general words are *prima facie* to be taken in a restricted

---

[3] *Jacobs* v *Morris*, [1901] 1 Ch 261; [1902] 1 Ch. 816
[4] [1903] 2 Ch. 268.
[5] See p 27, *supra*
[6] [1895] 1 Q B. 749.

sense ", and Rigby, L J. (at p 755), said : " You must give the words you find in the instrument their general meaning unless you can see with reasonable plainness that that was not the intention of the testator or settlor." So unless the law can find some evidence of a different intention, it will act on the principle that words are to have their ordinary meaning and a man must be taken to mean what he says. Contrast two cases : In *Harrison* v. *Blackburn*[7] there was an assignment by way of mortgage of " all and every the household goods and furniture, stock-in-trade and other household effects whatsoever, and all other goods, chattels and effects now being, or which shall hereafter be in, upon or about the messuage, etc., and all other personal estate whatsoever " of the mortgagor. These words (" and all other ", etc) were held to be *ejusdem generis* with the specific words and therefore did not pass the lease of the house in which the goods were. Whereas in *Ringer* v. *Cann*,[8] where the words were practically the same, the lease was held to pass partly on the ground that it was a creditors' deed and it must be assumed to have been intended to pass everything of value, and partly because the deed provided that the assignees should pay the rent for a limited period. This showed an intention that the omnibus words should not be restricted. The same presumption is applied where the general words mention something which is clearly not *ejusdem generis* with the specific words; this is taken to show that the former are not intended to be restricted. A debtor assigned to his creditors " all his stock-in-trade, book and other debts, goods, securities, chattels and effects whatsoever, except the wearing apparel of himself and family ". Now the wearing apparel is clearly not *ejusdem generis* with what preceded it; there was therefore no reason to suppose that the assignor meant anything less than he said, and that therefore a contingent interest would pass under the words he had used. It will now be apparent that unless there is a genus or category there can be no

---

[7] (1864), 7 C B (N S.) 678.   [8] (1838), 3 M & W 343.

application of the *ejusdem generis* rule. The specific words must refer not to different objects of widely differing character, but to something which can be called a class or kind of objects. In a case previously cited [9] the words " war, disturbance or other cause " comprise a category of violent acts attributable to human agency; but " plate, linen and other goods and chattels in the coach-house and stables " do not make up a category excluding horses,[10] and the horses passed. " Loss of time from deficiency of men or owner's stores, breakdown of machinery or damage to hull or other accident preventing the work of the steamer " does not admit the principle of *ejusdem generis*.[11] " If the particular words exhaust a whole genus, the general words must refer to some larger genus ",[12] and are therefore not to be construed as restrictive. Thus a charterparty contained an exemption for all liability arising from " frost, flood, strikes . . . and any other unavoidable accidents or hindrances of what kind soever beyond their control ", delaying the loading of the cargo. It was held that the words " what kind soever " were intended to exclude the *ejusdem generis* rule, in other words, the particular words had completely described a genus of hindrances and the words " any other " . . . " what kind soever " opened a new and larger category of exceptions. The charterers were accordingly held not liable for delay in loading caused by a block of other ships in the port.[13] The words " et cetera " have been held to be too vague to invoke the *ejusdem generis* rule.[14] This rule is often applied in the construction of statutes and will be referred to in a later portion of this book.[15]

---

9 *Tillmanns & Co.* v. *S.S. Knutsford Co*, *supra*. Cf *Pestonjee Bhicajee* v. *Anderson*, [1938] 2 Madras L. J 906, at p 910, *per* Lord Romer.

10 *Anderson* v *Anderson*, *supra*

11 *Owners of S.S. Magnhild* v. *Macintyre*, [1920] 3 K. B 321

12 Per Willes, J , *Fenwick* v. *Schmalz* (1868), L. R. 3 C P 313, at p 315. Snowstorm not an accident within the meaning of the exceptions.

13 *Larsen* v *Sylvester & Co.*, [1908] A C 295

14 *Herman* v. *Morris* (1914), 35 T. L. R. 328, 574.

15 Cf. Maxwell, Interpretation of Statutes (8th ed), pp 289 ff *Infra*, pp. 180—184 For a recent example, cf *Evans* v *Cross*, [1938] 1 K. B. 694.

Exceptions, reservations and implied grants.—Following the description of the property granted there frequently occur expressly or impliedly other interests which are excepted or reserved out of the grant or are expressly or impliedly included with it. Express grants of interests, such as easements, appurtenant to the property conveyed call for no comment upon the principles of construction, since it is clearly a question of substantive law whether or not the interest is clearly defined. Exceptions and reservations are interests in favour of the grantor which are either retained out of the property granted or which are created by the grantee over the property granted and may be either express or implied Interests may be impliedly granted by the operation of Statute or Common Law to the grantee without actual mention in the conveyance. Taking these in their order : —

According to Coke [1] an exception is from part of a grant of something in being at the time of the grant, as a grant excepting timber, quarries and mines; whereas a reservation is of a thing not yet in being but created for the first time by the grant; for example, A demises his house to B for five years *reserving* such and such a rent. The latter only comes into existence with the demise, whereas the timber and mines were in existence before.[2]

An exception or reservation must be clearly expressed, perhaps more especially in the case of exception of mines. If there is no exception in a conveyance then everything passes to the grantee, both the surface and whatever is above or below it; such a conveyance cannot be construed as merely intended to pass the surface [3] On the other hand a clear exception ("the liberty of working the coal ") with nothing

---

[1] Co Litt 47a
[2] See *per* Scrutton, J., in *Jones* v *Consolidated Anthracite Collieries, Ltd* , [1916] 1 K. B 123, at p 135.
[3] *Mitchell* v *Mosley*, [1914] 1 Ch. 439, 452.

to cut down its *prima facie* meaning will be construed as equivalent to a right of property.[4]

On the other hand, where there was a reservation " to get and carry away coal " and for nearly 100 years the plaintiff and his predecessors had not worked the coal and the plaintiff in fact had at the end of that period taken a lease of certain of the coal from the defendant and now claimed an exclusive right to the coal, the Court held that the reservation was not an exception of minerals, but only a grant of the right to work them and there was nothing to show that the right was to be an exclusive one. The defendant therefore had not infringed the plaintiff's right.[5]

" It is a settled rule of construction ", said Stirling, L.J., " that where there is a grant and an exception out of it, the exception is to be taken for the benefit of the grantor and to be construed in favour of the grantee   If then the grant be clear but the exception be so framed as to be bad for uncertainty, it appears to us that on this principle the grant is operative and the exception fails "[6]   In that case the exception was of " a piece of land not less than forty feet in width commencing at the level-crossing over the railway at the point marked A on the said plan and terminating at the nearest road to be made by the purchaser or his assignee on the estate so as to give access to such roads from other lands belonging to the vendor "   There was no attempt to define the excepted land either by way of boundaries or colour so as to distinguish it from the rest of the land described in the conveyance and plan. The piece was held not to have been effectively excepted; it was both uncertain, was an estate *in futuro*, and offended the rule against perpetuities.

---

[4] *Duke of Hamilton* v *Dunlop* (1885), 10 App Cas. 813. All coal and mines of coal will eventually become vested in the Coal Commission by virtue of the Coal Act, 1938

[5] *Duke of Sutherland* v *Heathcote*, [1891] 3 Ch 504; [1892] 1 Ch 475, 483

[6] *Savill Bros , Ltd* v *Bethell*, [1902] 2 Ch 523, at p. 537 (*supra*, p 60) Cf *per* Holroyd, J., in *Bullen* v. *Denning* (1826), 5 B & C. 842, at p 850; *Cardigan (Earl of)* v *Armitage* (1823), 2 B & C. 197

By section 65 (2) of the Law of Property Act, 1925, " A conveyance of a legal estate expressed to be subject to another legal estate not in existence immediately before the date of the conveyance, shall operate as a reservation, unless a contrary intention appears ".

Implied reservations.—Reservations may be implied either from the circumstances enumerated in the grant or by reason of necessity. A reservation of necessity is uncommon and is usually regarded as confined to a way of necessity, that is an easement of way, when the property retained by the grantor becomes land-locked by virtue of the conveyance. This limit may be too narrow.[7]

Reservations implied from the terms of the grant are more common but cannot be classified as they depend upon the construction of the instrument; it must suffice to give some examples.

Where a building lease reserved to the lessor the right of building to any height on adjoining land, it was held that the reservation was to be construed as a grant by the lessee to the lessor of full right to build on the adjoining land.[8]

For many years two properties, W. L. and C., were owned by the same person, and property C. had used a path over W. L. This latter was subsequently sold. The agreement reserved to the vendor all rights of way hitherto exercised in respect of C. over W. L. The conveyance contained a similar reservation but was not executed by the purchaser who took possession of W. L. The Court held that the purchaser and his successors in title taking with notice of the reservation were bound to give effect to it as a reservation of an equitable easement. Had it been executed it would have been a legal reservation.[9] Execution by the grantee of the conveyance containing a reservation is now rendered

[7] Norton, pp. 190 ff
[8] *Foster* v *Lyons*, [1927] 1 Ch. 219
[9] *May* v. *Belleville*, [1905] 2 Ch 605

unnecessary for its operation by section 65 (1) of the Law of Property Act, 1925.

So where " all mines and veins of coal in and under " the land conveyed were excepted and reserved to the grantors, the exception enabled the grantors' successors in title to construct underground roads and to use them as they pleased. A mine is not only a bed of coal but the workings of coal, so the roads were part of the mine excepted.[10]

It is sometimes difficult to distinguish between an exception or reservation in a grant (the names are often confused and used indifferently in the cases) and a re-grant of some privilege or easement by the grantee to the grantor. In *May* v. *Belleville*[11] there was a true reservation. In *Pearce* v. *Watts*,[12] where there was this clause, " the vendor reserves the necessary land for making a railway through the estate to P ", there was an exception. In *Savill Bros.* v. *Bethell*[13] there was also a true exception. Both these exceptions were held void for uncertainty. These cases were distinguished by Swinfen Eady, J., in *South Eastern Ry.* v. *Associated Portland Cement Co.*,[14] whose judgment was affirmed by the Court of Appeal. In that case the railway bought a strip of land and agreed that the landowner might make a tunnel under the strip conveyed in order to join his severed lands. The site of the tunnel was not defined. The learned Judge held that this was not an exception, but the re-grant of an easement to the grantor, in whom was vested the right to select the site for the tunnel, and was therefore not void for uncertainty.

Implied grants.—By virtue of statute and of common law, certain rights may pass or be created under the conveyance without mention therein. That which is legally appendant

---

[10] *Batten-Pooll* v. *Kennedy*, [1907] 1 Ch 256.

[11] *Supra*, p 133.

[12] (1875), L R 20 Eq. 492.

[13] *Supra*, p. 60.

[14] [1910] 1 Ch 12. In the Court of Appeal the exception was regarded as a mere personal covenant passing to the assignee (*supra*, p 59).

or appurtenant passes by the conveyance to which it is annexed without mention.[15]   Prior to 1881 it was customary to add certain words, commonly called " the general words ", which had the effect of turning many privileges or quasi-easements enjoyed over land prior to the conveyance and retained by the grantor into appurtenant rights, and since that date these words have been implied in a conveyance by section 62 of the Law of Property Act, 1925.[16]

So, where a tenant of a farm had been accustomed to depasture his sheep on a neighbouring hillside owned by the grantor and the farm was sold in fee simple, the purchaser was held to be entitled to continue this practice as an implied grant in the nature of a *profit à prendre*.[17]   Even apart from the general words, which are not implied in a contract,[18] a quasi-easement which is continuous, apparent and reasonably necessary to the enjoyment of the land sold, will be converted into a legal easement under the rule in *Wheeldon* v. *Burrows*.[19]

Neither of these rules will enable the conveyance to operate as the grant of a right incapable of subsisting as an incorporeal hereditament.   So, where prior to conveyance the land had been benefited by the overflow from a tank on the land of the grantor, it was held that this was a temporary purpose of uncertain quality which could not be converted into a legal easement and so the conveyance did not operate to create any right in the grantee.[20]

"*All the estate*" *clause*.—Furthermore, by section 63 of the Law of Property Act, 1925, every conveyance made after December 31, 1881, is effectual to pass all the estate and

---

[15] Co. Lit. 121b
[16] Re enacting the Conveyancing Act, 1881, s 6.
[17] *White* v. *Williams*, [1922] 1 K. B. 727.
[18] *Re Peck and School Board for London*, [1893] 2 Ch 315.
[19] (1879), 12 Ch. D 31.
[20] *Bartlett* v. *Tottenham*, [1932] 1 Ch. 114. For a fuller account of the rules governing implied grants under these rules, cf. Norton, pp 273 ff.

right, title and interest in the property conveyed, but is
subject to any expressed contrary intention and has effect
subject to the terms and provisions of the conveyance. This
is sometimes referred to by conveyancers as the " all estate "
clause. In conveyances prior to 1882 it was usual to insert
this in all parcels; it is now unnecessary, but the Law of
Property Act allows it to be modified or limited by the terms
of the deed. Sometimes express words may be necessary to pass
the interest, as, for instance, a tithe rentcharge is not an
interest in the land itself, passing without more on a conveyance of the land.[21] So where a deed purported to settle
" all the estate ", etc , of the settlor, a mortgage was not
mentioned and was held not to be included in the settlement.
The words of the " all estate " clause are in general terms
and are just as liable to restrictions by the circumstances or
scope of the instrument as any other general words, or by
reference to recitals (see *supra*, pp. 103—107). " If upon the
whole scope of the instrument as to which especial regard
is to be had to what I call introductory recitals, it appears
it was not the intention to pass those properties, it will not
pass them."[22]

XIII.—OPERATIVE PART—THE HABENDUM

Purpose of habendum.—All parts of a deed before the
habendum are technically known as " the premises ".[1] These
have already been briefly described. Now a few words must
be said about the habendum, as it is called, in so far as it
has to do with construction. As Coke says[2]: " The office
of the premises of the deed is twofold: first, rightly to name
the feoffor and the feoffee; and secondly, to comprehend the

[21] *Public Trustee* v. *Duchy of Cornwall*, [1927] 1 K B 576. Tithe rentcharge is now extinguished by the Tithe Act, 1936
[22] *Williams* v *Pinckney* (1897), 67 L J Ch. 34, 39; *Gregg* v. *Richards*,
[1926] Ch 521, *supra*, pp 67, 126
[1] Shep Touch , p 74.
[2] Co Litt. 6a

certainty of the lands or tenements to be conveyed by the feoffment. . . . The habendum hath also two parts, *viz.*: first to name again the feoffee, and, secondly, to limit the certainty of the estate." So the office of the habendum is to limit the estate to be taken. The property named in the premises passes by the deed, the habendum limits the estate therein Thus an estate, which may be implied by law in the premises (*e.g.*, a grant to A (formerly) conferred by law an estate for life merely) may be controlled by the habendum, *e.g.*, "to have and to hold to the said A and his heirs". Most of the law on the subject is to be found in old books and cases [2a]; there is very little on the subject in the modern law. It will be sufficient to cite a few examples only. In one of the cases it was held that if no estate is mentioned in the premises, the grantee takes nothing under that part of the deed save what, if any, would be implied by law; " but if an habendum follow, the *intention* of the parties as to the estate to be conveyed will be found in the habendum, and consequently no implication or presumption of law can be made "; so if the intention expressed by the habendum be contrary to law, the intention cannot operate and the deed will be void.[3]

Relation of premises and habendum.—Though it is, of course, usual to name the grantee in the premises, still the name of the grantee in the habendum will be sufficient,[4] and the grantee will take for the estate limited thereby. On the other hand, it is said that parcels not mentioned in the premises but only in the habendum will not pass.[5] Sheppard says if Blackacre only is granted in the premises but the habendum mentions Blackacre and Whiteacre, only Blackacre will pass.[6] If the new matter in the habendum is implied

---

[2a] Cf. for instance, *Baldwin's Case* (1589), 2 Rep 23a
[3] *Goodtitle* v *Gibbs*, (1826), 5 B. & C. 709, at p 717.
[4] Shep Touch 75
[5] *S. C.*
[6] See 1 Dav. Prec (5th ed) 81

in the premises this rule will not apply. In *Gregg* v. *Richards*,[6a] Warrington, L.J , said: " Although I thoroughly agree that you cannot read a habendum as enlarging the description of the parcels, on the other hand, it seems to me that when you have the habendum in such terms as we have it here [' to hold the same,with benefit of all such easements and privileges in the nature of easements as are now subsisting in respect of the property hereby conveyed '], it is strong evidence that the parties to this conveyance acted on the assumption that the easements and privileges in the nature of easements then subsisting would pass to the purchaser and therefore that the words expressed in the statute [section 63 (1) of the Law of Property Act, 1925] would not be excluded from the description in the deed." A habendum is not absolutely necessary; if there is none, the grantee takes the estate limited in the premises.[7] If the parcels are repeated in the habendum it is nugatory, and " the habendum shall be construed as if there had been no such recital " as it does " something which is not its office and is superfluous and therefore all that recital shall be of no effect ".[8] By a sort of inverted rule of recital, however, the setting out of the parcels in the habendum may, if necessary, be used to explain the parcels set out in the premises.

- As, for instance, where A, seised of a reversion in fee simple upon a lease for life, leased the reversion to B, habendum—the land for twenty-one years, the words in the -habendum were held to explain those in the premises and created a good lease for twenty-one years after the death of the tenant for life.[9] So, also if there are limitations both in the premises and in the habendum, those in the latter will, if possible, be treated as explanatory of those in the former. As in *Pilsworth* v. *Jones* (1671), T. Jones 4; demise to A and

---

[6a] [1926] Ch. 521, at p. 533.
[7] See *per* Abbott, C J., in *Goodtitle* v *Gibbs, supra*
[8] *Carew's Case* (1585), Moore 222, *per* Manwood, C.B.
[9] *Throckmerton* v *Tracy* (1555), 1 Plow. 145.

his heirs, habendum to A and his heirs for three lives, the grantee was held to take for the three lives, there being no repugnancy; if the limitations are repugnant, the estate limited by the premises is to be accepted and that in the habendum rejected. "The habendum may enlarge the premises but not abridge the same." [10] Blackstone (2 Bl. Com. 298) indeed thought that the habendum may "lessen, enlarge, explain or qualify, but not totally contradict or be repugnant to the estate granted in the premises." In *Kendal* v. *Micfeild*,[11] however, Verney, M.R., said: "On the other hand, it is clear that the habendum never abridges the estate granted by the premises of the deed; it may indeed alter or vary it", thus agreeing with Coke. And Lord Davey said: "Although the habendum cannot retract the gift in the premises, it may construe and explain the sense in which the words in the premises should be taken" [12] So also if different persons be mentioned as grantee in the premises and the habendum, he who is mentioned only in the latter cannot take an immediate estate in the land granted; though he may take an estate in remainder. "When the habendum is to such a person as was not named in the premises of the deed it is but a nugation." [13]

XIV —COVENANTS

It is beyond the scope of this work to consider in detail the implications of the various covenants, express or implied, in conveyances, as for title, for quiet enjoyment, against incumbrances and the like, but a few words must be said about covenants in general and their nature, with special reference to their interpretation. A covenant should mean strictly an agreement under seal; it is commonly used of any

[10] Co Litt 299a.
[11] (1740), Barn Ch Rep 46, at p 47
[12] In *Spencer* v *Registrar of Titles*, [1906] A. C. 503, at p. 507.
[13] *Per* Manwood, J , *Anon.* (1573), 3 Leon. 32, lx

promise or stipulation, either executed or executory. No special form of words is necessary. "No particular technical words are necessary towards making a covenant."[1] "I think the only principle which these cases establish which is useful to the question before us is that covenant is a matter of intention and that any words will make a covenant, whether participial or not, if it can be clearly seen that such was the intention of the parties."[2]

Lord Blackburn said in *Russell* v. *Watts*[3]: "I take it to be clear that any form of words which, when properly construed, with the aid of all that is legitimately admissible to aid in the construction of a written document, indicate an agreement, forms, when under seal, a covenant." There are many examples in the books of forms of words which have been held to amount to a covenant. "Upon condition that" the lessee do certain things, in a lease. "Provided always and it is agreed that the lessor shall find timber" for repairs. "Doing, fulfilling and performing"; "yielding and paying"; "rendering" rent free; "the said farmhouse and buildings being previously put in repair and kept in repair by" the lessor; "to be paid" may amount to a covenant to pay; when a person "declares" in a deed he will do a thing, it amounts to a covenant by him that he will do it. So the expression of an intention on the part of a railway company in a lease of a station refreshment room that all trains on that line should stop at that station was held to be a convenant by the company not to prevent trains stopping[4] As to recitals operating as covenants, see *supra*, p 110

Does an engagement to serve imply a covenant on the part of the employer to find work for the employee? In *Turner* v. *Sawdon & Co.*[5] the defendants engaged the

---

[1] *Per* Lord Mansfield, C J , in *Lant* v. *Norris* (1757), 1 Burr 287, at p. 290.
[2] *Per* Pickford, L J , in *Westacott* v. *Hahn*, [1918] 1 K B 495, at p 505
[3] (1885), 10 App Cas. 590, at p 611
[4] *Rigby* v. *G W R* (1845), 14 M & W. 811.
[5] [1901] 2 K. B 653

plaintiff as a representative salesman for four years. Before the end of that period they refused to give the plaintiff any work to do, although willing to pay his wages The Court of Appeal held that there was no obligation on the defendants to give the plaintiff work. This was a retainer at fixed wages, and to construe it into an obligation to give work would be to convert the retainer into a contract to keep the servant in the service of his employer in such a manner as to enable the former to become an expert at his work Where the servant is to be paid by commission different considerations arise, as in *Turner* v *Goldsmith* [6] and *Bunning* v. *The Lyric Theatre* [7] where the opportunity of appearing as musical director and being announced as such in the programmes was part of the consideration. Some years later, McCardie, J., at *nisi prius*,[8] threw some doubt on *Turner* v. *Sawdon & Co.*, but the case before him was one where the plaintiff was debarred from earning commission on the profits of the company.

A covenant will not be implied unless from a reasonable construction of the terms of the contract or other document " an implication necessarily arises that the parties must have intended that the suggested stipulation should exist. It is not enough to say that it would be a reasonable thing to make such an implication. It must be a necessary implication in the sense that I have mentioned." [9] " It is not competent to the Court ", said Cockburn, C.J.,[10] " to make a contract for the parties which they have not thought fit to make for themselves or to import a covenant which does not arise by fair and necessary implication from the language they have used." For instance, in a contract by

---

[6] [1891] 1 Q B 544

[7] (1894), 71 L T 396

[8] In *Re an Arbitration between Rubel Bronze and Metal Co and Vos*, [1918] 1 K B 315.

[9] *Per* Lord Esher, M R , in *Hamlyn* v *Wood*, [1891] 2 Q. B 488, at p. 491, and *ibid*, *per* Kay, L J , at p 494

[10] *Smith* v *Mayor of Harwich* (1857), 2 C B (N s) 651, at p. 669.

a merchant with his retail customers it was agreed that in consideration of the latter exclusively dealing with him for their supplies, he would distribute the net profits for four years plus a sum of money among them. The merchant before the expiry of the four years sold his business and went into voluntary liquidation and had thus put it out of his power to carry on business. The retailer was held entitled to damages.[11]

So also where the plaintiff was deprived of the chance of earning money as agent of the defendants, a shipping firm, who had sold their ships. It was held that there was no agreement, express or implied, that the defendants should run ships at all, and the question, decided in the negative, was: "Does the contract give the plaintiff a right to a continuing benefit?"[12] On the other hand, there may be an implied contract that the defendant would continue business so as to supply the plaintiff with orders during the period of his agency.[13] In a theatrical contract there may be an obligation to allow an artiste to appear and perform.[14] Or again, there may be no implied covenants on the part of patentees to keep the patent on foot for the benefit of their assignees. In this case [15] Kay, J., said: "The Court ought to be extremely careful how it implies such a covenant in a well-considered deed when there are no words whatever which express that covenant in any way."

Where a covenant begins with words like "it is hereby agreed and declared" that some party or parties to the deed will do such and such a thing, the covenant is only by that person or persons although the deed may be executed by others besides. It is not a covenant by all of them. "Anything

[11] *Ogdens* v *Nelson*, [1905] A C 109
[12] *Lazarus* v. *Cairn Line* (1912), 106 L T 378.
[13] *Northey* v *Trevillion* (1902), 18 T L. R 648; *Reigate* v. *Union Manufacturing Co.*, [1918] 1 K B 592
[14] *Clayton & Waller, Ltd* v. *Oliver*, [1930] A C 209.
[15] *Re Railway and Electric Appliances Co* (1888), 38 Ch. D 597, at p. 608.

more absurd than to hold it was a covenant by all of them could not be imagined." [16]

As to implied warranties or "covenants in the law" the *locus classicus* is the judgment of Bowen, L.J., in *The Moorcock*. [17]

The implied covenant for quiet enjoyment arising from the relationship of landlord and tenant is not an unrestricted covenant which would cover an interruption of the lessee's enjoyment by reason of eviction of his lessor by title paramount. [18] The covenant only extends to the duration of the lessor's own estate This was decided in a case where the defendants with an eight and a half years' lease by mistake sub-let the premises for ten and a half years. At the end of the eight and a half years the defendants were evicted by the superior landlord. In an action by the sub-tenants for breach of the implied covenant for quiet enjoyment it was held that assuming that the covenant could be implied (it was not expressed, nor was "demise" used) the covenant was limited to the lessor's estate, *viz.*, eight and a half years. [19] When a tenant holds over on the expiration of a term and the facts do not exclude an implied agreement to continue on the old terms, the tenant will be taken to hold subject to all the covenants in the lease which are applicable to the new tenancy. [20] This implication arises from the surrounding circumstances and these circumstances are to be found in the conditions upon which the tenant held the premises under the old lease. [21] An illegal covenant is void unless it can be severed, and then it is only the illegal part that will be void

---

[16] *Per* Jessel, M R., in *Dawes* v. *Tredwell* (1881), 18 Ch. D. 354, at p 359
[17] (1889), 14 P D 64, at p. 68   Cf. Chitty, Contracts (19th ed), pp 117—120.
[18] *Jones* v. *Lavington,* [1903] 1 K. B 253; *Markham* v *Paget,* [1908] 1 Ch. 697, at p 718.
[19] *Baynes & Co* v *Lloyd & Sons,* [1895] 2 Q B 610
[20] *Wedd* v. *Porter,* [1916] 2 K B 91
[21] *Cole* v *Kelly,* [1920] 2 K B 106   The same would apply where one party only had signed the agreement *Rye* v *Purcell,* [1926] 1 K B 446

(see p. 150). A covenant will be void if the same person is both covenantor and covenantee either solely or with others.[22]

Mutual covenants.—Where the same document contains covenants by each party to it, the question often arises, Are the covenants dependent or independent? Can A bring an action on B's covenant without having first performed his own? Or is the performance of his own covenant a condition precedent to his right to bring an action on B's covenant? It is a question of the intention and meaning of the parties to be collected from the instrument.

The rules as to the dependency of covenants are contained in the notes to *Pordage* v. *Cole* [23] They are somewhat complicated and may perhaps be stated simply as follows:—

(1) If there is a time fixed for performance, and if event A must or may happen before event B, then the doing of B is not a condition precedent to the doing of A. " But such stipulations as relate to things to be done after payment is due are not, and cannot be, conditions precedent.''[24]

(2) If A and B are to be done simultaneously, neither of the parties can sue without showing that he has done, or offered to do, his part. Examples of this will be found in the cases set out *infra*. The everyday purchase of goods for cash is an example.

(3) If the time for doing A must happen *after* the time fixed for doing B, the doing of B is a condition precedent to the doing of A, and the party to do B cannot sue without showing that he has done or has offered to do B.

Many examples may be found in charterparties—as, for instance, the covenant to pay freight on delivery of the goods and the delivery is prevented or delayed owing to deviation

---

[22] *Ellis* v *Kerr*, [1910] 1 Ch. 529, *Napier* v. *Williams*, [1911] 1 Ch 361; *Ridley* v *Lee*, [1935] Ch 591.

[23] (1670), 1 Wms Saund. 319. 1 (ed 1871); see Norton, Deeds (2nd ed), Chap XXX

[24] *Per* Lord Blackburn speaking of a fire insurance policy in *London Guarantie Co* v *Fearnley* (1880), 5 App Cas. 911, at p. 916.

or non-arrival of the ship. Or, again, agreements that no right of action shall arise until recourse has been had to arbitration, and then only for any sum awarded by the arbitrator.[25]

(4) Where the dependency arises from the *nature* of the covenants, if A is the *sole* consideration for B, A must be done or be offered to be done before suing for B. That is to say, the covenants are dependent; but if A is only *part* of the consideration for B and the non-performance of A can be compensated by damages, an action can be brought in respect of B without averring performance or offer of performance of A. In other words, the covenants are independent. The leading case is *Boone* v. *Eyre*,[26] where the plaintiff conveyed a plantation in the West Indies with the slaves on it for cash and an annuity and covenanted that he was lawfully possessed of the slaves. The defendant covenanted that, the plaintiff well and truly performing all and everything therein contained on his part to be performed, he would pay the annuity. The covenant to pay the annuity was held not to depend on the performance by the plaintiff; in other words, the phrase "the plaintiff well and truly performing", etc., was not a condition precedent to the defendant's obligation to pay the annuity. If that were the case, as Lord Mansfield pointed out, and the defendant could show that a single one of the slaves did not belong to the plaintiff, he (the defendant) would be released from his obligation. This is manifestly absurd The defendant in such a case would have a remedy in damages

The ability of a singer to perform on the opening night of an opera season has been held to be a condition precedent to liability where there was an agreement to engage the plaintiff to sing at £11 a week for three months if the opera ran so

---

[25] See *per* Jessel, M.R , in *Dawson* v *Fitzgerald* (1876), 1 Ex D 260; *Scott* v. *Avery* (1855), 5 H. L. C. 811; *Caledonian Insurance Co* v *Gilmour*, [1893] A C 85, *Hallen* v. *Spaeth*, [1923] A C 684 Chitty, Contracts (19th ed), pp 200 ff.
[26] (1777), 1 H Bl 273n

long [27] Bankers undertook to pay sterling in exchange for silver, but stipulated that the goods in payment for which the sterling was required should be financed through them. This last was held a condition precedent.[28]

Though a covenant might be construed as a condition precedent while the agreement was executory, it is a different matter where one of the parties has received a substantial portion of the consideration. Then this party cannot insist that the condition is a condition precedent and he cannot any longer rely on its non-performance as such.[29] So where a master had had the services of his apprentice for some time and then ceased to do business, he cannot bring an action on the covenant by the apprentice to serve him.[30]

An engagement was to sing in theatres, halls and drawing rooms for fifteen weeks and to be at rehearsals for six days before the engagement began. The stipulation as to rehearsals was held not to be a condition precedent [31] A covenant by a husband in a separation deed to pay an annuity to a trustee for the wife and a covenant by the trustee with the husband that the wife would not molest him are independent covenants.[32] Contracts to supply goods and to pay for them are held to be independent contracts [33]—if it were otherwise and the supplier failed to supply, say one of many thousands of articles, he would have no remedy.

It is sometimes a matter of some nicety whether a clause introduced by a participle (e.g., "all arrears being paid") or by the words "to be" (e g., "the names of the vessels to be declared as soon as the wool was shipped") is or is not a mere qualification of the covenant to which it is attached.

---

[27] *Poussard* v *Spiers & Pond* (1876), 1 Q B. D. 410
[28] *Bank of China* v. *American Trading Company*, [1894] A. C 266.
[29] *Per* Parke, B , in *Graves* v *Legg* (1854), 9 Exch 709, at p 716; *Carter* v. *Scargill* (1875), L. R 10 Q. B. 564, at p 567
[30] *Ellen* v *Topp* (1851), 6 Exch. 424; 441
[31] *Bettini* v. *Gye* (1876), 1 Q. B D. 183
[32] *Fearon* v *Earl of Aylesford* (1884), 14 Q B D. 792.
[33] Cf *Macintosh* v *Midland Counties Ry* (1845), 14 M & W. 548.

In the former case it forms a condition precedent to liability under the qualified covenant, in the latter it does not.[34]

Lord Mansfield said[35]: " The distinction is very clear: where mutual covenants go to the whole of the consideration on both sides, they are mutual covenants, the one precedent to the other. But where they go only to a part, where a breach may be paid for in damages, it is a different thing." To take one or two examples. Where there were covenants by each purchaser of different lots of property, the first that he would keep a drainage mill in good order for draining the other lots, and the other that he would keep the dykes, ditches and drains on his lot properly cleansed, the plaintiff did not keep his ditches cleansed, nor did the defendant work his mill to keep the plaintiff's marshes from being flooded. The plaintiff brought an action for breach of covenant to work the mill. It was held that the intention of the parties was that the covenants should be dependent; i.e., that the performance of the plaintiff's covenant should be a condition precedent to his right of action, and therefore that he could not recover.[36] So where a defendant agreed with a company to hold office for seven years and for seven years thereafter not to compete with the plaintiffs in business A compulsory winding-up order was made against the company and the defendant's services were dispensed with and he began business on his own account. The company brought an action on his covenant to restrain him; held, that he was no longer bound by the restrictive covenant as the company could no longer perform their covenant to employ him for seven years. The covenants were interdependent.[37] " Covenants are to be construed as

---

[34] See per Pickford, L.J , in *Westacott* v. *Hahn*, [1918] 1 K B. 495, at p. 505, and the examples given in Norton, pp. 594—596

[35] In *Boone* v *Eyre* (1777), 1 H. Bl. 273n., quoted by Lord Hanworth M.R , in *Huntoon Co* v *Kolynos*, [1930] 1 Ch 528, at p. 548

[36] *Kidner* v. *Stimpson* (1918), 35 T L R. 63 Cf *Henman* v. *Berliner*, [1918] 2 K. B 236

[37] *Measures* v. *Measures*, [1910] 2 Ch. 248 Cf. *General Billposting Co* v *Atkinson*, [1909] A. C 118

dependent or independent according to the intention of the parties and the good sense of the case.'' [37]   On the other hand, contracts to supply goods on the one side and to pay for them on the other are independent.   There are not very many modern examples of this in the books as the Court has always leaned against independent covenants.

Covenant operating as assignment. — A covenant may operate as an assignment of property when acquired. In *Re Lind* [38] Bankes, L.J., said: '' The covenant which has to be considered is a covenant to assign after-acquired property.   The question which has to be determined is whether the existence of that covenant at the date of the bankruptcy created without more a mere liability within section 37 (8) of the Bankruptcy Act, 1883, which must be deemed to be a debt provable in the bankruptcy.   If it did, then the discharge in bankruptcy operated as a discharge from all liability under the covenant   If it did not, then the matter is one outside the Bankruptcy Acts altogether and the covenant is unaffected by the bankruptcy discharge.'' Following this case Maugham, J. (as he then was) held that covenants in an agreement between husband and wife and a lender for the payment of the income of settled property into a specified account effected an equitable assignment of that income, and further that, owing to the agreement, the husband had forfeited his interest in the settlement. [39]

Two important topics remain to be mentioned—covenants in restraint of trade and penalties and liquidated damages. These are treated in detail in works devoted to the law of contract,[1] consequently a very brief statement of them will be set out here.

---

[38] [1915] 2 Ch 345
[39] *Re Gillott's Settlement,* [1934] Ch 97
[1] Restraint of trade Chitty, Contracts (19th ed), pp. 301—316; Pollock, Contract (10th ed.), pp. 391—400, Dix, Competitive Trading, pp. 158—180; Penalties and liquidated damages : Chitty, Contracts, pp. 255—259; Pollock, Contract, pp. 512, 513; Dix, *op cit ,* pp 144—152

Covenants in restraint of trade.—It is said generally that contracts in restraint of trade are void as being against public policy. The question most generally arises from covenants restraining persons who have sold their business or persons employed in an existing business from competing in trade with either their successors in the business or with their employers after leaving the employment. A general restraint on liberty of action is and always was void, but a system of partial restraints was developed in the earlier law which led to much uncertainty and confusion. All that was really certain was that there could not be a restraint *in gross*. A mere deed is not by itself sufficient without more. As Baron Parke said [2]: " Therefore if there be simply a stipulation though in an instrument under seal, that a trade or profession shall not be carried on in a particular place, without any recital in the deed or without any documents showing circumstances which rendered such a contract reasonable, the instrument is void.'' The modern law is derived from Lord Macnaghten's opinion in *Nordenfelt* v *Maxim-Nordenfelt & Co.* [3] He said: " All interference with individual liberty of action in trading, and all restraints of trade of themselves, if there is nothing more, are contrary to public policy and therefore void. That is the general rule. But there are exceptions: restraints of trade and interference with individual liberty of action may be justified by the special circumstances of a particular case. It is a sufficient justification, and indeed it is the only justification, if the restriction is reasonable—reasonable, that is, with reference to the interests of the parties concerned, and reasonable with reference to the interests of the public, so framed and so guarded as to afford adequate protection to the party in whose favour it is imposed, while at the same time it is in no way injurious to the public.'' This is the test, and even so a restraint unlimited in time [4] or space [5] may be reasonable,

[2] *Mallan* v *May* (1843), 11 M & W 653
[3] [1894] A C 535, 565
[4] *Fitch* v *Dewes*, [1921] 2 A C. 158
[5] *Nordenfelt* v. *Maxim-Nordenfelt, supra.*

though the absence of a limit will be an element in determining the reasonableness of the restraint.[6] The question of reasonableness is one of law, but evidence of surrounding circumstances, such as the character and requirements of the business, may be given,[7] and consequently these considerations differ in different kinds of contracts. In *McEllistrim* v. *Ballymacelligott Co-operative Agricultural and Dairy Society*[8] there was an agreement to be bound by a rule of the society forbidding a member from selling milk to any creamery other than a creamery of the society or to any body or person who sold milk or manufactured butter for sale: the rule was held illegal as being in restraint of trade and as imposing a greater restraint on a member than was reasonably required for the protection of the society. Lord Atkinson (at p. 583) said: "The fact that a restraint of trade is imposed for an indefinite time does not necessarily render it unreasonable and void, since this might in the particular circumstances of a given case be involved in the question whether the restraint afforded no more than reasonable protection to the person in whose favour it was imposed."

It is impossible within the limits of this work to set out at length the various cases decided on either side of the line of reasonableness and fair protection both to the employer, the employed and the public. A very complete table is given in the late Sir Frederick Pollock's work,[9] pp. 404—408.

It is possible sometimes to sever a covenant of this sort. For instance, if the covenant were not to carry on business as a butcher after leaving the employment within ten miles of Croydon, Aberdeen and New York, the employer's business being only in Croydon.[10] The question is whether the

---

[6] *Vancouver Malt Co* v *Vancouver Breweries*, [1934] A C 181, 191
[7] *N. W Salt Co* v *Electrolytic Alkali Co*, [1914] A. C 461, 471, *Mason* v. *Provident Clothing Co.*, [1913] A. C. 724, 732   [8] [1919] A. C 548.
[9] Contracts (10th ed).
[10] Cf *Goldsoll* v *Goldman*, [1915] 1 Ch 292, *Putsman* v *Taylor*, [1927] 1 K. B. 637 See, however, the views of Moulton, L.J., in *Mason* v *Provident Clothing Co*, *supra*, at p 745, and of Younger, L J., in *Attwood* v *Lamont*, [1920] 3 K B 571, 593.

covenant is one covenant or several distinct ones. If the latter, the unreasonable covenant or covenants may be excised.

There is a different view taken when the covenant is not between master and servant or employee but between the vendor and purchaser of a business. Rather more freedom is permitted here, as the parties stand on an equal footing for bargaining.[11] One is not in a position to dictate to the other and to require him to limit his freedom of action with regard to the disposal of his skill or labour. A vendor of a business has presumably got what he demanded and is in a position to be restrained from competing with that which he has sold and been paid for. Again, the leading authority for this is the *Maxim-Nordenfelt Case* and Lord Watson's opinion[12] therein. After observing that it is to the public interest to allow a man who has built up a lucrative business to dispose of it to a successor to allow it to be efficiently carried on, his Lordship said: "That object would not be accomplished if, upon the score of public policy, the law reserved to the seller an absolute and indefeasible right to start a rival concern the day after he sold. Accordingly it has been determined judicially, that in cases where the purchaser, for his own protection, obtains an obligation restraining the seller from competing with him, within bounds which having regard to the nature of the business are reasonable and are limited in respect of space, the obligation is not obnoxious to public policy and is therefore capable of being enforced." In that case a covenant by the vendor not to manufacture guns and ammunition for twenty-five years was held not too wide. Where, however, the business sold was in London and consisted in dealing in imitation jewellery, a covenant covering both real and imitation jewellery not only in London but in some European countries also was too wide, though it was severable.[13]

---

[11] *English Hop Growers v Dering*, [1928] 2 K. B. 174
[12] At p 552
[13] *Goldsoll v Goldman, supra*

Penalty or liquidated damages.[1]—"The essence of a penalty is a payment of money stipulated as *in terrorem* of the offending party: the essence of liquidated damages is a genuine pre-estimate of damage."[2]   The practical difference between the two is that in an agreement to pay money which the Court holds to be merely a penalty, the agreement is not binding in that respect and the defendant will pay only the proper damages as estimated by a jury; whereas in a case where the parties have estimated the damage before breach or other cause of action, that will be the amount of damages payable by the party found to be liable.   For instance, if the breach is non-payment of a certain sum of money, a contract to pay a larger sum is *prima facie* penal, for it exceeds the real damage.[3]   On the other hand, where retailers had agreed not to sell tyres except at certain prices or under certain conditions and to pay £5 by way of liquidated damages for each tyre so sold by them, the House of Lords held that the £5 was a genuine pre-estimate of damage; the fact that proof of actual damage in a case of that kind would be difficult was an element in the presumption that the parties had made a genuine attempt to estimate it beforehand.[4] Where the sum named is found to be a penalty, it is ignored and the plaintiff is not debarred from recovering a larger sum than the amount of the penalty.[5]   If a single lump sum is made payable by way of compensation on the occurrence of one or more or all of several events some of which may occasion serious and others trifling damage, the presumption is a

---

[1] Cf Chitty, Contract (19th ed), pp. 255—259; Dix, Competitive Trading, pp 144—152

[2] Lord Dunedin in *Dunlop Pneumatic Tyre Co* v *New Garage and Motor Co*, [1915] A C. 79, where he lays down certain propositions of law derived from the cases (at pp. 86, 87)

[3] *Kemble* v *Farren* (1829), 6 Bing 141.

[4] *Dunlop Pneumatic Tyre Co* v *New Garage and Motor Co*, *supra*; *English Hop Growers* v *Dering*, [1928] 2 K. B. 174, *Imperial Tobacco Co.* v. *Parslay* (1936), 52 T L. R 585.

[5] *Wall* v *Rederiaktiebolaget Luggude*, [1915] 3 K. B 66; *Watts, Watts & Co* v *Mitsui & Co*, [1917] A C. 227.

penalty.[6] But where the sum is payable on a single event only, *e.g.*, non-completion of works by a fixed date, it will be regarded as liquidated damages [7]

XV.—MARRIAGE. CHILDREN. ISSUE

" *Married.*"—In a deed or will means lawfully married. Many of the cases turn upon marriages with a man's deceased wife's sister, not legal till the passing of the Deceased Wife's Sister's Marriage Act of 1907, or with a deceased brother's widow, made legal by the Deceased Brother's Widow's Marriage Act, 1921 A condition in absolute restraint of marriage is void as against public policy, but a condition subsequent in partial restraint is apparently valid and enforceable if accompanied by a gift over.[1] A testator often leaves an income to his widow subject to ademption or reduction if she marries again; or a man may provide by settlement for his daughter and her children, subject to forfeiture on her marriage at any time without the consent of certain named persons.

" *Unmarried* ".—This word is capable of two constructions. In its primary sense it means " without ever having been married ". " Unmarried and without issue " was held to be construed in its ordinary meaning of " without wife and without issue him surviving ".[2] In its secondary sense it means " without leaving a widow (or widower) ". So when the context was " unmarried and without lawful issue " it clearly pointed to an intention to use the expression in its

[6] *Elphinstone (Lord)* v. *Monkland Iron Co* (1886), 11 App Cas 332, at p 342, *Dunlop Pneumatic Tyre Co* v *New Garage and Motor Co.*, *supra.*
[7] *Law* v. *Redditch Local Board*, [1892] 1 Q. B 127, *Cellulose Acetate Silk Co.* v. *Widnes Foundry, Ltd* , [1933] A C 20
[1] *Re Whiting's Settlement*, [1918] 1 Ch 458 See Pollock, Contract (10th ed), pp. 390, 391
[2] *Re Reilly*, [1935] Ir R 352

secondary sense.[3] At one time some confusion was caused by what was called the rule in *Wilson* v. *Atkinson*.[4] In that case a widow re-married after having an illegitimate daughter and in a settlement of her property provided that the latter was to be held as if she had died intestate and " without having been married " ; it being declared that the illegitimate daughter should be treated for the purposes of the trust as if she were legitimate. The question was whether the words " without having been married " were intended to exclude children or not. The Court held that the fact that the illegitimate daughter was to be treated as legitimate clearly showed that legitimate children were to take, and that the addition relating to the illegitimate daughter was useless unless this was the assumption. In 1880 Jessel, M R., declared that no general rule was to be extracted from this decision.[5] Swinfen Eady, J , was also of the same opinion in *Re Smith's Settlement* [6] and held that the context in default of children and, in the event of the wife predeceasing the husband, for her statutory next-of-kin as if she had died intestate and " without ever having been married " *prima facie* excluded children, following *Clarke* v. *Colls* [7] where Lord Cranworth said " the words ' without ever having been married ' would exclude issue, which they obviously do in their ordinary meaning " So now " without having been married " means " never having been married " unless there is something in the context (as in *Wilson* v: *Atkinson*) or the circumstances which will justify the Court in departing from the plain and ordinary meaning of the words used.[8] So where a settlor settled property in trust for such person or persons as under the statutes for the distribution of the effects of intestates

---

3 *Re Jones, Last* v. *Dobson*, [1915] 1 Ch 246, 253
4 (1864), 4 D J & S 455
5 In *Emmins* v. *Bradford* (1880), 13 Ch D 493.
6 [1903] 1 Ch 373, 378
7 (1861), 9 H. L C 601, 612.
8 See *per* Vaughan Williams, L J , in *Re Brydone's Settlement*, [1903] 2 Ch. 84, at p. 92.

would have become entitled thereto at her death "had she died possessed thereof and intestate and without having been married", the Court of Appeal held that there was nothing to show that these last words had anything but their natural meaning, which excluded the issue of the wife. Younger, L.J., who dissented, thought the words ought to be confined to the contemplated marriage "as aforesaid" or "as now proposed".[9]

"*Children*".—In its primary meaning means descendants of the first degree, *i.e.*, not grandchildren. So in a marriage settlement, in default of children of the marriage, property was settled "for all and every the child or children of J. G." living at the decease of the survivor of the husband and wife. It was held that as there were children of J. G. living at the prescribed date, no grandchild of J. G. took any share; grandchildren being only a substitutional class to take only in the event of no child being alive at the date of distribution of the estate.[10]

A limitation to children will include a child *en ventre sa mère*. As to children *en ventre sa mère*, Lord Russell, in *Elliot* v. *Joicey*,[11] laid down certain rules as to the ability of persons to take who were "born" before or "living at" or "surviving" a particular point of time, and pointed out that in their ordinary meaning these words do not include children *en ventre sa mère*. The question in that case was whether a posthumous child can be said to be "issue him surviving" The learned Lord adopted the decision in *Villar* v. *Gilbey*[12] that there is no fixed rule that a child was born in the lifetime of the testator because it was *en ventre sa mère* at the time. This rule is limited to cases where that construction of "born" is necessary for the benefit of the unborn child.[13]

[9] *Re Ellis' Settlement*, [1920] 2 Ch 432, [1921] 1 Ch 230
[10] *Re Coley*, [1901] 1 Ch 40   [11] [1935] A. C 209.
[12] [1907] A. C. 139.
[13] See *Blasson* v *Blasson* (1884), 2 D. J & S. 665

"Born" includes "to be born" and *vice versa* unless there are special words in the context to indicate a contrary intention. So a remainder to the settlor's brother for life, with remainder to "the heirs male of his body *hereafter* to be begotten", did not prevent the brother from taking an estate tail, as the words did not confine it to the issue born after but would also include that already born.[14]

"Children" *prima facie* means legitimate children, but illegitimate children will take if properly described either expressly or impliedly by the context. In *Gabb* v. *Prendergast*[15] there was a settlement with limitations to all the children as well those already born as hereafter to be born to A and B These persons were married at the date of the deed, they never had any legitimate children but before marriage B had had children of whom A was the reputed father. It was held that the context showed that these children were intended to take. An illegitimate child, however, unborn at the date of the deed can never take. And a person born illegitimate but subsequently become legitimated cannot take under the will of a testator dying before the date of legitimation, if, apart from the legitimation, he would not have been entitled to take[16] (Legitimacy Act, 1926, s. 3 (1) and s. 20 (2).) As North, J., said[17]. "It is conceded that, according to law, the rest [illegitimate children] can take nothing, for the provision was made for illegitimate children, and they were not then even begotten." In *Ebbern* v. *Fowler*[17] there was a settlement in trust for E and after her death in trust for the children of E who attained twenty-one years of age or being daughters married under that age. A year before the settlement E married J K, who was her deceased sister's husband, and at that time within the prohibited degrees. At the date of the settlement E was *enciente*

---

[14] *Hebblethwaite* v *Cartwright* (1734), Cas. t Talb 31.

[15] (1855), 1 K. & J. 439.

[16] *Re Hepworth*, [1936] Ch. 750.

[17] In *Re Shaw*, [1894] 2 Ch. 573, overruled (not on this point) by C A. in *Ebbern* v *Fowler*, [1909] 1 Ch 578

and a child, who subsequently attained twenty-one years of age, was born a month after the settlement. E died without ever having been lawfully married   The Court of Appeal (overruling *Re Shaw*) held that the intention was to treat the children of E whether by J K or not as entitled to benefit, and, if so, the child begotten before but born after the settlement was entitled to take as being *in esse*. As an instance to the contrary, *Re Pearce* [18] may be cited. That was a case of a will which bequeathed property " to all or any of the children or child of F ". F had six illegitimate and two legitimate children. F and K were always received and regarded as husband and wife and the six illegitimate children (by K) as legitimate. The testatrix was proved to have believed the six children to be legitimate, but nevertheless the Court of Appeal held that only the two legitimate children were entitled to take under the will. The Court followed *Hill* v. *Crook* [19] and held that the fact that the testatrix was informed and believed that the six children were legitimate did not make any difference or constitute a further exception to those laid down by Lord Cairns,[20] where, after pointing out that a will might provide a dictionary for the meanings to be attributed to the expressions used and that this was the *prima facie* method of interpretation, said: " There are two classes of cases in which that *prima facie* interpretation is departed from. One class of case is where it is impossible from the circumstances of the parties that any legitimate children could take under the bequest.[21] The other class is of this kind, where there is upon the face of the will itself and upon a just and proper construction and interpretation of the words used in it, an expression of the intention of the testator to use the term ' children ' not merely according to its *prima facie* meaning of legitimate children, but according

---

[18] [1914] 1 Ch 254. Cf *Re Taylor*, [1925] 1 Ch. 739
[19] (1873), L. R 6 H L. 265
[20] *S C.*, p. 282
[21] *E g*, to the children of Jane, who had died a spinster.

to a meaning which will apply to and which will include, illegitimate children "

"*Issue*".—*Prima facie* means descendants and has thus a wider meaning than children. It is, however, frequently used to denote the latter. This being a special and restrictive interpretation, the onus of proving that "issue" means children lies on those who assert it.

"It is clearly settled that the word 'issue' unconfined by any indication of intention, includes all descendants. Intention is required for the purpose of limiting the sense of that word, restraining it to children only." [22] In that case there was a settlement on marriage of personal property, and after certain limitations it was to be "for his issue". The settlor had no children by the marriage, but he had children and grandchildren by a former marriage. It was held that the children and grandchildren living at his death were equally entitled *per capita* Where a marriage settlement is expressed to provide for "the issue of the intended marriage" or for "the issue of the marriage", the word "issue", is construed in its restricted meaning of "children".[23]

In *Re Birks* [24] twelve legacies contained gifts over to the issue of the legatees dying in the testator's lifetime. Except in one legacy, the gifts contained words which limited the meaning of issue to children. The exception contained no such restriction, but it was held that the restrictive meaning must apply to this legacy also. It was said by Lindley, M.R.[25]: "I do not know whether it is law or a canon of construction, but it is good sense to say that whenever in a deed or will or other document you find that a word used in one part of it has some clear and definite meaning, then the presumption is that it is intended to mean the same thing where, when

[22] *Per* Grant, M R , in *Leigh* v *Norbury* (1807), 13 Ves 340, at p 344.
[23] *Re Denis' Trusts* (1875), Ir. R. 10 Eq. 81, *Re Meade's Trusts* (1881), 7 L. R. Ir. 51
[24] [1900] 1 Ch 417
[25] *S. C* , p 418

used in another part of the document, its meaning is not clear." [26]

In *Re Swain* [27] a fractional share was left to each daughter of the testator. In the event of the death of either daughter leaving issue, "such issue shall take their mother's share" in the distribution. If either daughter died in the wife's lifetime without issue, the share of the deceased should be equally divided among the surviving children and issue of the deceased child, etc. A daughter died in 1914 having had two children; one of these children died in 1911 having two children. The testator's widow died in 1916. What was the meaning of "issue", used four times in the will? The first two words "issue" refer to the same persons and are contained in the gift which is substitutionary of the mother, then we have the death of either daughter "without issue" and the gift over in that event and finally the collocation of "children and issue" which is plain enough. The question really came down to the meaning of "issue" in the substitutionary gift, as the Court held that the word in the gift over had its primary meaning of descendants In the substitutionary gift the Court thought that standing alone it might have meant "children", but the meaning was ambiguous; it must, therefore, be construed in the light of the unambiguous meaning of "issue" in the gift over and therefore meant descendants, so that all issue of whatever degree who survived any daughter who died in the wife's lifetime took equally the share that daughter would have taken if she had survived the tenant for life (*i.e*, the widow of the testator).

The reference to a "parent" of "issue" may show that "issue" is intended to be used in the restricted sense, as was

[26] As to this, cf Lord Warrington in *Watson* v *Haggitt*, [1928] A. C 127, at p 130 (P C). "The truth is there is no rule of such general application as is contended for by the appellant. A difficulty or ambiguity may be solved by resorting to such a device but it is only in such cases that it is necessary or permissible to do so"

[27] [1918] 1 Ch 399 (compromised on appeal), 574 Cf *Ralph* v *Carrick* (1879), 11 Ch D 873, at p 888

said in *Re Swain*, cited above   Where the collocation was
" such issue shall take their mother's share ", standing alone,
it would have meant " children ".[29]   So in a deed of trust
" such issue should take such share as their parent would have
been entitled to ", excluded a grandchild of a child of the
marriage.[29]   And in a trust for children or such of them as
should be living at a certain time " and the issue of such of
them as might be then dead leaving issue, to be equally
divided among them share and share alike, but so as the issue
of any deceased child should take between them no more than
the parent would have taken if then living ", it was held
that " issue " meant children.[30]

---

[28] Cf *per* Shadwell, V.-C., in *Pruen* v *Osborne* (1840), 11 Sim. 132,
at p. 138.
[29] *Harrington* v. *Lawrence* (1814), cited *Pruen* v *Osborne* (1840), 11
Sim. 132, at p. 138
[30] *Anderson* v *St Vincent* (1856), 4 W. R. 304.

PART II

STATUTES

I.—The Nature of a Statute

A statute is the will of the Legislature, and we now proceed
to state some rules which guide the Courts in their construction of statutes "The expression ' construction ', as applied
to a document, at all events as used by English lawyers,
includes two things: first, the meaning of the words; and,
secondly, their legal effect, or the effect which is' to be given
to them. "The meaning of words I take to be a question of
fact in all cases, whether we are dealing with a poem or legal
document The effect of the words is a question of law." [1]
It may appear surprising that matters drafted so carefully
and with so much deliberation and consideration by experts
should need these rules. It might be considered that whereas
a layman in his written contracts, his deeds or his will may
be expected to express himself in loose or non-legal language
and consequently to expose these instruments to frequent
examination by the Courts, in the case of expert legal
draftsmen, whose work generally undergoes minute criticism
in Parliament before the Bill becomes law, this would not
happen, and that a statute would always state clearly and
beyond possibility of doubt exactly what it meant This is
unfortunately not the experience of lawyers or the Courts,
constantly engaged as they are in trying to unravel the
meaning and inconsistencies of our statute law; nor is the

---

[1] *Per* Lindley, L J , in *Chatenay* v. *Brazilian Submarine Telegraph Co* ,
[1891] 1 Q B 79, at p 85

experience of those who have had to deal with, *e.g.*, the Indian Codes, in any way different

II.—GENERAL RULES OF CONSTRUCTION

I. Same rule as in document.—It has been said that no further rules of construction should be placed upon statutes than upon any other legal document, and Bowen, L J.,[2] said: " The rules for the construction of statutes are very like those which apply to the construction of other documents, especially with regard to one crucial rule—*viz.*, that, if possible, the words of an Act of Parliament must be construed so as to give a sensible meaning to them. The words ought to be construed *ut res magis valeat quam pereat."* " It is said that the Court draws no distinction between statutes and other written documents. I am not prepared to say that this is true to the full extent."[3]

II. Statute read as a whole.—Next, the statute must be read as a whole and construction made of all the parts together. As Lord Halsbury said in *Leader* v. *Duffey*[4]: " All these refinements and nice distinctions of words appear to me to be inconsistent with the modern view, which is I think in accordance with reason and common sense, that, whatever the instrument, it must receive a construction according to the plain meaning of the words and sentences therein contained. But I agree that you must look at the whole instrument inasmuch as there may be inaccuracy and inconsistency; you must, if you can, ascertain what is the meaning of the instrument taken as a whole in order to give effect, if it be possible to do so, to the intention of the framer of it But it appears to me to be arguing in a vicious circle

---

[2] *Curtis* v *Stovin* (1889), 22 Q B D 512, at p 517

[3] *Per* Cozens-Hardy, M.R., in *Camden (Marquis)* v *I. R. C*, [1914] 1 K B 641, at p 648

[4] (1888), 13 App. Cas 294, at p 301 Cf *per* Lord Davey in *North Eastern Ry* v. *Hastings*, [1900] A. C. 260, at p 269, *Att -Gen* v. *Milne*, [1914] A C 765.

to begin by assuming an intention apart from the language
of the instrument itself and having made that fallacious
assumption to bend the language in favour of the presumption
so made." In *Canada Sugar Refining Co.* v. *R.*[5] Lord Davey
said: " Every clause of a statute should be construed with
reference to the context and other clauses of the Act, so as,
as far as possible, to make a consistent enactment of the whole
statute or series of statutes relating to the subject-matter."
So in the Employers' Liability Act, 1880, one section pre-
scribes that notice shall be " given ", which might be satisfied
by a verbal notice, whereas another section provides that the
notice shall be " served " on or " left " with another, thus
plainly implying that the notice is to be in writing Also
in the Workmen's Compensation Act, 1906, s. 2, the notice
of accident to be " given " is construed by the context as
meaning a notice in writing [6] This is the rule of construction
from context to which we shall return later. Next, the words
of a statute are to be interpreted as bearing their natural
meaning [7] Lord Macnaghten asked in *Mersey Docks and
Harbour Board* v. *Turner* [8]: " Why should we reject the plain
and ordinary meaning of words which we find in the statute? ",
And Scott, L.J., recently [9] said: " Where the words of an Act
of Parliament are clear, there is no room for applying any of
the principles of interpretation which are merely presumptions
in cases of ambiguity in the statute." So where the question
was whether a letting was within the Increase of Rent Act,
1920, and the contention that it was would, it was pointed
out, involve making the word " let " include the word " sub-
let ", Lord Warrington said [10]: " In my opinion the safer
and more correct course of dealing with a question of construction is to take the words themselves and arrive if possible

---

[5] [1898] A C 735, at p 741
[6] *Hughes* v. *Coed Talon Colliery Co* (1909), 78 L J K B 539
[7] *Att.-Gen* v *Milne*, [1914] A. C. 765.
[8] [1893] A. C. 468, at p. 477
[9] *Croxford* v. *Universal Insurance Co*, [1936] 2 K B 253, at p 281
[10] *Barrell* v. *Fordree*, [1932] A. C. 676, at p 682

at their meaning, without in the first instance reference to cases."

So in *Tuff* v. *Guild of Drapers* [11] Kennedy, L J , said: "I base my judgment on the simple ground . . that when an Act of Parliament says in terms as the Act of 1891 [Tithe Act, 1891] does here . . one ought to read it in its natural meaning without the insertion of the terms which it seems to me it is necessary to insert in order to support the appellant's intention . . . Speaking for myself, I think that one of the great dangers that may arise from such a course is that you are really framing what you think that Parliament ought to have said."

III. Intention of the Legislature predominates.—Further, the statute should be construed in a manner to carry out the intention of the Legislature. As Lord Blackburn said in *Edinburgh Street Tramways* v *Torbain* (1877), 3 App. Cas. 58, at p 68: "I quite agree that in construing an Act of Parliament we are to see what is the intention which the Legislature has expressed by the words, but then the words again are to be understood by looking at the subject-matter they are speaking of and the object of the Legislature, and the words used with reference to that may convey an intention quite different from what the self-same set of words used in reference to another set of circumstances and another object would or might have produced." Where the words are unambiguous this intention is best declared by the words themselves In order to make the words square with the intention, it has sometimes been found necessary to modify the actual expressions used "Courts of law have cut down or even contradicted the language of the Legislature when, on a full view of the Act—considering its scheme, its machinery and the manifest purpose of it—they have thought that a particular case or class of cases was not intended to fall within the taxing clause relied on by the Crown. A notable example

[11] [1913] 1 K B 40, at p 53 Cf *David* v *De Silva*, [1934] A C. 106.

is the case of *Colquhoun* v. *Brooks*,[12] decided nearly thirty years ago and always followed." [13]   In *Curtis* v. *Stovin* (*supra*), section 65 of the County Courts Act, 1888, gave power to the parties to apply for an order " that an action not exceeding £100 be tried in any Court in which the action might have been commenced ". The Court held that an addition was necessary to this clause, *viz* : " if the amount claimed had been such that it could have been commenced in a county court ". The Legislature had misdescribed the Court to which the transfer was to be made. A remarkable example is as follows. Under the Judgments Act, 1838, an insolvent imprisoned for debt might be liberated either on his own petition or on that of any of his creditors. The Bankruptcy Act, 1847, transferred the jurisdiction of the Insolvency Commissioners to the county courts, and provided that " if an insolvent petitions " certain procedure was to be followed, but omitted all reference to the case where the petitioner was a creditor   The Court held that the latter was intended to be included, and, in order to avoid injustice, the words " if an insolvent petitions " were held to be an example of the general intention expressed by such a phrase as " if a petition be presented ".[14] In a very recent case, the question was whether under the Dentists Act, 1921, the General Medical Council could delegate its disciplinary powers to an executive council· Luxmoore, J , held that the sub-section permitting the Council to delegate its functions applied only in respect of matters in which the General Medical Council was not required to act itself, and said [15] : " Having regard to the

---

[12] (1889), 14 App. Cas 493
[13] *Per* Lord Loreburn, L C , in *Drummond* v. *Collins*, [1915] A C 1011, at p 1017. Cf *per* Lord Shaw in *Shannon Realties* v *Ville de St Michael* [1924] A C 185, 192, and *per* Scott, L.J , in *Barber* v. *Pigden*, [1937] 1 K B 664, at p 677, who held that the intention of the Law Reform Act, 1935, was to sweep away an " old fiction of the common law "
[14] *R* v. *Dowling* (1857), 8 E. & B 605   Cf. *The Derfflinger and other ships*, [1919] P. 264
[15] *General Medical Council* v *United Kingdom Dental Board*, [1936] 1 Ch. 41, 48.

object with which the Act of 1921 was passed and to .the position before its passing, I think sub-section 4 of section 16 ought not to be construed in the widest sense of the words used in it, but as conferring power on the General Council to act by an executive committee only in respect of those matters in which the General Council is not required to act itself " In another recent case [16] in the Court of Appeal, Romer, L J., held that the literal construction of the words " lump sum " in section 8 (3) (iii) of the Workmen's Compensation Act, 1925, must be rejected and the words read as meaning the lump sum which would have been payable if there had been no redemption of the weekly payments.

It may reasonably be asked—How is the intention of the Legislature to be discovered? "Intention of the Legislature" has been described by a high authority as "a common but very slippery phrase" [17] which, popularly understood, may signify anything from intention embodied in the positive enactment to speculative opinion as to what the Legislature probably would have meant, although there has been an omission to enact it; and of course care must be taken to avoid the "vicious circle" described by Lord Halsbury in *Leader* v. *Duffey*.[18] The intention of the Legislature must not be assumed or surmised. As Lord Haldane said in *Lumsden* v. *I. R. C.* [19]: "But a mere conjecture that Parliament entertained a purpose which, however natural, has not been embodied in the words it has used, if they be literally interpreted, is no sufficient reason for departing from the literal construction." "In a Court of law or equity, what the Legislature intended to be done or not to be done can only be legitimately ascertained from what it has chosen to enact either in express words or by reasonable and necessary implication." [20]

---

[16] *Swan* v. *Pure Ice Co*, [1935] 2 K. B 265.
[17] *Per* Lord Watson in *Salomon* v. *Salomon*, [1897] A C. 22, at p. 38.
[18] *Supra*, p 162
[19] [1914] A C 877, at p 892, and *per* Lord Parmoor, at p. 924.
[20] *Per* Lord Watson in *Salomon* v *Salomon* (*supra*)

IV. Policy and object of statute.—Next, if possible the construction adopted should be in accordance with the policy and object of the statute in question. This is possibly only another way of stating the rule just mentioned and must be confined to cases where the policy and object of the Legislature are clear from the statute itself. The danger of these rules concerning " intention ", " object ", " policy " and so on, is that they may open the door to individual bias or opinion or result in guessing at the intention.[21] As to general words in a statute which have no very definite meaning, " we must look at the object to be attained ", *per* Lindley, M.R., in *Nutton* v. *Wilson* (1889), 22 Q. B. D. 744; and Lord Halsbury in *Fox* v. *Oakes* (1890), 15 App. Cas. 506: " It is impossible to contend that the mere fact of a general word being used in a statute precludes all enquiry into the object of the statute or the mischief which it was intended to, remedy."

In *Watney, Combe* v. *Berners*[22] Lord Haldane said: " No doubt general words may in certain cases be properly interpreted as having a meaning and scope other than the literal or usual meaning They may be so interpreted where the scheme appearing from the language of the Legislature read in its entirety points to consistency as requiring the modification of what would be the meaning apart from any context, or apart from the purpose of the legislation as appearing from the words which the Legislature has used or apart from the general law." The statute 34 Edw. 3, c. 1, conferred on justices jurisdiction to make orders binding to be of good behaviour " pillors and robbers ". Held, that all persons who were disturbers of the peace were included.[23]

As a corollary to this rule, the Courts have sometimes extended the meaning of words. For instance, they have held bicycles to be " carriages " within the provisions of the Highway Act, 1835, with respect to " furious driving ",

---

[21] *Per* Lord Haldane in *Lumsden* v *I. R. C. (supra),* at p 892.
[22] [1915] A. C. 885, at p. 891
[23] *Lansbury* v *Riley,* [1913] 29 T. L R. 733

though not so held with regard to taxation,[24] and tricycles propelled by steam were held to be locomotives within the Locomotives Act, 1865, though not invented when that Act was passed.[25] Similarly a private Act of 1790 provided that certain proprietors were not to be rated for a ferry either for parliamentary or parochial rates. This exemption was held to include income tax, though it was not imposed till after 1790.[26] On the other hand, tableaux vivants or "living pictures" were held not to be an infringement under the Fine Arts Copyright Act, 1862, of paintings. "Copying and reproducing by any means" in the Act have for their object the protection of painters from depreciation of their works by means of something of a character similar to that of which they were the authors. Section 6, providing for the forfeiture of copies, could not possibly apply to living pictures, and "reproduction" means something in which if the original author of the painting had himself produced it, he might have had the copyright.[27] But in *Simpson* v *Teignmouth Bridge Co.*,[28] where a local Act authorised the levy of a toll on a "coach, chariot, hearse, chaise, berlin, landau and phaeton, gig, whisky, car, chair or coburg and every other carriage hung on springs", a bicycle was held to be not within the Act. But Edison's telephone was held to be a "telegraph" within the Telegraph Acts, 1863, 1868 and 1869, and a conversation through the telephone is a "message" or at all events a "communication" received by a telegraph and therefore a "telegram" within these Acts.[29]

In construing a private Act however (the Plymouth Corporation Act, 1898), the Court of Appeal refused to give

24 *Williams* v *Ellis* (1880), 49 L J M C 47 Cf *Dock Co at Kingston-upon-Hull* v. *Browne* (1831), 2 B & Ad 43, 58, where "port" was construed in an extended, popular sense
25 *Taylor* v *Goodwin* (1879), 4 Q B D. 228.
26 *Pole-Carew* v *Craddock*, [1920] 3 K. B. 109, *Gissing* v *Liverpool Corporation*, [1935] Ch. 1.
27 *Hanfstaengl* v. *Empire Palace*, [1894] 1 Ch 1, at p 8, *per* Kay, L J
28 (1903), 72 L J K B 204
29 *Att.-Gen* v. *Edison Telephone Co* (1881), 6 Q B D. 244

a general meaning to a section of the Act so as to extend the powers of the corporation to selling their ancient corporate lands without the leave of the Local Government Board.[30]

Two recent cases may be cited in this connection. Both concern provisions of Finance Acts, where duty was payable on certain imported goods. In the first, the Finance Act, 1928, s. 9 (1) imposed an import duty on imported " buttons finished or unfinished " Button blanks nearly spherical in shape made of trocas shell and pierced with one hole were imported The Court held that in construing the meaning of " unfinished ", it should consider the object of the section of the Finance Act, which was to protect the English button trade. In this case the Court held that the bulk of the work on the finished buttons had been done abroad.[31]

The second case is *Powell Lane Manufacturing Co.* v. *Putnam* [32] There the question was whether strawboard of varying thicknesses imported from Holland was " packing or wrapping paper " within section 11 (1) of the Finance Act, 1926. It was argued that, except possibly with regard to the thinnest quality, nobody in 1926 called the Dutch product " packing or wrapping paper "—it being in fact used for making, in England, corrugated paper. It was also urged that in an ambiguous enactment of a taxing Act the presumption should be in favour of the subject. The Court held that section 11 was passed in order to enable " packing or wrapping paper ", by whatever name it was called, to be taxed because it was in competition with the English product, and accordingly, anything which would substantially correspond to what the Legislature meant by " packing or wrapping paper " would come within the tax. So in *Att.-Gen.* v. *Beauchamp* [33] the respondent was held liable to the penalty imposed by section 2 of 2 & 3 Vict. c 4, though he was not the printer and though the words " or published " did not occur

---

[30] *Re Plymouth Corporation and Walter*, [1918] 2 Ch 354
[31] *Newman Manufacturing Co* v *Marrables*, [1931] 2 K B 297.
[32] [1931] 2 K B 305   [33] [1920] 1 K B 650

in the last line of the section before " by him or her ", as this would carry out the obvious intention of the Legislature, *viz* , to make two distinct classes of persons liable, the printers and the publishers. "It is always necessary in construing a statute and in dealing with the words you find in it to consider the object with which the statute was passed: it enables one to understand the meaning of the words introduced into the enactment." [34] So also Brett, M.R., in *Lion Insurance Association* v *Tucker*,[35] said: "Grammatically they [the words of a statute] may cover it [the case in question] but whenever you have to construe a statute or document you do not construe it according to the mere ordinary general meaning of the words, but according to the meaning of the words as applied to the subject-matter with regard to which they are used, unless there is something which obliges you to read them in a sense which is not their ordinary sense in the English language as so applied." A case which went to the House of Lords [36] will further illustrate this point. Under the Poor Law Officers' Superannuation Act, 1896, such officers' pensions were inalienable and the question arose whether the guardians, their officers and servants could contract themselves out of the Act, which contained no express provision on the subject. The House was of opinion that to allow contracting out would be against the purpose and scheme of the Act which it was important to consider. Lord Cave, L.C., said [37] : " I base my decision on the whole scope and purpose of the statute and upon the language of the sections to which I have specifically referred." Lord Sumner, who dissented from the opinion of the majority, said [38] : " Personally, I think it not an unwholesome rule of con-

---

[34] *Per* Channell, J , in *Reigate R. D. C* v *Sutton District Water Co* (1908), 99 L. T. 168, at p. 170. *Cf Gaby* v. *Palmer* (1916), 85 L J. K. B. 1240, 1244, *per* Lord Reading, C J

[35] (1883), 12 Q B D. 176, at p. 186

[36] *Guardians of Salford Union* v *Dewhurst*, [1926] A C. 619.

[37] *S C.*, p 624.

[38] *S C*, p 633

struction (and construction is the whole of our task) to say that just as we are bound by the language of the Legislature, so we must abstain from putting upon the Legislature anything which is not clearly what it has said, for this very good reason, that it is so extremely apt to make judicial ideas as to what is good for the public or within the vague confines of public policy do duty, instead of a literal and unimaginative interpretation of the Legislature's own words." These words of Lord Sumner contain the essence of the danger of judicial interpretation of statutes, especially those bearing on social reform or social services. In the case just cited the majority, acting on their view of the scope and object of the statute, were for prohibiting contracting out, but Lord Sumner, in the absence of a prohibition in the statute, declined to imply it on the ground that public policy demanded it. Sir Samuel Evans, P., uttered much the same warning in *Re H.M.S. Temple and H.M.S. Usk*,[39] when he said: "By every rule of interpretation that can apply to such a matter [Naval Prize Acts], the Court is bound to confine its exposition within the very letter of the statute, if that letter speaks an intelligible language" And Mr Justice Willes, in *Abel* v. *Lee* (1871), L R 6 C. P. 365, at p. 371, said: "But I utterly repudiate the notion that it is competent to a Judge to modify the language of an Act in order to bring it in accordance with his views of what is right or reasonable."

V. Words construed in popular sense.—General statutes will be *prima facie* presumed to use words in their popular sense (see *per* Lord Esher, M R., in *Clerical, etc., Assurance Co* v. *Carter* (1889), 22 Q. B. D. 444, 448). If they are used in connection with some particular business or trade, they will be presumed to be used in a sense appropriate to such business or trade In the case of statutes, unlike deeds, there is no opportunity to call

---

[39] (1917), 86 L J. P. 127

persons conversant with the business or trade referred to
in order to enable the Court to decide on the meaning
of the terms employed [40] Hence the necessity, *inter alia*,
of appending - interpretation clauses to statutes, and of
Interpretation Acts to provide the Courts with a dictionary.
At the same time, it will also be presumed that words
in statutes are used precisely and exactly, not loosely or
inexactly.[41] In illustration: The question was the meaning
of " adjoining " in a New Zealand Act (section 282 of the
Municipal Corporations Act of 1920). The Privy Council [42]
said that the primary meaning of " adjoining " was " con-
terminous ", and in a statute it should be given that meaning
unless the context showed that it was used in a looser sense
as equivalent to " near or neighbouring ". Lord Macmillan [43]
quoted with approval the words of Lord Hewart, C.J., in
Spillers, Ltd. v *Cardiff (Borough) Assessment Committee*,[44]
where the learned Chief Justice said. " It ought to be the
rule and we are glad to think that it is the rule that words
are used in an Act of Parliament correctly and exactly and
not loosely and inexactly Upon those who assert that the
rule has been broken, the burden of establishing their proposition lies heavily. and they can discharge it only by
pointing to something in the context which goes to show that
the loose and inexact meaning must be preferred." So, in
a remarkable case in 1922 turning on the unrepealed section 2
of the Gaming Act, 1835, Lord Birkenhead [45] said: " There
is indeed no reason for limiting the natural and ordinary
meaning of the words used " So in *Unwin* v. *Hanson* [46] the

---

40 Cf *per* Cozens-Hardy, M R , in *Camden (Marquis)* v *I R. C* , [1914]
1 K B 641, at p 647

41 Cf *Law Society* v *United Service Bureau*, [1934] 1 K B 343, and
s 2 of the Interpretation Act

42 *New Plymouth Borough Council* v *Taranaki Electric Power Board*,
[1933] A C 680

43 *S C* , at p 682

44 [1912] 3 K B 533

45 In *Sutters* v *Briggs*, [1922] A. C 1.

46 [1891] 2 Q. B 115.

question was whether the words " pruned or lopped " included
cutting off the tops of trees   The Court of Appeal held that
" lop " in its popular sense meant " cutting off branches
laterally ", and Lord Esher, M.R , said [47] : " If the Act is
directed to dealing with matters affecting everybody generally,
the words used have the meaning attached to them in the
common and ordinary use of language   If the Act is one
passed with reference to a particular trade, business or transaction and words are used which everybody conversant with
that trade, business or transaction knows and understands
to have a particular meaning in it, then the words are to
be construed as having that particular meaning though it
may differ from the common or ordinary meaning of the
words "   So " children " may include illegitimate children [48];
" gas ",[49] " spirits ",[50] " Bohea tea ",[51] " five miles square ",[52]
" gin ",[53] " grain ",[54] have been construed in the popular
or commercial sense of those words

In *Caledonian Ry* v *North British Ry* [55] Lord Selborne,
L C , said : " There is always some presumption in favour of
the more simple and literal interpretation of the words of a
statute . . .   The more literal construction ought not to
prevail if (as the Courts below have thought) it is opposed
to the intentions of the Legislature as apparent by the statute,
and if the words are sufficiently flexible to admit of some
other construction by which that intention will be better
effectuated "   And in a more recent case [56] the Privy Council
said : " Where the words of a statute are clear, they must,
of course, be followed, but in their Lordships' opinion where

[47] *S C.*, at p 119
[48] *R* v *Hodnett* (1786), 1 T R 96   *Supra*, p 156
[49] *Stanley* v *Western Insurance Co* (1868), L R 3 Ex 71
[50] *Att .Gen* v *Bailey* (1847), 17 L J Ex 9
[51] *Two Hundred Chests of Tea* (1824), 9 Wheat 430
[52] *Robertson* v *Day* (1881), 5 App Cas 63, 69
[53] *Webb* v *Knight* (1877), 2 Q B D 530.
[54] *Cotton* v *Vogan*, [1896] A C 457.
[55] (1881), 6 App Cas 114, 121, 122
[56] *Shannon Realties* v *St Michael* (*Ville de*), [1924] A C 185.

alternative constructions are equally open, that alternative is
to be chosen which will be consistent with the smooth working
of the system which the statute purports to be regulating and
that alternative to be rejected which will introduce uncertainty, friction or confusion into the working of the system."

*VI. Words are taken to be used in the sense they bore at
the time the statute was passed.*[57]

So Lord Esher[58] said: "The first point to be borne in
mind is that the Act [6 & 7 Will. 4, a private Act] must be
construed as if one were interpreting it the day after it was
passed. . . . The word 'action' mentioned in the section
was not applicable when the Act was passed to the procedure
of the Admiralty Court Admiralty actions were then called
'suits' or 'causes'; moreover, the Admiralty Court was not
called and was not one of His Majesty's Courts of Law."

VII. Same words bear the same meaning.—It is said to
be a rule of construction that it is presumed that the same
words are used in the same meaning in the same statute
and that consequently a change of language is some indication of a change of intention on the part of the Legislature.
The presumption is, however, of the slightest. Cleasby, B,
said in 1869[59]: "It is a sound rule of construction to
give the same meaning to the same words occurring in
different parts of an Act of Parliament." "Where the
Legislature has used the same words in a similar connection
in two statutes it may be presumed in the absence of any
context indicating a contrary intention that the same meaning
attaches to the words in the latter as in the former statute."[60]
But there are very many instances where the application of
this rule is impossible or would result in injustice or absurdity

[57] *R* v. *Casement*, [1917] 1 K B. 98, 139.
[58] In *The Longford* (1889), 14 P D. 34, quoted by Collins, M R, in
The Burns, [1907] P 137
[59] In *Courtauld* v. *Legh* (1869), L R. 4 Ex 126, 130
[60] *Lennon* v. *Gibson & Howes, Ltd*, [1919] A. C. 709, *per* Lord Shaw.

In the Real Property Limitation Act of 1833 the word "rent" was used in two different senses throughout· (i) as rent charged on land, and (ii) as rent reserved under a lease [61] So the Offences against the Person Act, 1861, s. 57, which deals with bigamy, enacts : " Whosoever, being married, shall marry any other person during the life of the former husband or wife . . shall be guilty of felony ", the word " marry " is obviously used in two different senses.[62] The same words may often receive a different interpretation in different parts of the same Act for " words used with reference to one set of circumstances may convey an intention quite different from what the self-same set of words used with reference to another set of circumstances would or might have produced." [63] There are also many instances of a change of language without an intention to change the meaning in the same statute.   In *R.* v. *Buttle,*[64] Blackburn, J., said . " When the Legislature changes the words of an enactment, no doubt it must be taken *prima facie* that there was an intention to change the meaning."   But the same learned Judge four years [65] previously observed that the Legislature " to improve the graces of the style and to avoid using the same words over and over again " employs different words without any intention to change the meaning   So the difference in language between the Bankruptcy Act of 1849 and that of 1869 was held not to have intended any change in the law,[66] and " made " was held to have the same meaning as " taken " in the *Bradlaugh Case* [67] with reference to the provisions of the Parliamentary Oaths Act, 1866   Lindley, M.R., in *Re Birks,*[68] speaking of a settlement and not of a statute, said: " I do not know

[61] *Doe d Angell* v. *Angell* (1846), 9 Q. B 355
[62] *R v Allen* (1872), L R 1 C C R 367, 374
[63] *Per* Lord Blackburn in *Edinburgh Street Tramways* v *Torbain* (1877), 3 App Cas 58, at p 68
[64] (1870), L R 1 C C R 248, 252
[65] In *Hadley* v *Perks* (1866), L R 1 Q B 444, 457.
[66] *Per* Mellish, L J , in *Re Wright* (1876), 3 Ch. D. 70, 75
[67] *Att -Gen* v *Bradlaugh* (1884), 14 Q B. D. 667
[68] [1900] 1 Ch 417, at p 418 *Supra,* p 158

whether it is law or a canon of construction but it is good sense to say that whenever in a deed or will or other document you find that a word used in one part of it has some clear and definite meaning, then the presumption is that it is intended to mean the same thing where, when used in another part of the document, its meaning is not clear." But Lord Warrington, in the Privy Council case of *Watson* v *Haggitt*,[69] said · "The truth is there is no such rule of general application as is contended for by the appellant A difficulty or ambiguity may be solved by resorting to such a device, but it is only in such cases that it is necessary or permissible to do so."

VIII. Statute if clear must be enforced —The next general rule to notice is that if the language of a statute is clear, it must be enforced though the result may seem harsh or unfair and inconvenient. Lord Birkenhead in *Sutters* v. *Briggs*[70] said. "The consequences of this view will no doubt be extremely inconvenient to many persons. But this is not a matter proper to influence the House unless in a doubtful case affording foothold for balanced speculation as to the probable intention of the Legislature." The argument from hardship is a dangerous one; there are few statutes which do not produce hardship or inconvenience on some classes of the community,[71] and in fact the rules of construction may entail such an interpretation to be placed on the words of a statute as may fairly be said not to be within the intention of the Legislature The same risk is run, as we saw, in the case of documents. A man, like the Legislature, must be taken to mean what he says; if he has chosen inapt language for the expression of that intention, he has only himself to blame for it. There are, however,

---

[69] [1928] A C 127, at p 130
[70] *Supra*, p 172
[71] Cf *Keyser* v *British Railway Traffic and Electric Co.*, [1936] 1 K. B. 224

some evidences of intention in the case of statutes not open in the case of deeds—as we shall subsequently see.

"Where the language of an Act is clear and explicit, we must give effect to it whatever may be the consequences, for in that case the words of the statute speak the intention of the Legislature." [72]

So Lord Herschell speaking of an Act, which placed the burden of removing a wreck on the owner of the wrecked vessel for the benefit of the public, said . "But a sense of the possible injustice of legislation ought not to induce your Lordships to do violence to well-settled rules of construction, though it may properly lead to the selection of one rather than the other of two possible interpretations of the statute." [73]

IX. Construction to avoid absurdity.—Statutes will be construed as far as possible to avoid absurdity. This is sometimes called the presumption against absurdity As we shall see later, the Courts have been accustomed to act on certain basic rules, which the text-writers call presumptions, in applying the canons of construction to statutes. We have seen some of these already, *e g.*, that the Courts will assume that the draftsman of the Act used language in its precise and logical meaning; that words are used in their ordinary, popular sense, and so on. The presumption against absurdity, or the leaning of the Court against a construction which would produce one, is only a branch of the larger rule that a statute, like a deed, should be construed in a manner to give it validity rather than invalidity—*ut res magis valeat quam pereat.* A good recent example of the presumption against absurdity is *Bishop* v *Deakin.*[74] There the defendant was convicted and sentenced to imprisonment for more than three months. An action was brought for a declaration that he was disqualified from acting

---

[72] *Warburton* v *Loveland* (1831), 2 D & Cl. (H L) 489
[73] *Arrow Shipping Co* v *Tyne Commissioners*, [1894] A. C 508, at p 516
[74] [1936] 1 Ch. 409, 414

C.D S

12

as an elected member of a local authority under section 59 (1) of the Local Government Act, 1933. Clauson, J., said: " If the section is to be read as providing that a person is disqualified from being a councillor if he was convicted within five years before his election, it may well be that he is so disqualified when he acts as a councillor at a date later than five years from the date of the conviction. In that case the effect of the disqualification operating would be that he would cease to be a councillor, but he would be eligible at once for re-election to the vacant office, the five years having expired before the new election. I cannot think that the Legislature intended such a whimsical result." So where a statutory form of oath which contained the name of King George III was to be taken by certain persons, and it was argued that the obligation to administer it lapsed with the death of that monarch, it was pointed out that the name George was intended to designate the reigning sovereign, and it afforded an instance " in which the language of the Legislature must be modified, in order to avoid absurdity and inconsistency with its manifest intentions." [75] So an Act (Poor Removal Act, 1795), which provided that a sick pauper's order for removal might be suspended in the case of any pauper " who should be brought before " the justices for that purpose, did not mean physically brought before them, which might be impossible or absurd in the case of a sick pauper.[76] So in *The Longford* (*supra*, p. 174) an Act provided that " no action should be brought against certain shipowners for damage unless a month's notice of action was given ". It was held inapplicable to proceedings *in rem* in Admiralty, for, if such notice were necessary, the proceedings would be nullified by the departure of the ship to avoid seizure

In the case of possible alternative meanings, one which would lead to an absurdity and one which would avoid it, the rule is clear; but when there is no alternative, the Court is

---

[75] Per Parke, B., in *Miller* v. *Salomons* (1852), 7 Ex. 475.
[76] *R* v. *Everdon* (1807), 9 East 101. Cf. *Fowler* v *Padget* (1798), 7 T R 509.

bound to construe the words in their natural sense whatever the consequences; the danger of adopting any other course being to turn the Court into legislators instead of interpreters. This is a very important warning and it would be an interesting study to see how far legislation from statutes is actually effected by judicial decision The warning occurs very often in the cases. " If the precise words used are plain and unambiguous, we are bound to construe them in their ordinary sense, even though it does lead to absurdity or manifest injustice. Words may be modified or varied where their import is doubtful or obscure, but we assume the functions of legislators when we depart from the ordinary meaning of the precise words used, merely because we see, or fancy we see, an absurdity or manifest injustice from an adherence to their literal meaning." [77] "If the words of an Act are clear, you must follow them, even though they lead to a manifest absurdity. The Court has nothing to do with the question whether the Legislature has committed an absurdity." [78] This question of absurdity arose very recently in the case of *Altrincham Electric Co.* v. *Sale U. D. C.* [79] The meaning of the word in dispute was "undertaking", occurring in clause 58 of the Ashton-on-Mersey Lighting Order, 1896. The majority of the Court of Appeal held the word to apply only to that part of the undertaking acquired by the respondents, as otherwise an absurd and manifestly unintended result would be arrived at in the matter of the price to be paid. The majority in the House of Lords was of opinion that " the undertaking " meant the whole undertaking. Lord Thankerton,[80] referring to *River Weir Commissioners* v. *Adamson*,[81] said that there was no ambiguity in

[77] *Per* Jervis, C.J., in *Abley* v *Dale* (1851), 20 L J. C. P 233, at p. 235.
[78] *Per* Lord Esher in *R.* v *Judge of City of London Court*, [1892] 1 Q. B. 273, at p. 290. Cf *Central London Ry* v. *Inland Revenue Commissioners*, [1937] A C. 77, where Lord Macmillan spoke of " the incongruous result " under the Income Tax Act, 1918, and the General Rules thereunder.
[79] (1936), 34 L. G. R. 215
[80] S. C , p. 227
[81] (1877), 2 App. Cas. 743.

the use of the word in its natural signification. Lord Macmillan [82] quoted Lord Bramwell in *Hill* v. *East and West
India Dock* [83] : " I should like to have a good definition of
what is such an absurdity that you are to disregard the plain'
words of an Act of Parliament. It is to be remembered that
what seems absurd to one man does not seem absurd to
another " The same learned Lord, speaking in a tax case
earlier than that just cited,[84] said : " However anomalous
an enactment may be, it must be applied by the Courts
according to its terms, unless these terms are susceptible
according to the accepted canons of construction of an interpretation which avoids the anomalies." He quoted Lord
Herschell in *Colquhoun* v. *Brooks* [85] as pointing out that where
the natural meaning of words would lead to " strangely
anomalous " results, it is legitimate to examine their statutory
context in order to see whether they ought to be construed as
they would be if read alone.

So also Lord Halsbury some years previously had said [86] :
" But a Court of law has nothing to do with the reasonableness
or unreasonableness of a provision except so far as it may help
them in determining what the Legislature has said."

X Expressio unius and ejusdem generis rules applied.—
As in the interpretation of Deeds, so in that of Statutes
the doctrines of *expressio unius exclusio alterius* (as to which
see p 66, *supra*) and *ejusdem generis* (p. 127, *supra*) apply.
As examples of the former, an Act imposed a rate on houses,
buildings, works, tenements and hereditaments, but exempted
" land ", the latter evidently meant land without buildings,
houses or works upon it [75] So in the Poor Relief Act of 1601,

---

[82] *S C* , p 235
[83] (1884), 9 App Cas 448, at p. 464
[84] *Astor* v. *Perry*, [1935] A C 398, at pp 416, 417
[85] (1889), 14 App Cas 493.
[86] *Cooke* v *Charles A Vogeler*, [1901] A. C. 102, at p. 107.
[75] *R.* v *Midland Ry.* (1855), 4 E & B 958 The Act in question was
a local one for lighting the town of Chesterfield · *Crayford* v *Rutter*, [1897]
1 Q B 650

a poor-rate was imposed on occupiers of "lands", houses, tithes and "coal mines"; the words were construed to exclude mines other than coal mines as the Legislature evidently intended the word "lands" not to include any mines at all.[76] So the word "person" may or may not include "corporations" according to the context[77]; for the allied doctrine of *noscitur a socus* (*infra*, p. 182) may also be applied. So section 17 of the Statute of Frauds requiring writing for the sale for £10 or upwards of "goods, wares and merchandise" was held not to apply to stocks and shares or the certificates of them.[78] So the word "entertainment" was held to relate to bodily comfort and not to mental enjoyment, as, for instance, a theatrical "entertainment" in section 6 of the Refreshment Houses Act, 1860, where the words were "for public refreshment, resort and entertainment".[79] So the repealed statute 7 & 8 Geo. 4 made it a felony to break and enter a "dwelling, shop, warehouse or counting house". The words were held to be confined to something of the same kind as a warehouse, somewhere where goods could be sold and not a mere workshop.[80] In *Lowe* v. *Dorling*,[81] Farwell, L.J., said: "The generality of the maxim '*expressum facit cessare tacitum*' which was relied on renders caution necessary in its application. It is not enough that the express and the tacit are merely incongruous, it must be clear that they cannot reasonably be intended to co-exist. In *Colquhoun* v. *Brooks*[82] Wills, J., says: "I may observe that the method of construction summarised in the maxim '*expressio unius exclusio alterius*' is certainly one which requires to be watched. . . . The failure to make the *expressio* complete very often arises

[76] *Lead Smelting Co* v. *Richardson* (1762), 3 Burr. 1341.
[77] *Law Society* v. *United Service Bureau*, [1934] 1 K B 343
[78] *Tempest* v *Kilner* (1846), 3 C B 249; *Freeman* v *Appleyard* (1862), 32 L J. Ex 175
[79] *Muir* v. *Keay* (1875), L R 10 Q B. 594
[80] *R* v. *Sanders* (1839), 9 C & P 79
[81] [1906] 2 K B 772, at p 784
[82] (1887), 19 Q B D. 400, at p. 406

from accident, very often from the fact that it never struck the draftsman that the thing supposed to be excluded needed specific mention of any kind " Lopes, L.J., in the Court of Appeal,[83] said: " The maxim *expressio unius exclusio alterius* has been pressed upon us. I agree with what is said in the Court below by Wills, J., about this maxim. It is often a valuable servant but a dangerous master to follow in the construction of statutes or documents. The *exclusio* is often the result of inadvertence or accident and the maxim ought not to be applied where its application, having regard to the subject-matter to which it is to be applied, leads to inconsistency or injustice."

Some examples of the *ejusdem generis* rule as applied to statutes may be given. This rule is based on that of *noscitur a sociis*. There must first be a category, as Farwell, L.J., explained in *Tillmans & Co.* v. *S.S. Knutsford Co.*[84] In the well-known case of *Powell* v. *Kempton Park Racecourse Co.*,[85] section 1 of the Betting Act, 1853, prohibited the keeping of a " house, office, room or other place " for betting with persons resorting thereto. The question was whether Tattersall's ring on a racecourse was a " place ". The House of Lords, by a majority, held that the *ejusdem generis* rule applied and that the words " or other place " meant a place similar to a " house, office or room " and did not apply to an uncovered enclosure adjacent to the racecourse, the public going there to bet with bookmakers, who were admitted on the ordinary terms and with no special rights in the enclosure.

So in *Att.-Gen.* v. *Brown*,[86] by section 43 of the Customs Consolidation Act, 1876, the importation of " arms, ammunition, gunpowder, or any other goods " may be prohibited by proclamation. A proclamation under the Act purported to

---

[83] (1889), 21 Q. B D. 52, at p 65.
[84] [1908] 2 K. B. 385. Cf. *Pestonjee Bhicajee* v. *Anderson* (1938), 2 Madras L J. 906, at p. 910, *per* Lord Romer. See this rule with regard to deeds discussed *ante*, pp 127—130.
[85] [1899] A. C 143.
[86] [1920] 1 K B. 773.

prohibit the importation of pyrogallic acid, and the question was whether the proclamation was valid. Sankey, J. (as he then was) applied the *ejusdem generis* rule and held that the acid was not one of the class of articles, the importation of which was prohibited by the Act.] Where the hull of a vessel was damaged by a boiler being negligently lowered into the hold, the damage was held not covered by a policy of insurance against perils of the sea or *ejusdem generis* therewith.[87] Under the Patents Act of 1883, s. 32, threats of an action for infringement were, under certain circumstances, rendered actionable if made " by circulars, advertisements or otherwise ". A threat by letter was held sufficient to satisfy the section although it could not be called either a circular or an advertisement.[88] In section 62 of the Charitable Trusts Act, 1853, " cathedral, collegiate (or) chapter schools or other schools " are mentioned, the Court of Appeal held that the words " or other schools " must be taken to mean schools of the same character as those mentioned in the section, Lindley, M.R., saying, " I cannot conceive why the Legislature should have taken the trouble to specify in this section such special schools as cathedral, collegiate and chapter, except to show the type of school they were referring to, and in my opinion other schools must be taken to mean other schools of that type." [89] The Road Traffic Act, 1930, s. 48 (1), defines a " traffic sign " to include " all signals, warning sign-posts, direction posts, signs or devices ". The Court held that the word " devices " must be construed as something *ejusdem generis* with the preceding words and, therefore, that a white painted line on a road was not a traffic sign.[89a]

General words following particular words will not be taken to include anything of a superior class to that to which

---

[87] *Stott (Baltic) Steamers, Ltd.* v. *Marten,* [1916] A C. 304 See *per* Lord Atkinson, pp. 310, 311. *Inland Revenue Commissioners* v *Smyth,* [1914] 3 K. B 406 Contrast *The Stranna* (1938), 54 T. L. R. 393.

[88] *Skinner & Co.* v. *Shew & Co,* [1893] 1 Ch 413.

[89] *Re Stockport, etc, Schools,* [1898] 2 Ch 687.

[89a] *Evans* v *Cross,* [1938] 1 K B. 694.

the particular words belong. For instance, where the statute
of Westminster the Second (13 Edw. 1, c. 41) began with
" abbots " and finished with " other religious houses ", bishops
were not included for they are superior to abbots, and the
" other religious houses " must mean those inferior to those
mentioned before [90] But where words are obviously used in
a wide sense, their meaning ought not to be qualified on
account of their association with other words.[91] So the
insertion of such words as " or things of whatever description " would exclude the rule [92]

III.—Omissions

Supply of omissions—The Court should not take upon
itself to supply omissions as this is to assume the function
of a legislator above referred to. But the Courts have
occasionally taken it upon themselves to do so Perhaps
one of the best known instances of an omission in a
statute occurs in Lord Tenterden's Act (the Statute of
Frauds Amendment Act, 1828), which enacts that no action
shall be brought on a representation to the intent that a
person " may obtain credit, goods or money upon ", unless
the representation is in writing. The text is obviously
imperfect. Lord Abinger was for rejecting the word " upon "
as nonsense; Parke, B., thought the Court was at liberty to
read the phrase by transposition " may obtain goods or money
upon credit ", or that " such representations " might be
supplied after the word " upon ".[1] There was also a notable
omission in section 33 of the Fines and Recoveries Act, 1833,
where the second part of the section omits to provide for the
case of a protector of a settlement in lieu of one convicted
of treason or felony, though such a one is mentioned in the

[90] According to Coke's opinion in 2 Inst. 457. Cf *Archbishop of Canter-
bury's Case* (1596), 2 Co Rep 46 a.
[91] *Provost, etc , of Glasgow* v. *Glasgow Tramway Co.,* [1898] A. C. 631,
and *per* Lord Halsbury, at p 634.
[92] *Att.-Gen* v *Leicester Corporation,* [1910] 2 Ch. 359, 369, *per* Neville, J.
[1] *Lyde* v *Barnard* (1836), 1 M & W. 101, 115

earlier part of the section   Lord Lyndhurst, L.C., accordingly thought the words "in lieu of the person who shall be convicted" ought to be supplied rather than to adopt a construction which would have deprived the preceding words of all meaning [2] Speaking of the Finance Act, 1922, Lord Macmillan in *Astor* v. *Perry* [3] said: "The possible extra-territorial effects of the section [20] were obviously not thought out and the task of reconciling the resulting conflict which the Legislature has omitted to perform is imposed upon your Lordships." While not strictly an omission, section 6 of the Intestates' Estates Act, 1890, refers to the "testamentary" expenses of an intestate. This is obviously a mistake and is taken to mean the expenses in obtaining representation to and administration of an intestate's estate. [4] Sometimes the Court has refused to imply an accidental omission of words (*e.g.*, section 9 of 18 & 19 Vict. c 108—omission of "serious personal injury" in the penalty clause) on the ground that it is not for them to take upon themselves "the office of the Legislature" [5] Similarly, under the Shop Hours Act, 1892, a section enacts that if a young person is employed for a longer period than seventy-four hours a week, the employer is liable to a penalty. Another section provides that a notice must be exhibited to show how many hours a young person may be employed under the Act, no penalty being provided in default   The respondent had not employed a young person for more than seventy-four hours a week, but had not exhibited the statutory notice and had been summoned for employing a young person contrary to the Act. The Court held that it could not read the provisions of the former section into the latter. [6] So, licensing justices were held to have no authority to make the renewal of a licence con-

---

[2] *Re Wainwright* (1843), 1 Phil 261.
[3] [1935] A C 398, at p. 416
[4] *Re Twigg's Estate*, [1892] 1 Ch 579
[5] *Underhill* v *Longridge* (1859), 29 L. J M C 65 Maxwell, p 239, seems to think that the decision in this case turned upon the penal character of the statute, *sed quære*.
[6] *Hammond* v *Pulsford*, [1895] 1 Q B 223

ditional on the applicant giving an undertaking as to the conduct and management of the premises in respect of matters not covered by the grounds for refusing the renewal of the licence, and Collins, M.R., said[7]: "In my judgment it is not competent for this Court to introduce by implication only a provision directly contradictory of an unambiguous enactment addressed to the very point itself. If we are at large to draw inferences and make implications, why are we to leave out the inference arising from the fact that the Legislature has not only abstained from enacting this sixth ground of refusal, but has by the limitation to five other grounds directly excluded it?" In a case under the Poor Law Loans Act, 1871, a question of the mode of repayment of loans borrowed by the guardians arose, and Lord Davey said[8]: "It seems to me that the whole argument of the appellants really comes to the old and apparently ineradicable fallacy of importing into an enactment which is expressed in clear and apparently unambiguous language, something which is not contained in it by what is called implication from the language of a proviso which may or may not have a meaning of its own."

As to implied repeals, see *infra*, p. 243.

IV.—RETROSPECTIVE EFFECT OF STATUTES

1. The natural and ordinary way to regard statutes is as affecting something in the future and as not affecting what has gone before.—" Prima facie ", said Scrutton, L.J.,[1] " an Act deals with future and not with past events. If this were not so, the Act might annul rights already acquired, while the presumption is against the intention." And in the same case[2] Greer, L.J , said: " There are numerous cases which

---

[7] *R.* v *Dodds*, [1905] 2 K. B. 40, at p. 49.

[8] *West Derby Union* v *Metropolitan Life Assurance*, [1897] A C 647.

[1] *Ward* v *British Oak Insurance Co*, *Ltd.*, [1932] 1 K B. 392, at p 397. Cf. *Re Nautilus Steam Shipping Co.*, [1936] Ch 17, 28, *per* Romer, L.J.

[2] *S C*, at p 398.

clearly show that the Courts lean against so interpreting an Act as to deprive a party of an accrued right." In that case the question arose on the construction of the Third Party (Rights against Insurers) Act of 1930, s. 1 (1), which provided that if the insured became a bankrupt, and thereafter incurred a liability by reason of an accident on the road, his rights against the insurer should pass to the third party to whom the liability had been incurred. The Act was held not to affect cases where liability had been incurred before July 10, 1930, when the Act came into operation. So Wright, J., in *Re Athlumney*[3] said: " Perhaps no rule of construction is more firmly established than this, that a retrospective operation is not to be given to a statute so as to impair an existing right or obligation, otherwise than as regards a matter of procedure,[4] unless that effect cannot be avoided without doing violence to the language of the enactment. If the enactment is expressed in language that is fairly capable of either interpretation, it ought to be construed as prospective only." Lindley, L.J., in *Lauri v. Renad*,[5] not only states the law in much the same way, but adds an important subordinate rule when he says: " It is a fundamental rule of English law that no statute shall be construed so as to have a retrospective operation, unless its language is such as plainly to require such a construction, and the same rule involves another and subordinate rule to the effect that a statute is not to be construed so as to have a greater retrospective effect than its language renders necessary." In *Re Hale's Patent*[6] section 8 of the Patents and Designs Act, 1919, was held not retrospective, the tribunal for determining the user of an invention by the Government being merely changed from the date of the Act Likewise the Act of 1923, which removed the limitation of £100 in respect of a claim under the Workmen's Compensation Acts against a company being wound up, was held

---

[3] [1898] 2 Q B. D. 547, at p 551.
[4] As to this, see *infra*, p. 190.
[5] [1892] 3 Ch. 402, at p 421.
[6] [1920] 2 Ch 377.

not to be retrospective as there appeared no intention to make it so.[7] Two cases under section 2 of the Gaming Act of 1835 may be noticed. As is well known, this section remained unrepealed, one might almost say undetected, for many years, when in 1922 it was repealed by the Gaming Act of that year, which provided that "no action shall be entertained" on a cause of action arising out of the Gaming Act, 1835, s 2. The Act of 1922 was held not to be retrospective in respect of actions begun before the passing of the Act, though judgment was not given till after the Act had come into force,[8] nor in respect of a writ issued after the Act came into force on a cause of action which had arisen before that date.[9] In the latter case the plaintiff's cause of action was held not to have been divested by the Act of 1922.

In *West* v. *Gwynne* [10] the question was whether section 3 of the Conveyancing and Law of Property Act, 1892, ought to be applied to a lease of the year 1874. That section of the Act prohibited the exaction of a fine for a licence or consent to assign a lease unless there was an express provision to the contrary contained in the lease. This Act was an amending Act to the principal Act, the Conveyancing Act of 1881, and by section 14 (9) of that Act, the provisions of the section were to apply to leases made either before or after the commencement of that Act, *viz.*, January 1, 1882. The Court of Appeal felt compelled to hold that the section was applicable to the old lease by reason of the retrospective clause just cited; and Buckley, L.J., said [11]: "As a matter of principle an Act of Parliament is not without sufficient reason taken

---

[7] In *Re Snowdon Colliery Co* (1925), 94 L J Ch 305

[8] *Beadling* v. *Goll* (1922), 39 T L R 128. Cf *Smithies* v. *National Association of Operative Plasterers*, [1909] 1 K B 310

[9] *Henshall* v *Porter*, [1923] 2 K B 193 Cf. *Moon* v *Durden* (1848), 2 Ex 22

[10] [1911] 2 Ch 1

[11] S C , at p 12 Cf *Barber* v *Pigden*, [1937] 1 K B. 664, where the effect of ss 3 (b) and 4 (1) (b) of the Law Reform Act, 1935, was held to give a retrospective effect, as to the non-liability of a husband for his wife's torts

to be retrospective. There is, so to speak, a presumption that it speaks only as to the future. But there is no like presumption that an Act is not intended to interfere with existing rights. Most Acts of Parliament in fact do interfere with existing rights. To construe the section I have simply to read it, and looking at the Act in which it is contained, to say what is its fair meaning." Even in an Act which is held to be retrospective, "That is a necessary and logical corollary of the general proposition, that you ought not to give a larger retrospective power to a section, even in an Act which is to some extent intended to be retrospective, than you can plainly see the Legislature meant ".[12] So in *Hitchcock* v. *Way* [13] the Wine and Beerhouse Amendment Act, 1870, which provided that every person convicted of felony " should for ever be disqualified from selling spirits by retail ", and if he should take out or have taken out a licence for that purpose it should be void, was held to apply to a man who had been convicted before, but had obtained a licence after, the Act was passed, apparently on the ground that the object of the Act was to ensure that beerhouses were not kept by men of bad character, in order to protect the public.

II. Presumption against retrospectivity.—In some of the cases cited, the presumption against retrospectivity has been applied in order to preserve accrued rights. As Lord Wright said in *Re A Debtor* [14]: " A matter of substantive right which has become *res judicata* cannot be upset by a general change in the law, in the absence of precise intention to make the change so retrospective being evidenced in the Act." In *Allen* v. *Gold Reefs of West Africa* [15] Lindley, L J., dealing with the argument that a company's articles could not be altered retrospectively on this

[12] *Per* Bowen, L J., in *Reid* v. *Reid* (1886), 31 Ch. D. 408
[13] (1837), 6 A. & E. 943
[14] [1936] 1 Ch. 237, at p 243. Cf *Ward* v *British Oak Insurance Co*, *Ltd*, *supra*, p. 186.
[15] [1900] 1 Ch. 656, at p. 673.

ground, said that existing rights dependent on alterable articles must necessarily be affected by their alteration, "such rights are in truth limited as to their duration by the duration of the articles which confer them". In *The Colonial Sugar Refining Co.* v. *Irving*,[16] the Australian Commonwealth Judiciary Act of 1903 had abolished a right of appeal to the Privy Council from the Supreme Court of Queensland, but this was held not to apply retrospectively to a suit pending when the Act was passed and decided by the Supreme Court after that date. Lord Macnaghten said: "To deprive a suitor in a pending action of an appeal to a superior tribunal which belonged to him as of right is a very different thing from repealing procedure." But it must be a "vested right" in order to raise the presumption. The Patents Act of 1888 and the Register of Patent Agents Rules, 1899, created and regulated the registration of patent agents. Prior to 1888, anybody could call himself a patent agent and practice as such, and the question arose in *Starey* v. *Graham*[17] as to whether this was an "acquired right" or not. Channell, J., said[18]: "Before the passing of the Act, everybody had a right to call himself a patent agent, that is to say, the law did not forbid him to do so. A right enjoyed in that way is not within the meaning of this saving clause a 'right acquired', otherwise it is obvious that such a clause would nullify the operation of any Act in which the clause was inserted."

III. There are no vested rights in Procedure.—Nobody, it is said, has a vested right in procedure, and this maxim holds good in this connection, *i.e*, there is no presumption that a change in procedure is *prima facie* intended to be prospective and not retrospective. Lord Macnaghten drew the distinction, for example, in *Colonial Sugar Refining*

---

[16] [1905] A C. 369.
[17] [1899] 1 Q. B 406   Cf. *Abbott* v. *Minister for Lands*, [1895] A C. 425, 431.   [18] S. C., at p. 411.

Co. v. *Irving* (*supra*) and it occurs in very many cases. The Public Authorities Protection Act, 1893, provides (*inter alia*) that an action must be brought against a public authority or officer within six months of the default complained of. This was held in *The Ydun* [19] to be a matter of procedure only and that an action was barred after six months from the date of default. An Act passed during the Great War (Increase of Rent and Mortgage Interest Act of 1915) prohibited the calling in of mortgages or of foreclosing them so long as certain conditions were fulfilled. A mortgagee holding a mortgage of 1910, before the Act came into operation, issued a writ for foreclosure or sale. The question was whether the Act of 1915 operated retrospectively. It was held that it did, inasmuch as the Act placed in suspense as a war measure a particular form of remedy normally open to mortgagees and that it therefore related merely to procedure. [20]

IV. Retrospective effect may be express or implied.— We have so far seen that retrospective effect may be supplied either by express enactment (cf. *West* v. *Gwynne*, *supra*, and 23 & 24 Vict. c. 38, s. 12) [20a] or by implication and that this latter is the much more frequent method. The presumption is against such operation (except as to procedure in which nobody has a vested right) especially where it would affect vested or acquired rights. Another presumption to the opposite effect has been suggested   It is said that where an Act contains a clause postponing its operation for a certain period, it is an indication that the Legislature intended it to have a retrospective action, because it gives time for proceedings to be taken in respect of causes of action already accrued and if the litigant neglects or omits to take advantage of that opportunity he must take the consequences of being

---

[19] [1899] P. 236   Cf. *Wright* v. *Hale* (1860), 6 H & N. 227, 232, *per* Wilde, B.

[20] *Welby* v. *Parker*, [1916] 2 Ch. 1.

[20a] Enacting that clause 32 of 22 & 23 Vict c 35 shall operate retrospectively.

caught by the retrospective effect, if any, of the new Act. In *Re Athlumney* [21] Wright, J., said: "One exception to the general rule [*i e.*, that a retrospective intent is not to be assumed] has sometimes been suggested, *viz.*, that where as here [section 23 of the Bankruptcy Act, 1890] the commencement of the operation of the Act is suspended for a time, that is an indication that no further restriction upon retrospective operations is intended." The learned Judge went on to discuss the cases on the point, and suggested that the supposed rule applied, if at all, to cases [22] within Lord Tenterden's Act,[23] *viz.*, that a verbal promise to pay was of no avail if made before the Act, as the latter applied to past as well as to future transactions. These cases are sometimes justified as a matter of evidence. The Act in question is merely an amendment to the Statute of Frauds, which provides that a contract shall be unenforceable unless certain evidence is forthcoming. It is, however, to be observed that the principle of the cases just cited was followed by Lord Campbell, C.J., in a somewhat similar case, in that it also related to limitation, in *R. v. Leeds and Bradford Ry.*[24] There an award obtained in 1850, three years after the damage was done in 1847, was held ineffectual, as in 1848 the Summary Jurisdiction Act was passed providing that awards must be applied for and obtained within six months from the time the damage was sustained. The Act came into operation six weeks after it was passed. Lord Campbell said: "If the Act had come into operation immediately after the time of its being passed, the hardship would have been so great that we might have inferred an intention on the part of the Legislature not to give it a retrospective operation, but when we see that it contains a

---

[21] *Supra*, p 187

[22] *Towler v Chatterton* (1829), 6 Bing. 258; *Hilliard v. Lenard* (1829), M. & M 297. Cf. the criticism of these cases by Rolfe, B , in *Moon v. Durden* (1848), 2 Ex. 33

[23] Statute of Frauds Amendment Act, 1828.

[24] (1852), 21 L J M C. 193, at p 195. Cf *per* Pollock, C B., in *Wright v Hale* (1860), 30 L. J Ex. 40.

provision suspending its operation for six weeks, that must be taken as an intimation that the Legislature has provided that as a period of time within which proceedings respecting antecedent damages or injuries might be taken before the proper tribunal . . . A certain time was allowed before the Act was to come into operation and that removes all difficulty. The case of *Towler* v. *Chatterton* is strongly in point." The rule is at least doubtful and, further, as Wright, J., pointed out in *Re Athlumney*, the phrase "shall have been", usual in former statutes to suggest an inference of retrospectivity, is common form in modern drafting where there is no question of such an effect. There seems no other modern case in which the matter has come under review.

Another class of statutes is also held free from the general presumption against retrospective effect, *viz.*, declaratory Acts. When a statute is passed either to supply an omission in a previous Act or to explain a previous Act, the later statute is taken to relate back to the time when the earlier was passed. So where by a "gross mistake" the rate per weight (per cwt) of a duty was omitted from one statute and almost immediately afterwards supplied by another,[25] the latter was held to have reference to the former and "they must be taken together as if they were one and the same Act" Also in *Att.-Gen* v. *Theobald*[26] stamp duty was held to be payable on voluntary settlements, though the litigation in which the terms of one such was involved was begun before the relevant Act (Customs and Inland Revenue Act, 1889, s. 11) was passed.

V. Statutes sometimes have a retroactive effect on contracts —The emergency legislation in the Great War supplied numerous examples of "frustrated" contracts as, for instance, *Metropolitan Water Board* v. *Dick, Kerr & Co.*,[27] *Bank Line*

---

[25] 53 Geo 3, c. 33, and 53 Geo. 3, c 105; *Att -Gen.* v. *Pougett* (1816), 2 Price 381.

[26] (1890), 24 Q B. D 557

[27] [1917] 2 K. B. 1.

v. *Capel*,[28] and *Marshall* v. *Glanvill*.[29] A change in the law
may have a similar effect as in *Baily* v. *De Crespigny*,[30] where
a railway company under its compulsory powers acquired
a piece of land belonging to the lessor, on which he had
covenanted that neither he nor his assigns would build, and
erected a station thereon. The lessor was held not liable to
the lessee on this covenant. The rule is thus stated by Lord
Holt· "The difference where an Act of Parliament will
amount to a repeal of a covenant and where not, is this:
where a man covenanted not to do a thing which was lawful
for him to do and an Act of Parliament comes after and
compels him to do it, there the Act repeals the covenant and
vice versa; but where a man covenants not to do a thing which
was unlawful at the time of the covenant, and afterwards an
Act makes it lawful, the Act does not repeal the covenant."[31]

Perhaps the apparent, not real, retrospective effect of
statutes upon wills should be noticed. Suppose a man makes
a will in 1920 and dies in 1930 and between those dates
a statute is passed which renders one or some of the dispositions in his will illegal or abortive—does the will or the statute
take effect? By section 24 of the Wills Act, 1837, all wills
now take effect as if they had been executed immediately
before the death of the testator. The question has arisen in
cases on the Apportionment Act, 1870, and the Married
Women's Property Acts. In holding that a will, made before
the first of these, was affected by the Act Jessel, M R., said[32]:
"It is said that testators make their wills on the supposition
that the state of the law will not be altered, and it is contended
that this will ought to be construed as it would have been
under the old law (*i e.*, as speaking from the date of the will).
The answer is that a testator who knows of an alteration in

---

28 [1919] A. C 435
29 [1917] 2 K B 87
30 (1869), L. R 4 Q. B. 180.
31 *Brewster* v *Kitchell* (1678), 1 Lord Raymond 317, 321   Cf. Chitty,
Contracts (19th ed), pp. 147, 148.
32 *Hasluck* v *Pedley* (1875), L. R 19 Eq 271, at p. 273   Cf. *Constable*
v *Constable* (1880), 11 Ch. D 685, *Re Bridges*, [1894] 1 Ch 297, 302.

the law (as this testator must be presumed to have done) and does not choose to alter his will, must be taken to mean that his will shall take effect under the new law." So with regard to the Married Women's Property Act, 1882, a will was made by a married woman before, but came into force after, the Act, and Lindley, L.J., said[33]: "The testatrix by her will, construed as it would have been when she made it, gave the appellant half her residuary estate. We can find nothing in the Act to alter this construction." The Court refused to give the Act a retrospective operation. And such another will has been held valid to pass a married woman's separate property acquired by her as such under the Act,[34] and section 3 of the Married Women's Property Act, 1893, has been held to apply to every married woman dying after the passing of the Act, whether her will was made before or after that date.[35]

V.—AIDS TO CONSTRUCTION

These correspond to the evidence which can be used to enable the Court to discover the intention of the maker of a document and which is summarised at pp 31—36, *supra*. We now have to see what the Courts can summon to their aid in the construction of statutes As in the case of documents, these aids or evidence naturally fall into two categories—*viz.*, Internal and External.

(1) *Internal.*—(a) Just as in deeds, so in statutes, the meaning is to be sought for in the expressions used in the statute itself. It has been previously pointed out that the intention is to be collected from the words used in a deed read as a whole and that the deed itself is in the first instance to supply the key to its own meaning A statute contains rather more aids to its own construction than does an ordinary deed. The latter

---

[33] *Re Bridges, supra,* at p 300.
[34] *Re Bowen,* [1892] 2 Ch 291
[35] *Re Wythe,* [1895] 2 Ch 116

may, and often does, contain precise recitals of what has been agreed to be done or what the object of the maker is, and, as we saw,[1] these may furnish a valuable guide to the intention, especially in the case of ambiguity. Now a statute used to begin with a recital of the object of the Legislature—called the preamble—see, for example, the long preamble to the Statute of Frauds. This has fallen into disuse, and in the Law of Property Act, 1925, there is no preamble at all. Sometimes there is a very short one : " Whereas it is expedient to amend the law of libel " (51 & 52 Vict. c. 64 (1885)); compared with Fox's Act (32 Geo 3, c. 60 (1792)) : " Whereas doubts have arisen whether on the trial of an indictment or information for the making or publishing any libel, where an issue or issues are joined between the king and the defendant or defendants, on the plea of not guilty pleaded, it be competent to the jury impanelled to try the same and to give their verdict upon the whole matter in issue : Be it therefore enacted," etc Before the preamble comes the title: " An Act for the better security of the Crown and Government of the United Kingdom "; " An Act to consolidate the enactments relating to Conveyancing and the Law of Property in England and Wales " Acts are now divided into sections; these sometimes have headings, also marginal notes at the side, or in some cases (not frequent in this country) illustrations appended Sometimes rules are appended to the Act and frequently interpretation sections defining the meaning of various expressions used in the statute. With all these to pray in aid, it looks *prima facie* as if the interpreter of a statute had an easier task than the interpreter of a deed or other written document, and as if the several sources of information open to the former would more than compensate for the lack of oral evidence which, as we saw,[2] is under some circumstances open to the latter, but not in the interpretation of statutes. " No case has been called to our attention ",

---

[1] *Ante*, p. 100
[2] *Ante*, pp 31—36; 53—58.

said Cozens-Hardy, M.R.,[3] on the question whether expert
evidence could be adduced as to the meaning of the words
" nominal rent ", " and I do not believe there is any case in
which dealing with a modern statute any such evidence has
been admitted. The duty of the Court is to interpret and give
full effect to the words used by the Legislature and it seems to
me really not relevant to consider what a particular branch
of the public may or may not understand to be the meaning
of these words." The multitude of decisions past and present
on statutes, however, does not encourage one to think that
there is any substance in the supposition that the interpretation of statutes is in any way easier than that of deeds
and documents.

(b) If the words are plain, there is of course no difficulty.
What does create a difficulty (to be referred to later [4]) is the
question, When are the words plain? What is plain to one
mind may be just the reverse to another. If the words are
not plain, the first thing to do is to consider the *object* and
scope of the Act.[5] This involves a consideration of the
context, the setting in which the disputed words are placed
and the design of the whole statute. This has been referred
to under the General Rules.[6] The *locus classicus* on this
subject, in fact the case from which a large part of the rules
of interpretation are derived, is *Heydon's Case*. This
celebrated case, reported by Lord Coke [7] and decided by the
Barons of the Exchequer in the sixteenth century, laid down
the following rules: " That for the sure and true interpretation of all statutes in general (be they penal or beneficial,
restrictive or enlarging of the common law) four things are
to be discerned and considered: (1) what was the common law
before the passing of the Act; (2) what was the mischief and

[3] In *Camden (Marquis)* v *I. R C*, [1914] 1 K. B 641, at p 647.
[4] *Post*, p 292
[5] *Guardians of Salford Union* v *Dewhurst*, [1926] A C 619, *Metropolitan Coal Co* v. *Pye*, [1936] A. C 343.
[6] *Ante*, p. 164
[7] (1584), 3 Co Rep 8.

defect for which the common law did not provide, (3) what remedy the Parliament hath resolved and appointed to cure the disease of the commonwealth; (4) the true reason of the remedy.   And then the office of all the Judges is always to make such construction as shall suppress the mischief and advance the remedy, and to suppress subtle inventions and evasions for the continuance of the mischief and *pro privato commodo*, and to add force and life to the cure and remedy according to the true intent of the makers of the Act *pro bono publico*"   Probably legislation was less frequent and less involved in the sixteenth century than it is to-day; but so far as they can be applied to modern legislation, these rules are in force to-day and often form a valuable guide to interpretation.   For a recent example of this, Lord Halsbury, in *Eastman Photographic Co.* v. *Comptroller of Patents* (where the question was whether the word " Solio ", used as a trade mark, was an invented or a descriptive word) said [8] " Among the things which have passed into canons of construction recorded in *Heydon's Case*, we are to see what was the law before the Act was passed, and what was the mischief or defect for which the law had not provided, what remedy Parliament appointed, and the reason of the remedy."   He then proceeded to quote Turner, L J ,[9] who said: " We have therefore to consider not merely the words of this Act of Parliament, but the intent of the Legislature to be collected from the cause and necessity of the Act being made, from a comparison of its several parts and from foreign (meaning extraneous) circumstances, so far as they can justly be considered to throw light on the subject "

(c) The construction is therefore to be in harmony with the intention.[10]   Further, no addition to or omission from the words is to be made unless on grounds justifiable as carrying out the intention of the Legislature.   So in *Vickers* v. *Evans* [11]

---

[8] [1898] A C 571, at p 573.
[9] In *Hawkins* v *Gathercole* (1855), 6 D. M & G 1, at p 21
[10] *Ante,* p 164.
[11] [1910] A C 444, at p 446

Lord Loreburn, speaking with reference to the words in the Workmen's Compensation Act, 1906, " the amount of the weekly payment may be increased to any amount . . which the workman would probably have been earning . . . if he had remained uninjured ", said: " The arguments urged seem to me quite insufficient to lead us to read these words (' would have been earning in his actual employment under the same employer ') into the Act of Parliament. The question is what would the workman probably have been earning Those are the only provisions in the Act." He also said in the same case [12]: " We are not entitled to read words into an Act of Parliament unless clear reason for it is to be found within the four corners of the Act itself." So an order for the protection of the earnings of a deserted married woman by the Matrimonial Causes Act, 1857, s 21, might be discharged by the magistrate who made it. This was held not to apply to his successor, although the magistrate who made the order was dead.[13] Really the same thing under another name is an *omission*. As Bramwell, L.J., said in *Ex p. Welchman* [14]: " Whether the draftsman had it in mind or not is another question; but very often the Courts have to discover what provision has been made for the happening of an event which was not in the contemplation of the person who drew the Act." In *Crawford* v *Spooner* [15] the Privy Council said: " We cannot aid the Legislature's defective phrasing in an Act, we cannot add and mend, and by construction make up deficiencies which are left there; for this as Lord Brougham said [16] would mean that the Judges do not construe the Act but alter it " Nor must the Court alter a word of the statute so as to produce a *casus omissus* which it may then proceed to supply [17]

[12] *S C.*, p. 445
[13] *Ex p Sharpe* (1864), 5 B & S 322
[14] (1879), 11 Ch D 48, at p 55
[15] (1846), 6 Moore P. C. 9
[16] In *Gwynne* v *Burnell* (1840), 7 Cl & F 696
[17] *Per* Lord Halsbury in *Mersey Docks and Harbour Board* v *Henderson* (1888), 13 App Cas 595, at p 602

(d) Next, a change of language is some, though possibly slight, indication of change of intention on the part of the Legislature. For instance, if a later statute *in pari materia* with an earlier contains a difference in language, it is generally a fair presumption that the difference is intentional. In *Dickenson* v. *Fletcher*,[18] Brett, J., said: "Where two statutes dealing with the same subject-matter use different language, it is generally a fair presumption that the alteration in the language used in the subsequent statute was intentional" "When the Legislature", said Cockburn, C.J.,[19] "in legislating *in pari materia* and substituting certain provisions for those which existed in an earlier statute, has entirely changed the language of the enactment, it must be taken to have done so with some intention and motive." There are, however, many instances to the contrary. In 1845 the Judicial Committee of the Privy Council said[20]: "It is certainly to be wished that, in framing statutes, the same words should always be used in the same sense", but the Legislature does not comply in very many cases. Blackburn, J., thought the Legislature changed the words but not the meaning to "improve the graces of the style and to avoid using the same word over and over again."[21] And in *Re Wright*,[22] Mellish, L.J., referring to the difference in language in the Bankruptcy Act, 1849, and the repealing Act of 1869 said: "Every one who is familiar with the present Act knows that the language of the former Acts has been very much altered in many cases where it could not have been intended to make any change in the law." Where a word of doubtful meaning has once been judicially interpreted it will be taken to bear that meaning in subsequent statutes unless a contrary intention is indicated. It is always assumed that the Legislature uses precise language and also

---

18 (1873), L. R. 9 C. P. 1, at p 8
19 In R. v Price (1871), L. R 6 Q. B. 411, at p 416
20 Casement v Fulton (1845), 5 Moore P. C 130, at p 141
21 Hadley v. Perks (1866), L. R 1 Q. B 444, at p 457
22 (1876), 3 Ch D. 70, at p 78, *supra*, p. 175.

that it knows the state of the law In an Act of 1894 the word "wreck" had received a judicial interpretation. The House of Lords decided that it must bear the same interpretation in the later Act of 1925 unless the later Act indicated a contrary intention,[23] and Lord Buckmaster said: "It has long been a well established principle to be applied in the consideration of Acts of Parliament that where a word of doubtful meaning has received a clear judicial interpretation, the subsequent statute which incorporates the same word or the same phrase in a similar context must be construed so that the word or phrase is interpreted according to the meaning that has previously been assigned to it "[24] It may be here noticed that the repealed part of an Act is still part of the history of the new Act and may be referred to as such This will be dealt with more fully when external aids to construction are discussed (*post*, pp. 228—233).

Again, in private Acts of Parliament, *e g.*, railway Acts, the special clauses, generally inserted for the protection of special private interests, have no effect on the construction of a general clause. Such clauses are " in the nature of private arrangements, not inserted by the Legislature as part of a general scheme of the legislation which it desires to express, but they are in the nature of private contracts and ought not to have any effect upon the construction of a general clause." [25]

The consequences of the proposed construction should be considered. This will often supply the rule of construction to be followed, for this consideration of consequences will most probably be controlled by one or more of the presumptions which figure largely in this subject and which will be dealt with later (*post*, pp 263—280).

[23] Cf James, L.J , in *Ex p Campbell* (1870), L R 5 Ch App 703, 706; Lord Halsbury in *Webb v Outrim*, [1907] A C. 81, at p. 89
[24] *Barras v Aberdeen Steam Trawling and Fishing Co* , [1933] A C 402, at p. 411
[25] *Per* Lord Cairns in *East London Ry v Whitchurch* (1874), L R 7 H. L. 81, at p 89

Title.—The *Title* of Acts was added probably about 1495. There is often a long title and a short one. It may be amended by the House of Lords at any stage at which amendments are admissible, when alterations in a bill have rendered an alteration in the title necessary, and in the House of Commons since 1854 either in committee or on report or the third reading of the bill. In 1896 an Act was passed, the Short Titles Act, to facilitate citation of an Act, and nowadays the House of Lords requires all Acts to have a short title in addition to the formal long one   For example, the 15th of Geo. 5, c. 20, is entitled " An Act to consolidate the enactments relating to Conveyancing and the Law of Property in England and Wales "—a comparatively succinct " long " title.   By section 209 (1) of the Act it is provided : " This Act may be cited as the Law of Property Act, 1925 ", by which name it is of course known to the legal profession.   In 1840 Tindal, C.J., thought that neither the title nor the marginal notes could be used to assist in construction.[26]   In 1868 Willes, J., was of the same opinion on the ground that the title was not part of the Act.[27]   The older decisions were to the same effect.[28]   The rule against resorting to the title does not, however, seem to have been invariably observed and the title was used by Sir John Nicholl, M.R., in *Brett* v. *Brett* [29] to settle the question whether the 25 Geo 2, c. 6, applied to all wills and codicils or only to those of real estate.   The title made it quite clear that it was the latter, and there are several other similar cases.[30]   It is, however, now settled as the modern view that the title is an important part of the Act. This change in the law has been effected by the fact that the title is now, as mentioned above, subject to amendment by

---

[26] *Birtwhistle* v *Vardill* (1840), 7 Cl. & F. 895, 929
[27] *Claydon* v *Green* (1868), L R 3 C P. 511, 522
[28] See *per* Lord Coke in *Powlter's Case* (1611), 11 Co Rep. 33; Lord Hardwicke in *Att -Gen* v *Lord Weymouth* (1743), Ambler 22, Lord Cottenham in *Hunter* v. *Nockolds* (1849), 1 M & G 640
[29] (1826), 3 Addams 210
[30] For these and history of the Title, see Craies' Statute Law (4th ed), pp 175—177

both Houses and is not simply inserted at the discretion of the draftsman. So Lord Macnaghten, speaking of the Workmen's Compensation Act after reading the title, said. "It has been said that you cannot resort to the title of an Act for the purpose of construing its provisions. Still as was said by a very sound and careful Judge, 'the title of an Act of Parliament is no part of the law, but it may tend to show the object of the Legislature.' Those were the words of Wightman, J., in *Johnson* v. *Upham* (1859), 2 E. & E. 263, and Chitty, J., observed in *East and West India Docks Co.* v. *Shaw, Savill & Albion Co.* (1888), 39 Ch D. 531, that the title of an Act may be referred to for ascertaining generally the scope of the Act. Surely, if such a reference is ever permitted it must be permissible in a case like this, where Parliament is making a new departure in the interest of labour, and legislating for working men presumably in language that they can understand." [31] So also Lindley, M.R., in *Fielden* v. *Morley Corporation*,[32] referring to the Public Authorities Protection Act, 1893, said: "I read the title advisedly because now and for some years past the title of an Act of Parliament has been part of the Act In old days it used not to be so, and in the old books we are told not to regard it, but now the title is an important part of the Act and is so treated by both Houses of Parliament." And Lord Moulton in *Vacher* v. *London Society of Compositors* [33] said: "The title is part of the Act itself and it is legitimate to use it for the purpose of interpreting the Act as a whole and ascertaining its scope."

It is not certain if the short titles under the Act of 1896 come within these decisions, but there seems no good reason why they should not, as they are pre-eminently part of the Act being enacted in a section thereof It is not of course suggested that if the enacting section is clear it is to be

---

[31] *Fenton* v *Thorley*, [1903] A. C 443, at p 447.
[32] [1899] 1 Ch 1, at p. 3
[33] [1913] A C 107, at p 128

controlled by the title. Like all difficulties in statute construction, the title is only to be prayed in aid where the words or object of some particular provision are not clear.

The Preamble.—As pointed out above, most modern statutes have either a very short preamble or none at all. This was not the old practice, *e g.*, the preamble to 5 Geo. 3, c 26, covers eighteen pages. Lord Thring [34] said: "The proper function of a preamble is to explain certain facts which are necessary to be explained before the enactments contained in the Act can be understood." These long preambles were sometimes very useful, *e.g.*, the Refreshment Houses Act of 1860 made it an offence for a publican to allow bad characters "to assemble and meet together" in his house. The preamble showed that the object of the Act was the suppression of disorderly conduct, not the denial of all entertainment to persons of bad character who might be permitted to enter, take refreshment and stay there a reasonable time for that purpose [35] Lord Alverstone, C.J., in *L.C.C* v. *Bermondsey Bioscope Co* ,[36] said: "I very much regret that the practice of inserting preambles in Acts of Parliament has disappeared; for the preamble often helped to the solution of doubtful points." It will be now clear that a preamble in a statute stands in very much the same position as a recital in a deed; some statutes have both

So if the meaning of an enactment is not clear "the preamble may be resorted to to explain it." [37] The utility of it is to show the intention of the Legislature. "If any doubt arises from the terms employed by the Legislature, it has always been held a safe means of collecting the intention to call in aid the ground and cause of making the statute and

---

[34] Thring, p. 92
[35] *Belasco* v. *Hannant* (1862), 3 B. & S. 13. See, generally, Maxwell (8th ed), pp 40—46, and *per* Farwell, L J , in *Fletcher* v *Birkenhead Corporation*, [1907] 1 K. B. 205, at p 218
[36] [1911] 1 K. B 445
[37] *Per* Buller, J , in *Crespigny* v *Wittenoom* (1792), 4 T R. 793.

to have recourse to the preamble, which, according to Chief Justice Dyer, is ' a key to open the minds of the makers of the Act, and the mischiefs which they intended to redress '." [38]

It is clear that when the enacting words or sections are free from doubt, there is no scope for the preamble to operate at all. If the enacting words or section are doubtful, the preamble may be appealed to in order to fix the scope and intention of the Legislature, and may have the effect of either limiting or extending the words or section as best suits the conclusion drawn from it as to the ambit and object of the legislation in question. Thus 4 & 5 Ph & M c. 8 made the abduction of all girls under sixteen penal, though the preamble only referred to heiresses and other rich girls. The Transportation Act, 1824, recited that transported felons in New South Wales, after obtaining remissions of their sentences, sometimes " by their own industry acquired property in the enjoyment whereof it was expedient to protect them ", and proceeded to enact that every such felon should be entitled to sue for the recovery " of any property, real or personal, acquired since his conviction " The enacting words were held not to be limited by the preamble merely to property acquired by the felon's own exertions, but were to extend to, e.g., property acquired by inheritance [39] So a limited preamble cannot control the enacting words when the latter are plain and free from doubt, and the reverse case also applies. The preamble may be more extensive than the enacting words, as, for example, 3 W. & M. c. 14, s 3, which gave creditors an action of " debt " against the devisees of their debtors. The preamble recited that it was not just that by the contrivance of debtors their creditors should be defrauded of their debts, but that it had often happened that after binding themselves by bonds " or other specialties "

---

[38] *The Sussex Peerage Claim* (1844), 11 Cl & F 143, quoted with approval by Lord Halsbury, L.C., in *Income Tax Commissioners* v. *Pemsel*, [1891] A C. 531, at p. 542.
[39] *Gough* v *Davies* (1856), 25 L. J Ch 677

they had devised their property. The section, in spite of the generality of the preamble, was held not to authorise an action for breach of covenant or for the recovery of money not strictly a "debt" [40]

The House of Lords has dealt with this question in a modern case. In *Powell* v. *Kempton Racecourse Co.*[41] Lord Halsbury said: "Two propositions are quite clear, one that a preamble may afford useful light as to what a statute intends to reach, and the other, that if an enactment is itself clear and unambiguous, no preamble can qualify or cut down the enactment." [42] Also Lord Davey [43]: "But, further, I am of opinion that the argument itself is illegitimate if it is sought thereby to cut down the language of the enactment according to its plain and natural meaning or to restrict the enactment to the particular matter set forth in the preamble. ' Undoubtedly '—I quote from Chitty, L.J.'s, judgment words with which I cordially agree—' it is a settled rule that the preamble cannot be made use of to control the enactments themselves where they are expressed in clear and unambiguous terms.' But the preamble is a key to the statute and affords a clue to the scope of the statute when the words construed by themselves without the aid of the preamble are fairly capable of more than one meaning." It remains to add that under the Statute Law Revision Act of 1890 a number of the preambles to existing Acts have been repealed and their omission from the Revised Edition of the Statutes authorised. The object is economy, but it may be at the expense of obscuring the history and meaning of legislation. The repeal of the preamble in no way affects the construction of the statute [44]

Marginal notes.—Though formerly these formed no part

---

40 *Wilson* v *Knubley* (1806), 7 East 128
41 [1899] A C. 143 *Supra*, p 182
42 *S C*, at p 157
43 S. C , at p. 184
44 *S C*, [1897] 2 Q B. 242, *per* A. L Smith, L.J , at p 269

of the Act, they now appear on the rolls of Parliament, which are the official record of our statutes. At one time Sir George Jessel, M.R., thought they were the subject of motion and amendment in Parliament, but he afterwards withdrew that opinion,[45] and Baggallay, L J , said in *Att.-Gen.* v *Great Eastern Ry.*[46]: "I never knew an amendment set down or discussed upon the marginal notes to a clause The House of Commons never has anything to do with a marginal note." The matter has come up in two recent cases. In *Re Woking U. D. C. (Basingstoke Canal) Act, 1911,*[47] Phillimore, L.J., said: "I am aware of the general rule of law as to marginal notes at all events in general Acts of Parliament, but that rule is founded, as will be seen on reference to the cases, upon the principle that these notes are inserted not by Parliament or under the authority of Parliament, but by irresponsible persons. Where, however, in section 10 of this Act, and in some other recent local and personal acts which have come under my cognisance, the marginal notes are mentioned as already existing and established, it may well be that they do form part of the Act of Parliament." And more recently Lord Hanworth, M.R., in *Nixon* v. *Att.-Gen.,*[48] referring to the Superannuation Act of 1859, said. "The marginal notes of section 3 refer to 'existing rights', and of section 12 to 'right'. It was contended that these catch words could be used to explain the meaning of sections upon which they appear. For my part I cannot allow this. As explained by Baggallay, L.J., in *Att -Gen.* v. *Great Eastern Ry.* (*supra*) marginal notes are not part of an Act of Parliament The Houses of Parliament have nothing to do with them, and I agree with the learned Lords Justices in that case that the Courts cannot look at them." This seems to be the last word on the subject, and marginal

---

[45] In *Venour* v *Sellon* (1876), 2 Ch D 525, withdrawn in *Sutton* v *Sutton* (1882), 22 Ch D 511, 513.

[46] (1879), 11 Ch D 449, *Claydon* v *Green* (1868), L R 3 C P. 511

[47] [1914] 1 Ch 300, at p 322

[48] [1930] 1 Ch 566, at p 593

notes, at least in a general Act of Parliament, afford no aid to its construction

Headings.—These are in some modern statutes prefixed to sections or sets of sections and are regarded as preambles to those sections. This is stated in Maxwell [49] and was quoted with approval by Farwell, L.J., in *Fletcher* v. *Birkenhead Corporation,* [50] who added: " Taking the doctrine so expressed as a guide in such a case I cannot read prefatory words of this kind so as to strike out plain words, but only for the purpose of explaining doubtful expressions in the body of the section " The same rule, in fact, as applies to preambles, as stated above. So Lord Darling in delivering the judgment of the Judicial Committee in *Martins* v. *Fowler* [51] said " It is clear that such headings as those referred to [headings to sections] may be regarded as preambles to the provisions following them. This is so stated in Maxwell on Interpretation of Statutes and has received judicial authority from Farwell, L.J., in *Fletcher* v. *Birkenhead Corpn.* [52] and also from the Privy Council in *Union Steamship Co. of New Zealand* v *Melbourne Harbour Trust Commissioners,* [53] to mention no others." Avory, J., in *R.* v. *Hare,* [54] expressed a decided opinion against the admission of headings and notes. He said: " Headings of sections and marginal notes form no part of the statute. They are not voted on or passed by Parliament but are inserted after the Bill has become law. Headnotes cannot control the plain meaning of the words of the enactment, though they may, in some cases, be looked upon in the light of preambles if there is any ambiguity in the meaning of the sections on which they throw light."

---

[49] 8th ed., p 46
[50] [1907] 1 K B 205, at p. 218.
[51] [1926] A C. 746 (P C.).
[52] *Supra*
[53] (1884), 9 App. Cas 365
[54] [1934] 1 K B 354

Punctuation.—Punctuation is regarded as a kind of *contemporanea expositio* (see *infra*, p. 236) but not as forming part of the statute itself. Lord Esher, M.R., said [55]: " In an Act of Parliament there are no such things as brackets any more than there are such things as stops " It seems, however, that in the vellum copies which have been printed since 1850 there are some cases of punctuation. In *Barrow* v *Wadkin* [55a] a question as to who are natural-born subjects arose under section 3 of 13 Geo. 3, c. 21 of 1773. The crucial words were " aliens duties customs and impositions ". Sir John Romilly, M.R., by whom the case was heard, referred to the 1774 edition of the statutes, which read " aliens, duties, customs and impositions ", but another edition read " aliens' duties, customs and impositions ". On the general construction of the statute, the latter was adopted as expressing the intention. Sir John Romilly had inspected the Parliament Roll, which was in his keeping as Master of the Rolls, and found it contained no punctuation. Punctuation is avoided, if possible, as it gives rise to difficulties, particularly with regard to amendments made in the passage of a bill through Parliament, when the wording may be materially altered, but sometimes the punctuation is not altered in accordance with the amendments made.

Rules.—These, when made under the authority of an Act and after the commencement of the Interpretation Act, 1889 (*i.e*, on and after January 1, 1890), are by section 31 of that Act to have the same meanings with respect to expressions used therein as in the Act of Parliament under which they are made, unless a contrary intention appears. Technically these are external aids to construction and should perhaps have been noticed later, but as these rules are often directed to be read as part of the Act, they are practically incorporated with it. These rules may therefore be called in to aid the construction of any doubtful expressions in the

[55] *Duke of Devonshire* v *O'Connor* (1890), 24 Q. B D 468.
[55a] (1857), 24 Beav. 327.

Act itself. As was said by the Court of Appeal in *Ex p. Wier*,[56] "recourse may also be had to rules which have been made under the authority of the Act, if the construction of the Act is doubtful on any point, and if we find in the rules that any particular construction has been put on the Act, it is our duty to adopt and follow that construction." In the case of a conflict between the rules and the sections of the Act, and reconciliation is impossible, the subordinate provision must give way, and the rules would be regarded as subordinate to the section, especially as the rules may themselves be called in question as being *ultra vires* the Act, which itself cannot of course be open to the same objection.[57]

Interpretation clauses.—In many modern Acts there is an interpretation clause, part of the Act which provides that certain words used in the Act shall have certain meanings For instance, in the Law of Property Act, 1925, section 205 contains thirty-one clauses assigning meanings to words and expressions used in the Act. In some of these clauses it will be noticed that " mean " is used; *e.g.*, clause (xv): " ' Minister ' means the Minister of Agriculture and Fisheries." In others the word " include " is employed; *e g.*, clause (xxiii): " ' Rent ' includes a rent service or a rentcharge, or other rent ", etc. In the former the definition is taken to be explanatory and therefore restrictive; in the latter, the definition is extensive. The practice, which is modern, of inserting these interpretation clauses has not escaped frequent judicial censure. Lord Blackburn approved of the " objection of the old school of draftsmen to the introduction of interpretation clauses ",[58] and Cockburn, C.J., said seventy-four years ago: " I hope the time will come when we shall see no more of interpretation clauses, for they frequently lead to confusion."[59] That time

---

[56] (1871), 6 App. Cas 879, *per* James and Mellish, L JJ. Cf *Re Andrew* (1876), 1 Ch D 358
[57] See further, p. 280, *infra*
[58] In *Mayor, etc., of Portsmouth* v *Smith* (1885), 10 App Cas. 364, at p. 374.
[59] *Wakefield* v *West Riding, etc., Ry.* (1865), 6 B. & S. 801.

has not yet come. The chief fault in these clauses is that frequently the draftsman attempts to legislate under guise of a definition—as, for instance, in " saying that things are what they are not " by saying that " a dwelling-house " shall mean " a part of a dwelling-house ".[60] The ordinary meaning of a word is not taken away by an interpretation clause. In discussing the meaning of " street " in section 157 of the Public Health Act, 1875, Lord Selborne said [61]: " An interpretation clause of this kind is not meant to prevent the word receiving its ordinary, popular and natural sense whenever that would be properly applicable, but to enable the word as used in the Act when there is nothing in the context or the subject-matter to the contrary, to be applied to some things to which it would not ordinarily be applicable." So where the word " street " was again discussed in *Nutter* v. *Accrington Local Board* [62] and the interpretation clause stated that it should " apply to and include any highway not being a turnpike road ", Cotton, L.J., said: " The interpretation clause is not retroactive. It does not say that the word ' street ' shall be confined to any highway not being a turnpike road . . . (and after quoting the clause) That is enlarging, not restricting, the meaning of ' street '; that is to say, that which, independently of the Act of Parliament, in ordinary language is properly a street, does not cease to be so because it is part of a turnpike road." So an interpretation clause is not necessarily to be applied every time a word defined in it occurs in the Act. The clause in truth declares what the meaning is to be or what may be included in it where the circumstances require that it should bear that meaning or have that ambit. " An interpretation clause ", said Lush, J,[63] " should be used for the purpose of interpreting

---

[60] *Per* Esher, M.R , in *Bradley* v. *Baylis* (1881), 8 Q B D 210, at p 230
[61] In *Robinson* v. *Barton-Eccles Local Board* (1883), 8 App Cas 798, at p. 801, referring to s 4, the interpretation clause in the Public Health Act, 1875
[62] (1879), 4 Q B D 375, at p 384.
[63] *R.* v. *Pearce* (1880), 5 Q B D. 386, at p. 389

words which are ambiguous or equivocal and not so as to
disturb the meaning of such as are plain." So the words
" any person " in the Solicitors Act were held not to include
a body corporate, but only such person as could become a
solicitor, in spite of section 2 of the Interpretation Act, which
says that " person " shall include a body corporate " unless
a contrary intention appears ".[64]

Provisoes.—These are clauses of exception or qualification
in an Act, excepting something out of, or qualifying something
in, the enactment which, but for the proviso, would be within
it. These can generally be identified by the words " Provided
that "—or " this section does not apply to ", etc. Unless
of necessity, a proviso is never construed as enlarging the
scope of the enacting words. It must be construed with
reference to the preceding parts of the clause to which it is
appended [65] and as subordinate to the main clauses of the Act
Though framed as a proviso, such a clause may exceptionally
have the effect of a substantive enactment,[66] though, as
Lush, J., said in *Mullins* v. *Treasurer of Surrey*,[67] " the
natural presumption is that, but for the proviso, the enacting
part of the section would have included the subject-matter
of the proviso ". Two modern cases may be cited as to this.
In *West Derby Union* v. *Metropolitan Life Assurance Co.*,[68]
Lord Watson said. " I am perfectly clear that if the language
of the enacting part of the statute does not contain the provisions which are said to occur in it, you cannot derive those
provisions by implication from a proviso. . . . I think your
Lordships would be adopting a very dangerous and certainly
unusual course if you were to import legislation from a proviso
wholesale into the body of the statute, although I perfectly
admit that there may be and are many cases in which the

[64] *Law Society* v *United Service Bureau*, [1934] 1 K. B 343 Cf.
Chesterman v *Federal Commissioner of Taxation*, [1926] A C. 128
[65] *Ex p Partington* (1844), 6 Q. B 649
[66] *E g*, *Rhondda U. D C* v. *Taff Vale Ry*, [1909] A. C. 253, 258
[67] (1880), 5 Q. B D 173
[68] [1897] A C 647, at p. 652

terms of an intelligible proviso may throw considerable light on the ambiguous import of the statutory words." Moulton, L.J., voices a different warning in *R.* v. *Dibdin* [69] when he said, in considering the meaning of section 1 of the proviso to section 1 of the Deceased Wife's Sister's Marriage Act, 1907: "The fallacy of the proposed method of interpretation is not far to seek. It sins against the fundamental rule of construction that a proviso must be considered with relation to the principal matter to which it stands as a proviso. The Courts . have frequently pointed out this fallacy and have refused to be led astray by arguments such as those which have been addressed to us, which depend solely on taking words absolutely in their strict literal sense, disregarding the fundamental consideration that they appear in a proviso."

Schedules.—To many Acts of Parliament schedules are appended These may be merely forms or examples of the way in which an enactment is intended to be carried out in practice or may contain provisions important in themselves. For instance, section 39 of the Law of Property Act, 1925, enacts that "for the purpose of effecting the transition from the law existing prior to the commencement of the Law of Property Act, 1922, to the law enacted by that Act (as amended) the provisions set out in the First Schedule to this Act shall have effect" for certain purposes set forth in the section. It should perhaps be stated that the Act of 1925 almost entirely repeals *inter alia* Part I of the Act of 1922. The First Schedule accordingly contains practically an Act of Parliament in itself The other Schedules contain the ordinary matters of Schedules—namely, forms and examples. As Brett, L J , said [70]. "A schedule in an Act is a mere question of drafting, a mere question of words The schedule is as much part of the statute and is as much an enactment as any other part." If there is any contradiction the earlier

[69] [1910] P 57, at p 125
[70] In *Att -Gen.* v *Lamplough* (1878), 3 Ex D 214, at p. 229.

enacting clause would prevail, for " it would be quite contrary to the recognised principles upon which Courts of law construe Acts of Parliament to .   restrain the operation of an enactment by reference to the words of a mere form given for convenience sake in a schedule ".[71]   It has also been held that the words in a schedule cannot be construed so as to enlarge the words in a private Act.[72]   Sometimes the forms set out in Schedules are imperative and must be strictly followed and employed in instruments under the Acts to which they relate.   The best known example is the form prescribed in the Schedule to the Bills of Sale (1878) Amendment Act, 1882.   A bill of sale need not be " a verbal and literal transcript of the statutory form ",[73] but must not materially depart therefrom whether or not the departure alters the legal effect.   The Merchant Shipping Act, 1894, ss. 31 and 320, refers to certain compulsory forms to be employed in mortgages and forms of ticket for steerage passengers

Illustrations —It is not the general practice to append illustrations to sections of British Acts of Parliament.   Indian and Colonial Acts are, however, full of them.   The Indian Contract Act, Indian Penal Code, Indian Evidence Act, Transfer of Property Act and Specific Relief Act are examples. In speaking of the construction of the Straits Settlement Ordinance (III of 1893), which generally corresponds to the Indian Evidence Act, Lord Shaw, giving the judgment of the Judicial Committee, said: " Their Lordships are of opinion that in the construction of the Evidence Ordinance it is the duty of a Court of law to accept, if it can be done, the illustrations given as being both of relevance and value in the construction of the text.   The illustrations should in no case be rejected because they do not square with ideas possibly

71 *Per* Lord Penzance in *Dean* v. *Green* (1882), 8 P. D. 79, at p. 89.   Cf. also *per* Lord Denman in *R* v *Baines* (1840), 12 A & E 210, at p 226.
72 *Laird* v. *Trustees of Clyde Navigation* (1879), 6 Rettie (Sc.) 756, 785.
73 *Per* Lord Macnaghten in *Thomas* v. *Kelly* (1888), 13 App. Cas. 506, at p 520   Cf *Burchell* v. *Thompson*, [1920] 2 K B. 80, and Chitty, Contracts (19th ed), pp. 926-7, and the cases there cited.

derived from another system of jurisprudence as to the law with which they or the sections deal, and it would require a very special case to warrant their rejection on the ground of their assumed repugnancy to the sections themselves. It would be the very last resort of construction to make any such assumption. The great usefulness of the illustrations, which have, although not part of the sections, been expressly furnished by the Legislature as helpful in the working and application of the statute, should not be thus impaired." [74]

(ii) *External.*—(a) *Dictionaries.*—These are not generally resorted to as a means of elucidating the construction of statutes, and their use has sometimes been deprecated. For instance, in *Midland Ry.* v. *Robinson* the question arose as to the meaning of the word " mine ". In the House of Lords, Lord Herschell cited Dr. Johnson's definition, but Lord Macnaghten said: " It seems to me that on such a point the opinions of such Judges as Kindersley, V.-C., Turner, L.J., and Sir George Jessel are probably a safer guide than any definitions or illustrations to be found in dictionaries." [1] But dictionaries may afford some help, for, as Lord Coleridge said in *R.* v. *Peters* [2]: " I am quite aware that dictionaries are not to be taken as authoritative exponents of the meanings of words used in Acts of Parliament, but it is a well-known rule of Courts of law that words should be taken to be used in their ordinary sense, and we are therefore sent for instruction to these books." Cozens-Hardy, M.R., said [3]. " It is for the Court to interpret the statute as best it may. In so doing the Court may no doubt assist themselves in the discharge of their duty by any literary help they can find, including of course the consultation of standard authors and reference to well-known and

---

[74] *Mahomed Syedol Ariffin* v *Yeoh Ooi Gark*, L R. 43 I A 256, at p. 263; [1916] 2 A. C 575.

[1] (1889), 15 App Cas. 19, at p 34

[2] (1886), 16 Q. B D 636, at p 641.

[3] *Camden (Marquis)* v. *I. R. C* , [1914] 1 K. B 641, at p 647.

authoritative dictionaries." So books of authority may be referred to in order to show the accepted meaning of terms used at the time the statute was passed. Thus "political crime" was defined after consulting Mill and Stephen as to its meaning [4]; so was "direct taxation" [5] in the British North America Act of 1867, by reference to standard works on political economy.

(b) *Text-books.*—A text-writer of established repute, as, for example, Lord Coke, may have a great influence on the construction of a statute, especially if the statute contain no interpretation clause of its own. "Although the text-books do not make law, they show more or less whether a principle has been generally accepted" [6] So Tindal, C.J., speaking of the statute 16 Edw. 1, c. 31, said: "We must look, however, not only at the statute, but to the commentary of Lord Coke, which has been uncontradicted to the present day. . . . When we see the authority of so great a writer not only uncontradicted but adopted in all the digests and text-books, we can scarcely err if we adhere to his opinion." [7] So in *Mayor, etc. of Newcastle v. Att.-Gen.* [8] the House of Lords unanimously adopted Lord Coke's exposition of a clause in the 39 Eliz. c. 3; and in *R. v. Ritson,* [9] in discussing the meaning of "forge" in section 20 of the Forgery Act, 1861, Kelly, C.B., said. "There is no definition of the word 'forgery' in the statute on which this indictment is framed, but the offence has been defined by very learned authors, and we find among them no conflict of authority." The definition in the text-books was adopted by the Court. The practice of eminent conveyancers may also influence construction. James, L J., once described this as "to be looked upon as part

---

[4] *Re Castioni,* [1891] 1 Q B 149.
[5] *Bank of Toronto v Lambe* (1887), 12 App. Cas 575, at p 581
[6] Per Jessel, M R., in *Henty v Wrey* (1882), 21 Ch D 332, at p 348
[7] In *Strother v Hutchinson* (1837), 4 Bing. N. C. 83
[8] (1845), 12 Cl. & F. 402.
[9] (1869), L R 1 C C. R. 200. Cf. Cozens-Hardy, M.R , in *Camden (Marquis) v I R C , supra.*

of the common law ",[10] and in *Bassett* v. *Bassett*[11] Lord Hardwicke relied on the practice of conveyancers as to the construction of 10 Will. 3, c. 22. If a construction has become a settled practice of conveyancers in, *e g.*, Scotland or a British possession, this construction will not be rejected because it does not coincide with the prevailing ideas or conceptions in this country.[12]

(*c*) *Intention of the framer.*—This has already been partially dealt with under the general rules [13] and the danger of guessing at the intention pointed out. In *London County Council* v. *Aylesbury Dairy Co*[14] Wright, J., spoke as follows: " But the mere fact that it might have been better to extend the section to those cases and that one can apparently gather that such an intention was probable is not enough to justify us in putting a construction upon the section which would necessitate reading into it words which the appellants' counsel has invited us to read in It is clear to my mind that we should, as the Court of Queen's Bench said in *Underhill* v. *Longridge*,[15] " be taking upon ourselves the office of the Legislature. . I am the more strongly driven to this conclusion because the proceeding here is penal, involving penal consequences, and without making the alteration in section 14 which we are asked to make, it could not be prosecuted at all." And speaking of the Moneylenders Act, 1900, Farwell, L.J , said [16]: " These considerations (*i e.*, the evil to be stamped out) are germane to the question of the meaning of the Act (*Heydon's Case*), but it is obvious that the paramount intention to prevent oppression and to forge fetters to be imposed on moneylenders are so vague and general that the Courts have little, if anything, to guide them beyond

[10] In *Re Ford and Hill* (1879), 10 Ch D. 365, at p. 370.
[11] (1744), 3 Atk. 206, 208
[12] *Natal Bank* v. *Rood*, [1910] A C. 570
[13] See p 164, *supra*
[14] [1898] 1 Q B 106
[15] (1859), 29 L J M C. 65
[16] *Sadler* v. *Whiteman*, [1910] 1 K. B 868, at p 886

the words of the Act read literally: in many cases one can say that the Legislature never intended such and such a result to follow, but it is difficult to draw any such conclusions from an Act of this nature."

(d) *Reports of Royal Commissions.*—In the recent case of *Assam Railways and Trading Co., Ltd.* v. *C I. R.,*[17] learned counsel proposed to cite the report of the Royal Commissioners on Income Tax in 1920 to interpret the meaning of section 20 of the Finance Act, 1920. Lord Wright, in giving the judgment of the Judicial Committee, spoke as follows[18]: " It is clear that the language of a minister of the Crown in proposing in Parliament a measure which eventually becomes law is inadmissible and the report of commissioners is even more removed from value as evidence of intention, because it does not follow that their recommendations were accepted." Later, the learned Lord referred to the *Solio Case,*[19] where Lord Halsbury, in his opinion in the House of Lords, had referred to the report of a royal commission, and said: "'The Lord Chancellor was there referring to the report of a commission that had sat to enquire into the working of the earlier Act, which had been superseded by the Act actually being construed by the House, but Lord Halsbury refers to the report not directly to ascertain the intention of the words used in the Act as he says, ' no more accurate source of information as to what was the evil or defect which the Act of Parliament now under construction was intended to remedy could be imagined than the report of that commission '. Lord Halsbury, it is clear, was treating the report as extraneous matter to show what were the surrounding circumstances[20] with reference to which the words were used, so

---

[17] [1935] A C. 445 (P C)
[18] S C, p 458
[19] *Eastman Photographic Co* v *Comptroller of Patents,* [1898] A C. 571, at p 575
[20] Cf Fletcher Moulton, L J, in *Macmillan* v *Dent,* [1907] 1 Ch 101, at p. 120, quoted *infra,* p. 222

that the case came within the principle stated by Lord Langdale " (in the case of *Gorham* v. *Bishop of Exeter*[21]). So that neither debates on the Bill or the history of the changes it underwent nor reports of commissions are admissible as showing intention, though according to Lord Wright the latter may be evidence of surrounding circumstances under which the Act was passed. Speeches in Parliament have in the past sometimes been admitted in evidence, as, *e.g.*, in *R.* v. *Bishop of Oxford*,[22] and *S. E. Ry.* v. *Railway Commissioners*.[23] The former was disapproved in *Julius* v. *Bishop of Oxford*,[24] and these cases are opposed to the opinion of Willes, J.,[25] and to the decisions in *R.* v. *Hertford College*[26] and *Administrator General of Bengal* v. *Prem Lal Mullick*[27] and to the judgment set out above.

(*e*) *Parliamentary history of the Act* —This corresponds to the " surrounding circumstances " which may be prayed in aid in construing deeds and other instruments as we previously saw. It is to some extent permitted by the rules in *Heydon's Case* (p. 197, *supra*), and is important where, as very often happens, it is impossible to ascertain the meaning of the Act or a section of it from the wording of the enactment alone. How far is it permissible to have recourse to outside sources for the purpose of discovering this meaning? Some have been already indicated. In *Keates* v. *Lewis Merthyr Consolidated Collieries*, [1911] A C 641, at p 642, Lord Atkinson said: " In the construction of a statute it is of course at all times and under all circumstances permissible to have regard to the state of things existing at the time the statute was passed and to the evils which, as appears from its provisions, it was designed to remedy." And Lord Lindley in *Murray*

---

[21] (1850), 5 Ex 630
[22] (1879), 4 Q. B. D. 525, Bramwell and Baggallay, L.JJ
[23] (1880), 5 Q B D. 217, 236, Cockburn, C J.
[24] (1880), 5 App Cas 214, Earls Cairns and Selborne
[25] In *Millar* v *Taylor* (1769), 4 Burr 2303, 2332.
[26] (1878), 3 Q. B. D 693, 707.
[27] (1895), L. R. 22 I. A. 107.

v. *I. R. C.*, [1918] A. C. 541, 549, said: " I think reasons can be conceived why the Legislature should have desired to impose the tax in this way ", and proceeded to state the reasons In this section we shall endeavour to explain how the construction may be influenced by the state of the law both *before* and *after* the date of the statute in question. As Lord Blackburn said [28]: " In all cases the object is to see what is the intention expressed by the words used. But from the imperfection of language it is impossible to know what that intention is without inquiring further and seeing what the circumstances were with reference to which the words were used and what was the object appearing from those circumstances which the person using them had in view. For the meaning of words varies according to the circumstances with respect to which they are used " And in *Eastman Photographic Co.* v. *Comptroller-General of Patents* [29] Lord Halsbury said: " To construe the statute now in question it is not only legitimate but highly convenient to refer both to the former Act and to the ascertained evils to which the former Act had given rise, and to the later Act which provided the remedy." The Legislature is presumed to know the existing state of the law,[30] hence the constant practice of the Courts to examine the pre-existing state of the law to discover the intention of the superimposed legislation. By this means it may be possible to discover the intention of the later legislation. A good example of this method is disclosed in *The Claim of the Viscountess Rhondda* [31] to be summoned to the House of Lords. Very shortly put, the Viscountess contended that, now that the sexes are upon a footing of equality, the Sex Disqualification Act of 1919 entitled her to be summoned. The law was examined at great length by Lord Birkenhead sitting on the Committee of Privileges, and he showed that

---

[28] *River Wear Commissioners* v *Adamson* (1877), 2 App Cas. 743
[29] [1898] A C 571, at p 575
[30] *Per* Lord Blackburn in *Young* v *Mayor, etc , of Leamington* (1883), 8 App Cas 517, at p 526
[31] [1922] 2 A C 339.

a peeress as such had no right at common law to a summons, not merely a right she was unable to exercise by reason of her sex disqualification. Parliament could not have intended to have effected such a radical change in our constitution by a side-wind as it were, and this could not have been within its contemplation in passing the Act of 1919. The legal history of the matter was expressly stated by Lord Birkenhead to be referred to for the purpose of aiding the interpretation of the Act of 1919, as being authorised by the doctrine of *Stradling* v *Morgan*.[32] It will have been gathered that the ideal method of interpretation is the language of the statute itself, uncontrolled by any outside influences, and this is the case where the words are said to be plain and unambiguous. Like all aids to construction, history is only to be invoked where the words are not plain. Baron Alderson said: " We do not construe Acts of Parliament with reference to history ",[33] and Farwell, L.J.[34]. " The mischief sought to be cured by the Act of Parliament must be sought in the Act itself. Although it may perhaps be legitimate to call history in aid to show what facts existed to bring about a statute, the inferences to be drawn therefrom are exceedingly slight." It does not appear, however, that either the learned Baron or the learned Lord Justice intended their remarks to apply to the parliamentary history of a statute, but only to outside influences which may have led to the introduction of the measure. In *Read* v. *Bishop of Lincoln*[35] Lord Halsbury said that the terms of the Rubric could only be ascertained when considered in relation to the circumstances existing when they were framed, and that works on ecclesiastical history and practices might properly be consulted. In the well-known case of *Bank of England* v. *Vagliano*,[36] Lord Herschell said · " I think the proper course is in the first instance to

---

[32] (1560), 1 Plowden 209, and cf Turner, L J , in *Hawkins* v *Gathercole* (1855), 6 De G M & G 1, 22

[33] In *Gorham* v *Bishop of Exeter* (1850), 5 Ex 630, at p 667.

[34] In *R* v. *West Riding C C* , [1906] 2 K B 670

[35] [1892] A C 644, 652, 653, 665.   [36] [1891] A C 107, at p 144.

examine the language of the statute and ask what is its natural meaning uninfluenced by any considerations derived from the previous state of the law and not to start with enquiring how the law previously stood and then, assuming that it was probably intended to leave it unaltered, to see if the words of the enactment will bear an interpretation in conformity with this view.   . I am of course far from asserting that resort may never be had to the previous state of the law for the purpose of aiding in the construction of the provisions of the code   If for example such a provision be of doubtful import, such resort will be perfectly legitimate." With reference to the earlier part of his Lordship's remarks, as quoted, it should be noted that he was referring to a consolidating statute, viz., the Bills of Exchange Act, 1882. We shall return to the subject later.

In *Macmillan* v. *Dent*,[37] a question of copyright, Fletcher Moulton, L.J., said: " In interpreting an Act of Parliament you are entitled and in many cases bound, to look at the state of the law at the date of the passing of the Act—not only the common law but the law as it then stood under previous statutes—in order properly to interpret the statute in question. These may be considered to form part of the surrounding circumstances under which the Legislature passed it and in the case of a statute, just as in the case of any other document, you are entitled to look at the surrounding circumstances at the date of its coming into existence, though the extent to which you are allowed to use them in the construction of the document is a wholly different question." So Lord Herschell, in considering the effect of the Admiralty Jurisdiction Acts of 1868 and 1869, detailed the history of the Acts and came to the conclusion that the Admiralty Court had jurisdiction over the claim in question at the time they were passed [38] And in *Re Mayfair Property Co* [39] Lindley, M R.,

---

37 [1907] 1 Ch. 101, at p 120.
38 *Mersey Docks and Harbour Board* v. *Turner*, [1893] A C 468.
39 [1898] 2 Ch. 28, at p. 35.

said: "In order properly to interpret any statute it is as necessary now as it was when Lord Coke reported *Heydon's Case*, to consider how the law stood when the statute to be construed was passed, what the mischief was for which the old law did not provide, and the remedy provided by the statute to cure that mischief."

(i) *Earlier Acts.*—What assistance is it permissible to draw from Acts prior to the date of the Act under construction? No such assistance is to be derived from prior Acts proceeding on different lines and relating to a different subject-matter, and the Court will also decline to regard judicial decisions under such differing Acts. In *Inland Revenue Commissioners* v. *Forrest*,[40] Lord Macnaghten, in discussing the wording of two revenue Acts, said: "The two Acts differ widely in their scope; and even if they happen to deal with the same subject their wording is not the same. It was argued, indeed, that the language was 'practically identical'; but that expression, to my mind, involves an admission that the language is different." So in *Re Lord Gerard's Settled Estates*[41] the Court of Appeal was of opinion that the Settled Land Acts formed a code applicable to the subject-matter with which they dealt, and that a decision on the Lands Clauses Act, 1845, could not be used to aid the interpretation of those Acts, as the Act of 1845 was passed with a different object and was concerned with a different subject-matter. It is, therefore, laid down that in order to be available as a guide the prior Statute must be *in pari materia*—have relation to the same subject-matter as the Act under discussion

So we have to consider when is a statute said to be *in pari materia* with another? It is obviously wrong to say that a Customs Act stands in this relation, without more, to an Income Tax Act because they are both concerned with

[40] (1890), 15 App Cas 334, 353
[41] [1893] 3 Ch 252 Cf Lord Loreburn, L C , in *Kydd* v *Liverpool Watch Committee*, [1908] A. C 327, at p 330

taxes or levies. " Par " means not " similar " or " like "
but " identical " or " the same ". The answer seems to
be: Can the statutes alleged to be *in pari materia* with
the statute in question fairly be said to form one system
of legislation with it? A learned American Judge has
said that statutes are *in pari materia* which relate to
the same person or thing, or to the same class of persons
or things. When statutes are thus connected or form
a code (as in the case of a consolidation Act) they are
" to be taken together as forming one system and as interpreting and enforcing each other ".[42] Somewhat earlier Lord
Mansfield, in *R. v Loxdale*,[43] had said: " Where there are
different statutes *in pari materia*, though made at different
times, or even expired and not referring to one another, they
shall be taken together and construed together as one system
and as explanatory of each other " The fact that this principle of Lord Mansfield's has been adopted by the Court of
Appeal in 1907 [43a] probably impliedly overrules the *dictum* of
Lord Russell, C J., in *R. v. Titterton* [44] that " it is proper to
refer to earlier Acts *in pari materia* only where there is an
ambiguity "; though it may be said that where the words of
a statute are perfectly clear and unambiguous there is no
need of recourse to other aids, whether those aids are statutes
in pari materia or anything else.[45] In the case before Lord
Mansfield, he held that the Acts concerning church leases,
those concerning bankrupts, and all statutes providing for the
poor are to be considered as forming one system. All statutes
as to certificates to be taken out by solicitors form a system,[46]

---

[42] *Palmer's Case* (1784), 1 Leach C. C (4th ed), 355
[43] (1758), 1 Burr 445, at p 447 Cf. *Ex p. Copeland* (1853), 22 L J
Bank 21, and *per* Farwell, L J., in *Goldsmiths Co* v. *Wyatt* (1907), 76
L J K B 161, at p 169, *Victoria City* v *Bishop of Vancouver*, [1921] 2
A C 384 Cf the principle applied in *Stoomvaart Maatschappy Nederland*
v. *P. & O. S N Co* (1882), 7 App Cas 795, 816, *per* Lord Blackburn.
[43a] In *Macmillan* v *Dent, supra*, p 222   [44] [1895] 2 Q B. 67.
[45] Cf *per* Scott, L J , in *Croxford* v *Universal Insurance Co* , [1936]
2 K B 253, at p 281, *supra*, p. 163
[46] *Davis* v *Edmondson* (1803), 3 B & P 382

as also the Railways Act, 1873, and Order LV of the Supreme Court of Judicature Act, 1875 (see R. S. C, Order LXV) were *in pari materia* in that they both gave power to judicial tribunals to deal with the question of costs [47]

Consolidating Acts are Acts to comprehend in one statute the provisions contained in a number of statutes and which codify the law on some subject as far as they go, as, for instance, the Bills of Exchange Act, 1882. By these Acts a number of prior statutes are usually repealed but reproduced in substance, it being, as we shall see, a presumption that it is not the intention of the Legislature to alter the law by a consolidating Act unless that intention plainly appears.[48] These prior statutes, though repealed, are regarded as *in pari materia* with the consolidating Act and the judicial decisions on them as applicable to substantially the same provisions contained in the repealing Act. So in *Mitchell* v. *Simpson*[49] Lord Esher, M.R., speaking of the Sheriffs Act, 1887, said: "The Act of 1887 is a consolidation Act and the provision in question is in substantially the same terms as that of the Act of Geo. 2 and therefore in order to determine the meaning of the provision, we must consider to what the Act of Geo. 2 was applicable." The same view was adopted by the House of Lords in the well-known case of *Smith* v. *Baker*,[50] where the construction of a section of the County Courts Act, 1888, was (*inter alia*) in question. Lord Watson referred to *Clarkson* v. *Musgrave*,[51] a decision on the repealed County Courts Act of 1875, holding that decision equally applicable to the section of the 1888 Act Eight years previously, however, Lord Watson had expressed the opinion[52] that it was an extremely hazardous procedure "to refer to provisions which

[47] *Re Foster* (1881), 8 Q B D 515, 522.
[48] Cf *Swan* v. *Pure Ice Co*, [1935] 2 K B. 265, 274.
[49] (1890), 25 Q. B. D. 183, at p. 188
[50] [1891] A. C 325, at p. 349
[51] (1881), 9 Q B. D. 386
[52] In *Bradlaugh* v *Clarke* (1883), 8 App. Cas. 354, at p. 380

have been absolutely repealed in order to ascertain what the Legislature intended to enact in their room and stead ''.

The rule must, therefore, be applied carefully, and it can probably only be safely so applied where the provisions of the repealed Act are substantially reproduced in the consolidating statute. Lord Watson again in 1895, in giving the judgment of the Judicial Committee on an appeal from India,[53] said: ''The respondent maintained the singular proposition that, in dealing with a consolidating statute, each enactment must be traced to its original source, and, when that is discovered, must be construed according to the state of circumstances which existed when it first became law. The proposition has neither reason nor authority to recommend it. The very object of consolidation is to collect the statutory law bearing upon a particular subject, and to bring it down to date, in order that it may form a useful code applicable to the circumstances existing at the time when the consolidating Act was passed.'' But the fact that the Act in question is a codification of the pre-existing law does not, of course, enable the Court to brush aside any provision in it which alters that law. ''The object and intent of the statute of 1893 [the Sale of Goods Act] was no doubt simply to codify the unwritten law applicable to the sale of goods; but in so far as there is an express enactment, that alone must be looked at and must govern the rights of the parties even though the section may have to some extent altered the prior common law.''[54] In the recent case of *Notts County Council* v *Middlesex County Council*,[55] section 89 of the Poor Law Act, 1930, was in question. The Court pointed out that the Act of 1930 was a consolidating Act and there was no reason for thinking that there was any intention to change the previous law. ''It could not be altered without plain

[53] *Administrator-General of Bengal* v. *Prem Lal Mullick* (1895), L R. 22 I A. 107, at p. 116

[54] *Per* Cozens-Hardy, M R., in *Bristol Tramways* v *Fiat Motors*, [1910] 2 K B 831.

[55] [1936] 1 K. B. 141, *per* Lord Hewart, C J., at p 145.

words, and these words, so far from being plain in favour of the view that an alteration was made, seem to me plainly to show that no alteration was intended "

Some statutes contain clauses providing that the statute in which they are contained shall be read *with* another and prior statute as if the two were a single Act. For instance, the Merchant Shipping Act, 1906, is to be read as one with the Merchant Shipping Act, 1894 (see *Charing Cross Electric Supply Co.* v. *London Hydraulic Power Co.*, [1914] 3 K. B. 772). The effect of such a provision is that the Court must construe each and every part of each Act as if the two Acts were one Act. If it is found on examination that there is some clear discrepancy between the provisions of the two Acts, then it will be necessary to hold that the later Act has modified something to be found in the earlier.[56] So where the Weights and Measures Act, 1889, was to be read with the Sale of Food (Weights and Measures) Act of 1926, and coal had been delivered in less quantity than as described on the weight ticket, and no notice had been served upon or sent to the appellant in accordance with section 12 (6) of the latter Act, it was held that the condition precedent to action had not been fulfilled. There was found to be no discrepancy between the two Acts, and that being so, every part of each of them was to be construed as if contained in one Act [57] By section 13 of the Municipal Elections Act, 1875, it was provided that " This Act, so far as is consistent with the tenor thereof, shall be construed as one with the Municipal Corporations Act, 1835, and the Acts amending it." By section 142 of the Act of 1835 a provision was made for amending inaccuracies. It was argued that this provision should be applied to inaccuracies in nomination papers under the later Act. The argument was rejected, Lord Coleridge, C.J., saying [58]: " These terms (*i e.*,

[56] See *per* Lord Selborne in *Canada Southern Ry.* v. *International Bridge Co* (1883), 8 App Cas 723, 727.
[57] *Phillips* v *Parnaby*, [1934] 2 K. B 299 Cf. *Norris* v *Barnes* (1872), L. R 7 Q B 537; *Hart* v *Hudson Bros*, [1928] 2 K B 629.
[58] *Mather* v. *Brown* (1876), 1 C. P. D 596, at p. 601.

those of section 142) do not seem to me to extend the operation
of the amending section in the earlier Act to a document
which had no existence then, and therefore could not
have been in the contemplation of the Legislature " And
Lindley, J., in the same case said he had found authorities
showing that a mere incorporation by reference of a former
Act does not extend all the provisions of the earlier to the
later Act [59]

(ii) *The construction of statutes in pari materia.*—If
two statutes are *in pari materia,* any judicial decision as to
the construction of one " is a sound rule of construction
for the other ".[60]   So that " when a particular form of
legislative enactment which has received authoritative interpretation, whether by judicial decision or by a long course
of practice, is adopted in the framing of a later statute, it is
a sound rule of construction to hold that the words so adopted
were intended by the Legislature to bear the meaning which
had been so put upon them." [61]   In other words, the Legislature being presumed to know the state of the law at the time
of the passing of any Act, must be taken to know the interpretation which has been placed upon words and expressions
in prior Acts.   If the Legislature employs those same words
and expressions in later Acts, it is to be assumed, in the absence
of anything appearing to the contrary, that it intended to
employ those words and expressions in the accepted sense.

The Legislature may itself interpret, as by Interpretation
Acts, or by interpreting sections to individual Acts, or by
subsequent legislation *in pari materia.*   In considering a
question of liability for assessment to excess profits duty
and the provisions of the Finance Acts, 1915—1920, Lord
Sterndale, M.R., said [62]: " I must treat this exposition in

[59] *S C ,* at p 602
[60] *Per* Buller, J , in *R v Mason* (1788), 2 T R 586
[61] *Per* Griffith, C J., in *D'Emden v Pedder* (1904), 1 Austr. C L. R 91,
at p 110, adopted by P C. in *Webb v Outrim,* [1907] A. C 81, 89
[62] *Cape Brandy Syndicate v I. R. C ,* [1921] 2 K B. 403, at p 415.

the Act of 1916 in the same way as if it had been given by a Court binding on me compelling me to construe the Act of 1915 in a way I could not otherwise have done." We shall return to consider how far subsequent legislation is a legitimate guide in interpreting a prior statute.

Or the statute *in pari materia* with the one under consideration may have received a *judical* interpretation. On the assumption mentioned above, the words and expressions in the later statute will be presumed to bear the meanings that have been judicially determined. For example, the question arose whether sandstone was a mineral within section 70 of the Railway Clauses Consolidation (Scotland) Act, 1845, and Lord Loreburn, L.C., said [63]: " I desire to add that in my opinion the decisions in 1818 [64] and 1841 [65] as to the meaning of the word ' minerals ' in private conveyances are of the greatest importance in interpreting this statute. When an Act of Parliament uses a word which has received a judicial construction, it presumably uses it in the same sense. The Act merely says what shall be deemed to be reserved out of the conveyance. . . . The Court has to determine what the words mean in the vernacular of the mining world, the commercial world and landowners only at the time when the purchase was effected and whether the particular substance was regarded as a mineral." Cf. *per* Lord Halsbury in *Lord Provost of Glasgow* v *Farie*.[66] So in *Barras* v. *Aberdeen Steam Trawling and Fishing Co.*[67] Lord Buckmaster said: " It has long been a well-established principle when applied in the consideration of Acts of Parliament that where a word of doubtful meaning has received a clear judicial interpretation, the subsequent statute which incorporates the same word or the same phrase in a similar context must be construed so that

[63] *North British Ry* v *Budhill Coal and Sandstone Co*, [1910] A. C. 116, at p 127
[64] *Menzies* v. *Earl of Breadalbane* (1818), 1 Shaw App (Sc.) 225
[65] *Duke of Hamilton* v. *Bentley* (1841), 3 Dunlop (Sc) 1121
[66] (1888), 13 App Cas 657.
[67] [1933] A. C 402, at p. 411.

the word or phrase is interpreted according to the meaning that has previously been assigned to it."

But a subsequent Act of Parliament does not alter the law by placing an *erroneous* construction on the former Act. This was laid down in 1788,[68] and the decision adds that where it is gathered from a later Act that the Legislature attached a certain meaning to certain words in an earlier corporate statute, this would be taken as a legislative declaration of its meaning. Lord Sterndale, M.R., in *Cape Brandy Syndicate* v. *I. R. C*,[69] said: "I quite agree that subsequent legislation if it proceeded on an erroneous construction of previous legislation cannot alter the previous legislation, but if there be any ambiguity in the earlier legislation then the subsequent legislation may fix the proper interpretation which is to be put upon the earlier."

In *Ormond Investment Trust* v. *Betts* [70] Lord Buckmaster adopted this statement of the law by Lord Sterndale and held that as section 26 of the Finance Act, 1924, was founded on an erroneous assumption as to the effect of Rule 1 of Case V of the Income Tax Act, 1918, it could not be referred to as an authority in interpretation. So in an early case where an Act provided a certain rate of pay for appraisement in cases of distress for rent "whether by one broker or more", this was taken not to abrogate the earlier law that appraisement should be by two brokers [71]

This rule of construction holds good also in the case of a Dominion or Colonial Act *in pari materia* with an English Act. "An Act of a colonial legislature where the English law prevails must be governed by the same rules of construction as prevail in England, and English authorities upon an Act *in pari materia* are authorities for the interpretation of

---

[68] *Dore* v. *Gray* (1788), 2 T. R 358

[69] *Supra*, at p 414

[70] [1928] A. C. 143, at p. 156. See also *per* Lord Atkinson at pp. 163—166; *Port of London Authority* v. *Canvey Island Commissioners*, [1932] 1 Ch. 446, at p 492, *per* Lawrence, L J.

[71] *Allen* v *Flicker* (1839), 10 A & E. 640.

the colonial Act." [72]   In 1899, however, Sir Henry Strong, delivering the judgment of the Privy Council in *Grand Trunk Rail. Co.* v. *Washington*,[73] declined to hold that the Canadian Court of Appeal (Ontario) was justified in regarding as *in pari materia* Dominion Acts for the regulation of provincial railways with an Act of Parliament. "As these are enactments emanating from a different legislative body from that which passed the statute to be interpreted, and cannot be said to be *in pari materia* with that, their Lordships are unable to see that they ought to have any influence upon the question to be decided arising exclusively upon the Dominion Act, and relating only to Dominion railways"

Although, as we have seen, it is legitimate to consult previous statutes *in pari materia* as an aid to the construction of a later Act, it is not legitimate to treat the Act *in pari materia* as if it were incorporated wholly in the later Act. The two are not to be treated as one Act unless the Legislature distinctly or impliedly says so, and it generally says so distinctly where it is intended that the two shall form in fact one statute. A good instance of an illegitimate use of a statute *in pari materia* is the *Casanova Case*,[74] where the Judge of the colonial Court acted on a subsequent statute *in pari materia* and which prescribed certain evidence as being sufficient to justify seizure of a slave ship, as enabling him without more to decide on the provisions of an earlier statute on which the action was brought. The Judicial Committee decided that "the learned Judge was not at liberty to use the rule of evidence introduced by that subsequent statute as applicable to the case before him. It was perfectly competent to him to refer to that statute as an Act that recognised the fact of having an unusual number of water-casks on board as a

---

[72] *Per* Dr. Lushington in *Catterall* v *Sweetman* (1845), 9 Jur. 954, approved by the P. C. in *Trimble* v *Hill* (1880), 5 App Cas. 342

[73] [1899] A. C. 275, at p 280. Cf as to a Dominion Taxing Statute *Armstrong* v *Estate Duty Commissioners*, [1937] A. C 885 (P. C), *per* Lord Maugham

[74] (1866), L. R. 1 P. C 268, at p 277.

circumstance of suspicion, but the learned Judge was not at liberty to take that circumstance *per se*, as a Judge applying the Act of 5 & 6 Will. 4, c. 60 (the later Act) might have done. He was bound to take it in conjunction with all the other circumstances of the case."

(iii) *Subsequent Acts.*—From some of the citations quoted above it will be apparent that subsequent Acts may be used as aids to interpretation. This has been referred to already under the head of legislative exposition—that is to say, the Legislature either deliberately sets out in the later Act the exposition of the earlier for the express purpose of explaining it or, more frequently, does so by implication, *i.e.*, by giving a definite meaning to the same or a similar expression which was unexplained in the earlier Act [1] This is sometimes called "Parliamentary Exposition". But it must be remembered that it is the Courts of law, and not the Legislature, who are the authorised expositors of the statute law; so that in truth a "parliamentary exposition", though a powerful argument, is *only* an argument for a particular construction and is generally not necessarily conclusive. Of course, if the later Act definitely says that such and such a word or expression in an earlier Act is to have such and such a meaning, our Courts have no option but to obey; but this is not what is generally known as "parliamentary exposition". It has been said [2] that, except as parliamentary exposition, subsequent Acts cannot be relied on as an aid to construction, and there is an opinion of A. L Smith, J ,[3] that a statute cannot be construed by the light of subsequent statutes. But it has often been done and Magna Charta has been construed in the light of a subsequent statute [4] So, too, the expression "wilful default" in section 299 of the repealed Merchant Shipping Act of 1854 was construed with reference to a similar expres-

---

[1] As in *Battersby* v. *Kirk* (1836), 2 Bing. N. C 584, 609.
[2] Craies (4th ed), p 137.
[3] In *Ward* v *Folkestone Waterworks* (1890), 62 L. T. 325.
[4] *Rolle* v *Whyte* (1868), 37 L J. Q. B. 105.

sion in the 25 & 26 Vict. c. 63 of 1863,[5] and there are several more examples in the older cases. The modern cases seem also to support this view. Lord Esher, in *Gas Light and Coke Co.* v. *Hardy* (1886), 17 Q B. D. 619, at p. 621, said: "Now I will not say it is impossible to ascertain the interpretation of an Act passed in 1847 by reading an Act which was passed in 1871; if the Legislature has clearly put a construction on the former Act in the later Act, then, for myself, I think one may use the later Act." In *Ormond Investment Co.* v. *Betts,*[6] an income tax case, Lord Atkinson said: "Sargant, L J., seems to hold that a legislative interpretation of the statute of 1918 is to be found in this section 26 of the Act of 1924 and therefore the case comes within a well-recognised principle dealing with the construction of statutes, namely, that where the interpretation of a statute is obscure or ambiguous or readily capable of more than one interpretation, light may be thrown upon the true view to be taken of it by the aim and provisions of a subsequent statute." And in the same case Lord Buckmaster[7] quoted Lord Sterndale, M.R., with approval when the latter said[8]: "I think it is clearly established in *Att.-Gen* v. *Clarkson*[9] that subsequent legislation may be looked at in order to see the proper construction to be put upon an earlier Act where that earlier Act is ambiguous. I quite agree that subsequent legislation if it proceeded on an erroneous construction of previous legislation cannot alter that previous legislation; but if there be any ambiguity in the earlier legislation then the subsequent legislation may fix the proper interpretation which is to be put upon the earlier." The rule thus seems to have the approval of the House of Lords

---

[5] *Grill* v *General Screw Collier Co* (1866), L R 1 C P 611. Cf *Dore* v. *Gray, supra,* p 230.

[6] [1928] A C 143, at p 164

[7] *S C ,* p 156

[8] In *Cape Brandy Syndicate* v *I R C ,* [1921] 2 K. B 403, at p. 414 Cf *Port of London Authority* v *Canvey Island Commissioners,* [1932] 1 Ch. 446, 474.

[9] [1900] 1 Q B. 156.

(*f*) *Cases* —Our reports are full of decisions upon statutes, and the citation of cases on the construction of statutes may be of equal importance as on any other question of law. "Under our system", said Lord Sankey, L.C.,[1] " decided cases effectively construe the words of an Act of Parliament and establish principles and rules whereby its scope and effect may be interpreted." As we have seen (*supra*, p. 197) primarily the words themselves are to be construed as they stand; it is only if and when those actual words have been already construed by a competent Court in the same or a closely analogous statute that there will be any scope for case-law except as laying down general principles. It is probably on this ground that reference to cases has in the first instance been deprecated.[2] So in *R. v. Titterton*[3] Lord Russell, C.J., quoted Lord Campbell, C.J., in *Wray v Ellis*[4]: " There can be little use in referring to cases where a similar question has arisen on Acts differently framed, for they only illustrate the general principle which is not in dispute." These general principles will receive but slight elucidation from decisions on the special language used in particular statutes—and conversely, a decision on special language will scarcely be of service if applied to other words in a different Act. As Cotton, L.J., said[5]: "The question for our consideration is, what is the true meaning of the language which the Legislature has employed? Cases on the construction of other Acts or instruments generally give very little help to the Court, but if there is any principle laid down we ought not to disregard them in considering a different Act or instrument." If the numerous cases on statutes in the reports are examined they will be found to fall into three classes:—

---

[1] *Re Aeronautics in Canada*, [1932] A C 54, at p 70
[2] *Per* Lord Warrington in *Barrell v. Fordree*, [1932] A. C. 676, 682; *Fry v Salisbury House Estate, Ltd*, [1933] A C 432, *per* Lord Dunedin at p 441, and Lord Warrington, at p. 451; *Shotts Iron Co v Fordyce*, [1930] A C 503, 508, 511, 515.
[3] [1895] 2 Q B. 61, at p. 67
[4] (1859), 1 E & E 288.
[5] In *Reid v. Reid* (1886), 31 Ch. D. 402, at p 405.

. (a) Those which lay down a general principle or principles
—such, for instance, as *Heydon's Case.*

(b) Those which decide which of the established principles
should be applied to particular enactments. This is
a matter upon which Judges may differ Some
illustrations of this will be found in Section XI
(*infra*). One Judge may hold that a particular
principle (say, the Literal Rule) should be applied;
another may hold that the Mischief Rule ought to
be applied in the same case; or the Court may hold
that the Mischief Rule, having regard to the object
of the statute, should be applied as, *e.g.,* in *Powell
Lane Manufacturing Co.* v. *Putnam.*[6]

(c) Those which decide whether the accepted construction
of a statute includes or excludes a particular state
of facts. This may be illustrated by the cases on
evasion of taxing statutes (see p. 307, *infra*)

Of these the first class is the most important; but in the case
of a consolidating Act, all three may become of great
importance and influence. A consolidating statute, being
merely a codification, will almost certainly adopt language
which has already received judicial interpretation; the case
law, therefore, on this language will be most valuable. As
Chitty, J., said in considering a section of a consolidating
Act, *viz.,* the Bankruptcy Act, 1883: " I think it is legitimate
in the interpretation of the sections in this amending and
consolidating Act to refer to the previous state of the law for
the purpose of ascertaining the intention of the Legislature." [7]
In the case of a codifying statute, the proper course is " to
examine the language of the statute, uninfluenced by any
considerations derived from the law as it previously stood ",[8]
and not to assume that the Legislature did not intend to alter

---

6 [1931] 2 K B 305
7 *Re Budgett,* [1894] 2 Ch 557
8 *Per* Lord Herschell in *Bank of England* v. *Vaghano,* [1891] A C. 107,
at p 144

the previous law. Again, where a particular judicial construction has been put upon the words of a statute, the Legislature, being assumed to know the law, will be taken to have used those words in subsequent legislation in the sense judicially determined.[9] "There is a well-known principle of construction, that where the Legislature uses in an Act a legal term which has received judicial interpretation, it must be assumed that the term is used in the sense in which it has been judicially interpreted"[10]—unless, of course, a contrary intention appears. Where this is the case, the Courts will not disturb the construction which has thus affected the subsequent legislation unless that construction was clearly wrong.[11] Lord Sankey, L.C., thought[12] that decided cases as authorities were in danger of extending the terms of a statute and of diverting attention from what it enacted to what had been said about it by Judges. In the case cited, a question arose on the British North America Act and very numerous decisions on that Act had been cited at the Bar. The remarks of the Lord Chancellor were, it is submitted, addressed to the policy of the statute. In such a case, it is undoubtedly the fact that the words of an Act may be overlaid with *dicta* of Judges about it and its policy or intention. It may be better, in those circumstances, to "get back to the words of the Act itself and to remember the object with which it was passed".[13]

(g) *Usage* and *contemporanea expositio* —We saw (*supra*, p. 80) that it was permissible in the case of an ambiguous deed to call in aid of a decision as to intention, the Acts of the parties or their representatives under the deed in question.

---

9 Cf. *per* James, L.J., in *Ex p Campbell* (1871), L R 5 Ch. 703, 705; *Barras* v *Aberdeen Steam Trawling Co.*, [1933] A C 402, 411.

10 *Jay* v *Johnstone*, [1893] 1 Q B. 25, 28

11 *Lancashire and Yorkshire Ry.* v. *Bury Corporation* (1889), 14 App. Cas. 417

12 *Re Aeronautics in Canada* (*supra*, p 234).

13 *Ibid.*

The title, marginal notes and punctuation in an Act were regarded merely as *contemporanea expositio*, " which, though useful as a guide to a hasty inquirer, ought not to be relied upon in construing an Act of Parliament ".[1] A construction which has been long and publicly acted upon will not be lightly disturbed.[2] For instance, when the powers of justices under section 25 of the Summary Jurisdiction Act, 1848, were in question, the practice under the Criminal Law Act of 1827 (7 & 8 Geo. 4, c. 28) was adopted as showing " a contemporaneous expression of the effect of 7 & 8 Geo. 4, c 28, s. 10," and the Court held that the statute of 1848 should be construed in the same way.[3] So in a Canadian case concerning the conclusive character of a probate, the Privy Council said: " Their Lordships, however, think that they cannot consider this matter now as *res integra*. They cannot disregard the practice of the Canadian Courts with respect to it for the last seventy years . . It appears to their Lordships that, by the uninterrupted practice and usage of the Canadian Courts since 1801, the law has received an interpretation which does not affix to the grant of probate that binding and conclusive character which it has in England . . . their Lordships therefore think that they ought not to advise Her Majesty that a different construction ought now to be put on the law." [4] In *Gorham* v. *Bishop of Exeter*,[5] Lord Campbell said: " Were the language obscure instead of being clear, we should not be justified in differing from the construction put upon it by contemporaneous and long-continued usage "

Lord Campbell here implies that if the meaning is plain, it is not legitimate to resort to any such aid, and the cases are in accordance with this view, for in *Magistrates of Dunbar*

---

[1] *Per* Willes, J , in *Claydon* v. *Green* (1868), L. R. 3 C P 511, at p 522
[2] See, however, *per* Lord Eldon in *Att.-Gen.* v *Bristol* (1820), 2 Jac & W. 321.
[3] *R* v *Cutbush* (1867), L R 2 Q B 379
[4] *Migneault* v. *Malo* (1872), L. R 4 P C 123.
[5] (1850), 15 Q B 52, at p. 73.

v. *Duchess of Roxburgh* [6] Lord Brougham said: "Where the' statute uses words of doubtful import, the acting under it for a long course of years may well give an interpretation to that obscure meaning and reduce that uncertainty to a fixed rule . . . but it is quite plain that against a plain statutory law no usage is of any avail." And Chitty, J:,[7] held that neither usage nor practice for eighty years would render the Crown liable for bridge tolls from which it was clearly exempted by the Post Office Management Act, 1837. In order to prevail the construction or practice must have been generally and universally acquiesced in. "We understand that in acting upon the statute in Ireland a practice has been prevalent, though not universal, which is at variance with our opinion as to its proper construction. We conceive that the meaning of the Act is so clear that we ought not to give any weight to the practice." [8]

The more modern cases may shortly be considered, there being, it is submitted, a balance of weighty learned opinion so far in favour of regarding both usage and *contemporanea expositio* as aids to construction, at least in cases of ambiguity. In *Trustees of Clyde Navigation v. Laird* [9] it was in question whether navigation dues were legally payable on timber floated up the river Clyde in logs chained together. From 1858 to 1882 dues had been levied and had been paid without protest under the Clyde Navigation Consolidation Act, 1858. On this question of non-resistance as a guide Lord Blackburn said [10]: "I think that raises a strong *prima facie* ground for thinking that there must exist some legal ground on which they (the merchants) could not resist. And I think a Court should be cautious, and not decide unnecessarily that there is no such ground. If the Lord President means no more than this when

6 (1835), 3 Cl & F. 325, at p 354
7 In *Northam Bridge Co* v *R* (1886), 5 L. T. 759
8 *Per* the Judges consulted by the H L in *Bank of Ireland* v *Evans'* *Charity* (1855), 5 H. L C 405.
9 (1883), 8 App Cas 658
10 *S C*, at p. 670.

he calls it 'contemporanea expositio of the statutes which is almost irresistible', I agree with him." Lord Watson, on the other hand, in the same case [11] said: "I have only to add that in my opinion such usage as has in this case been termed 'contemporanea expositio' is of no value whatever in construing a British statute of the year 1858. When there are ambiguous expressions in an Act passed two or three centuries ago, it may be legitimate to refer to the construction put upon these expressions throughout a long course of years by the unanimous consent of all parties interested as evidence of what must presumably have been the intention of the Legislature at that remote period. But I feel bound to construe a recent statute according to its own terms when these are brought into controversy, and not according to the views which interested parties may have hitherto taken." In *Assheton-Smith* v. *Owen*,[12] a somewhat similar case concerning port dues, Cozens-Hardy, L.J., thought the doctrine of *contemporanea expositio* could not be applied in construing Acts comparatively modern, although Stirling, L.J., said: "I will only add that the rates and dues were paid by the plaintiffs' predecessors in title in respect of ships laden or unladen at Port Dinorwic without dispute for a long period and down to a time shortly before bringing this action. This circumstance, though it may not preclude the plaintiff from questioning the right to levy rates or dues, yet as pointed out by Lord Blackburn in *Trustees of Clyde Navigation* v *Laird*.[13] may well render the Court cautious in holding that such right does not exist." Lord Loreburn, in *West Ham Union* v. *Edmonton Union*,[14] said: "Great importance is to be attached to these authorities [those by which the lower Court had considered itself bound] on the strength of which many transactions may have been adjusted and rights determined But where they are plainly

---

[11] *S C*, at p 673 Adopted by Farwell, L J , in *Sadler* v *Whiteman*, [1910] 1 K B. 868, at p 892
[12] [1906] 1 Ch. 179, at p. 212
[13] *Supra*, p 238.
[14] [1908] A. C. 1, at p 4

wrong, especially where the subsequent course of judicial decisions has disclosed the weakness of the reasoning on which they are based, and the practical injustice in the consequences which must flow from them, I consider it is the duty of this House to overrule them, if it has not lost the right to do so by itself expressly affirming them."

Where no such transactions have taken place or rights determined on the faith of a particular construction having been placed on the words of a statute by judicial decision, the rule will not apply,[15] and in *Pate* v *Pate*[16] Lord Sumner declined to follow earlier cases on the construction of a statute and said: "This is not one of those cases in which inveterate error is left undisturbed because titles and transactions have been founded on it which it would be unjust to disturb" This consideration may sometimes arise in cases where the action of the Legislature may have been guided in subsequent legislation by the decisions placed on earlier enactments; as, for instance, section 46 of the Railways Clauses Consolidation Act, 1845. This section had received a certain construction in a case in 1857 [17] and again in 1860,[18] and arose in 1889 in *Lancashire and Yorkshire Ry.* v. *Bury Corporation*,[19] where Lord Herschell said: "And there are, as it seems to me, special reasons why a judgment so given should not be disturbed, unless it be clearly shown to have proceeded upon an erroneous view of the law, inasmuch as the clause which there received construction was contained in an enactment which did not of itself produce any legal results; it only had effect if incorporated by a subsequent Act of the Legislature in statutes giving powers to railway companies. And one cannot but see that the construction put upon an enactment of that description may well have affected the action of the

---

15 *Goldsmiths' Company* v *Wyatt*, [1907] 1 K. B. 108
16 [1915] A. C. 1100, at p. 1108.
17 *North Staffordshire Ry* v *Dale* (1857), 8 E. & B 836.
18 *Newcastle Turnpike Trustees* v *North Staffordshire Ry* (1860), 5 H & N 160.
19 (1889), 14 App. Cas. 417.

Legislature in subsequent cases, when they had to consider what obligations they should or should not impose upon the railway companies to whom they were giving powers. At the same time, if it could be established that the decision was manifestly erroneous, your Lordships would be bound to give effect to that view, and to hold that the statute must be construed according to its natural meaning, notwithstanding the interpretation which had been so long ago placed upon it by eminent Judges.''

This doctrine is no doubt but an instance of *stare decisis* of which perhaps the leading modern example is *Hanau* v. *Ehrlich*,[20] in which the House of Lords in 1912 refused to disturb decisions since 1829 on the ambiguous words in section 4 of the Statute of Frauds, though they plainly thought the decisions were at least doubtful, and Lord Loreburn said [21]: " To my mind when doubtful words in a statute have for a long period been decided in a particular sense we ought not to reopen the matter if we can help it." And there are other examples.[22]

VI.—Repeals

More than a century ago Tindal, C J , said: " The effect of repealing a statute is to obliterate it completely from the records of the Parliament as if it had never been passed ; and it must be considered as a law that never existed except for the purpose of those actions which were commenced, prosecuted and concluded whilst it was an existing law." [1] This is the law to-day under the Interpretation Act, 1889.[2] Generally a statute is definite as to what it repeals by its enactment. There is now nearly always a schedule appended to the

---

[20] [1912] A C. 39.

[21] *S C* , p 41

[22] *E g* , *Cohen* v *Bayley-Worthington*, [1908] A C 97, *Tancred, Arrol & Co.* v. *Steel Co of Scotland* (1890), 15 App Cas. 125, *Lucas* v *Dixon* (1889), 22 Q. B. D 357

[1] In *Kay* v. *Goodwin* (1830), 6 Bing 576 Cf *Lemm* v. *Mitchell*, [1912] A. C. 400, *Hosie* v *C. C of Kildare*, [1928] Ir. R 47

[2] S. 38 (2)

statute setting out the Acts repealed, as, for instance, the Seventh Schedule to the Law of Property Act, 1925, which contains a list of over forty Acts either wholly or partially repealed by the Act of 1925   It is when a question of the unexpressed intention of the Legislature arises that the difficulty is caused   If a statutory right becomes vested upon the completion of a certain matter but not before that, no right will have been acquired if the statute conferring the right is repealed before the matter is complete.   But it may be far from the intention of the Legislature to *undo* something that has been done under a statute by means of another and repealing statute.   An Act of 1819 provided for the stopping of a bridle path, vesting the soil of it in the owner of the land over which it passed in exchange for land taken for making a turnpike road as a substitute for the bridle path.   The Act of 1819 was repealed by an Act of 1856, and the question arose as to whether the bridle path, abolished by the Act of 1819, was restored.   Romer, J., held it was not.   " When the Act of 1856 was passed and the Act of 1819 repealed it was not, in my judgment, at all the intention of the Legislature or the effect of the Act of 1856 to undo that which had already been done during the continuance of the prior Act, or to revive these ways which had once for all been put an end to and discontinued as private ways." [3]   Similarly rights acquired under a statute will not be taken away by the repeal of the statute conferring them   Sometimes a clause to this effect is inserted in the repealing statute, but this is really unnecessary both by the common law and now by section 38 (2) of the Interpretation Act   A good modern instance is furnished by *Lemm* v. *Mitchell*.[4]   A Hong Kong Ordinance of 1895 had abolished the action for criminal conversation.   A subsequent ordinance of 1908 had repealed the ordinance of 1895 and had by its retrospective effect given a right of action for criminal

---

3 *Gwynne* v *Drewitt*, [1894] 2 Ch 616
4 [1912] A C. 400. Cf *Jacques* v. *Withey* (1788), 1 H. Bl. 65; and per Coleridge, J , in *Hitchcock* v. *Way* (1837), 6 A & E 943, at p. 947.

conversation committed before the enactment of the ordinance of 1908. The respondent after 1908 brought an action for criminal conversation committed before 1908, but it appeared that he had already brought such an action before the enactment of 1908 and in the then state of the law judgment had been given against him. The Privy Council held that this gave the defendant a vested right which was a bar to an action on the same facts brought after the ordinance of 1908. This is also an example of a repealing enactment expressly reviving an earlier enactment.

As soon as a landlord in view of a sale of his property gave his tenant notice to quit, the latter acquired a right to compensation for his agricultural holding under section 11 of the Agricultural Holdings Act, 1908, although it had been repealed.[5] But a mere right existing at the date of a repealing statute is not a " right accrued " within the meaning of the usual saving clause.[6]

The Courts lean against implying a repeal. " Unless two Acts are so plainly repugnant to each other that effect cannot be given to both at the same time, a repeal will not be implied. Special Acts are not repealed by general Acts unless there is some express reference to the previous legislation or unless there is a necessary inconsistency in the two Acts standing together "[7] This pronouncement was quoted with approval in a case[8] which furnishes an excellent example of the doctrine. A city corporation was by a private Act protected from any liability for damage which a tramway company authorised by the Act might sustain through acts of the corporation or exercise of its powers. Later the corporation were authorised by another private Act to lay an aqueduct along a main road and were empowered to break up roads and cross

[5] *Hamilton Gell* v *White*, [1922] 2 K B 422   The Court of Appeal held that the case came within s 38 of the Interpretation Act, 1889
[6] *Abbott* v *Minister of Lands*, [1895] A C 425
[7] *Kutner* v *Phillips*, [1891] 2 Q B 267, at p 272, *per* A L. Smith, J
[8] *Aberdeen Suburban Tramways Co* v *Aberdeen Magistrates*, [1927] S C 683.

under or over them, on making compensation to persons injured thereby. The tramway company sued for damage caused by the construction of the aqueduct, but they were held barred by the provisions of the earlier Act, the special provisions of which had not been impliedly repealed by the general provisions of the later Act. Here of course both Acts were private Acts, but the general provisions as to compensation in the later Act gave it, for this purpose, the character of a general Act This is an example of a rule as to implied repeal sometimes summed up in the phrase *generalia specialibus non derogant*—general words or provisions do not affect special words or provisions. " Where general words in a later Act are capable of reasonable and sensible application without extending them to subjects specially dealt with by the earlier legislation . . . that earlier and special legislation is not to be held indirectly repealed, altered or derogated from, merely by force of such general words, without any indication of a particular intention to do so." [9] So the Judicial Committee in *Barker* v. *Edgar* [10] said that the presumption is that a subsequent general enactment is not intended to interfere with a special enactment, unless the intention to do so is very clearly manifested. The general language of the Acquisition of Land (Assessment of Compensation) Act of 1919 was held, in the absence of clear words, not to affect the special provisions of the Blackpool Improvement Act, 1917, a private Act. [11] So the Housing Act of 1925 was held not to override the special provisions of the London Open Spaces Act of 1893 with regard to Hackney Marshes. [12] And the general provisions of the Married Women's Property Act, 1882, allowing a married woman to dispose by will of her real and personal property as if she were a *feme sole*, were held not to override the special provision in the Gift for Churches Act, 1803, which enacted that a gift by will for the

---

9 *Per* Lord Selborne in *Seward* v. *The Vera Cruz* (1884), 10 App Cas 59, at p. 68.
10 [1898] A C 754
11 *Blackpool Corporation* v *Starr Estate Co* , [1922] 1 A. C. 27
12 *R.* v *Minister of Health*, [1936] 2 K B 29.

purpose of erecting a church could not be made by a married woman without the concurrence of her husband.[13]

So where a clause from a public Act, as, for instance, the Railway Clauses Act, 1863, has been incorporated in a private Act, and the public Act is subsequently repealed, this fact does not imply a repeal of the private Act.[14] Parliament cannot, save by express words, bind itself not impliedly to alter a statute by subsequent legislation, nor can it bind itself as to the form of subsequent legislation.[15] It does sometimes happen, therefore, that the provisions of one statute are so inconsistent with the provisions of a similar but later one, that the Courts admit an implied repeal.

In a recent case Farwell, J., said. " It is well settled that the Court does not construe a later Act as repealing an earlier Act unless it is impossible to make the two Acts or the two sections of the Act stand together, i.e., if the section of the later Act can only be given a sensible meaning if it is treated as impliedly repealing the section of the earlier Act." [16] In *Ellen Street Estates* v *Minister of Health* [15] the Court of Appeal held that section 46 of the Housing Act of 1925, so far as it was inconsistent with the similar Act of 1919, had impliedly repealed the later Act. In *Re Chance* [17] Farwell, J., thought that if possible it was his duty to read section 195 (2) and (3) of the Law of Property Act, 1925, so as not to effect a repeal of an earlier Act, the Judgments Act, 1864, s 4.

An order made under the Judicature Act, 1875, which enacted that all costs in the High Court shall be in the discretion of the Court and that, where an action is tried with a jury, the costs shall follow the event unless otherwise ordered, was held to repeal that portion of the Limitation Act,

---

13 *Re Smith's Estate* (1887), 35 Ch D. 589, 595, *per* Stirling, J.

14 *Jenkins* v. *Great Central Ry* (1912), 81 L J K. B. 24

15 *Ellen Street Estates* v. *Minister of Health*, [1934] 1 K B. 590, 596 Cf. *Smith* v. *Benabo*, [1937] 1 K B 518

16 In *Re Berrey*, [1936] 1 Ch 274.

17 [1936] 1 Ch. 266, 270.

1623, which deprived a successful plaintiff of his costs in an action of slander where he did not recover at least 40s. damages.[18] A complicated case of repeal is the following: The Judicature Act, 1873, came into operation in 1875, and by section 45 of that Act there was an appeal from the county court in an Admiralty action to the Divisional Court, but not further, except by leave of the Divisional Court. The County Courts Act, 1875, which came into operation on the next day in 1875, in section 10 allowed a further appeal without leave of the Divisional Court, if that Court altered the judgment of the county court in an Admiralty action. Thus the later Act must be taken to have impliedly repealed section 45 of the Judicature Act So far it is clear. The County Courts Act of 1888 repealed section 10 of the County Courts Act, 1875, but provided that it should not revive any enactment not in force at the commencement of the Act of 1888. Therefore, it was held that although the County Courts Act of 1875 was repealed, the relevant provisions of the Judicature Act, 1873, were not revived. Therefore, as the appeal before the Court of Appeal was without leave from a judgment of the Divisional Court altering a judgment of the county court in an Admiralty action, it was competent.[19]

Where an Act passed after 1850 contains a clause repealing a repealing enactment, no enactment previously repealed is revived unless there are express words of revivor.[20] This supersedes the old canon of construction and alters the presumption as to the intention to revive a defunct law. So, on the old theory, if a person became liable to a penal law which expired or was repealed before he was convicted, he could not be punished, although the prosecution was begun while the law was still in force, unless the repealing Act contained " a special clause to allow it "[21] And, further, if an offence was punishable under a certain statute and was

18 *Garnett v Bradley* (1878), 48 L. J Ex. 186 ; 3 App. Cas 944
19 *The Dart*, [1893] P 33.
20 Interpretation Act, 1889, s 11 (1)
21 *Miller's Case* (1764), 1 W. Bl 450

committed before, but not tried till after the passing of a
statute repealing the former one, but imposing new penalties
for the commission of the offence in question, the prisoner
could not be punished under either statute.[22]   Now by the
Interpretation Act,[23] unless a contrary intention appears, a
repeal does not affect the previous operation of any enactment
so repealed or anything duly done or suffered under it.   A
"contrary intention" was held to exist in an Irish case [24]
where the Court said: "The result is the full legal effect
of repeal as stated in *Kay* v. *Goodwin* [25] must follow, *viz.*,
that the Act is taken to have been obliterated from the statute
book, when as here the action was not commenced, prosecuted
and concluded while the Act of 1920 was in force"   The Acts
referred to were the Criminal Injuries (Ireland) Act of 1920,
repealed by the Damage to Property (Compensation) Act of
1923.   By-laws made under Acts subsequently repealed are
themselves repealed unless expressly preserved under the new
law.

Instead of repealing an entire Act, the repeal may be of
certain sections or clauses only   It cannot be said that "where
a particular clause in an Act is repealed the whole Act must
be read as if the clause had never been enacted".[26]   So a
Court is entitled to look at the repealed portion of an Act to
see what is the meaning of what remains in the Act, otherwise it would follow that an Act of Parliament, which at one
time had one meaning, would by the repeal of some one
clause in it have some other meaning.[27]   Where provisions
of one statute are incorporated by reference into a second
statute and the first is repealed by a third statute, the pro-

---

[22] *R* v *M'Kenzie* (1820), R. & R. 429
[23] S 38 (2) (b); *Bennett* v *Tatton*, [1918] W N. 291.
[24] *Hosie* v *C C of Kildare*, [1928] Ir. R. 47   Cf *Henshall* v. *Porter*
(1922), 39 T. L R 409, McCardie, J.
[25] (1830), 6 Bing. 576, *supra*, p 241
[26] *Att -Gen* v. *Lamplough* (1878), 3 Ex. D. 214, at p. 233, *per*
Kelly, C.B.
[27] *S. C.*, p 227, *per* Bramwell, B.

visions incorporated into the second remain intact. "There is a rule of construction that where a statute is incorporated by reference into a second statute, the repeal of the first statute by a third does not affect the second." [28] This is now provided for by the Interpretation Act. [29]

Penal Acts.—A difficulty sometimes arises, especially in the case of penal Acts : Did the Legislature intend to amend or add to the existing law or did it intend to abolish the existing law and start afresh? If each Act has its definite object, each being restricted to that object, they are clearly not in conflict. An Act which merely imposes a new form of punishment or procedure for what is already an offence, is regarded as cumulative and not as superseding the existing law   For instance, the Metropolitan Police Act, 1839, by one section (section 47) empowered a magistrate to impose a fine of not more than forty shillings for an offence, and by another section (section 77) empowered him to commit the offender to prison if the fine were not paid   The Metropolitan Police Act of 1864 repealed the former section and substituted for it the same fine and power to commit to prison for not more than three days. This was held not to impliedly repeal the latter section, and that a magistrate could lawfully impose a fine of forty shillings and commit to prison for one month in default. [30] The Interpretation Act [31] provides that if an offence is punishable under more than one Act or under an Act and at the common law, the offender may, unless a contrary intention appear, be punished under either, but shall not be punished twice for the same offence. An Act which alters the quality and incidents of an offence, would be construed as impliedly repealing the old law, *e.g* , making what was

---

28 *Per* Brett, L J., in *Clarke* v   *Bradlaugh* (1881), 8 Q. B D. 63
29 S 38 (1)
30 *R* v. *Hopkins*, [1893] 1 Q B 621   Cf *Wyatt* v *Gems* [1893] 2 Q B. 225 , *Keep* v *St Mary s, Newington,* [1894] 2 Q B 524
31 Section 33

formerly a felony into a misdemeanour.[32] Or again, where the penalty is altered in degree but not in kind; thus, by 5 Geo. 1, c. 27, a fine of £100 and three months' imprisonment was imposed for a first offence, and a fine at discretion and twelve months' imprisonment for a second offence. The 23 Geo. 2, c. 13, increased the punishment for a first offence to a fine of £500 and twelve months' imprisonment, and for a second a fine of £1,000 and two years' imprisonment. The object of both statutes was to prevent the export of silk and woollen goods and the emigration of the workmen The later statute was held to have impliedly repealed the earlier.[33] It has been said by authority that if a later statute describes an offence created by an earlier one and affixes a different punishment or varies the procedure, as, for instance, giving an appeal where none existed previously—the earlier statute is impliedly repealed thereby.[34] " Where the same offence is re-enacted with a different punishment, it (the subsequent enactment) repeals the former law."[35] In *Fortescue* v. *Bethnal Green Vestry*[36] the Metropolitan Management Act of 1855, which imposed a penalty not exceeding £5 (without specifying any minimum) and a further penalty of forty shillings a day for a continuance of the offence, upon any owner or occupier who did not after fourteen days' notice remove projections from his house, was held to impliedly repeal an Act of 1817 (57 Geo. 3, c. 29) which imposed a penalty of not less than forty shillings or more than £5 on any owner or occupier who did not immediately remove such projections upon notice to do so.

An offence may, of course, fall within two distinct enactments but this seems to afford no ground for attempting to give a secondary construction to one of these enactments

---

[32] *Per* Lord Esher, *Lee* v *Dangar*, [1892] 2 Q B 348

[33] *R.* v *Cator* (1802), 4 Burr 2026

[34] *Per* Lord Campbell in *Michell* v *Brown* (1859), 28 L J M C 55

[35] *Per* Lord Abinger in *Att.-Gen.* v *Lockwood* (1842), 9 M & W 378, at p 391.

[36] [1891] 2 Q B 170, 178, approving *Att.-Gen* v *Lockwood* (*supra*) Cf *Smith* v *Benabo*, [1937] 1 K. B. 518

in order to exclude the offence from one or other of them. Thus, an enactment which prohibited under penalty any person concerned in the administration of the poor laws from supplying goods ordered for the relief of any pauper, was held not to be construed as excepting a poor law guardian, merely on the ground that another provision expressly made such officers liable to a much higher penalty for supplying a workhouse with goods.[37] But there can be only one conviction for a fresh act of the same nuisance under the Nuisances Removal Act, 1855.[38]

VII.—DISCRETIONARY OR OBLIGATORY PROVISIONS

"*May*" *and* "*shall*" *or* "*must*".—The distinction between discretionary or compulsory powers was drawn by Sir Arthur Channell in giving the judgment of the Judicial Committee in *Montreal Street Rail. Co.* v. *Normandin*[1]: "The question whether the provisions in a statute are directory or imperative has frequently arisen in this country, but it has been said that no general rule can be laid down and that in every case the object of the statute must be looked at . . When the provisions of a statute relate to the performance of a public duty and the case is such that to hold null and void acts done in respect of this duty would work serious general inconvenience or injustice to persons who have no control over those entrusted with the duty, and at the same time would not promote the main object of the Legislature, it has been the practice to hold such provisions to be directory only, the neglect of them, though punishable, not affecting the validity of acts done." Where a statute, as often, gives a discretionary power, the discretion must be exercised according to common sense and to justice; it must be a judicial discretion "and not the mere whim or caprice of the person to whom it is entrusted on the

---

[37] *Davies* v *Harvey* (1874), L. R. 9 Q B 433.
[38] *Edleston* v. *Barnes* (1875), 45 L J M. C 73
[1] [1917] A. C. 170, at p. 174.

DISCRETIONARY OR OBLIGATORY PROVISIONS.

assumption that he is discreet ".[2]   The discretion if conferred is not necessarily exhausted by a single exercise of
it as was at one time the presumption; for by the Interpretation Act[3] it may be exercised from time to time as occasion
requires, and if given to the holder of an office, may be
exercised by the holder for the time being of the office; unless
in each case a contrary intention appears   When powers are
conferred as, for instance, for making a railway, it is the
duty of the promoters if they proceed to exercise those powers,
to keep strictly within them and " not to be guided by any
fanciful view of the spirit of the Act which confers them ".[4]
So in *R.* v. *St Pancras*,[5] the vestry declined to grant a
superannuation allowance to a retiring officer, being influenced
by the idea that they had no discretion as to amount.   The
words of 29 & 30 Vict c 31, s. 1, allowed " an annual
allowance not exceeding two-thirds of his then salary ".   It
was held that this involves a power to grant a sum of less
than two-thirds of his salary, but " they must fairly consider
the application and exercise their discretion on it fairly and
not take into account any reason for their decision that is not
a legal one ".   So it was held that section 7 of the Education
Act, 1902, does not allow the Board of Education to dis-
criminate between provided and non-provided schools or to
decide questions of law.   If its decision is based on a wrong
interpretation of the statute, the Court can interfere and
review it.[6]

The difficulty about the word " may " is that it is
sometimes or in some circumstances construed as not discretionary but imperative.   In other words, can " may " ever
mean " must "?   In an old case it was actually said that
" may be done " in cases of public or private right is always

---

[2] *Per* Willes, J., in *Lee* v *Bude, etc*, *Ry* (1871), L. R 6 C P 576, 580
[3] S. 32 (1) (2).
[4] *Per* Turner, L J, in *Tinkler* v *Wandsworth D B. W* (1858), 2
De G & J. 261, at p 274
[5] (1890), 24 Q B. D. 371, at p 375
[6] *R.* v. *Board of Education*, [1910] 2 K. B. 165.

to be understood as "must be done".[7] Thus the County
Courts Act, 1850 (13 & 14 Vict. c. 61, s. 13) provided
that in certain actions, the Court "may direct that the
plaintiff shall recover his costs". This was held not to be
permissive but obligatory. "When a statute confers an
authority to do a judicial act in a certain case, it is imperative
on those so authorised to exercise the authority when the case
arises and its exercise is duly applied for by a party interested
and having the right to make the application. For this
reason we are of opinion that the word 'may' is not used to
give a discretion, but to confer a power upon the Court and
Judges, and that the exercise of such power depends, not upon
the discretion of the Court or Judges, but upon proof of the
particular case out of which such power arises."[8] So by the
Arbitration Act, 1889, s. 5, where one of the parties does not
appoint an arbitrator after notice to do so, the Court "may"
on the application of the party who gave the notice, appoint
an arbitrator. The Court is bound to do so if applied to for
that purpose.[9] Again, the Weights and Measures Act, 1889,
by section 13 provided that an inspector "may take" certain
specified fees. This was held obligatory and the inspector had
a duty to take these fees.[10] In *Re Baker*[11] a power was
given by the Bankruptcy Act, 1883, s. 125 (4), to transfer
the administration of an insolvent estate from the Chancery
Division to the Court of Bankruptcy. The question was
whether it was a power that must be exercised. Cotton, L.J.,
said: "I think that great misconception is caused by saying
that in some cases 'may' means 'must'. It can never
mean 'must' so long as the English language retains its
meaning; but it gives a power and then it may be a question
in what cases, where a Judge has a power given to him by the

---

    [7] *R* v. *Barlow* (1693), Carth. 293; cited in *R* v. *Bishop of Oxford*
(1879), 4 Q. B. D. 245, 258.
    [8] *McDougal* v *Paterson* (1851), 6 Ex. 337, note.
    [9] *Re Eyre and Leicester Corporation*, [1892] 1 Q. B. 136.
    [10] *R.* v *Roberts*, [1901] 2 K. B. 177.
    [11] (1890), 44 Ch. D. 262.

word 'may', it becomes his duty to exercise it.   . . In my opinion there is given by the word 'may' a power, to the exercise of which there is a discretion, and there is not here enough to show that it was the duty of the Judge to exercise that discretion." [12]

It therefore appears that the word "may" always gives a power; but the further question whether, given the power, there is a duty to exercise it, must depend on the words creating the power. If the donee has nobody's interest to consult but his own, the power is permissive merely, but if a duty to others is at the same time created, the exercise of power will be imperative.   "The question whether a Judge or public officer to whom a power is given by such words is bound to use it upon any particular occasion or in any particular manner must be solved *aliunde*, and in general it is to be solved from the context, from the particular provisions, or from the general scope and objects, of the enactment conferring the power." [13]

So, by section 138 of the County Courts Act, 1888, "may order" are enabling words, but where a legal right to possession has been established on the part of the landlord, it is the *duty* of the Judge to make an order for possession. "'May' does not mean 'must'; 'may' always means 'may' 'May' is a permissive or enabling expression but there are cases in which for various reasons as soon as the person who is within the statute is entrusted with the power, it becomes his duty to exercise it." [14]   So the provisions of the Customs Consolidation Act, 1876, enacted that when goods become liable to forfeiture (as, for instance, a certain mixture of oils which was illegal), the vehicle conveying the goods shall also be forfeited (section 202)   The Act by section 226 laid down that on the appearance of the owner of the goods, the justices

---

[12] *S C*, pp 270, 271.

[13] *Per* Lord Selborne in *Julius* v *Bishop of Oxford* (1880), 5 App Cas, at p 235

[14] *Per* Talbot, J, in *Sheffield Corporation* v *Laxford*, [1929] 2 K B 180, at p. 183.

may proceed to the examination of the matter and "may condemn" the goods. The Act was held to give the justices no discretion to refuse to forfeit the vehicle on the ground of hardship to an innocent owner, as, *e.g.*, when the vehicle was used under a hire-purchase agreement with the owner.[15]

Similar considerations arise with regard to the expression "it shall be lawful". The leading case is *R.* v. *Bishop of Oxford*[16] or (in the House of Lords) *Julius* v. *Bishop of Oxford*.[17] The Church Discipline Act, 1840, s. 3, provided that "it shall be lawful for the Bishop to issue a commission" under certain circumstances. The question was whether it was within his discretion to do or abstain from doing so, or whether he was under a duty to do so. The House of Lords held that the Bishop had complete discretion in the matter. Lord Cairns said[18]: "Where a power is deposited with a public officer for the purpose of being used for the benefit of persons who are specifically pointed out and with regard to whom a definition is supplied by the Legislature of the conditions upon which they are entitled to call for its exercise, that power ought to be exercised and the Court will require it to be exercised." An extract from Lord Selborne's speech is set out above. Lord Blackburn said[19]: "I am not aware that it has ever in any previous judgment been laid down, and I think that in all the cases in support of the position so laid down and all the other cases of which I am aware in which words in terms empowering have been held to be imperative, are to be supported on a different principle." . . "But I cannot agree with the Court of Queen's Bench that whenever the statute is for the public good or of general interest and concern, powers conferred by enabling words are *prima facie* to be considered powers which must be exercised."

---

15 *De Keyser* v *British Railway Traffic and Electric Co.*, [1936] 1 K B 224.

16 (1879), 4 Q. B D. 245, 525.

17 (1880), 5 App. Cas. 214.

18 *S. C*, p 225

19 *S C.*, p. 241 and p 245

. . . " In fact in every case cited (where it has been held that the power must be exercised) it has been on the application of those whose private rights required the exercise of the power." [20]

"*Must*".—" Must " is naturally *prima facie* imperative and admits of no discretion, and so is " shall ". For instance, the Public Health Act, 1875, s. 174 (2) provides that every contract made by an urban authority under the Act of the value of over £50, " shall specify some pecuniary penalty in case the terms of the contract are not duly performed ". This enactment was held to be obligatory and not directory merely.[21] In a recent case, however, *Re Turner's Will Trusts*,[22] it was held that the words in section 31 of the Trustee Act, 1925, " the trustees shall pay the income ", though imperative, were part of and ancillary to the statutory power of maintenance conferred on the trustees by the section. Further, that section 69, which gave powers to apply the income, if no contrary intention were expressed, applied to section 31, and therefore where a contrary intention is expressed in the instrument creating the trust, it is to prevail.

" *Or* " *and* " *And* ".—In order to carry out the intention of the Legislature, it has sometimes been necessary to read one of these conjunctions for the other. The 43 Eliz. c. 3, which spoke of property to be employed for the maintenance of " sick *and* maimed soldiers ", was held to apply to soldiers who were sick *or* maimed, and not only to those who were both. By 1 James 1, c. 15, it was made an act of bankruptcy for a trader to leave his dwelling-house " to the intent *or* whereby his creditors might be defeated or delayed ". If a creditor called at a trader's house for payment while the trader was out for an hour, the Act, read literally, would have applied. This of course would have been an absurd construction, the

---

[20] *S C.*, p 244
[21] *British Insulated Wire Co* v *Prescott U. D C*, [1895] 2 Q. B. 463
[22] [1937] Ch 15.

intention of the Legislature being that an absence from home
would be an act of bankruptcy only if coupled with the
design of delaying or defeating creditors, and was so
construed.[23]   As an example of the converse, a Turnpike Act
imposed a toll on every carriage drawn by four horses and
another on every horse, laden or not laden, but not drawing,
and provided that not more than one toll should be charged
for repassing on the same day " with the same horses *and*
carriages ".   The question was whether the *same* carriage
repassing on the same day with *different* horses was liable to a
second toll.   It was held in the negative, as the toll was
imposed on the carriage and it was immaterial whether it was
drawn by the same or by different horses.   This involved
reading the " and " as " or ".[24]

In a recent case, a private Act, the Liverpool Corporation
Act, 1921, gave power to constables to arrest without warrant
" any loose, idle *or* disorderly person " under certain circumstances   The majority of the Court of Appeal held that in
order to justify arrest without warrant it must be shown that
the person so arrested belonged to the class of " loose, idle
and disorderly " persons   Scott, L J (p. 268) thought the
words in the Liverpool Act had been miscopied from a City
of London Police Act of 1839, where the words were " loose,
idle *and* disorderly person ", and the words in the Liverpool
Act should be read accordingly.[24a]

VIII —PRIVATE ACTS

Private Acts.—Besides legislating for the public generally,
Parliament passes annually a large number of private Acts
permitting individuals or corporations to do things which they
would not be able to do by the Common Law: for example,
to acquire land for a railway, to construct a tramway; to

---

23 *Fowler* v *Padget* (1798), 7 T R 509
24 *Waterhouse* v *Keen* (1825), 40 R R 858
24a *Ledwith* v *Roberts*, [1937] 1 K B 232.

impose a new rate on the inhabitants of a district; to construct a harbour; and numerous other objects   So a private Act is one which affects the interests of particular localities, persons or corporations, and is not of a public general character. These Acts are brought into Parliament by petition, and the proceedings partake largely of a judicial character as the promoters appear as suitors for the Bill and are usually represented by counsel before the select committee to which the Bill will have been referred   The opponents of the measure will be likewise represented and heard.   Every Act passed since 1850 is now to be considered a public Act unless the contrary is declared therein.[25]   As to Acts before this date the question may still arise as to whether they are public or private, the importance of this being generally a question of mode of proof.   In 1849 Wigram, V.-C., said.   " Whether an Act is public or private does not depend on any formal consideration as to whether it has a clause declaring that it shall be deemed a public Act, but upon the substantial considerations of the nature of the case."[26]   Sometimes Acts of a local nature have been held to be public Acts on account of the public interest of their subject-matter.   It was often the practice to insert in a private Act a clause providing that the Act should be judicially noticed, but this does not necessarily make the Act a public one, the object of the clause being merely to facilitate proof.   " But though the Act be public, it is of a private nature.   The only object of the proviso for making it a public Act is that it may be judicially taken notice of instead of being specially pleaded, and to save the expense of proving an attested copy.   But it has never been held that an Act of a private nature derives any additional weight or authority from such a proviso "[27]   An Act may even be partly public and partly private.[28]

---

[25] Interpretation Act, s. 9
[26] *Duncan* v. *Paver* (1849), 5 Hare 415
[27] Per Lord Alvanley in *Hesse* v *Stevenson* (1803), 3 B & P 565
[28] Per Lord Holt, C J , in *Ingram* v. *Foote* (1701), 12 Mod. 613   Cf. *R* v *London County Council*, [1893] 2 Q B. 454

As to the construction of private Acts. Lord Halsbury
said in *Herron* v *Rathmines and Rathgar Improvement Commissioners* [29]: "It may be stated generally that Parliament
in passing a private Act looks to the public advantage and
security and looks to the interference with private rights
Where a work of any kind has to be constructed, Parliament
has made an elaborate set of provisions, intended to secure to
the public the advantages which the promoters propose as the
reason for legislation and as the consideration for the rights
of the persons affected, or sought to be affected, by the intended
legislation   In dealing with the latter class of questions it has
been said that the particular provisions may rather be regarded
as words of contract to which the Legislature has given its
sanction, than as the words of the Legislature itself ". Lord
Esher, M.R., was of opinion that there was ordinarily no
difference between the modes of construing a public and a
private Act, the only difference being that if there were any
doubt as to its meaning, a private Act is to be strictly
construed. " In the case of a private Act which is obtained
by persons for their own benefit, you construe more strictly
provisions which they allege to be for their benefit, because
the persons who obtain a private Act ought to take care that
it is so worded that that which they desire to obtain for
themselves is plainly stated in it." [30] This rule will hardly
apply where the Act, though in form local or personal, is
obtained for a public purpose and not for private profit, as
in *Stewart* v. *Thames Conservancy*,[31] where the words of
the Thames Conservancy Act, 1894, exempting certain properties from payment of " all parliamentary rates, taxes and
payments whatsoever " were held impliedly to exempt those
properties from payment of income tax to the Crown. Not
only may the provisions of a private Act be regarded as a
contract, they may also be regarded as a conveyance, as in

---

[29] [1892] A C 498, at p 501.
[30] *Altrincham Union* v *Cheshire Lines Committee* (1885), 15 Q. B D. 597.
[31] [1908] 1 K B 893

the case of private Acts, such as estate Acts, passed as a
method of assurance. "A law thus made, though it binds
all parties to the Bill, is yet looked upon rather as a private
conveyance than as a solemn Act of the Legislature" [32] The
method of construction of such private Acts will, therefore,
be that applied to the construction of conveyances and contracts according to the intention of the parties, and the
surrounding circumstances at the date of enactment may be
looked at as in the case of an agreement.[33] In *Harper* v.
Hedges [34] Scrutton, L J., speaking of the construction of
private Acts as contracts, said: "So far as persons not
concerned in the Act are concerned, the Act is read strictly
against the promoters; so far as the promoters themselves are
concerned, it is read as a contract between them and is to be
construed accordingly." And in *Savin* v. *Hoylake Ry.*[35] the
plaintiff had agreed with the promoters to pay the costs of
obtaining the Act, which contained the usual clause directing
the promoters to pay the costs. The plaintiff argued that
this clause abrogated his agreement with the promoters,
but Pollock, C.B., said: "A private Act of Parliament
is in the nature of an agreement between the parties;
why, then, may not an agreement be made in derogation
of that private Act, provided the agreement be not
inconsistent with the public interest?" As there is
a presumption against interference with private rights
by private Acts of Parliament, any words authorising
such interference are jealously scrutinised. As Tindal, C J.,
said [36]: "It is to be observed that the language of these Acts

[32] Blackstone, 2 Comm 344; *Hornby* v *Houlditch* (1737), cited 1
T. R 96, 97
[33] *Townley* v *Gibson* (1789), 2 T. R 705, *Rowbotham* v. *Wilson* (1860),
8 H L C 347, 363
[34] (1923), 93 L J. K. B 116.
[35] (1865), L R 1 Ex 9 Cf *G W Ry* v. *Waterford and Limerick Ry*
(1881), 17 Ch D 493, at p 504, *per* James, L J
[36] In *Parker* v *G W Ry.* (1844), 7 Scott N R. 835, at p. 870; *Stour-
bridge Canal Co* v *Wheeley* (1831), 2 B. & Ad 792, *per* Lord Tenterden,
at p 793

of Parliament is to be treated as the language of the promoters of them. They ask the Legislature to confer great privileges upon them, and profess to give the public certain advantages in return. Therefore, Acts passed under such circumstances should be construed strictly against the parties obtaining them, but liberally in favour of the public."

So in a recent case before the Judicial Committee on appeal from New Zealand Lord Tomlin said [37] · " In the first place it is to be observed that this is a private Act of Parliament passed with a strictly limited purpose as indicated in the preambles and accordingly it would be contrary to accepted canons of construction to give to the Act, unless compelled by unambiguous language, an effect which would unnecessarily alter the rights of the parties, if the language employed is capable of any other construction." And Lord Fitzgerald said in *Scottish Drainage, etc. Co.* v. *Campbell*,[38] speaking of private Acts which purport to impose a charge on private individuals: " I have always understood with reference to private Acts, as contradistinguished from public Acts of Parliament, that if a charge is imposed upon the person of an individual it must be so imposed in clear and express terms, and not left to implication." And, conversely, clear and unequivocal words are required before persons can by a private Act be deprived of a right to do what they were doing for reward before the Act came into force.[39] " If a public company, or any private individuals, obtain an Act of Parliament which they say enables them to take away the common law rights of any person, they are bound to show that it does it with sufficient clearness." [40]

Though in many cases of Acts affecting only private individuals it has been, as we have seen, customary to speak

[37] *Barton* v. *Moorhouse*, [1935] A. C 300

[38] (1889), 14 App. Cas. 139, 149.

[39] *Bournemouth-Swanage Motor Road and Ferry Co* v *Harvey & Sons*, [1929] 1 Ch. 686

[40] *Per* Mellish, L J., in *Clowes* v *Staffordshire Potteries, etc., Co.* (1873), 8 Ch. App 125

of these as contracts or bargains between the parties, in the
case of public undertakings, though authorised by private
Acts, these expressions are not appropriate. In the case of
railways, canals, gasworks, waterworks and similar public
utility undertakings, their Acts are not merely Parliamentary
contracts, they are conditional powers, which may or may
not be exercised. If they are exercised, certain duties
emerge, but if they are not exercised, generally speaking,
their exercise cannot be compelled by a sort of decree for
specific performance as in a contract. In *R.* v *York and
North Midland Ry.*[41] it was said: " It is said that a railway
Act is a contract on the part of the company to make the line
and that the public are a party to that contract and will be
aggrieved if the contract may be repudiated by the company
at any time before it is acted upon. Though commonly so
spoken of, railway Acts, in our opinion, are not contracts,
and ought not to be construed as such: they are what they
profess to be and no more: they give conditional powers
which, if acted upon, carry with them duties, but which, if
not acted upon, are not either in their nature or by express
words imperative on the companies to whom they are granted."
On the other hand, third parties, or the public, may have
rights under an Act of this description. In *Davis* v *Taff
Vale Ry* [42] the former was sued by the railway company
for rates in excess of those laid down in the Barry Dock and
Railways Act, 1888, and the company contended that this
Act was merely a contract between two railway companies
concerning exchange of traffic and did not affect rates to be
paid by the public. On this argument, Lord Watson said [43]:
" The provisions of a railway Act, even when they impose
mutual obligations, differ from private stipulations in this
essential respect, that they derive their force and existence,

---

[41] (1852), 1 E. & B 858, at p. 864 Cf. *Corbett* v. *S. E. Ry.*, [1905]
2 Ch. 280, 286; [1906] 2 Ch 12, 20
[42] [1895] A. C. 542
[43] *S. C*, at p. 552.

not from the agreement of the parties, but from the will of the Legislature; and when provisions of that kind are not limited to the interests of the parties mutually obliged, but impose upon both of them an obligation in favour of third parties, who are sufficiently designated, I am of opinion that the obligation so imposed must operate as a direct enactment of the Legislature in favour of these parties and cannot be regarded as a mere stipulation *inter alios* which they may have an interest, but no title, to enforce. These observations are not meant to apply to any case where a private contract, made between two companies, is scheduled and confirmed by the Act; because in such a case the form of the enactment might be held to indicate that it is to operate as a contract, but not otherwise." With regard to this last sentence in the opinion of Lord Watson, private Acts often contain provisions for the protection of particular interests or individuals in which the public has no concern and which either party to the bargain may waive.[44] So it is the common practice to schedule to private Acts agreements made between the promoters and other persons and to declare in the Act that such agreements are valid and binding; thus making these agreements part of the statute in order to avoid all questions of *ultra vires* or illegality. In fact, by this method it may be possible to create rights unknown to the law and unenforceable by the ordinary law of contract, as, for instance, as offending against the rule against perpetuities.[45] In cases of this sort, the rules for the construction of statutes will be applied, not those applicable to the construction of contracts.

---

[44] *Per* Phillimore, L J., in *Att -Gen* v. *N. E Ry.*, [1915] 1 Ch 905, at p 917

[45] *Sevenoaks Ry* v. *L. C & D. Ry* (1879), 11 Ch D 625, *Manchester Ship Canal Co* v *Manchester Racecourse Co* , [1900] 2 Ch 352; [1901] 2 Ch. 37, 50.

IX.—Presumptions

To assist in the construction of statutes, the Courts have from time to time laid down numerous presumptions on which to found a *prima facie* approach to the consideration of a statute. These are very numerous, nearly thirty are enumerated in the index to Maxwell; they also vary very much in their force and influence; indeed, this fluctuation varies from time to time and is said to be stronger or weaker according to the view taken by the Court of the particular statute in question. To this we shall return later.[1] Several have been already referred to incidentally. Some of these presumptions may be shortly stated:—

(1) *The Legislature does not make mistakes.*—As Lord Halsbury said in *Commissioners of Income Tax* v. *Pemsel*[2]: " But I do not think it competent for any Court to proceed upon the assumption that the Legislature has made a mistake. Whatever the real fact may be, I think a Court of law is bound to proceed on the assumption that the Legislature is an ideal person that does not make mistakes." In *Bristol Guardians* v. *Bristol Waterworks*,[3] Lord Loreburn pointed out that owing to a draftsman's blunder the water company under its special Act of 1862 could charge what it liked to certain workhouses: " It is quite true that in construing private Acts the rule is to interpret them strictly against the promoters and liberally in favour of the public, but a Court is not at liberty to make laws, however strongly it may feel that Parliament has overlooked some necessary provision or even has been overreached by the promoters of a private Bill "

(2) *The Legislature knows the practice.*—The Local Government Board had dismissed an appeal by an owner

---

[1] See p. 297, *infra*
[2] [1891] A. C. 531, at p 549
[3] [1914] A C. 379, at p. 387

against whom a closing order had been made under the House and Town Planning, etc , Act, 1909, without disclosing the contents of their inspector's report or allowing the appellant to be heard. - The Court of Appeal thought this was contrary to natural justice and allowed the appeal; but Hamilton, L.J., in a dissenting judgment, said [4]: "I think it is a sound inference to be drawn as a matter of construction that the Legislature, aware, as I take it to have been, of the practice of these inquiries and its incidents, intended that the local inquiry which it prescribed should be the usual local inquiry and that the usual incidents should attach in default of any special enactment, including the incident that the Board would treat the report as confidential." The House of Lords reversed the decision of the Court of Appeal, Lord Moulton saying [5]: "In the present case, however, the Legislature has provided an appeal, but it is an appeal to an administrative department of State and not to a judicial body."

(3) *The Legislature does not intend what is inconvenient or unreasonable.*—"Unless Parliament has conferred on the Court that power" (*i.e.*, to make a foreigner resident abroad a bankrupt) "in language which is unmistakable, the Court is not to assume that Parliament intended to do that which might seriously affect foreigners who are not resident here and might give offence to foreign governments." [6] In *R.* v. *Tonbridge Overseers,* [7] Brett, M.R., said: "With regard to inconvenience, I think it is a most dangerous doctrine. I agree that if the inconvenience is not only great but what I may call an absurd inconvenience in reading an enactment in its ordinary sense, whereas if you read it in a manner of which it is capable, though not its ordinary sense, there

---

[4] *R* v. *Local Government Board, Ex p Arlidge,* [1914] 1 K B. 160, at p 197
[5] *S. C.,* [1915] A C 120, at p. 150
[6] *Per* Lindley, M R , in *Re A. B & Co ,* [1900] 1 Q. B. 541, at p 544; affirmed *sub nom Cooke* v. *Charles A Vogeler & Co ,* [1901] A. C 102.
[7] (1884), 13 Q B D. 339, at p 342

would not be any inconvenience at all, there would be reason why you should not read it according to its ordinary grammatical meaning. If an enactment is such that by reading it in its ordinary sense you produce a palpable injustice, whereas by reading it in a sense it can bear, though not exactly its ordinary sense, it will produce no injustice, then I admit one must assume that the Legislature intended that it should be so read as to produce no injustice."

(4) *Words are presumed to be used in their popular sense in statutes* —See p. 171, *supra*

(5) *The same meaning attaches to the same expression throughout the Act* —See p. 174, *supra*.

(6) *The Legislature does not intend any alteration in the existing law except what it expressly declares.*—" The general rule in exposition is this, that in all doubtful matters, and where the expression is in general terms, the words are to receive such a construction as may be agreeable to the rules of common law in cases of that nature, for statutes are not presumed to make any alteration in the common law further or otherwise than the Act does expressly declare " [8]

So, for instance, a mercantile agent, entitled to pledge goods in his possession by the consent of the owner under section 2 (1) of the Factors Act, 1889, is confined to transactions entered into as a mercantile agent and is not entitled to effect a pledge of household furniture not in the way of trade,[9] and where railways and other undertakings are given statutory powers which will " injuriously affect " private rights, and it is provided that full compensation is to be made for the exercise of these powers, it is generally to be understood that this provision applies to damage which

---

[8] *Per curiam Arthur* v *Bokenham* (1708), 11 Mod 150; *per* Lord Wright in *Secretary of State for India* v. *Bank of India, Ltd* (1938), L R 65 I A. 286   [9] *Waddington* v. *Neale* (1917), 96 L T 786.

would have been actionable but for the grant of statutory powers [10]; though, of course, there may be cases where the common law right is taken away by the statute. Where a horse had taken fright while passing along a road near a railway, by reason of the noise of the railway engines, the Court held that the Legislature must be presumed to have known that the railway would pass near the highway and that the public using the highway would suffer inconvenience thereby; but it was not unreasonable to suppose that this inconvenience was intended in order that the greater part of the public should benefit from the railway and that therefore the statute took away the common law right arising from the annoyance.[11]

So on section 159 of the Hastings Improvement Act, the question was whether the words "any ground" in the Act were to be construed as confined to any *made* ground, it being argued that to read it literally would put upon the owners of unmade ground an obligation which did not rest upon them at common law. Reading, C.J., thought the intention of the Legislature was to protect the public from danger and therefore that the obligation under the Act extended to an owner of unmade ground.[12]

On the contrary, the Vexatious Actions Act, 1896, which authorises the Court to order a litigant, who indulges in persistent and vexatious legal proceedings, to first obtain leave to proceed with his litigation, was held not to apply to criminal proceedings.[13]

In *Leach* v. *R.*,[14] in the House of Lords, the question arose whether a wife was not only a competent but also a compellable witness in a case in which her husband was indicted.

---

10 See *per* Cockburn, C J., in *New River Co* v *Johnson* (1860), 2 E & E 435, at p 442

11 *R* v *Pease* (1832), 4 B & Ad 30; *L. B. & S. C. Ry.* v *Truman* (1885), 11 App. Cas 45; *Cowper-Essex* v *Acton Local Board* (1889), 14 App Cas. 153.

12 *Gaby* v *Palmer* (1916), 85 L J K B. 1240, 1244.

13 *Re Boaler*, [1915] 1 K. B 21

14 [1912] A C 305. See p 299, *infra*.

It was said by the House of Lords that the common law right of a wife to refuse to give evidence against her husband could only be taken away by a definite and positive enactment to the contrary, and not by an inference from an ambiguous section such as section 4 of the Criminal Evidence Act, 1898.

In *R*. v. *Russell* (*Earl*) [15] although, as we shall see, there is a presumption against extending jurisdiction beyond the limits of the United Kingdom, the section (57) of the Offences against the Person Act, 1861, was held to extend to the case where the bigamous marriage took place beyond the King's dominions.

(7) *Mens Rea.*—In the criminal law, it has been a cardinal maxim that a guilty mind or *mens rea* must be proved before the penalty provided by the law can be inflicted. As Cave, J., said in the well-known case of *R* v *Tolson* [16] "At common law an honest and reasonable belief in the existence of circumstances which, if true, would make the act for which a prisoner is indicted an innocent act, has always been held to be a good defence. This doctrine is embodied in the somewhat uncouth maxim: '*Actus non facit reum, nisi mens sit rea*' . . . So far as I am aware, it has never been suggested that these exceptions do not equally apply in the case of statutory offences unless they are excluded expressly or by necessary implication." And Stephen, J., in the same case [17]: "Crimes are at the present day far more accurately defined, by statute or otherwise, than they formerly were. The mental element in most crimes is marked by one of the words 'maliciously', 'fraudulently', 'negligently' or 'knowingly'." And Wills, J. [18]: "Although *prima facie* and as a general rule, there must be a mind at fault before

[15] [1901] A. C 446 See p 274, *infra*.
[16] (1889), 23 Q. B. D 168, at p 181, but cf *R* v. *Wheat*, [1921] 2 K. B 119, where it is said "The principle is stated too widely The Court must pay strict regard to the wording of the statute"
[17] *S C*, at p 187
[18] *S. C.*, at p. 173

there can be a crime, it is not an inflexible rule, and a statute may relate to such a subject-matter and may be so framed as to make an act criminal whether there has been any intention to break the law or otherwise do wrong, or not . and in such a case the substance of the enactment is that a man shall take care that the statutory direction is obeyed, and that if he fails to do so he does so at his peril." " *Mens rea* may be dispensed with by statute, although the terms which should induce us to infer that it is dispensed with must be very strong." [19] So the statute must in each case of a statutory offence—and these have increased and are increasing rapidly—be examined to discover if knowledge or a guilty mind is of the essence of the offence or not.[20] As Goddard, J., said recently [21]: " With the complexity of modern legislation one knows that there are times when the Court is constrained to find that by reason of the clear terms of an Act of Parliament, *mens rea* or the absence of *mens rea* becomes immaterial and that if a certain act is done, an offence is committed whether the person charged knew or did not know of the act." Many statutes, especially recent ones, do not require a *mens rea* in order to justify a conviction under their provisions. For instance, in *Hobbs* v. *Winchester Corporation*,[22] the defendant was convicted under section 117 of the Public Health Act, 1875, as a person in whose possession or on whose premises unsound meat intended for human consumption was found, although he may not have known of its unsoundness. So a publican would be guilty of an offence under the Licensing Act if he sold liquor to a drunken person whom he had no reason to think was drunk, and also if his servant in his absence and contrary to his orders did so, provided the servant was acting in the course of his employment.[23]

---

[19] *Per* Cockburn, C J., in *R* v. *Sleep* (1861), L & C 44, at p 52
[20] *R* v *Prince* (1875), 44 L J M C 122.
[21] *Evans* v *Dell* (1937), 53 T. L R 310, 313   Cf. *Chajutin* v. *White-head,* [1938] 1 K B. 506.   [22] [1910] 2 K. B. 471.
[23] *Cundy* v *Lecocq* (1884), 13 Q. B. D 207; *Police Commissioner* v. *Cartman,* [1896] 1 Q. B. 655; *Williamson* v. *Norris,* [1899] 1 Q. B. 7, *Brooks* v. *Mason,* [1902] 2 K B 743.

(8) *Vested rights, public or private, are not taken away; at least without compensation.*—In *Re Cuno* [24] Bowen, L.J., said: " In the construction of statutes you must not construe the words so as to take away rights which already existed before the statute was passed, unless you have plain words which indicate that such was the intention of the Legislature." And in *Randolph* v *Milman*,[25] where the question arose as to whether the right of prebendaries of cathedrals to vote at the election of proctors was taken away by the Ecclesiastical Commissioners Act, 1840, a right which the prebendaries had enjoyed from time immemorial, the Court said: " We agree with the principle of the law stated by Sir Roundell Palmer at the outset, that vested rights are not to be taken away without express words or necessary intendment or implication; and upon adverting to the statute, it will be found that there is no express extinction of the right here claimed, and no necessary implication or intendment to that effect." And the like is laid down in more recent cases. For instance, in *Turton* v. *Turnbull*,[26] a question under the Agricultural Holdings Act, 1923, Scrutton, L J., said: " As by the Act he (the landlord) is being deprived of his common law rights, I think we must construe the Act with some liberality in his favour or scrutinise the tenant's claim with some strictness " The Court has held that the Law of Distress Amendment Act, 1908, s. 1, must be strictly complied with, as the statute was one depriving the landlord of his common law rights.[27] Brett, M.R., in *Att.-Gen.* v. *Horner*,[28] said: " It is a proper rule of construction not to construe an Act of Parliament as interfering with or injuring persons' rights without compensa-

---

[24] (1889), 43 Ch. D. 12, at p 17; *Forbes* v *Ecclesiastical Commissioners* (1872), L. R. 15 Eq. 51, 53.

[25] (1868), L. R. 4 C. P 107.

[26] [1934] 2 K. B 197, *West Ham Corporation* v *Benabo*, [1934] 2 K B 253

[27] *Druce* v *Beaumont Property Trust, Ltd*, [1935] 2 K B 257

[28] (1884), 14 Q B D. 245, at p. 257; cited with approval by Greer, L J, in *Consett Iron Co* v. *Clavering*, [1935] 2 K B 42, at p 58 Cf *West Midlands Joint Electricity Board* v *Pitt*, [1932] 2 K B 1.

tion unless one is obliged to so construe it." Lord Atkinson in *Central Control Board* v *Cannon Brewery Co* ,[29] referring to what he described as a canon of construction of statutes well recognised, said: "That canon is this : that an intention to take away the property of a subject without giving him a legal right to compensation for the loss of it is not to be imputed to the Legislature unless that intention is expressed in unequivocal terms." The Judicial Committee has also spoken to the same effect, for in *Colonial Sugar Refining Co.* v. *Melbourne Commissioners* [30] they said they ought to apply the principle that a statute should not be held to take away a private right of property, which in this case the appellants had acquired by limitation, without compensation unless the intention to do so was expressed in clear and unambiguous terms. So, the presumption is that a litigant is not deprived of his right of appeal.[31]

(9) *The jurisdiction of the Superior Courts is not enlarged, nor ousted, except by express enactment.*—The Admiralty Court Act, 1861, s. 7, gave the Admiralty Court jurisdiction over "any claim for damage done by a ship ". The question arose whether this gave that Court jurisdiction in a case of personal injury caused by a collision. The Court said[32] : "It is impossible to suppose that the Legislature can have intended under a general enactment like the present, as it were by a side wind, to effect so material a change in the rights and relative positions of the parties concerned in such an action "

---

[29] [1919] A C 744, at p 752, quoted in *Marshall* v *Blackpool Corporation*, [1933] 1 K B. 688 This judgment of the Divisional Court was restored by the House of Lords, [1935] A C. 16, *Bournemouth and Swanage Motor Road and Ferry Co* v *Harvey & Sons*, [1929] 1 Ch 686, at p 697, *per* Scrutton, L J
[30] [1927] A C 343
[31] *Mackay* v *Monk*, [1918] A. C 59
[32] *Smith* v *Brown* (1871), L R. 6 Q B. 729, *Seward* v *The Vera Cruz* (1884), 10 App. Cas. 59; *Att.-Gen.* v *Sillem* (1864), 10 H L C 704

Likewise as to ousting the jurisdiction. In *Albon* v. *Pyke*,[33] Tindal, C.J., said: "The general rule undoubtedly is that the jurisdiction of the superior Courts is not taken away except by express words or necessary implication." Lord Salvesen said: "A general rule applicable to the construction of statutes is that there is not to be presumed without express words, an authority to deprive the Supreme Court of a jurisdiction which it had previously exercised or to extend the privative jurisdiction of the Supreme Court to the inferior Courts."[34]

For instance, it does not follow that because authority is vested in some body, for example a commissioner of taxes, authorised to determine a question of distress, the jurisdiction of the High Court to try an action for illegal distress is ousted.[35] The matter was thus summarised by Willes, J., in *Wolverhampton New Waterworks Co.* v. *Hawkesford*[36]: "There are three classes of cases in which a liability may be established founded upon a statute. One is, where there was a liability existing at common law, and that liability is affirmed by a statute which gives a special and peculiar form of remedy different from the remedy which existed at common law: there, unless the statute contains words which expressly or by necessary implication exclude the common law remedy, the party suing has his election to pursue either that or the statutory remedy. The second class of cases is, where the statute gives the right to sue merely, but provides no particular form of remedy; there the party can only proceed by action at common law. But there is a third class, *viz.*, where a liability not existing at common law is created by a statute which at the same time gives a special and particular remedy for enforcing it. . The remedy provided by the statute must be followed, and it is not competent to the party to pursue the course applicable to cases

[33] (1842), 4 M & G 421, at p. 424
[34] *Dunbar* v *Scottish County Investment Co*, [1920] S C 210
[35] See *Shaftesbury* v. *Russell* (1823), 25 R R. 534
[36] (1859), 6 C B. (N s.) 336, at p. 356

of the second class." Dealing with the facts of the particular
case before him the learned Judge said [37]: " Reading the 21st
section by the aid of the light thrown upon it by the subsequent sections, it appears to me that the remedy was intended
to be enforced only in the particular mode prescribed against
persons who are shareholders " And where a statute provides
a particular remedy for an infringement of a right of property
thereby created or re-enacted, the jurisdiction of the Court
of Chancery to protect that right by injunction is not excluded
unless the statute expressly so provides, as the jurisdiction of
that Court is not limited to cases in which there is a right
at law.[38] " The true principle is that where a duty imposed
by the Act is not intended for the benefit of any particular
class of persons, but for that of the public generally, no right
of action accrues by implication to any person who suffers
no more injury from its breach than the rest of the public.
Where a specific remedy is provided by statute, proceedings
must be taken to enforce it, and if no specific remedy is so provided the proper course is to proceed by indictment.   A public
injury is indictable, but it is not actionable unless the sufferer
from the breach has sustained some direct and substantial
private and particular damage beyond and in excess of that
suffered in common with the rest of the public." [39]   In *Monk*
v. *Warbey* [40] the question of remedy open to a person injured
by the driver of a motor car who was not insured arose on a
consideration of section 35 (1) of the Road Traffic Act, 1930.
It was held that the penalties prescribed by that Act were
not the only remedy, and Greer, L.J., said [41]: " *Prima facie*
a person who has been injured by a breach of a statute has
a right to recover damages from the person committing it,

---

37 *S. C*, at p 357.
38 *Per* Farwell, J , in *Stevens* v *Chown*, [1901] 1 Ch. 894, quoting
Turner, L J., in *Emperor of Austria* v. *Day* (1861), 3 D. F & G. 217, at
p 253   Cf *R* v *Buchanan* (1846), 8 Q B. 883, 887
39 Maxwell, p. 345, and the cases there cited
40 [1935] 1 K. B. 75.
41 *S. C.*, p. 81.

unless it can be established by considering the whole of the Act that no such right was intended to be given." The learned Lord Justice went on to quote from the judgment of Atkin (then L.J), in *Phillips* v. *Britannia Hygienic Laundry Co.*[42]: "One question to be considered is, Does the Act contain a reference to the remedy for the breach of it? *Prima facie*, if it does, that is the only remedy. But that is not conclusive. The intention as disclosed by its scope and wording must still be regarded, and it may still be that, though the statute creates the duty and provides the penalty, the duty is nevertheless owed to individuals."

But where a statute gave a right to recover expenses in a Court of summary jurisdiction from a person not otherwise liable, it was held that there was no right to come to the High Court for a declaration of the existence of such a right, except by way of appeal. The litigant could only proceed in the summary Court, and Lord Watson said: "The Legislature . . . has therefore by plain implication enacted that no other Court has any authority to entertain or decide these matters "[43]

The commonest ouster of the jurisdiction of the Courts is to be found in provisions to refer disputes to arbitration. For instance, section 33 of the Tramways Act of 1870, providing that disputes should be referred to arbitration, was held to oust the jurisdiction of the Courts with regard to differences falling within its terms.[44] Under section 2 (1) of the Workmen's Compensation Act, 1897, notice of an accident is to be given as soon as possible and a claim for compensation has to be made within six months of the occurrence of the accident. More than six months after the accident the workman filed a request for arbitration. He

---

[42] [1923] 2 K B. 832, at p 841.

[43] *Barraclough* v. *Brown*, [1897] A C. 615

[44] *Norwich Corporation* v. *Norwich Tramways*, [1906] 2 K. B 119, *Crisp* v *Bunbury* (1832), 34 R R 747. As to the liberty of the parties to agree upon a particular mode of reference, cf *G W. Ry* v *Waterford and Limerick Ry* (1881), 17 Ch D 493, at p 504, *per* James, L J

was held entitled to do so as there was no limitation in the Act with regard to arbitration.[45] In a recent case, the Wheat Commission claimed that the appellants were importers of " German middlings " and that this product was " flour " within the Wheat Act of 1932, and that therefore the appellants were liable to make quota payments A bylaw made by the Wheat Commission to the effect that the Arbitration Act, 1889, shall not apply to proceedings under the Act was held to be *ultra vires* and invalid, as the Wheat Commission was a public authority and there were no express words in the Wheat Act ousting the jurisdiction of the Courts.[46] It is sometimes provided that a reference to arbitration should be a condition precedent to the right to commence an action.[47] In such cases the statutory procedure alone can be followed.

(10) *The Crown is not affected by statutes unless expressly named therein.*—For instance, locomotives owned by the Crown and driven by servants of the Crown on Crown service are not affected by the Locomotives Act, 1865,[48] nor do the provisions of the Rent Restriction Acts, 1920 and 1923, apply to premises owned by the Crown.[49]

(11) *Operation confined to United Kingdom.*—Though many offences have been extended to render liable British subjects committing them in any part of the world,[50] the presumption is that, if the statute is silent on the point, the

---

[45] *Powell* v *Main Colliery Co.*, [1900] A. C. 366.
[46] *R W. Paul, Ltd* v *Wheat Commissioners*, [1937] A. C. 139.
[47] *Cayzer, Irvine & Co* v. *Board of Trade*, [1927] 1 K. B 269
[48] *Cooper* v *Hawkins*, [1904] 2 K. B 164.
[49] *Wirral Estates* v *Shaw*, [1932] 2 K. B 247.
[50] *E g.*, treason and treason felony, breaches of the Foreign Enlistment Act, homicide, bigamy, slave dealing; offences committed in or in relation to the Indian Native States and other countries within the provisions of the Foreign Jurisdiction Act, 1890 See Craies, Chap VIII Colonial statutes have no extra-territorial effect, even as regards British subjects unless such power has been conferred on the colony by some Imperial authority Cf *Macleod* v *Att.-Gen for N. S W.*, [1891] A. C 455. This power has in several instances been granted.

intention of the Legislature is to confine the operation of a
statute to the territorial limits of the United Kingdom and
also does not include foreigners

For instance, it was said by Lord Halsbury, L C., in
Macleod v. *Att.-Gen. of N. S. W.*[51]: " All crime is local.
The jurisdiction over the crime belongs to the country where
the crime is committed, and except over her own subjects,
Her Majesty and the Imperial Legislature have no power
whatever." This is, as noted below, subject to exceptions.

Before 1861 a person married in England, who subsequently in the spouse's lifetime went through a form of
marriage abroad, was not indictable in this country and this
was the argument in *Earl Russell's Case* in 1901 before the
House of Lords. The words of section 57 of the Offences
against the Person Act, 1861, are: " Whosoever, being married,
shall marry any other person during the life of the former
husband or wife, whether the second marriage shall have taken
place in England or Ireland, or elsewhere, shall be guilty of
felony "; and it was contended that this could not be applied
to a second marriage which took place in the United States
of America as " elsewhere " must be construed as meaning
" elsewhere within the United Kingdom or the King's
Dominions ". The House of Lords summarily rejected this
argument.[52] Lord Brougham, in *Jefferys* v. *Boosey*,[53] said.
" Generally we must assume that the Legislature confines its
enactments to its own subjects over whom it has authority
and to whom it owes a duty in return for their obedience.
Nothing is more clear than that it may also extend its provisions to foreigners in certain cases and may without express
words make it appear that such is the intendment of these
provisions But the presumption is rather against the exten-
sion and the proof of it is rather upon those who would
maintain that such is the meaning of the enactment." It has

---

[51] [1891] A. C 455, at p 458
[52] *R* v *Russell (Earl)*, [1901] A C. 446
[53] (1854), 4 H L. C 815, at p 970.

been held that the provisions of the Fatal Accidents Acts, 1846 and 1864, apply for the benefit of the representatives of a deceased foreigner at least as against an English wrong-doer.[54] So an act of bankruptcy must have taken place within the jurisdiction and our Courts have no jurisdiction to make a receiving order against a foreigner resident abroad, who, without coming into this country, has here a place of business and has contracted debts.[55] A British subject domiciled in France made an unattested will valid in that country and admitted to probate here. It was held that it effectually exercised a general testamentary power of appointment over the trust funds of an English settlement.[56]

An Act of 4 & 5 Will. 4 abolished certain weights and measures, and by section 21 it was enacted that any contract made by such weights and measures shall be null and void. The question was whether a contract of sale made in this country after the passing of the Act for goods to be weighed and measured according to the old scale was void if the goods were not to be weighed, measured and delivered in this country, but in Africa. Parke, B., said [57]: "The Act applies to those contracts only which are to be performed by the commodities being measured in the United Kingdom. Otherwise a contract made in China would have to have English weights and measures sent out there." On the other hand, the provisions of the statute against slave trading (5 Geo. 4, c. 113) by "any person" was held not to be confined to acts done by British subjects in furtherance of the slave trade in England or the British colonies, but to apply to such acts done by British subjects in places not part of the British dominions.[58] Before the passing of the legislation legalising marriage with a deceased wife's sister in 1907 a

[54] *Davidson* v *Hall*, [1901] 2 K B 606

[55] *Re A B & Co*, [1900] 1 Q B 541, 544; *sub nom Cooke* v *Charles A Vogeler & Co.*, [1901] A. C 102, *Re Debtors*, [1936] 1 Ch 622

[56] *Re Simpson*, [1916] 1 Ch 502

[57] *Rosseter* v. *Cahlmann* (1853), 8 Ex 361, at p 363.

[58] R. v *Zulueta* (1843), 1 C & K. 215.

British subject made such a marriage in Denmark where it
was valid; the Court held the Danish marriage invalid, and
Lord Campbell said [59]: " It is quite obvious that no civilised
State can allow its domiciled subjects or citizens by making
a temporary visit to a foreign country to enter into a contract
to be performed in the place of domicil, if the contract is
forbidden by the law of the place of domicil as contrary to
religion or morality or to any of its fundamental institutions."
So one X, describing herself as a widow, married D, an
Englishman in 1904   She had in 1898 married a domiciled
Frenchman, but this marriage had been annulled in France
on a ground not recognised here   The marriage of 1904 was
held to be bigamous [60]   Many more instances of the kind
might be cited from authorities on private international law.

(12) *Statutes do not violate the principles of international
law.*—" Every statute is to be so interpreted and applied, as
far as its language admits, as not to be inconsistent with
the comity of nations or with the established principles of
international law "[61]   Terms in British Acts sometimes
receive a limited construction in accordance with what is
assumed to be a conflict with international law.   " The
Judges may not pronounce an Act *ultra vires* as contravening
international law, but may recoil, in case of ambiguity, from
a construction which would involve a breach of the ascertained and accepted rules of international law."[62]   Some
examples of the rule have been illustrated from the cases
of foreigners (*ante*, p. 276)   So a foreign subject, not prohibited from engaging in the slave trade by the laws of his
own country, recovered damages in our Courts for the wrongful
seizure by a British man-of-war of a cargo of slaves [63]; as
the Act of Parliament, which authorised the commanders of

---

[59] *Brook* v. *Brook* (1858), 9 H. L C 193
[60] *Ogden* v *Ogden*, [1908] P 43
[61] *Bloxam* v. *Favre* (1883), 8 P D 101; 9 P D 130
[62] Craies, p 71; *Rochefoucauld* v *Boustead* (1896), 66 L J Ch 75
[63] *Madrazo* v *Willes* (1820), 3 B. & Ald 353

our ships of war to seize and prosecute " all ships and vessels engaged in the slave trade ", was construed as tending not to affect the rights of foreigners, as otherwise it would have been contrary to the law of nations   So also in *Santos* v. *Illidge*,[64] a contract for the purchase of slaves to be performed in Brazil was held to be actionable in this country as the contract was not unlawful in Brazil and was not then prohibited by our statutes.   Our law respects diplomatic privilege   Accordingly no representative of a foreign power at our Court can be sued while he is an ambassador nor within a reasonable time after his recall during which he might remain in this country.[66]   Real property is always subject to the laws of the State in which it is situated. Accordingly, as " the territory and soil of England . . . is governed by all statutes which are in force in England " [67] and it makes no difference whether the owner of the soil be domiciled in England or elsewhere, nor whether the interest in the land is a chattel interest or a freehold interest, a will disposing of either of these interests in realty must be validly executed and attested in accordance with English law [68]; whereas personalty is practically always governed by the law of the domicil of its owner and not by the law of its situation. Thus the Legacy Duty Act, 1796, imposing a duty on legacies given by a " will of any person out of his personal estate " and the Succession Duty Act, 1853, imposing a duty on every " disposition of property " whereby " any person " became " entitled to any property " on the death of another, were held not to apply either in the case of a deceased foreigner or even to a deceased British subject domiciled abroad, though the property was in England.[69]

[64] (1860), 8 C B (N S) 861
[66] *Musurus Bey* v *Gadban*, [1894] 2 Q. B 352
[67] *Per* Lord Selborne in *Freke* v. *Lord Carbery* (1873), L R 16 Eq. 466.
[68] *Pepin* v. *Bruyère*, [1902] 1 Ch. 24
[69] *Wallace* v *Att.-Gen* (1865), 1 Ch. App 1, *Harding* v *Queensland Commissioners of Stamps*, [1898] A C. 769, 774. As to liability for Income Tax, see *Colquhoun* v *Brooks* (1889), 14 App Cas. 493, and for estate duty, *Winans* v. *Att -Gen* , [1910] A. C. 27.

(13) *A person must not be permitted to impair the obligation of his contract by his own act, or to profit by his own wrong; and a statute will be construed in this sense, if possible* —So it was held that the Vaccination Act of 1867, which authorised a summons to a parent " to appear with his child ", was complied with by the appearance of the parent without the child, for otherwise the parent could defeat the object of the statute by refusing to produce his child.[70]

The Gaming Act of 1710, which enacted that securities given for money lost at play should be " utterly frustrate, void and of none effect, to all intents and purposes ", was held to be confined to the drawer and any person claiming under him from recovering from the loser, but did not affect an innocent indorsee for value, who might sue the drawer This construction involved holding the securities voidable against certain persons, but valid against others; and a *bona fide* holder of such securities is still protected at the present day.[71] So, although the Infants' Relief Act, 1874, s. 1, makes all contracts entered into by infants for the supply of goods which are not necessaries absolutely void, the infant cannot recover any money he has paid for them, if he has used or consumed them. Lord Coleridge, C.J., said on this section: " No doubt the words of the Infants' Relief Act, 1874, are strong and general; but a reasonable construction ought to be put upon them. . When an infant has paid for something and consumed or used it, it is contrary to natural justice that he should recover back the money which he has paid." [72] If the infant has in fact taken no benefit under such a contract, he would probably be able to recover his money.[73]

The Bankruptcy Act of 1893 enacted that voluntary

[70] *Dutton* v *Atkins* (1871), L R 6 Q B. 373
[71] *Edwards* v *Dick* (1821), 4 B. & Ald. 212, *Woolf* v *Hamilton*, [1898] 2 Q B 337
[72] *Valentini* v. *Canali* (1889), 24 Q B D 166.
[73] *Pearce* v. *Brain*, [1929] 2 K B 310

settlements made by a person who became bankrupt within two years thereafter should be void as against the trustee in bankruptcy. "Void" was held to be "voidable", so that the title of a purchaser for valuable consideration from the donee before avoidance could not afterwards be defeated by the trustee.[74] And the 13 Eliz. c. 5 similarly does not affect a *bona fide* conveyance for valuable consideration, although it was made with intent to defeat an execution creditor.[75]

These cases, which might be multiplied, imply that the Courts in adopting the construction in accordance with the presumption, were of opinion that by so doing they were carrying into effect the intentions of the Legislature. Hence the restricted construction placed upon the various statutes involved. If, however, the Court is of opinion that the intention of the Legislature can only be effected by a strict construction of the sections of the Acts, combined with the language and structure of their provisions, words abridging or avoiding the effect of instruments and contracts will receive their primary and natural meaning. For instance, a bill of sale *must* be in accordance with the form in the schedule to the Act and no material deviation is allowed See *supra,* p. 214.

X.—RULES AND ORDERS

It is very common to find the Legislature giving power to certain individuals or bodies to make rules under a statute in order to carry its provisions into effect, and it is usual in modern legislation to confine the efforts of the Legislature to the laying down of general principles and to delegate to others the power of making rules and orders in order to settle details of the procedure necessary to give effect to the general principles embodied in the Act. This is particularly the case with Orders in Council. The modern statute often consists of a short enactment setting out

---

[74] *Re Brall,* [1893] 2 Q. B 381
[75] *Wood v Dixie* (1845), 7 Q. B. 892.

the object of the legislation and the rest, possibly even the date of the coming into force of the Act, is left to Orders in Council or to regulations issued by a Government Department. Hence the phrase " government by Whitehall ". Much has been written in opposition to this type of legislation,[1] and in the opinion of many, too much is left to the discretion of Ministers and their departments. From a practical point of view, the method has the disadvantage of obscuring discovery of when or if certain provisions of the Act have come into force, for the relevant Orders in Council are not always readily available to the ordinary layman Regulations and bylaws under statutory powers are in the same category, which is sometimes called Subordinate Legislation,[2] from the fact that these powers are derived from and are controlled by the statute by which they are created. The more important of the rules affecting these matters may be shortly stated:—

(i) Statutory powers may be exercised as soon as the statute conferring them is passed, unless a contrary intention appears therein; but if the statute is not to come into force immediately on its enactment, then these powers shall not come into operation until the Act does so—subject to two exceptions· (a) if a contrary intention appears in the Act; (b) if the exercise of the power or powers is or are necessary to bring the Act into operation.[3]

(ii) Where an Act passed after 1890 confers a power or imposes a duty, unless a contrary intention appears the power may be exercised and the duty shall be performed from time to time as occasion requires.[4] This rebuts the presumption which formerly existed that such powers were exhausted after a single exercise of them. The same rule applies to successive holders of an office.[5] Statutory rules, regulations and bylaws

---

[1] Cf. for instance, Lord Hewart's powerful indictment of this method in " The New Despotism ".

[2] See Craies (4th ed), Part II, Chap III

[3] Interpretation Act, 1889, s 37

[4] Interpretation Act, 1889, s 32 (1)

[5] *Ibid* , s 32 (2).

may be rescinded, revoked, amended or varied within the same powers[6]: "Where a statute enables an authority to make regulations, a breach of the regulation or regulations made under the Act becomes for the purpose of obedience or disobedience a provision of the Act. The regulation is only the machinery by which Parliament has determined whether certain things shall or shall not be done."[7]

(iii) If the statute is repealed, the bylaws made under it are naturally repealed also.

(iv) Expressions used in these Orders in Council, rules, regulations and bylaws shall, unless the contrary intention appears, have the same meanings as in the Act confirming the power to make them[8]

(v) Owing to the delegated or derived authority of these Orders, rules, regulations and bylaws, the Courts will generally not give effect to them unless they are satisfied that all conditions precedent to their validity have been fulfilled, e.g., has the Order, etc., been made and promulgated in accordance with the statute; and has the rule-making power been exercised in accordance with the provisions of the statute by which it was granted. The statute may, of course, direct as to the former that the Orders, etc , should be judicially noticed, or may expressly prohibit inquiry into the latter—but neither of these are common or probable. Speaking of the rules made under the Patents Act, 1888, Lord Herschell said[9]: "I own I feel very great difficulty in giving to this provision that they shall be of the same effect as if they were contained in this Act any other meaning than this, that you shall for all purposes of construction or obligation or otherwise treat them exactly as if they were in the Act." This opinion,

6 *Ibid* , s. 32 (3). This rule does not extend to Orders in Council, orders, warrants, schemes or letters patent, etc Contrast the different wording in s. 32 (3) and s 37

7 *Per* Lord Alverstone, C J., in *Willingale* v *Norris*, [1909] 1 K B. 57, at p 64.

8 Interpretation Act, 1889, s 31

9 *Institute of Patent Agents* v *Lockwood*, [1894] A C 347, at p. 360.

in the view of Lord Dunedin in the case to be cited, precluded inquiry as to whether the rules were *ultra vires* or not. In the *Minister of Health* v. *R., Ex p. Yaffé,*[10] an order of the Minister under an improvement scheme in Liverpool was in question. Under the Housing Act, 1925, when such an order was made confirming an improvement scheme, "the order of the Minister, when made, shall have effect as if enacted in this Act". It was held by the House of Lords that these words do not preclude the Court from questioning the order of the Minister where the scheme which is *presented* to him for confirmation is inconsistent with the provisions of the Act. The case of *Institute of Patent Agents* v. *Lockwood* (*supra*) was distinguished on the ground that in that case the draft rules had been laid on the table in Parliament for forty days previous to their promulgation; whereas in *Yaffé's Case* there was no parliamentary manner of dealing with the confirmation of the scheme.[11] The House of Lords held the scheme to be *intra vires*, but held that, had it been *ultra vires*, the order of confirmation would not have saved it. In *Re Bowman*[12] a question of a clearance order under the Housing Act, 1930, arose. The Court held that it would entertain an application under section 11 (3) of that Act by a person aggrieved by a clearance order who desires to question its validity on the grounds mentioned in the sub-section, *viz.*, that the order is not within the powers given by the Act, or that some requirement of the Act has not been complied with, or *possibly* on the ground that there is *no* evidence to support the order, but *not* on the ground that the evidence is insufficient to support the order.

Rules cannot repeal or contradict express provisions in the Acts from which they derive their authority, and "if the Act is plain, the rule must be interpreted so as to be reconciled with it, or, if it cannot be reconciled, the rule must give way

---

[10] [1930] 2 K. B 98, [1931] A C 494.
[11] Cf. *S. C., per* Lord Dunedin, at p 503
[12] [1932] 2 K. B 621

to the plain terms of the Act ".[13] This is also the case with an
Act passed subsequently to the making of the rules (unless
the later Act was clearly passed with a different object in
view) and then the rules and the subsequent Act will stand
together [14] As to the ground on which bylaws may be
declared to be *ultra vires*, see Craies, pp. 272—281 They
must be made, sanctioned and published in the manner
authorised by the statute; they must not be repugnant to the
general law of the land, nor to the statute from which they
derive their power, and they must be certain and not
unreasonable As to the second of these, Channell, J., in
White v. *Morley*,[15] said: "A bylaw is a local law, and may
be supplementary to the general law; it is not bad because
it deals with something which is not dealt with by the general
law, but it must not alter the general law by making that
lawful which the general law makes unlawful, or that
unlawful which the general law makes lawful." And Lord
Hewart, C.J., said in a recent case [15a]: "A bylaw is not
repugnant to the general law merely because it creates a new
offence and says that something shall be lawful which the law
does not say is unlawful It is repugnant if it makes
unlawful that which the general law says is lawful."
Apparently the Courts are averse to holding a bylaw
bad for unreasonableness. "They ought to be supported
if possible. They ought to be, as has been said,
' benevolently interpreted ' [16] and credit ought to be given
to those who have to administer them that they will
be reasonably administered " [17] And in *Salt* v. *Scott*

---

[13] *Per* James, L J., in *Ex p Davies* (1872), 7 Ch App 526, 529.

[14] See *King* v. *Charing Cross Bank* (1890), 24 Q B D. 27, where the
question was whether the County Courts Act, 1888, s 127, was inconsistent
with R S C of 1883, O XXIX, rr 1, 8A

[15] [1899] 1 Q B 34, at p 39, approved in *Thomas* v *Sutters*, [1900]
1 Ch 10 Cf. *Scott* v *Pilliner*, [1904] 2 K B 855, at p 858, *per* Lord
Alverstone, C J

[15a] *L M. & S Ry* v *Greaves*, [1937] 1 K. B 367, at p 376, quoting
Channell, J., in *Gentel* v *Rapps*, [1902] 1 K B 160, 165.

[16] See *infra*, p 287

[17] *Per* Lord Russell, C J , in *Kruse* v. *Johnson*, [1898] 2 Q B. 91.

Hall [18] Channell, J , said· " The Court does not now readily interfere to set aside as unreasonable and void bylaws which a local authority has deliberately adopted, for it recognises that the local authority is itself the best judge as to whether a particular bylaw is required in its district or not." A railway or tramway company will not be *intra vires* in framing bylaws imposing penalties with respect to the production of tickets and the like in the absence of any intent to defraud So a passenger who travelled accidentally beyond the station to which he had paid his fare cannot be compelled by a bylaw to pay from the starting-point unless the company can prove an intent to defraud. [19] And a bylaw providing that a passenger shall be guilty of an offence who leaves a tramcar without paying his fare, no fare having been demanded, is *ultra vires* as being against the general law and is also unreasonable. [20]

Where powers are conferred on, for instance,' a company to do something which it would have been legal for it to have done without those special powers, those powers may be regarded and construed in either of two ways, clearly defined in the judgment of Lindley, L.J., in *London Association of Shipowners* v. *London and India Docks.* [21] He said: " The Legislature has expressly conferred on the company many powers which the company as owner of property could have exercised without any express statutory authority. Whenever this is the case, the powers expressly given must be treated either as superfluous, or as purposely inserted in order to define, that is, to limit the right conferred and as implying a prohibition against the exercise of the more extensive rights which the company might have by virtue of its owner-

---

[18] [1903] 2 K B 245, at p 249
[19] *Dearden* v. *Townsend* (1865), L R 1 Q B 10; *Huffam* v *North Staffordshire Ry* , [1894] 2 Q B 821
[20] *London Passenger Transport Board* v *Sumner* (1936), 52 T L. R 13 Cf , however, *Hanks* v *Bridgman*, [1896] 1 Q B 253, where a tramway passenger had lost his ticket and refused to pay again He was convicted under a by-law which required passengers to deliver up their tickets on demand   [21] [1892] 3 Ch 242, at p 251.

ship of property. That the latter is the true mode of regarding statutory powers conferred on bodies created for public purposes and authorised to acquire land for such purposes cannot, I think, admit of any doubt."

XI.—METHODS OF CONSTRUCTION

Having dealt with the general rules of construction as derived from the authorities and the aids to which the Courts resort to assist them in coming to their decisions, we finally have to examine the methods adopted by the Courts in applying these authorities and aids. It has been said that a defect in the consideration of the law of interpretation is that *dicta* of the Judges, as to which very numerous examples have been given in the foregoing pages, are too much relied upon and that what we should attend to is not what the Judges *say* about the law, but what they *do*; or how do they carry their statements of the law into effect in their judgments. In other words, what methods of approach to construction do they adopt? These we shall attempt to summarise in this chapter. We must first briefly notice two methods of construction now practically obsolete:—

(a) *Beneficial construction.*—For instance, as we have seen, the Courts are somewhat slow to condemn municipal bylaws as invalid, on the ground that those entrusted to administer them will probably do so in a proper manner, and also that these persons are best fitted to judge of local requirements.[1] So a bylaw made by a local authority under section 157 of the Public Health Act, 1875, though containing no power to exempt from certain building restrictions, was not held unreasonable and void on that ground, the Court saying that the justices might in exceptional cases think there was no need to enforce the bylaw.[2] On the other hand, a somewhat similar bylaw under the Public

---

[1] *Kruse* v *Johnson*, [1898] 2 Q. B. 91, *per* Lord Russell, C.J.
[2] *Salt* v *Scott Hall*, [1903] 2 K. B. 245.

Health (London) Act, 1891, which required every landlord of a lodging-house to have his house cleansed and lime-washed once a year in April, was held bad as it did not provide for notice being served on landlords that the bylaw had not been complied with before they could become liable under the bylaw.[3] It is to be doubted if any Court would at the present day admit to being swayed by benevolence alone; if it finds that the statute was intended to effect a definite result, as, for example, the Workmen's Compensation Act, 1897, the Court will as far as possible construe the statute in the light of that intention.[4] To supply beer at a public-house to a drunken man and his sober companion, who ordered and paid for the beer, is to " sell " liquor to a drunken man within the repealed Licensing Act, 1872, s. 13.[5] So Acts which gave a " single " woman who had an illegitimate child an action against the putative father for maintenance were held applicable to a widow, and to a married woman living apart from her husband.[6] So, statutes which required notice before action for anything " done " under them, were construed to include omissions as well as commissions of acts.[7] The Engraving Copyright Act, 1734, which protected copyright in engravings by piratically engraving, etching, or otherwise or " in any other manner " copying them, was extended to copies taken by photography.[8] The words " where annual contributions have been made " were held to cover a case where efforts had been made to contribute, so as not to deprive a servant of a corporation of her pension.[9]

(b) *Equitable construction* —This was a doctrine formerly used to extend a remedial statute, so that cases which did not

---

[3] *Stiles* v *Galinski*, [1904] 1 K. B 621.

[4] *Lysons* v *Knowles*, [1901] A C. 79, *Fleming* v *Lochgelly Iron and Coal Co* (1902), 4 F. 890

[5] *Scatchard* v *Johnson* (1888), 57 L J M C 41.

[6] *R* v *Wymondham* (1843), 2 Q B. 541; *R.* v *Collingwood* (1848), 12 Q. B. 681

[7] *Edwards* v. *Islington* (1889), 22 Q. B D. 338; *Harman* v. *Ainslie*, [1904] 1 K B 698   [8] *Gambart* v. *Ball* (1863), 14 C B (N S) 306

[9] *Gissing* v *Liverpool Corporation*, [1935] Ch 1

fall within its literal interpretation should be included, in order to comply with the object or " mischief " of the Act.[10] For instance, " charitable use " under the 43 Eliz. c. 46 was construed by the Court of Chancery to cover a number of subjects not usually included in that expression [11] And Byles, J., said that " within the equity " of a statute meant the same thing as being " within the mischief " of it.[12] But the expression has been used in other senses, particularly in the case of old statutes. For instance, the Statute of Westminster II, c. 31, which gave a bill of exceptions to the rulings of Judges of the Common Pleas, was held to be applicable to all Judges, both of the Superior and Inferior Courts.[13] The Statute of Gloucester (6 Edw. 1, c. 11), in speaking of London, was held to have intended to include all cities and boroughs equally, London having simply been named for pre-eminence.[14] In more modern statutes, the doctrine has been applied. Though the Limitation Act, 1623, by section 3 enacted that certain actions should be brought within six years " and not after ", it was held that where an action had been brought within the six years, but had abated owing to the death of a party, the representative of the latter had a reasonable time—generally a year—from the grant of administration to commence a fresh action, though the six years had long ago expired.[15] And the same equitable construction was given to the provisions of the Civil Procedure Act, 1833, which, in language identical with that used in the statute of 1623, limited the time for bringing actions on bonds and other specialties to twenty years.[16] So on the

10 Co Litt 24 b.
11 *Per* Lord Halsbury, L C , in *Income Tax Commissioners* v. *Pemsel*, [1891] A C. 531, at p 542.
12 *Shuttleworth* v *Le Fleming* (1865), 19 C. B (N s) 703.
13 *Strother* v *Hutchinson* (1837), 4 Bing. N. C 83.
14 2 Inst 322
15 *Curlewis* v *Earl Mornington* (1857), 7 E & B 283, *Rhodes* v *Smethurst* (1840), 6 M & W 353, *Atkinson* v *Bradford Building Society* (1890), 25 Q B D 377, *Re Tidd*, [1893] 3 Ch. 154
16 *Sturgis* v *Darell* (1860), 29 L. J Ex 472; *Wakefield, etc , Bank* v *Yates*, [1916] 1 Ch. 452.

ground that it would be a fraud on the party who has partly performed a contract, unenforceable under the Statute of Frauds for want of writing, to refuse specific performance, the Court did and does compel performance of such part-performed contracts under certain conditions in spite of the positive provisions of the statute.[17]

Lord Bacon long ago condemned this doctrine and it is now discredited.[18] All modern statutes are considered as framed on equitable as well as strictly legal doctrines. In *Edwards* v *Edwards*[19] Mellish, L.J., said: " If the Legislature says that a deed shall be ' null and void to all intents and purposes whatsoever ', how can a Court of Equity say that in certain circumstances it shall be valid? The Courts of Equity have given relief on equitable grounds from provisions in old Acts of Parliament, but this has not been done in the case of modern Acts, which are framed with a view to equitable as well as legal principles."[20] And Lord Cairns, in speaking of a taxing Act, said[21]. " In other words, if there be admissible in any statute what is called an equitable construction, certainly such a construction is not admissible in a taxing statute where you simply adhere to the words of the statute."

(c) *Modern methods.*—There are three methods of judicial approach to the construction of a statute, viz., (i) the Literal; (ii) by employing the Golden Rule; (iii) by considering the Mischief that the statute was designed to obviate or prevent.

The Literal method has been set out and illustrated at pp. 172, 176, *supra.*

[17] *Att.-Gen.* v *Day* (1794), 1 Ves. Sen. 221; *Maddison* v *Alderson* (1883), 8 App. Cas. 467; *Rawlinson* v. *Ames*, [1925] Ch 96, *Stimson* v *Gray*, [1929] 1 Ch 629; and Chitty, Contracts (19th ed), pp. 251-2
[18] Cf per Jessel, M.R , in *Ex p Walton* (1881), 17 Ch. D. 750, Vaughan Williams, J , in *Re English, Scottish and Australian Bank*, [1893] 3 Ch. 385
[19] (1876), 2 Ch D. 291, at p. 297.
[20] Quoted with approval by Lord Cozens-Hardy, M R., in *Re Monolithic Building Co., Ltd.*, [1915] 1 Ch 643, 665.
[21] *Partington* v. *Att.-Gen.* (1869), L R. 4 H. L. 100, at p. 122

. The Mischief Rule is set out in *Heydon's Case* and the more recent cases adopting it   See pp. 197, 198, *supra*.

The Golden Rule, as it was called by Jervis, C.J.,[1] was enunciated by Lord Wensleydale in *Grey* v. *Pearson*[2] in 1857.

It is as follows ·—" In construing wills and indeed statutes and all written instruments, the grammatical and ordinary sense of the words is to be adhered to, unless that would lead to some absurdity, or some repugnancy or inconsistency with the rest of the instrument, in which case the grammatical and ordinary sense of the words may be modified so as to avoid that absurdity and inconsistency, but no further." This is in fact a corollary to the Literal Rule. Lord Blackburn in 1881[3] spoke in approbation of the rule and added: " I agree in that completely, but in the cases in which there is a real difficulty this does not help us much, because the cases in which there is a real difficulty are those in which there is a controversy as to what the grammatical and ordinary sense of the words used with reference to the subject-matter is.   To one mind it may appear that the most that can be said is that the sense may be what is contended by the other side, and that the inconsistency and repugnancy is very great, that you should make a great stretch to avoid such absurdity, and that what is required to avoid it is a very little stretch or none at all   To another mind it may appear that the words are perfectly clear—that they can bear no other meaning at all, and that to substitute any other meaning would be not to interpret the words used, but to make an instrument for the parties—and that the supposed inconsistency or repugnancy is perhaps a hardship—a thing which perhaps it would have been better to have avoided, but which we have no power to deal with." The words of Lord Blackburn will find illustration in the cases to be quoted.

---

[1] In *Mattison* v. *Hart* (1854), 14 C. B. 385
[2] 6 H L C 61, at p. 106
[3] *Caledonian Ry* v *North British Ry.* (1881), 6 App Cas 114, at p 131

The methods illustrated.—Vacher v. *The London Society of Compositors* [4] is an example of the employment of all three methods of approach. The question there was whether under section 4 (1) of the Trade Disputes Act, 1906, *any* tortious act by trade unions was protected or only such tortious acts as were committed in contemplation or furtherance of a trade dispute. The House of Lords took the former view and, in delivering their opinions, Lord Macnaghten [5] adopted the Golden Rule from *Grey* v. *Pearson* [6]; Lord Atkinson [7] followed the Literal approach and the case of *Cooke* v. *Charles A. Vogeler* [8]; while Lord Moulton [9] discussed the history of the statute and applied the Mischief method.

Again, Judges may disagree as to the plain meaning. This may be illustrated by the case of *Ellerman Lines* v. *Murray*,[10] where the question was the wages to be paid to seamen thrown out of employment by the wreck of their ship. Section 1 of the Merchant Shipping (International Labour Convention) Act, 1925, was said by their Lordships to be perfectly plain, but Lords Dunedin, Tomlin and Macmillan disagreed as to what the plain meaning was. Judicial opinions may also differ as to the proper presumption to be applied In *R.* v. *Halliday*,[11] a case of the validity of a regulation under the Defence of the Realm Act, 1914, Lord Finlay thought the restraint imposed was a measure of precaution and was in the interests of the whole nation, and therefore right and proper Lord Atkinson thought the restraint was imposed because the presumption was that unless restrained, a foreigner would communicate with the enemy Lord Shaw held it illegal to intern a man without trial, and that it was impossible to presume that Parliament had left in the hands of the Government the entire body of laws protective of liberty.

---

[4] [1913] A C. 107
[6] *Supra*
[8] [1901] A C 102, at p 107
[10] [1931] A C 126
[5] *S. C*, at p 117.
[7] *S C*, at p 121
[9] *S C*, at p 130
[11] [1917] A C 260

The Literal or "plain meaning" rule must be adopted ": even if absurd ".[12] This method of approach was common and important when statutes were not framed in wide and general language as they are to-day.   Again, the case of *Ellerman Lines* v. *Murray* [12a] may be examined and the contrasting views of the Judges compared.   In the Court of Appeal, Scrutton and Greer, L.JJ., thought the section clear and unambiguous, and refused to call in aid the preamble. Slesser, L.J,[13] dissenting, quoted Dyer, C.J,[14] as to the utility of the preamble, and relied on the mischief of the Act.   In the House of Lords Lord Dunedin thought the Act must be taken as it stood and there was no ambiguity; Lord Blanesburgh relied on the mischief of the Act, while Lord Macmillan thought there was no ambiguity and that therefore there could be no resort to extraneous aids, such as the preamble.   In *Croxford* v. *Universal Insurance Co.*[15] Scott, L.J., agreed that section 10 of the Road Traffic Act, 1934, was plain, but disagreed with Slesser, L J., as to what it meant. Professor Willis is of opinion that the Literal approach is never a really controlling factor to-day.[15a]   But in *R.* v. *Hare*[16] the question was whether a woman could be convicted of an indecent assault on a boy under section 62 of the Offences against the Person Act, 1861: "Whosoever . . . shall be guilty of . . . any indecent assault upon any male person ".   The section was headed " unnatural offences " and one might have thought it inapplicable to a woman   The Court, however, convicted, pointing out that a woman might be included in the word " whosoever ", a general term, and that the meaning was too plain·to need any reference to a possibly controlling context.   The Court here applied the Literal Rule to a statute framed (in 1861)

---

[12] See *per* Jervis, C J., in *Abley* v *Dale*, 11 C B. 378, at p. 391.
[12a] *Supra, sub nom* in C. A *The Croxteth Hall, The Celtic*, [1930] P 197.
[13] [1930] P , at p 212, 215.   [14] See p 205, *supra*.
[15] [1936] 2 K B 253, 280, 281
[15a] Canadian Bar Review, Vol XVI, p. 11
[16] [1934] 1 K. B. 354.

in wide and general terms. On the other hand, up to the Law Reform (Married Women and Tortfeasors) Act, 1935, the Literal Rule was constantly adopted by the Courts in order to confine the operation of the Married Women's Property Acts to the exact words of the statutes in disregard of the scheme of legislation in the direction of the emancipation of women. This may be seen in its latest example: *Edwards* v. *Porter.*[17]

Mischief Rule.—The Mischief Rule is based on *Heydon's Case* (*supra*, p. 197) and is designed to carry into effect the object and purpose of the statute This method of approach is easy to apply when the objects and reasons of the Act are set out therein—as, for instance, in the Statute of Frauds—but difficult to apply when these are wanting. It is, however, a method much resorted to in approaching the construction of all types of statutes. We have had some examples already. In *Duncan* v. *Aberdeen County Council,*[18] section 11 of the Poor Law (Scotland) Act, 1934, was held by Lords Blanesburgh and Atkin to be " a remedial section intended specially to benefit a class of persons entitled in the view of the Legislature to exceptional consideration ". And Lord Thankerton thought the section " alters not only the standard of adequacy of outdoor relief but also the standard of poverty which is to give the legal right to that relief ". A further illustration of this method is *Powell Lane Manufacturing Co.* v *Putnam*[19] (*supra*, p. 169) where the Court held that the object of section 11 (1) of the Finance Act, 1926, was to tax packing or wrapping paper which, when imported, would be in competition with the English products. So the words of Lord Selborne in *Caledonian Ry.* v. *North British Ry.*[20] (*supra*, p. 173), where he said that the Literal method ought

[17] [1925] A. C. 1.
[18] (1936), 106 L J. P. C. 1.
[19] [1931] 2 K. B. 305
[20] (1881), 6 App. Cas 114, 121, 122

not to prevail if the words of the statute are sufficiently flexible to admit of another construction which will better carry out the intention. In *Newman Manufacturing Co.* v. *Marrables* [21] (*supra*, p. 169) the object of section 9 (1) of the Finance Act, 1928, was held to be to protect the English button trade. Again, in *Guardians of Salford Union* v. *Dewhurst* [22] (*supra*, p. 170) Lord Cave, L.C., based his opinion on the scope and purpose of the statute as well as on the language, whereas Lord Sumner preferred the "literal and unimaginative interpretation of the Legislature's own words".

The Court will sometimes apply the Literal Rule when it thinks the matter in hand should be covered by the Act, or adopt the mischief or object method if it is of opinion that the matter should fall outside the Act,[23] as in *Ledwith* v. *Roberts*.[24]

The Golden Rule.—The Golden Rule permits the plain meaning to be departed from if a strict adherence to it would result in an absurdity. This has already been referred to, *supra*, p. 291. Of course, absurdity or not may be largely a matter of opinion. Absurdity is said by Lord Macnaghten to be one of the two causes justifying a departure from the ordinary and natural sense of the words of an enactment.[25] In *Ex p. Walton* [26] Jessel, M.R., after quoting Lord Blackburn's quotation of Lord Wensleydale's Golden Rule (*supra*), proceeded to consider the object of the Bankruptcy Act, 1869, and whether a literal construction would be absurd or inconsistent with the object of the Act.

All methods discussed.—Sometimes the Court discusses all

---

21 [1931] 2 K B 297

22 [1926] A C 619, 624, 633.

23 *Banbury* v *Bank of Montreal*, [1918] A C 626, at p 691, *per* Lord Atkinson

24 [1937] 1 K B 232, at p. 270 ff , where Scott, L.J , used the history of the poor law to restrict the meaning of "loiter". *Supra*, p 256.

25 *Vacher* v *London Society of Compositors*, [1913] A C. 107, at p 118.

26 (1881), 17 Ch D 746 Cf *The Ruapehu*, [1927] P 47, at p. 54.

these three approaches, as in *Vacher* v. *London Society of Compositors (supra)*, or it may occasionally adopt the Literal Rule as against the Mischief Rule, as in *Ellerman Lines* v. *Murray*. A good example is *Law Society* v. *United Service Bureau*,[27] where the words of the Solicitors Act, 1932, in question were "any person who wilfully pretends to be qualified to act as a solicitor" were held not to be applicable to a corporate body, "any person" being held to be confined to "any person who could become a solicitor". Avory, J., was conscious that in adopting this construction the Court was not giving full effect to considerations based on the mischief aimed at by the Act. Or the Mischief Rule may be preferred to the Literal, as in *Duncan* v. *Aberdeen County Council* and *Powell Lane Manufacturing Co.* v. *Putnam*, already referred to. Occasionally the adoption of one or the other method of approach may result in a difference of opinion. In *Rowell* v. *Pratt*[28] the question of the privilege of a return to the Potato Marketing Board by a grower was in question. In the Court of Appeal, Greer, L.J., who dissented from the judgment of the majority, thought that the policy of section 17 of the Agricultural Marketing Act, 1931, was to protect producers who were obliged to give information to the Board from having that information disclosed to their trade rivals. Slesser and Scott, L.JJ., held that the document would not be privileged at common law and that privilege being well settled, statutes do not alter the common law further than they expressly declare, and further that the Courts have jealously guarded their powers of compulsion against the encroachments of privilege. The case went to the House of Lords,[29] who held that the information may only be disclosed in a legal proceeding under the Act, the provision being unambiguous and reasonable. Lord Wright said[30]. "But if the words properly

---

[27] [1934] 1 K B 343, 349
[28] [1936] 2 K B 226.
[29] [1938] A. C. 101.
[30] *S C.*, p 105

construed admit of only one meaning, the Court is not entitled to deny the words that meaning, merely because the Court feels that the result is not in accordance with the ordinary policy of the law or with what seems to be reasonable " And Lord Maugham thought the object of the provision was to avoid disclosure to competitors and that it was not correct to say that there was a presumption that the secrecy attaching to the return was not intended to be applicable if its production was called for in a legal proceeding, unless the Legislature has in plain language declared the contrary. The matter should be decided without any presumption either way.

Employment of Presumptions. — Besides these three methods of approach, there are others applied to particular types of statutes. We have already referred to Presumptions (p. 263) as aids to construction. These are specially liable to fluctuation and, as was previously said, this fluctuation is stronger or weaker according to the view taken by the Court of the particular statute in question They are frequently employed to control the intention of the Legislature and are particularly important in construing statutes relating to social reforms, or involving penalties, and taxing Acts. If the Court knows and sympathises with the purpose of the Act, it will apply a presumption to bring the case before it within the Act. Thus in *Shannon Realties* v. *Ville de St. Michael*,[31] Lord Shaw said: " Where the words of a statute are clear, they must of course be followed, but, in their Lordships' opinion, where alternative constructions are equally open, that alternative is to be chosen which will be consistent with the smooth working of the system which the State purports to be regulating and that alternative is to be rejected which will introduce uncertainty, friction or confusion into the working of the system " Thus in *Powell Lane Manufacturing Co.* v. *Putnam*,[32] a product not within

---

[31] [1924] A C 185, at p. 192.
[32] *Supra.*

the words of the Act was presumed to be within its purpose or mischief The history of the section was set out from the excise point of view. So, too, in *Astor* v. *Perry*,[33] another taxing case, the House of Lords discovered a scheme or purpose in the legislation (Finance Act, 1922, s. 20 (1))—referring to the words of Lord Herschell in *Colquhoun* v *Brooks* [34] These two cases are perhaps somewhat unusual generally in the matter of a taxing Act the subject has the benefit of the doubt and, unless the words of the taxing statute are perfectly clear, he escapes (see *infra*, p 305).

A difficult question to answer is this : If the Court decides to approach the construction by presumption, which presumption will it adopt? In *R.* v. *Halliday* (*supra*) the majority of the Law Lords held the regulation legal in the interests of the realm, for securing the public safety, without suspending the Habeas Corpus Act They also held that it must not be assumed that the powers conferred by the Act on the Executive would be abused [35] On the other hand Lord Shaw [36] thought the regulation illegal in that it made the Government a party, a judge and an executioner at the same time, and that there could be no repeal of liberties by implication. In *Croxford* v. *Universal Insurance Co.* (*supra*) Slesser, L J , thought that if the effect of section 10 of the Road Traffic Act, 1934, was to make the position of insurers worse before 1935 than after that date, it was a ridiculous position, and it must be presumed that such was not the intention of the Legislature, and, replying to the argument of counsel that legislation taking away common law rights should be strictly construed, said that " the Landlord and Tenant Acts and the Workmen's Compensation Acts must be construed in favour of the classes of persons for whose benefit they were passed ". On the other

---

[33] [1935] A C. 398; see *per* Lord Macmillan, at p 416
[34] (1889), 14 App Cas. 493, 506.
[35] [1917] A C 260, *per* Lord Finlay, at p. 268, Lord Atkinson, at p 273; and Lord Wrenbury, at p 308
[36] *S. C* , at p 285

hand Scott, L.J., thought the words clear and that there was
no scope for any principles of interpretation "which are
merely presumptions in cases of ambiguity". In *Edwards
v. Att.-Gen. for Canada*[37] the question arose whether a woman
by reason of her sex was disqualified from being summoned
by the Governor-General to the Senate of Canada. It was
decided by the Judicial Committee that the word " person "
in section 24 of the British North America Act, 1867, includes
members of both sexes, and that the provisions of that Act
should be given a large and liberal interpretation, " so that
to a certain extent the Dominion may be mistress in her own
house " It was pointed out that in England women were
under a common law disability to hold public office It is
a somewhat difficult question to decide whether, given the
presumption relevant to the case, the Court will apply it,
In other words, is the relevant presumption fluctuating either
up or down—has it increased or declined in force with Judges
—or is it static?

Presumption against deprivation of rights.—Is the presumption, for instance, against taking away rights at common
law falling into disuse?

It is indeed still employed, as, for instance, in *Leach v.
R*,[38] where the question was whether a wife was a compellable
witness against her husband in a criminal case under section 4
of the Criminal Evidence Act, 1898. Lord Loreburn, L.C.,
said[39]: " It is a fundamental and old principle to which the
law has looked, that you ought not to compel a wife to give
evidence against her husband in matters of a criminal kind.
. . It seems to me that we must have a definite change in
the law in this respect, definitely stated in an Act of Parliament, before the right of this woman can be affected." Lord
Halsbury[40] said " That you should introduce a new system

---

37 [1930] A C 124, 143
38 [1912] A C. 305
39 S. C , p 309
40 S C , p. 311

of law without any specific enactment of it, seems to me to be perfectly monstrous ''. And Lord Atkinson [41]: '' The principle that a wife is not to be compelled to give evidence against her husband is deep-seated in the common law of this country, and I think if it is to be overturned, it must be overturned by a clear, definite and positive enactment, not by an ambiguous one such as the section relied upon in this case.'' In *Rowell* v. *Pratt* (*supra*) we saw from the judgments the same anxiety to preserve common law rights as against a plea of privilege of non-disclosure. The presumption against change was adopted in *Viscountess Rhondda's Claim*,[42] where the Committee of Privileges held that as the Viscountess had no right at common law to a summons to the House of Lords, it could not be presumed that Parliament intended such a radical change in the constitution by the '' side wind '' of the Sex Disqualification Act, 1919. So also in the case of the claim of women graduates of the University of Edinburgh to vote at the election of a Member of Parliament for the University.[43]

In a very recent case [44] before the Judicial Committee on an appeal from the High Court of Bombay, the question arose as to whether in addition to the statutory indemnity under section 21 of the Indian Securities Act, 1920, the Government had a common law right of indemnity Lord Wright, in delivering the judgment of their Lordships, said [45]: '' A statute is *prima facie* to be construed as changing the law to no greater extent than its words or necessary intendment require. Section 21 was not in the Act of 1886. If it had been intended by the insertion of that section in the Act of 1920 to abrogate the common law indemnity existing under the repealed Act (of 1886), the Legislature would, it seems, have used words clearly expressing that

[41] *S. C.*, p. 311.
[42] [1922] 2 A C. 339
[43] *Nairn* v. *University of St Andrews*, [1909] A. C. 147
[44] *Secretary of State for India* v *Bank of India, Ltd* (1938), L R. 65 I A. 286, at p. 298.   [45] *S C.*, p. 298.

intention, so as to secure that, save as provided by section 21, there should be no right of indemnity. Their Lordships see no reason to justify reading in or implying such words. On the contrary, they construe section 21 as giving an added statutory right, which is different from, and in no way inconsistent with, the common law right."

In spite of doubt expressed by some writers, there seems ground for saying that the presumption against the deprivation of common law rights without clear and definite enactment still holds good   One learned writer says: " To assume that there is an intention not to interfere with common law rights is to assume a proposition that is in direct contradiction to the truth." He was speaking of the common law assumption that a landowner may use his land as he pleases, subject only to the law of nuisance, and also of the liberty of the individual in the matter of contracts, and continued: " But the fundamental assumption of modern statute law is that the landowner holds his land for the public good " [46] There is no doubt that modern legislation as to Housing, Slum Clearance, Development and many other matters relating to social reform or improvement do press very hardly on the landowner, who is forced to surrender or submit to a diminution in the value of his property for little or no compensation. In many cases no mere money return can compensate for loss of ancestral possessions, privacy and peaceful surroundings. How far, then, is the presumption " no confiscation without compensation " of value to-day? The presumption is noticed at p. 269, *supra*. Its value is to restrict confiscatory legislation. The case of *R.* v. *Minister of Health* [47] in the Court of Appeal illustrates this. This case is referred to at p. 283 above and the judgment of the Court of Appeal was reversed by the House of Lords [48] on the ground that the party who

---

[46] Dr W. Ivor Jennings in *Courts and Administrative Law*, 49 Harv. Law Review, 426.
[47] *R* v *Minister of Health, Ex p. Yaffe*, [1930] 2 K B 98
[48] [1931] A C. 494

succeeded in the Court of Appeal could only hold the judgment in his favour if he could show that the improvement scheme was a scheme not contemplated or provided for by the Act in question (section 40 of the Housing Act, 1925). The judgments in the Court of Appeal contain the following points relevant to the presumption. It was a clearance scheme and the landlord was the party aggrieved. Lord Justice Scrutton remarked that the scheme framed by the Ministry of Health proposed only to pay Yaffé (the landlord) the value of the land and nothing for his buildings, and the learned Lord Justice thought he was entitled to a writ of prohibition. He continued [49]: " The present Act enables a Minister to take away the property of individuals without compensation on certain defined conditions In my view those conditions must be strictly complied with and only the very clearest words can give final validity to an order which does not comply with the prescribed statutory conditions." And Lord Justice Greer [50]: " It is argued on behalf of the Minister that if none of these things had happened [i.e., conditions precedent to the confirmation of the scheme] the Minister could make an order which, when made, would have effect as if enacted in the Act. This would mean that owners might be dispossessed of their property merely by the *ipse dixit* of the Minister and that the provisions put in the Act for the protection of owners and ratepayers might be wholly disregarded."

Barring subject from Courts —As to the presumption against barring the subject from the Courts (see p 270, *supra*), the case just cited both in the Court of Appeal and the House of Lords may serve as an example—the trend of modern social legislation is probably to restrict the jurisdiction of the Courts. In *Chester* v. *Bateson*,[51]

---

[49] [1930] 2 K B , at p 145.
[50] *S. C* at p 156
[51] [1920] 1 K B 829.

Regulation 2ᴀ (2), purporting to have been made under the authority of the Defence of the Realm Act, 1914, provided that steps should not be taken without the consent of the Minister for possession or ejectment in the case of a tenement in which a munition worker was living, and situate in an area declared by order of the Ministry of Munitions to be a "special area". A breach of this regulation was made a criminal offence. The regulation thus barred a landlord from the Courts except with the consent of the Minister. Darling, J., relied on *R. v. Halliday* [52] and thought that this disability could only be imposed by direct enactment of the Legislature itself, and that "so grave an invasion of the rights of the subject was not intended by the Legislature to be accomplished by a departmental order such as this one of the Minister of Munitions". The Vexatious Actions Act, 1896, furnishes an example of barring a subject from the Courts for the purpose of preventing vexatious or frivolous litigation. (Cf. *Re Boaler*, [1915] 1 K B. 21, at p. 36, *per* Scrutton, J.).

In *R. W. Paul, Ltd.* v. *Wheat Commissioners* [53] a bylaw under the Wheat Act, 1932, set up a special arbitration tribunal to which the Arbitration Act, 1889, was not to apply. This bylaw was held to be *ultra vires* and invalid as there was no express power in the Act to oust the jurisdiction of the Courts but only a power to make bylaws.

Liberty of subject.—The presumption against interference with the liberty of the subject is probably still the most firmly established of all. Even this is, however, not universal, especially in time of national emergency, as we saw in the case of *R. v. Halliday*, [54] where, though the majority of the House of Lords thought the regulation under the Defence of the Realm Act valid as necessary for the public safety in a time of danger, Lord Shaw entered an emphatic protest against what

---

[52] [1917] A C, at p 287, *per* Lord Shaw
[53] [1937] A C 139, 153-5
[54] *Supra*, p. 292

he called " the violent exercise of arbitrary power "   In the
War Measures Act, 1914, and the Immigration Act, 1915, the
Legislature definitely interferes with the liberty of persons
of enemy origin in war-time and foreign-born immigrants
in time of peace.   So in *Ronnfeldt* v *Phillips*,[55] a war-time
case, a Regulation under the Defence of the Realm Regulations prohibited a person from residing in a particular locality
where a military authority suspects him of acting in a manner
prejudicial to the public safety.   Scrutton, L.J., said: " The
Courts were always anxious to protect the liberty of the
subject.   They did so both in the interests of the subject
himself and in the interests of the State.   In time of war
there must be some modification in the interests of the State."
And in *Hudson Bay Co.* v. *Maclay*,[56] Greer, J., holding that
a similar regulation, empowering the Shipping Controller to
give directions as to the use of ships and to prohibit any ship
from putting to sea without his licence, was not *ultra vires*,
said: " Under circumstances such as these the notion that
there is any effective presumption that Parliament did not
intend to interfere with the liberty or property of the subject
becomes so thin as to be describable as the shade of a shadow,
and disappears altogether when we find in the statute express
words which show that the Legislature expressly authorised
particular regulations which would of necessity restrict the
liberty of the subject and his freedom to enjoy his normal
rights over his real and personal property."   Reference may
also be made to Lord Parker's words in *The Zamora*[57]:
" Those who are responsible for the national security must
be the sole judges of what the national security requires."

Penal statutes, formerly " strictly " construed when many
offences were capital or made convicts liable to transportation, are now given their ordinary meaning, and there are
no longer any special rules concerning their construction

---

[55] (1918), 35 T L R 46, at p. 47
[56] (1920), 36 T L R 469, at p 475
[57] [1916] A C 77, at p 107.

Blackburn, J., said [58]: " When the Legislature imposes a
penalty, the words imposing it must be clear and distinct."
The reference to penal statutes in *Heydon's Case (supra,
p. 197)* is to statutes which create some disability or forfeiture, " none of them are statutes creating a crime and I
think it is altogether a mistake to apply the resolutions in
Heydon's Case to a criminal statute which creates a new
offence. The distinction between a strict construction and
a more free one has, no doubt, in modern times almost
disappeared, and the question now is what is the true construction of the statute? I should say that in a criminal
statute you must be quite sure that the offence charged is
within the letter of the law." [59] The distinction now means
little more than " that penal provisions, like all others, are
to be fairly construed according to the legislative intent as
expressed in the enactment, the Courts refusing on the one
hand to extend the punishment to cases which are not clearly
embraced in them, and on the other equally refusing by any
mere verbal nicety, forced construction or equitable interpretation to exonerate parties plainly within their scope ".[60]
The person against whom it is sought to enforce the penalty
is entitled to the benefit of any doubt which may arise on the
construction of a statute of this character.[61] " You ought
not to do violence to the language in order to bring people
within it, but ought rather to take care that no one is brought
within it who is not brought within it by express language." [62]

The question of *mens rea* in criminal statutes has been
dealt with *supra*, at pp. 266, 267.

Taxing Acts.—Just as the Court was formerly inclined to

[58] *Willis* v *Thorp* (1875), L. R. 10 Q. B 383, at p. 386.
[59] *Per* Pollock, C B , in *Att .Gen.* v *Sillem* (1863), 2 H. & C 431,
at p 509.
[60] Sedgwick, Statutory Law (2nd ed), p 282, cited by Bramwell, B ,
in *S. C* , at p 531.
[61] *L C. C.* v *Aylesbury Dairy Co* , [1898] 1 Q B 106, at p 109, *per*
Wright, J.
[62] *R.* v. *Chapman*, [1931] 2 K. B. 606; *per* Huddleston, B , in *Rumball*
v. *Schmidt* (1882), 8 Q B. D. 603, at p. 608

construe penal statutes "strictly" and not to admit a construction not plainly warranted by their words, so, too, formerly the Courts "leaned against" taxing Acts, and the onus was heavily on the Crown to prove that the subject ought to be taxed. The reason may have been that taxation was regarded more or less in the light of a penalty or that taxes were originally imposed to benefit certain privileged persons, generally those in favour at Court. Taxing Acts are now construed as any others. In *Att.-Gen.* v *Carlton Bank* [63] Lord Russell, C.J., said. " In the course of the argument reference was made on both sides to the supposed special canons of construction applicable to a Revenue Act. For my part I do not accept the suggestion I see no reason why special canons of construction should be applied to any Act of Parliament and I know of no authority for saying that a taxing Act is to be construed differently from any other Act." And Lord Hanworth, M R., in *Dewar* v. *Inland Revenue Commissioners*,[64] said: " Either in the clear words of a taxing statute the subject is liable or if he is not within the words, he is not liable." He referred to Lord Sumner's opinion [65] · " The Crown does not tax by analogy but by statute." There would seem, therefore, to be some presumption in favour of the taxpayer, and the Courts no doubt adopt a restrictive approach for the most part to the construction of taxing statutes. Lord Tenterden, in *Dock Co. at Kingston-upon-Hull* v. *Browne*,[66] said: " These rates are a tax on the subject and it is a sound general rule that a tax shall not be considered to be imposed (or at least not for the benefit of a subject) without a plain declaration of the Legislature to impose it." The presumption in favour of the subject was held to be overridden by the object of the taxing statute (Finance Act, 1926), and it was held that

---

[63] [1899] 2 Q B 158, at p. 164.
[64] [1935] 2 K. B 351, at p 360.
[65] *Ormond Investment Co* v *Betts*, [1928] A C. 143, at p 158
[66] (1831), 2 B & Ad 43, 58 (port dues), quoted with approval by Vaughan Williams, L J , in *Assheton-Smith* v *Owen*, [1906] 1 Ch. 179, 205.

section 11 " was passed to enable packing and wrapping paper by whatever name it was called to be taxed " because it was in competition with the English product, and anything which would substantially correspond to what the Legislature meant by " packing or wrapping paper " would come within the tax.[67]

So, the object of the Finance Act, 1928, was considered in deciding the meaning of " unfinished "—" buttons finished or unfinished " The object being found to be to protect the English button trade [68] And in *Astor* v. *Perry* [69] the scheme of a taxing statute was examined in order to find the subject liable. This is, as we have seen, quite a legitimate method in the case of other statutes and, as taxing Acts are to be construed in the same way as others, this method is legitimate in their case also.

Evasion.—Speaking of taxing Acts suggests the subject of Evasion, since this occurs chiefly in connection with this kind of enactment. From time to time devices have been invented to avoid payment of taxes; for example, the formation of trusts in order to avoid payment of income tax, and so on. So general has this form of evasion become that in the current year (1938) sections of the annual Finance Act have been specifically designed to prevent this. How have the Courts dealt with the matter? Grove, J , said [70]: " The word ' evasion ' may mean either of two things. It may mean an evasion of the Act by something which, while it evades the Act, is within the sense of it, or it may mean an evading of the Act by doing something to which the Act does not apply." The first of these methods suggests underhand dealing, the second merely the intentional avoidance of something disagreeable,[71] which is a wholly different thing.

---

[67] *Powell Lane Manufacturing Co* v. *Putnam*, [1931] 2 K B 305
[68] *Newman Manufacturing Co* v *Marrables*, [1931] 2 K B 297, 304
[69] [1935] A C 398, at p 416
[70] In *Att -Gen* v. *Noyes* (1881), 8 Q B D 125, at p 133
[71] *Per* Lord Hobhouse in *Simms* v *Registrar of Probates*, [1900] A C 323, at p. 334.

There is no obligation not to do what the Legislature has
not really prohibited and it is not evading an Act to keep
outside it.[72]

Thus where fraudulent renewals of successive bills of sale,
each given before the expiry of the period within which a bill
had to be registered under the Bills of Sale Act, 1854, were
made, the last one of the series having been registered within
the period was held valid, as the requirement of the Act had
been complied with, though its spirit had been evaded.[73] This
device in fraud of the revenue and obviously calculated to
defeat creditors is now of no avail (section 9 of the Bills of Sale
Act, 1878).   A construction which facilitates evasion will on
grounds of convenience be avoided if possible.   An Act
(9 Geo. 4, c. 61) prohibiting an innkeeper from allowing
gaming " in his house or premises " was held not to be
limited to his guests in the public rooms, but applied
also to himself and his friends in private rooms on the
premises [74] On the other hand, the sufficiency of a stamp on
a document produced in Court depends entirely on what
appears on the face of the document, as it would be most
inconvenient to spend time in holding a collateral inquiry
as to the sufficiency of the stamp.   This fact may, of course,
be taken advantage of to evade stamp duty, as in the case of
a cheque post-dated to the knowledge of the holder.[75]

Turning to the more recent cases, in *Bullivant* v. *Att.-Gen.
for Victoria* [76] Lord Halsbury said: " People are not bound
to continue in the same condition of things either as regards
their direct or indirect taxation, which will render either the

---

[72] Cf *Edwards* v *Hall* (1853), 25 L J. Ch 82, at p 84; *Macbeth* v.
Ashley (1874), L R. 2 Sc App 352, at p. 359

[73] *Smale* v *Burr* (1872), L R. 8 C. P 64

[74] *Patten* v. *Rhymer* (1860), 29 L. J. M C 189. Cf *Gallagher* v. *Rudd*,
[1898] 1 Q B. 114

[75] And therefore liable to an *ad valorem* duty as a bill of exchange ·
Gatty v *Fry* (1877), 2 Ex D 265, *Royal Bank of Scotland* v *Tottenham*,
[1894] 2 Q B. 715, where the test of admissibility was held to be whether
the document appears when tendered in evidence to be sufficiently stamped.

[76] [1901] A C 196, at p 202

consumption of articles in the one case or the property they have in the other, always liable to the tax " So where a son, a legatee of his father, was not paid his legacy within the executors' year, allowing the question of interest on his legacy to stand over and receiving none in the meantime, he was held not to be liable for surtax thereon [77] In *Levene* v. *Inland Revenue Commissioners* [78] Lord Sumner said: " It is trite law that His Majesty's subjects are free if they can to make their own arrangements so that their cases may fall outside the scope of the taxing Acts. They incur no legal penalties and, strictly speaking, no moral censure if, having considered the lines drawn by the Legislature for the imposition of taxes, they make it their business to walk outside them." In this view, there is nothing immoral in taking steps to evade a taxing statute.

In another case, before the Judicial Committee, [79] the deceased had covenanted to pay £200,000 to his children with $1\frac{1}{2}$ per cent. interest, the debt being payable at call. During his life, he regularly paid the interest but no principal. This diminished by £200,000 his net assets liable to duty at his death. The Judicial Committee, affirming the judgment of the High Court of South Australia, held that the arrangements conferred on the children complete ownership of the debt and was a non-testamentary disposition of property within the South Australian Succession Duties Act, 1893, s. 16 (corresponding to our Succession Duty Act of 1853, s 8) and was not subject to duty as the testator had died more than three months after the execution of the covenant. It was argued also that this scheme was an attempt to evade payment of the succession duty and was therefore liable to double duty under section 27 of the South Australian Act. The Judicial Committee negatived this argument and agreed with the observation of Way, C.J., [80] in the Court below that

---

[77] *Dewar* v. *Inland Revenue Commissioners*, [1935] 2 K B 351
[78] [1928] A C 217, at p. 227.
[79] *Simms* v *Registrar of Probates, supra.*
[80] *S C.,* at p. 337.

"evade means some device or stratagem, some arrangement, trust or other device (whether concealed or apparent) by which what is really part of the estate of the deceased is made to appear to belong to somebody else in order to escape payment of duty". The Duke of Richmond, in order that his successors should escape estate duty, effected disentailing assurances of his estates and charged the capital values of the interests of his successor and his successor's son with interest on the estates. These sums, with interest, were assigned to trustees to pay the income to the successor for life and after his death to his son. No interest was paid, but bonds were given for the interest due On the death of the Duke in 1903 the Inland Revenue claimed estate duty in respect of these estates. It was held that none was payable. The debts and incumbrances were held to have been incurred "wholly for the deceased's own use and benefit" (section 7 (1) (a), Finance Act, 1894) The sub-section was construed as meaning, not spending wholly on oneself, but as making oneself master of a sum of money over which he and he alone has the power of disposition. The said sums and interest amounted to more than the value of the estates which passed on the death of the Duke [81] Lord Shaw, who, with Lord Collins, dissented from the opinion of the majority of their Lordships, thought the scheme contravened both the letter and the spirit of the statute.[82] Finally, in *Inland Revenue Commissioners* v. *Westminster (Duke of)* [83] the Duke bound himself to pay a servant an annual sum irrespective of services rendered, and the Duke was allowed to deduct this payment from his taxable income. It may be doubted whether the House of Lords has not gone very far in this case, though they purported to found on the genuineness of the transaction. It is, however, hard to regard the annuity as anything more than remuneration for services,

[81] *Att.-Gen* v *Duke of Richmond and Gordon,* [1909] A C 466
[82] *S. C*, at p 487.
[83] [1936] A C. 1.

in other words, wages.   It also suggests that there can
nowadays be no such thing as an evasion of a taxing
Act, any such arrangement being within permissible limits.
The House has already declared evasion of a taxing statute to
be unblameworthy, actually or morally, and from the decision
in the *Duke of Westminster's Case* it certainly looks as if,
in revenue cases at any rate, the evasion of the spirit and
object of a taxing statute, with the undisputed intention of
avoiding taxation, will succeed.   Lord Atkin, who dissented
from the majority, said [84]: " It was not, I think, denied—
at any rate it is incontrovertible—that the deeds were brought
into existence as a device by which the respondent might avoid
some of the burdens of surtax.   I do not use the word device
in any sinister sense, for it has been recognised that the
subject, whether poor and humble, or wealthy and noble, has
the legal right so to dispose of his capital and income as to
attract upon himself the least amount of tax."

[84] *S C.*, at p 7.

INDEX.

CONSTRUCTION,
Deeds,
  according to modern dates, 86
  ambiguities and equivocations, 51—58
  contemporaneous interpretation, 82—85
  Court must not supply intention, 23
  document partly printed, 43
       to be construed as a whole, 38
  extrinsic evidence, when admissible to translate language, 31 (*and see* EVIDENCE).
  intended for one purpose, may take effect for another, 25—26
  intention to prevail, if words not clear, 24
  literal meaning depends on circumstances of parties, 28
       three senses of, 28
       to be taken, 27
  meaning of " children ", 156
      " issue ", 157
      " unmarried ", 153—155
  miscellaneous exceptions in grants, 69
      rules of, 63—70
      words construed against grantor, 67—70
  rules of, 21—51
  statutory rules of, 23
  technical terms to have legal meaning, 36
  transaction in more than one document, 40
  written contract and collateral agreement, 75, 77
Statutes,
  aids to, 195—141
    cases, 234—236
    earlier Acts, 223—228
    erroneous, of former Act, law not altered by, 230, 233, 241
    external, 215—241
    internal, 195—215
    statutes *in pari materia stare decisis*, 241
    subsequent Acts, 232—233
    usage, 236—241
  discretionary or obligatory provisions of, 250—256
  evasion of, 306
  general rules of, 162—184
  literal, presumption in favour of, 173
  meaning of, 161
  methods of, 286—310
    beneficial, 286
    equitable, 287
    " golden " rule, 294
    literal rule, 292
    mischief rule, 293
  of all parts read together, 162
  presumptions, 263—280, 296
  private Acts, 256—262

Printed in Great Britain by **The Eastern Press, Ltd**, *London and Reading*

BOOKS FOR LAW STUDENTS.

SUBJECT INDEX.

LIST E may be obtained post free. It contains a specimen page and summary of contents of every book in this catalogue.

SWEET & MAXWELL, LIMITED, 2 & 3 CHANCERY LANE, LONDON, W.C.2.

SUGGESTED COURSE OF READING FOR THE BAR EXAMINATIONS.

ELEMENTS OF CONTRACT AND TORT.
 CARTER'S Contracts and WINFIELD or SALMOND'S Torts; COCKLE and HIBBERT's Leading Cases

ROMAN LAW.
 HUNTER'S Introduction. SANDARS' Justinian. For final revision, GARSIA'S Roman Law in a Nutshell FARRIN'S Questions and Answers

CONSTITUTIONAL LAW AND LEGAL HISTORY.
 CHALMERS & ASQUITH SALANT THOMAS'S Leading Cases POTTER'S Legal History For final revision, GARSIA'S Constitutional Law and Legal History in a Nutshell GRIFFITH's Questions and Answers

CRIMINAL LAW AND PROCEDURE.
 HARRIS or KENNY'S Criminal Law, and WILSHERE'S Leading Cases For final revision, GARSIA'S Criminal Law in a Nutshell ROGERS' Questions and Answers

REAL PROPERTY.
 WATSON'S or HARGREAVES' Introduction TOPHAM or CHESHIRE on Real Property For revision, GARSIA'S Nutshell PHILLIPS's Q and A

COMMON LAW.
 INDERMAUR'S Common Law, or SALMOND on Contracts, and SALMOND or WINFIELD on Torts COCKLE's Leading Cases For final revision, WILSHERE'S Outline of Contracts and Torts or CONYERS' Contracts and Torts in a Nutshell, or O'CONNELL's Q and A on Contracts and PADLEY's Q and A on Torts FAY's Leading Cases

EVIDENCE AND PROCEDURE.
 PHIPSON'S Manual of Evidence, and COCKLE'S Cases on Evidence ODGERS' Pleading For final revision, GARSIA'S Procedure in a Nutshell, and Evidence in a Nutshell MILLER'S Questions and Answers on Evidence

EQUITY.
 SNELL or HANBURY RIVINGTON'S Epitome GARSIA'S Equity in a Nutshell RIVINGTON'S Questions and Answers

PRACTICAL CONVEYANCING.
 BURNETT'S Elements GARSIA'S and KRUSIN'S Nutshells

COMPANY LAW.
 CHARLESWORTH'S Principles BALFOUR'S Company Law in a Nutshell MILLNER'S Questions and Answers

SPECIAL SUBJECTS.
 Administration of Assets, GARSIA *Agency*, WILSHERE *Bills of Exchange*, JACOBS or WILLIS *Carriers*, WILLIAMS, BALFOUR *Carriage by Sea*, GARSIA *Damages*, GAHAN *Insurance*, PICARD *Interpretation* ODGERS *Landlord & Tenant*, WILSHERE *Libel & Slander*, BUTTON *Master & Servant*, SMITH, GARSIA *Mortgages*, STRAHAN *Partnership*, STRAHAN, BALFOUR *Sale of Goods* WILLIS, BALFOUR *Hindu Law*, DURAI

SUGGESTED COURSE OF READING FOR THE SOLICITORS' FINAL EXAMINATION.

FINAL REVISION.
> The Articled Clerk's Cram Book   See page 18   FAY's Leading Cases

COMPULSORY SUBJECTS.

REAL AND PERSONAL PROPERTY AND CONVEYANCING.
> WATSON's or HARGREAVES' Introduction   CHESHIRE on Real Property   GOODEVE on Personal Property   BURNETT's or GIBSON's Conveyancing   GARSIA's Real Property in a Nutshell   PHILLIPS's Questions and Answers

PRACTICE OF THE COURTS.
> GIBSON's Practice and GIBSON's County Court Practice   GARSIA's Procedure in a Nutshell

CRIMINAL LAW AND PROCEDURE.
> HARRIS's Principles of Criminal and Magisterial Law   WILSHERE's Leading Cases   GARSIA's Criminal Law in a Nutshell   ROGERS' Questions and Answers

WILLS, INTESTATE SUCCESSION, ASSETS AND DEATH DUTIES. PARRY's Succession

PROBATE AND DEATH DUTIES. GIBSON's Probate

INCOME TAX. ROWLAND

BANKRUPTCY.
> RINGWOOD's Principles of Bankruptcy
> GARSIA's Bankruptcy Law in a Nutshell

COMPANIES.
> CHARLESWORTH's Principles   BALFOUR's Company Law in a Nutshell

AGENCY.
EMPLOYMENT.
NEGOTIABLE INSTRUMENTS.
SALE OF GOODS.
> INDERMAUR's Common Law or CHARLESWORTH's Mercantile Law

PARTNERSHIP. STRAHAN   BALFOUR's Nutshell.

GENERAL LAW OF CONTRACT AND TORT.
> INDERMAUR's Principles of the Common Law   SALMOND or ANSON on Contracts   SALMOND or WINFIELD on Torts

PRINCIPLES AND RULES OF EQUITY.
> SNELL   RIVINGTON's Epitome

OPTIONAL SUBJECTS.

SHIPPING. MACLACHLAN's Law of Merchant Shipping
LOCAL GOVERNMENT. HART and WRIGHT & HOBHOUSE.
CONFLICT OF LAWS. BURGIN & FLETCHER and CHESHIRE.
DIVORCE. GIBSON

ADMINISTRATION OF ASSETS.

GARSIA'S Administration of Assets in a Nutshell.
39 pages   Price 3s. 6d. net.   1927
This has been written specially for the Bar Final Examinations
It embodies the changes made by the Administration of Estates
Act, 1925

ADVOCACY.

SINGLETON on Conduct at the Bar and some Problems of Advocacy. By J. E. SINGLETON, K.C.
44 pages.   Price 2s. 6d net   1933
   "We most strongly advise every Bar Student to add this
volume to his library "—*Law Journal.*

AGENCY.

BOWSTEAD'S Digest of the Law of Agency.
Ninth Edition.   By A. H. FORBES, Barrister-at-Law
485 pages.   Price £1 10s. net.   1938
   "The Digest will be a useful addition to any law library, and
will be especially serviceable to practitioners who have to advise
mercantile clients or to conduct their litigation, as well as to
students, such as candidates for the Bar Final Examination and
for the Consular Service, who have occasion to make the law of
agency a subject of special study "—*Law Quarterly Review*

WILSHERE'S Outline of the Law of Agency. By
A. M. WILSHERE, Barrister-at-Law   103 pages
Price 7s. 6d. net   1925
   "Should prove a valuable aid to students "—*Law Times.*

ARBITRATION.

BALFOUR'S Law of Arbitration and Awards in a Nutshell. By J A. BALFOUR, Barrister-at-Law.
127 pages.   Price 6s net.   1934
   "The matter is well classified and clearly set out, and is supported by numerous references to decided cases "
                         —*Incorporated Accountants' Journal.*

BANKRUPTCY.

The Articled Clerk's Cram Book. See page 18

RINGWOOD on Bankruptcy and Deeds of Arrangement. With an Appendix containing the Acts, Rules, etc. Seventeenth Edition, by A ROPER. Text 321 pages, Appendix 289 pages Price £1 2s 6d net. 1936

A Tutor's Opinion :-

"I have never been without a copy of 'Ringwood' for 25 years and I have long been of the opinion that it is the best book on Bankruptcy available to students"

"A reconstruction which appears to us to be well balanced and rounded and admirable in every respect One great improvement from a student's point of view is the narrative marginal précis which enables him on a first reading to follow the thread, and on a revision to recall the gist of the story The increased size of the book means that it has put on not fat but muscle The index is more exhaustive and the appendices more complete than ever before The book thus becomes of infinitely greater value to the practitioner."—*Law Quarterly Review*

"Candidates for examinations will find ,that a rather dull branch of the law has been expounded in attractive fashion."
—*Solicitors' Journal.*

GARSIA'S Bankruptcy Law in a Nutshell. Including Deeds of Arrangement and Bills of Sale. By M GARSIA, Barrister-at-Law Second Edition. 69 pages. Price 3s 6d net. 1937

This Edition, slightly enlarged and re-arranged, will continue to prove of assistance to the student wishing to ascertain any main principle of bankruptcy law and the section of the Bankruptcy Act in which it is embodied

BILLS OF EXCHANGE.

JACOBS on Bills of Exchange, Cheques, Promissory Notes, and Negotiable Instruments Generally, including a large number of representative forms, and a note on I O U's and Bills of Lading By BERTRAM JACOBS, Barrister-at-Law. Third Edition 264 pages. Price 10s. 6d. net. 1930

[continued

Bills of Exchange—*continued.*

"It appears to me to be a most excellent piece of work."

"After perusing portions of it I have come to the conclusion that it is a learned and exhaustive treatise on the subject, and I shall certainly bring it to the notice of my pupils."

WILLIS'S Law of Negotiable Securities. Contained in a Course of Six Lectures delivered by WILLIAM WILLIS, Esq., K.C., at the request of the Council of Legal Education. Fifth Edition, by A. W. BAKER WELFORD, Barrister-at-Law. 190 pages. Price 10s. net. 1930

"They are very much companion volumes. Judge Willis with his racy style and fresh outlook, proving a useful foil to Mr. Jacobs, with his measured and lucid survey of a difficult branch of the law."—*Annual Survey of English Law.*

CARRIERS.

BALFOUR'S Carriage of Goods by Land in a Nut-shell. By J. A. BALFOUR, Barrister-at-Law. 60 pages. Price 3s. 6d. net. 1934

Including the Road and Rail Traffic Act, 1933, and some cases on Carriage.

GARSIA'S Law relating to the Carriage of Goods by Sea in a Nutshell. As amended by the Carriage of Goods by Sea Act, 1924. Second Edition. By MARSTON GARSIA, Barrister-at-Law. 36 pages. Price 3s. net. 1925

Written with special reference to Bar Examinations.

COMMON LAW.

(See also Broom's Legal Maxims, p. 23, *post*).

ODGERS on the Common Law of England. Third Edition. By ROLAND BURROWS, LL.D., Reader in the Inns of Court. 2 vols. 1,521 pages. Price £2 10s. net. 1927

Odgers on the Common Law deals with Contracts, Torts, Criminal Law and Procedure, Civil Procedure, the Courts, and the Law of Persons.

WILSHERE'S INDERMAUR'S Principles of the Common Law. The Law of Contracts and Torts, with a Short Outline of the Law of Evidence. Re-written and enlarged by A M Wilshere, Barrister-at-Law.   Fourth Edition   816 pages. Price £1 10s net   1937

"It is clear in statement and makes as easy reading as the nature of the subject permits   The selection of matter to be treated is good—exactly the right emphasis is laid on fundamental principles, and they are presented with an accuracy of statement not always to be found in law books .   Painstaking labour is evident in every page, and the result is the student may read and the practitioner consult this book with confidence that his efforts will be repaid "—*Law Notes*

"I am very much pleased with the new edition, and shall place it on my list of approved text-books "

INDERMAUR'S Leading Common Law Cases; with some short notes thereon. Chiefly intended as a Guide to "Smith's Leading Cases." Tenth Edition. by E. A. Jelf, Master of the Supreme Court   With six illustrations by E. T. Reed   111 pages. Price 8s 6d net,   1922

COCKLE & HIBBERT'S Leading Cases in Common Law. With Notes, Explanatory and Connective, presenting a Systematic View of the whole Subject. By E Cockle and W. Nembhard Hibbert, LL D., Barristers-at-Law.   Second Edition.   962 pages Price £2 2s net.   1929

This book is on the same lines as Cockle's Cases on Evidence.   It contains 771 cases

Following is a short summary of its contents :—

Nature of the Common Law.	Void, etc., Contracts.	Negotiable Instruments.
Common Law Rights and Duties.	Quasi-Contracts.	Partnership.
Contract, including Contracts of Record.	Agency.	Sale of Goods.
	Bailments.	Torts.
Specialty Contracts.	Carriers.	Damages
Simple Contracts.	Landlord and Tenant.	Law of Persons.
	Master and Servant.	Conflict of Laws.

"Dr Hibbert is to be congratulated on the masterly manner in which he has re-edited Cockle's Leading Cases on Common Law The arrangement and printing are particularly clear, the choice of cases is marked by great discretion, and a short analysis of the

Common Law—*continued.*

law of various departments dealt with in the book is set forth with a view to refreshing the reader's knowledge on the subject before he turns to read the cases which are set out."—*Law Coach.*

"The present work has the merits of thoroughness, accuracy, systematic arrangement and a modern point of view."

—*Solicitors' Journal.*

SMITH'S Leading Cases. A Selection of Leading Cases in various Branches of the Law, with Notes. Thirteenth Edition. By Sir T. Willes Chitty, K.C., A. T. Denning and C. P. Harvey, Barristers-at-Law. 2 vols. Price £4 10s. net. 1929

This work presents a number of cases illustrating and explaining the leading principles of the common law, accompanied by exhaustive notes showing how those principles have been applied in subsequent cases.

COMPANIES.

The Articled Clerk's Cram Book. See page 18.

CHARLESWORTH'S Principles of Company Law. Illustrated by Leading Cases. By J. Charlesworth, Barrister-at-Law. Second Edition. 299 pages. Price 7s. 6d. net. 1938

"It would be difficult to recommend to a student a clearer and more helpful book on the Law of Companies."—*Law Times.*

"Gives a clear and vivid presentment of the principles of company law, with a judicious blend of illustrations and cases to make it an ideal book for Examination purposes. . . . we are convinced that a careful study of this new edition will produce the most satisfactory results in practice and in Examinations."—*Law Notes.*

BALFOUR'S Company Law in a Nutshell. By J. A. Balfour, Barrister-at-Law. 88 pages. Price 3s. 6d. net. 1933

SOPHIAN'S Companies Act, 1929, with Introduction, Notes and Index. 266 pages. Price 10s. 6d. net. 1929

MILLNER'S Questions and Answers on Company Law. By R. Millner, M.A., Barrister-at-Law. 5s. net. 1939

CONFLICT OF LAWS.

The Articled Clerk's Cram Book. See page 18.

SEYMOUR'S Conflict of Laws in a Nutshell. By G O. SEYMOUR, LL B. 52 pages. 3s 6d. net.
1938

BURGIN & FLETCHER'S Students' Conflict of Laws. An Introduction to the Study of Private International Law, based on Dicey Third Edition. 307 pages. Price £1 net
1937

HIBBERT'S Leading Cases on Conflict of Laws. By W. N. HIBBERT, LL.D., Barrister-at-Law 293 pages Price £1 1s. net.
1931

Compiled on the same lines as Cockle's Cases on Evidence It contains 200 cases and is an indispensable companion to all the text books on the subject.

CONSTITUTIONAL LAW AND HISTORY.

CHALMERS & ASQUITH'S Outlines of Constitutional Law. Fifth Edition. By CYRIL ASQUITH, K.C 510 pages Price 15s net.
1936

The section on the history of the Courts has been re-written and considerably expanded, and articled clerks will find it suitable for the intermediate examination

"If we are asked 'Is this a good cram book?' we must answer 'Yes' It is the book used by most pass students and satisfies their one desire—to be enabled to pass the examination "
—*Annual Survey of English Law, 1930*

"It is a mine of accurate information and we recommend it as a most convenient substitute for Anson and a wise substitute for Dicey "—*Canadian Historical Review*

"It contains a very great deal of information, ranging over the whole field of constitutional law Its style is very attractive, and its utility to the student is undoubted "—*Bell Yard*

SALANT'S Constitutional Laws of the British Empire. By E SALANT, LL B 240 pages. Price 10s 6d net. 1934

With an Appendix containing the Constitutions of Canada, Australia, South Africa and the Irish Free State, and the Statute of Westminster

"The book supplies a real need, and is an excellent introduction to all concerned with this wide subject "
—*Cambridge Law Journal*

THOMAS & BELLOT'S Leading Cases in Constitutional Law. With Introduction and Notes. Seventh Edition. By E SLADE, M A., Barrister-at-Law. 377 pages Price 10s 6d net. 1934

Some knowledge of the chief cases in constitutional law is now required in many examinations, and is obviously necessary to the thorough student of constitutional history. This book extracts the essence of the cases with which the student is expected to be familiar, preserving always something of the concrete circumstance that is so helpful to the memory It adds, where necessary, a short note to the individual case, and subjoins to each important group of cases some general remarks in the shape of a note The cases are so arranged as to be convenient for ready reference

TASWELL-LANGMEAD'S English Constitutional History. From the Teutonic Invasion to the Present Time. Designed as a Text-book for Students and others. Ninth Edition By A L POOLE, M.A., F.S.A., Fellow and Tutor, St. John's College, Oxford. 758 pages. Price 21s net 1929

"This is much more than a new edition The book is the only one which gives the law student exactly what he wants "
—*Annual Survey of English Law, 1929*

" 'Taswell-Langmead' has long been popular with candidates for examination in Constitutional History, and the present edition should render it even more so It is now, in our opinion, the ideal students' book upon the subject "—*Law Notes*

WILSHERE'S Analysis of Taswell-Langmead's Constitutional History. By A. M. WILSHERE, LL B, Barrister-at-Law. 133 pages. Price 6s. 6d net. 1929

GARSIA'S Constitutional Law and Legal History in a Nutshell. Including an Alphabetical Table of Writs and their Uses, a Comparative Table of the Constitutions of the Dominions. Third Edition. By M. GARSIA, Barrister-at-Law. 138 pages. Price 4s net. 1932

"I have looked over this book and find that it is admirably adapted for its purpose For almost any type of student it should be invaluable if judiciously used with the standard Text Book "
—*A Law Lecturer*

GRIFFITH'S Questions and Answers in Constitutional Law and Legal History. By D M GRIFFITH. Second Edition 86 pages Price 5s net. 1935

"Should prove very helpful to students who are seeking to master the subject for the purposes of their examination"
—*Law Notes*

CONTRACTS.

(See also Common Law.)

The Articled Clerk's Cram Book. See page 18.

WILSHERE'S Outline of Contracts and Torts. By A. M WILSHERE, Barrister-at-Law. Fourth Edition. 158 pages Price 7s. 6d net 1936

" This little book is an admirable starting point for the young student in his study of the law of Contract and Tort The simple but lucid style in which it is written will enable the student to get a quick grasp of the basic principles In short it is a book which should be read by all young students before tackling the larger works "—*Bell Yard*

CARTER on Contracts. Elements of the Law of Contracts By A. T CARTER, of the Inner Temple, Barrister-at-Law, Reader to the Council of Legal Education. Seventh Edition. 272 pages. Price 12s. 6d net. 1931

" We have here an excellent book for those who are beginning to read law "—*Law Magazine*

SALMOND & WINFIELD on Contracts. Principles of the Law of Contract By the late Sir JOHN W. SALMOND and P. H WINFIELD, Barrister-at-Law. 544 pages Price 30s net. 1927

"Exceedingly clear and accurate in its statement of the principles of the law of contract "—*Law Notes*

CONYERS' Contracts in a Nutshell. With Epitomes of Leading Cases. By A J CONYERS, Barrister-at-Law Second Edition 119 pages. Price 4s. net.
1934

"The work is thorough, covering the ground well in outline, and the selection of authoritative cases seems judicious"
—*Law Times.*

O'CONNELL'S Questions and Answers on Contracts. By M O'CONNELL, LL B 180 pages. Price 5s net.
1936

" This is one of the best books of its kind we have come across The answers do not merely answer the questions—they do more than that they teach the student "—*Law Notes*

CONVEYANCING.

The Articled Clerk's Cram Book. See page 18.

ELPHINSTONE'S Introduction to Conveyancing. By Sir HOWARD WARBURTON ELPHINSTONE, Bart. Eighth Edition, by HARRY FARRAR, Barrister-at-Law, Editor of Key and Elphinstone's Precedents in Conveyancing. [*In the press.*

"In our opinion no better work on the subject with which it deals was ever written for students and young practitioners"
—*Law Notes.*

PHILLIPS'S Questions and Answers. See REAL PROPERTY.

GARSIA'S Law relating to Conveyancing in a Nutshell. By M. GARSIA, Barrister-at-Law. 160 pages. 5s. net.
1939

KRUSIN'S Practical Conveyancing Forms in a Nutshell. By S. M KRUSIN, Barrister-at-Law. About 3s.
March 1939

BURNETT'S Elements of Conveyancing; with an Appendix of Students' Precedents. Sixth Edition, by J. F R BURNETT, Barrister-at-Law. Text 392 pages, Precedents 70 pages. Price 21s. net. 1937

This book is complementary to and extends the information in the books on Real Property. The reader is taken through the component parts of Purchase Deeds, Leases, Mortgage Deeds, Settlements and Wills, and the way in which these instruments are prepared is explained   Previous to this is a short history of Conveyancing, and chapters on Contracts for Sale of Land dealing with the statutory requisites, the form, particulars and conditions of sale, the abstract of title, requisitions, etc , and finally there is a chapter on conveyance by registration   The second part of the book contains STUDENTS' PRECEDENTS IN CONVEYANCING, illustrating the various documents referred to in the first part It is the only book containing a representative collection of precedents for students.

"Students of the present day are lucky in having such a pleasant path cut for them to the knowledge of real property law "—Law Times

"Students will find in this book a clear exposition of a difficult subject which solves most of their difficulties and deals with all the matters that concern them for examination purposes "—Law Notes

CRIMINAL LAW AND PROCEDURE.

The Articled Clerk's Cram Book. See page 18.

ODGERS on the Common Law. See page 6.

GARSIA'S Criminal Law and Procedure in a Nutshell. Sixth Edition. By M GARSIA, Barrister-at-Law. 132 pages. Price 4s net.   1937
Enumerates and classifies the more important crimes, gives a short history of the Criminal Courts and a brief outline of criminal procedure

"A well-planned digest of the Criminal Law and will be found to provide a good foundation for fuller study   "

HARRIS & WILSHERE'S Principles and Practice of the Criminal Law. Intended as a Lucid Exposition of the subject for the use of Students. Sixteenth Edition   By A M. WILSHERE, Barrister-at-Law. 687 pages. Price 15s. net   1937
"This Standard Text-book of the Criminal Law is as good a book on the subject as the ordinary student will find on the library shelves   .   The book is very clearly and simply written   No previous legal knowledge is taken for granted, and everything is explained in such a manner that no student ought to have much difficulty in obtaining a grasp of the subject   "
—Solicitors' Journal.

"   As a Student's Text-book we have always felt that this work would be hard to beat, and at the present time we have no reason for altering our opinion . . . "—Law Times

WILSHERE'S Elements of Criminal and Magisterial Law and Procedure. By A. M. WILSHERE, Barrister-at-Law. Fourth Edition. 354 pages. Price 15s. net. 1935

"It is a work eminently suitable for the Bar student and contains within its modest compass a surprisingly large amount of accurate information of practical utility "—*Law Quarterly Review*

WILSHERE'S Leading Cases illustrating the Criminal Law, for Students. Third Edition. 441 pages. Price 15s. net. 1935

"This collection of 208 cases has been skilfully selected so as to cover a very wide field and forms a most useful book of reference . . it is not intended to be a case-book and text-book in one, and therefore explanatory notes have been cut down to a minimum "—*Cambridge Law Journal*

ROGERS' Questions and Answers on Criminal Law. By P. H. T ROGERS, Barrister-at-Law. 99 pages. Price 5s. net 1936

"Would that all authors could concentrate in a bare hundred pages all the useful information which is to be found here . The questions are clear but sometimes tricky, and are just the type of questions which might be found in any examination paper "—*Police Journal*

DAMAGES.

GAHAN'S Handbook on the Law of Damages. By FRANK GAHAN, Barrister-at-Law, Reader in Common Law in the Law Society's School of Law. 204 pages. Price 15s. net 1937

DEEDS.

(See Interpretation)

DICTIONARY.

The Concise Law Dictionary. By P. G. OSBORN, Barrister-at-Law. Second Edition. 358 pages. Price 15s. net 1937

A book every student should have for general reference It deals with existing law and with legal history Legal maxims are translated, and there are glossaries of Latin, French and Early English words relating to the law There is also a list of abbreviations used in citing law reports.

"The student will find it an accurate and an extremely convenient reference book "—*Cambridge Law Journal*

ENGLISH LEGAL SYSTEM.

PHILLIPS' Principles of English Law and the Constitution. By O. H. PHILLIPS, M A., B C L , Barrister-at-Law   558 pages.   21s. net   1939

CONTENTS

Introduction—Law and the State   The English Legal System (English Law and its Sources—Elements of English Law—Main Branches of English Law); Constitution of the United Kingdom , Constitution of the British Empire

GRAVESON'S English Legal System in a Nutshell. By R H. GRAVESON, LL B   Price about 5s
March, 1939

EQUITY.

The Articled Clerk's Cram Book.   See page 18.

POTTER'S Introduction to the History of Equity and its Courts.   By HAROLD POTTER, LL.D , Ph.D. 105 pages.   Price 8s. 6d net.   1931

SNELL'S Principles of Equity.   Intended for the use of Students and Practitioners   Twenty-second Edition   By H. G. RIVINGTON, M A , Oxon   595 pages   Price £1 10s. net   1939

"In a most modest preface the editors disclaim any intention to interfere with Snell as generations of students have known it Actually what they have succeeded in doing is to make the book at least three times as valuable as it ever was before   Illustrations from cases have been deftly introduced, and the whole rendered simple and intelligible until it is hardly recognisable"
—*The Students' Companion*

(—— Adapted for Indian Students.   By S. C BAGCHI) Price £1 1s. net   1930

RIVINGTON'S Epitome of Snell's Principles of Equity.   Second Edition   By H. G RIVINGTON, M.A , and C. W RIVINGTON, B A   267 pages. 9s net.   1939

"It is an admirable summary of the principles, which are clearly set out with reference to statutes and cases   The print is so arranged that the main points catch the eye"
—*Cambridge Law Journal*

Equity—*continued.*

GARSIA'S Equity in a Nutshell. By M. GARSIA, Barrister-at-Law Second Edition. 96 pages Price 4s. net. 1933

"The matter is carefully drawn up and very clearly and systematically set out "—*Law Times.*

RIVINGTON'S Questions and Answers on Equity. By C W. RIVINGTON, B A , Barrister-at-Law. 108 pages Price 5s. net 1937

STORY'S Commentaries on Equity Jurisprudence. Third English Edition. By A E. RANDALL. 641 pages Price £1 17s 6d. net. 1920

WILSHERE'S Principles of Equity. Second Edition. By L B TILLARD, Barrister-at-Law. 590 pages. Price 12s. 6d. net. 1929

"Mr. Wilshere has succeeded in giving us a very clear exposition of these principles ' The book is far better balanced than the majority of text books, and the law is stated in its modern garb and is not, as in so many elementary works, almost lost to sight beneath a mass of historical explanatory matter "—*Sittings Review.*

WHITE & TUDOR'S. Leading Cases in Equity. A Selection of Leading Cases in Equity; with Notes. Ninth Edition. By E P HEWITT, K.C. 2 vols. Price £4 10s net. 1928

EVIDENCE.

COCKLE'S Leading Cases and Statutes on the Law of Evidence, with Notes, explanatory and connective, presenting a systematic view of the whole subject By ERNEST COCKLE, Barrister-at-Law. Sixth Edition By C. M. CAHN. Cases, 426 pages. Statutes, 120 pages. Price 18s 6d. net. 1938

This book and Phipson's Manual are together *sufficient* for all ordinary examination purposes, and will save students the necessity of reading larger works on this subject

By an ingenious use of black type the author brings out the essential words of the judgments and Statutes, and enables the student to see at a glance the effect of each section

"Of all the collections of leading cases compiled for the use of students with which we are acquainted, this book of Mr Cockle's is, in our opinion, far and away the best. The student who picks up the principles of the English law of evidence from these readable and logical pages has an enormous advantage over a generation of predecessors who toiled through the compressed sentences of Stephen's little digest in a painful effort to grasp its meaning Mr Cockle teaches his subject in the only way in which a branch of law so highly abstract can ever be grasped , he arranges the principal rules of evidence in logical order, but he puts forward each in the shape of a leading case which illustrates it Just enough of the headnote, the facts, and the judgments are selected and set out to explain the point fully without boring the reader ; *and the notes* appended to the cases *contain all the additional information that anyone can require in ordinary practice.*"—*Solicitors' Journal*

PHIPSON'S Manual of the Law of Evidence. Fifth Edition. By ROLAND BURROWS, K C, LL D 317 pages. With a supplement dealing with the Evidence Act, 1938 Price 12s. 6d net   1935-8

" The increasing popularity of this book is well deserved One might almost say that it has superseded all other elementary text-books, so general has its use become amongst students .   An excellent book, at a reasonable price , and its price is not an indication of its value and usefulness "—*Cambridge Law Journal*

" The way of the student, unlike that of the transgressor, is no longer hard The volume under review is designed by the author for the use of students To say that it is the best text-book for students upon the subject is really to understate its usefulness , as far as we know there is in existence no other treatise upon evidence which gives a scientific and accurate presentment of the subject in a form and compass suitable to students "
—*Australian Law Times*

BEST'S Principles of Evidence. With Elementary Rules for conducting the Examination and Cross-Examination of Witnesses. Twelfth Edition. By S. L PHIPSON, Barrister-at-Law 673 pages Price £1 12s. 6d. net   1923

"The most valuable work on the law of evidence which exists in any country "—*Law Times*

GARSIA'S Evidence in a Nutshell. By MARSTON GARSIA, Barrister-at-Law. Second Edition. 47 pages. Price 3s net   1935

Evidence—*continued.*

MILLER'S Questions and Answers on Evidence. By D. MILLER, Barrister-at-Law. 4s. net. 1939

WROTTESLEY on the Examination of Witnesses in Court. Including Examination in Chief, Cross-Examination, and Re-Examination. With chapters on Preliminary Steps and some Elementary Rules of Evidence. Second Edition. By F. J. WROTTESLEY, of the Inner Temple, Barrister-at-Law. 173 pages. Price 6s. net. 1929

This is a practical book for the law student. It is interesting, and is packed full of valuable hints and information.

EXAMINATION GUIDES AND QUESTIONS.

The Concise Law Dictionary (*ante*, p. 14) is an indispensable book of reference.

GARSIA'S Digest of Questions set at Bar Examinations during the past six years. 121 pages. Price 6s. net. [*In preparation.*

The questions are grouped logically under subjects, and references are given to text books where the answers will be found.

BROOKS'S All You Want for the Bar Final. A Condensed Cram Book, dealing with Torts, Contracts, Equity, Civil Procedure, Evidence, Pleading. Third Edition. By R. MILLNER, M.A., Barrister-at-Law. Price 5s. 6d. net. About March, 1939

The author claims that a full knowledge of the contents of this book is by itself sufficient for the purpose of answering all questions normally asked.

The Articled Clerk's Cram Book. By W. S. CHANEY, Solicitor, (*John Mackrell Prizeman*). 794 pages.

With a Supplement to September, 1936.   Price
17s. 6d. net   1932–6
   A collection of Notes on the various subjects which come
within the purview of the Solicitor's Final and Honours
Examinations   While it is thought that a knowledge of its
contents would in some cases probably suffice to enable a
Student to answer sufficient questions to secure a pass, it is only
intended as Notes on the general principles of the various subjects
covered, and spaces have been left to enable the Student to
add to these Notes as occasion offers
   Throughout the book epitomes of the leading cases are
given
   The following subjects are dealt with —

Property and	**Companies.**
Conveyancing.	**Practice.**
Contract.	**Criminal Law and**
Tort.	**Procedure.**
Equity.	**Private International**
Bankruptcy.	**Law**

**RUSHTON'S Guide to the Legal Examinations for.
Unarticled Clerks** of the London Chamber of
Commerce and the Royal Society of Arts. By
J. N RUSHTON, Solicitor. 94 pages.   Price 3s. 6d.
net.   1939
A useful guide, with hints as to study, and specimen examina-
tion questions

A Guide to the Legal Profession and London LL.B.
Containing the latest Regulations for the Bar and
articled clerks   With a detailed description of all
current Students' Law Books, and suggested courses
of reading   112 pages. Price 3s 6d. net   1933

EXECUTORS.

PARRY'S Law of Succession   See WILLS

**WALKER'S Compendium of the Law relating to
Executors and Administrators.** Sixth Edition,
embodying the effect of the Acts of 1925   By S E.
WILLIAMS, of Lincoln's Inn, Barrister-at-Law. 386
pages.   Price £1 5s. net   1926
   "We highly approve of Mr Walker's arrangement   .   . We
can commend it as bearing on its face evidence of skilful and
careful labour."—*Law Times*

Executors—*continued.*

GARSIA'S Administration of Assets in a Nutshell.
39 pages. 3s. 6d. net.   1927
    Excellent for final revision.

HINDU LAW.

DURAI'S Hindu Law in a Nutshell. By J. CHINNA
DURAI, Barrister-at-Law, Advocate, Madras. 124
pages. Price 5s. net.   1933

INCOME TAX.

NEWPORT on Income Tax Law and Practice. By
C. A. NEWPORT, F.C.R.A., Corporate Accountant,
Eleventh Edition, 329 pages. Price 10s. 6d. net.
                                                          1938
Written specially for examination students. It is illustrated
throughout by examples, and has an appendix of questions
and answers.
    "This book in a way breaks new ground . . . The volume
before us purposely assumes no prior knowledge, endeavours to
make the position clear by simple practical illustrations, and,
in the words of its author, 'so far as possible, anything
approaching the jargon almost inseparable from the subject has
been either avoided or accompanied by intelligible explana-
tions.'"—*Law Notes.*

INSURANCE LAW.

**PORTER'S Laws of Insurance: Fire, Life, Accident,
and Guarantee.** Embodying Cases in the English,
Scotch, Irish, American, Australian, New Zealand,
and Canadian Courts. Eighth Edition. 501 pages.
Price £1 12s. 6d. net.   1933

PICARD'S Elements of the Laws of Insurance,
Relating to all risks other than Marine. By
M. P. PICARD, Barrister-at-Law. 162 pages. Price
7s. 6d. net.   1935
A Concise outline, intended for the use of Students.
There is an appendix containing 69 leading cases, with a
concise statement of the principles for which each one is an
authority. This feature will be found invaluable for revision.
    "The author has well satisfied the demand for a small book for
students . . . The beginner has here a well-arranged text-book
which adequately explains the essential principles of insurance.
Over two hundred cases are cited ; the statements of facts are

models of compression, and there are copious quotations from judgments . The whole work is admirably done, and should prove a boon to students faced with insurance as a special subject "
—*Cambridge Law Journal*

INTERNATIONAL LAW.

(See also Conflict of Laws)

HOLLAND'S Lectures on International Law. By SIR T. ERSKINE HOLLAND, D.C.L K C Edited by T A. WALKER, LL.D. and W. L WALKER LL.B. Carnegie Fellow in International Law. 547 pages. £1 10s. net. 1933
A very readable work, designed especially for students, by the greatest authority of his time.

COBBETT'S Cases and Opinions on International Law. Vol. I "Peace." Fifth Edition By F. TEMPLE GREY, Barrister-at-Law. 365 pages. Price 16s. net. 1931
"The book is well arranged, the materials well selected, and the comments to the point Much will be found in small space in this book "—*Law Journal*

Vol II "War and Neutrality" Fifth Edition. By W. L. WALKER, LL.B., Barrister-at-Law, Carnegie Fellow in International Law. 579 pages. Price £1 5s. net. 1937
"Here is a welcome attempt to perform an important and impossible service, for what this volume aims to do is no less than to present war rights and duties recognised in 1937 "
—*Am Jl Int Law*

JACKSON'S Manual of International Law with Epitomes of Leading Cases and Conventions. A Guide to the Modern Practice of States By S JACKSON, LL B 163 pages Price 5s net 1933
"Very clearly and lucidly written and presents a good outline of the subject "—*Law Notes*

DAVISON'S Questions and Answers on International Law. By R DAVISON, LL B Price about 5s March, 1939

INTERPRETATION.

(See also Statutes)

ODGERS' Construction of Deeds and Statutes. By SIR CHARLES E. ODGERS, Barrister-at-Law, late

[21]

Interpretation—*continued*

Puisne Judge of the High Court at Madras. About
300 pages 15s net. 1939

BROOM'S Principles of Legal Interpretation. Reprinted from Broom's Legal Maxims 114 pages.
7s 6d net. 1937

JURISPRUDENCE.

SALMOND'S Jurisprudence; or, Theory of the Law.
By JOHN W. SALMOND, Barrister-at-Law. Ninth
Edition. By J L PARKER, Barrister-at-Law 731
pages. Price £1 5s. net. 1937

"Mr Parker has had a difficult task and on the whole he has
done it well He has found it necessary to re-write certain parts
of the text, for example, passages dealing with the Law of Property, where to leave the original untouched would have given
an inaccurate picture of substantive law, but apart from this his
operations on the text have been confined to excision and compression in places where this seemed possible without alteration
of the general sense, and the new matter which he has introduced
has been placed in notes and excursuses In his work of compression he has shown admirable skill "—*Law Quarterly Review*

HIBBERT'S Jurisprudence. By W. N. HIBBERT, LL D.,
Barrister-at-Law. 319 pages. Price 12s. 6d. net. 1932

A critical examination of the varying views of writers on
this subject and a statement of the Author's own views which
are the result of thirty-three years' teaching Where necessary
the historical aspect has been dealt with It is a book of the
greatest assistance to examination students.

"It goes almost without saying that Dr Hibbert's exposition is
lucid, in fact it is difficult to think of any recent work on the
same subject which 'puts over' an author's ideas with such
clarity and which must have succeeded in leaving a student
with so little doubt of what the teacher was trying to say "
—*Journal of the Society of Comparative Legislation.*

BARTLETT'S Questions and Answers on Jurisprudence. By L BARTLETT, LL B 112 pages Price
4s net. 1934

LANDLORD AND TENANT.

**WILSHERE'S Student's Law of Landlord and
Tenant.** By A M WILSHERE, Barrister-at-Law.
Price 4s net 1935

LEADING CASES.

(See also under Subjects)

FAY'S Students' Case Book. Leading Cases in a Nutshell. By E. S. FAY, Barrister-at-Law. Second edition 152 pages Price 4s. 6d net. 1937

250 Cases on

Constitutional Law—Criminal Law—Tort and Contract—Evidence—Real Property—Equity.

"The nuts are full of meat and for the price of a hundred 'gaspers' the purchaser certainly gets more than one substantial meal, after which he will feel so fit mentally that, full of bravado, he will ask, 'Where are those Examiners?'"
—*Law Notes*

"As pegs to hang fuller knowledge upon these neat little summaries could hardly be bettered."—*Justice of the Peace*

LEGAL HISTORY.

(See also Constitutional Law, Dictionary, Equity)

POTTER'S Short Outline of English Legal History. By HAROLD POTTER, LL.D, Ph D. Third edition. 285 pages Price 10s 6d net 1933

Intended more especially for the Bar Examinations, particular attention is given to the history of judicial institutions, sources of English Law and the history of Contract and Tort
"Very thoughtful and well-balanced."—*The Times*

POTTER'S Historical Introduction to English Law and its Institutions. By HAROLD POTTER, LL D. 575 pages Price £1 net 1932

"Dr Potter has written his present book with a view to the student s requirements for the Bar and University Examinations, but we are certain it will have a wider appeal It marks a noteworthy addition to the existing works on Legal History, and should enhance the author s growing reputation as one of the leading authorities on historical legal research."—*Law Notes*

"An excellent manual clearly expressing the basic principles of English Law and their development."
—*Annual Bulletin of Historical Literature*

LEGAL MAXIMS.

(See also Dictionary)

BROOM'S Selection of Legal Maxims, Classified and Illustrated. Ninth Edition. By W. J. BYRNE. 633 pages Price £1 12s 6d. net 1924

[23]

Latin for Lawyers. Contains (1) A course in Latin, in 32 lessons, based on legal maxims; (2) 1000 Latin Maxims, with translations, explanatory notes, cross-references, and subject-index; (3) A Latin Vocabulary. Second edition 300 pages. Price 7s. 6d. net

This book is intended to enable the practitioner or student to acquire a working knowledge of Latin in the shortest possible time, and at the same time to become acquainted with the legal maxims which embody the fundamental rules of the common law

COTTERELL'S Latin Maxims and Phrases. Literally translated, with explanatory notes. Intended for the use of students for all legal examinations. By J N. COTTERELL, Solicitor Third Edition. 82 pages Price 5s net.

LIBEL AND SLANDER.

BUTTON'S Law of Libel and Slander. By WILFRID A. BUTTON, Barrister-at-Law. 230 pages. Price 12s. 6d net 1935

In a Foreword, Lord Justice Greer says —

"The author has in my opinion succeeded in doing admirably what he set out to do, and I have no hesitation in recommending his little book"

"There was a real need for a book of modest dimensions on this important subject, which would be suitable for the use of students Mr Button has produced such a book, and has set out lucidly and accurately the leading principles, and illustrated them with a wealth of verbatim extracts from the Law Reports"
—*Cambridge Law Journal*

LOCAL GOVERNMENT.

WRIGHT & HOBHOUSE'S Outline of Local Government and Local Finance in England and Wales (excluding London). Eighth Edition With Introduction and Tables of Local Taxation. 267 pages Price 12s. 6d net 1937

"Lucid, concise, and accurate to a degree which has never been surpassed."—*Justice of the Peace.*

[24]

MASTER AND SERVANT.

GARSIA'S Law relating to Master and Servant in a Nutshell. Second Edition. 50 pages. Price 3s. 6d. net   1933
 "It covers the whole range of the law of Master and Servant, which is classified, digested and presented in a form well calculated for assimilation "—*Justice of the Peace*

SMITH'S Law of Master and Servant. Eighth Edition By C. M. KNOWLES, Barrister-at-Law 366 pages Price 25s. net   1931

MERCANTILE LAW.

CHARLESWORTH'S Principles of Mercantile Law. By J. CHARLESWORTH, Barrister-at-Law. 366 pages Fourth Edition. Price 8s 6d. net.   1938
 "The law is very clearly stated, and selected cases are set out in a summarised form for the purpose of illustrating the various propositions which are formulated Taking it all round, this is one of the best books of its type"
 —*Annual Survey of English Law, 1929*

SMITH'S Mercantile Law. A Compendium of Mercantile Law, by the late JOHN WILLIAM SMITH Thirteenth Edition. By H. C. GUTTERIDGE, Barrister-at-Law. 800 pages. Price £2 2s. net
CONTENTS—   1931

Partners.	Carriers.	Lien.
Companies.	Affreightment.	Bankruptcy.
Principal and Agent.	Bottomry.	Bills of Exchange.
Goodwill.	Insurance.	Sale of Goods.
Negotiable Instruments.	Guarantees	Debtor and Creditor.
	Stoppage in Transitu.	

 "We have no hesitation in recommending the work before us to the profession and the public as a reliable guide to the subjects included in it, and as constituting one of the most scientific treatises extant on mercantile law "—*Solicitors' Journal*

MORTGAGES.

HANBURY & WALDOCK on Mortgages. By H G. HANBURY and C H M. WALDOCK, Barristers-at-Law. 496 pages 25s net   1938
 "Surveyed as a whole, this book leaves an impression of clarity and completeness It presents an excellent survey of the modern law, with occasional illuminating excursions into the history of its developments "—*Solicitor*
 "Here is a book which will help many to take a keen interest in and get a vivid and lasting idea of our law of mortgages "—*Law Times*

PARTNERSHIP.

STRAHAN & OLDHAM'S Law of Partnership. By J. A. STRAHAN, Reader of Equity, Inns of Court, and N. H. OLDHAM, Barristers-at-Law. Fifth Edition. 264 pages. Price 10s net. 1927

"It might almost be described as a collection of judicial statements as to the law of partnership arranged with skill, so as to show their exact bearing on the language used in the Partnership Act of 1890, and we venture to prophesy that the book will attain a considerable amount of fame."—*Student's Companion*

BALFOUR'S Partnership Law in a Nutshell. By J. A. BALFOUR, Barrister-at-Law. 64 pages. Price 3s. 6d. net. 1934

PERSONAL PROPERTY.

WILLIAMS' Principles of the Law of Personal Property, intended for the use of Students in Conveyancing. Eighteenth Edition. Adapted to the Acts of 1925. By T. CYPRIAN WILLIAMS, of Lincoln's Inn, Barrister-at-Law. 739 pages. Price £1 10s. net. 1926

GOODEVE'S Modern Law of Personal Property. Eighth Edition. By HAROLD POTTER, LL.D., Solicitor and A. K. KIRALFY, LL.B. 702 pages. Price £1 2s 6d. net. 1937

"The new Goodeve may establish itself firmly as the most popular book on a very difficult subject, as it is undoubtedly the best."—*Jl Pub Teachers of Law*

"An able new edition effecting some rearrangement in a textbook of established reputation, amplifying it and bringing it thoroughly up to date."—*Law Times*

PLEADING.

(See Procedure.)

PRIVATE INTERNATIONAL LAW.

(See Conflict of Laws.)

PROCEDURE.

The Articled Clerk's Cram Book. See page 18
ODGERS on the Common Law. See page 6.

WILSHERE'S Outlines of Procedure in an Action.
With an appendix of specimen forms and precedents
of pleadings For the Use of Students By A M
WILSHERE, Barrister-at-Law. Fourth Edition. 220
pages. Price 15s net   1930
  "The author has made the book clear, interesting, and instructive, and it should be acceptable to students "—*Solicitors' Journal*

GARSIA'S Civil Procedure in a Nutshell. With numerous specimens and examples of Writs, Pleadings,
Summonses and Orders in use in the King's Bench
Division. Third Edition. With a chapter on the
New Procedure. 90 pages Price 4s. net.   1934
  "Should greatly assist the student in a final revision of procedure, and by reason of its clarity and conciseness should
help him to arrange his knowledge acquired from one of the
larger books "—*Law Notes*

FARRIN'S Questions and Answers on Civil Procedure. By R W FARRIN Second Edition. 68
pages. Price 3s 6d. net.   1935

JACKSON'S Precedents of Pleadings in Tort; drafted
in Fac-Simile for the use of Students By R. W
Jackson, Barrister-at-Law. 87 pages Price 2s. 6d
net   1933
  "Should prove very useful "—*Law Notes.*

REAL PROPERTY.

The Articled Clerk's Cram Book. See page 18

WATSON'S Introduction to the Law of Real Property. Second Edition By J A WATSON, LL.D,
Barrister-at-Law 296 pages. Price 15s net   1938
  "It is written in an accurate and attractive style throughout Beginning with an introductory historical sketch we are
taken through the whole subject, point by point—each separate
phase being explained in simple and accurate form The student
will acquire something very much more than a theoretical basis
for his knowledge, he steps at once into the practical application of the legal principles he is studying."—*Solicitors' Journal*

**HARGREAVES' Introduction to the Principles of Land
Law.** By A. D HARGREAVES, LL B 224 pages
Price 12s 6d net   1936
  "   . Its object is ' to present to the beginner the main principles
of English Land Law in such a way that at a later stage he may

Real Property—*continued*

approach the study of its details with an existing knowledge of it as a whole ' This object is admirably achieved , for the book is written in an attractive style and the law is clearly and precisely stated The most striking thing about the book is the natural and happy way in which the historical outlines and the modern rules are blended together to give a live impression of our law "

—*Journal of the Society of Public Teachers of Law, 1935*

WILLIAMS & EASTWOOD'S Principles of the Law of Real Property. Twenty-fifth Edition By R. A. EASTWOOD, Barrister-at-Law, Professor of Law at the University of Manchester. 554 pages. Price £1 7s 6d. net   1933

"The modern law of real property is, as he remarks in his concluding summary, a system of great complexity, but under his careful supervision 'Williams on Real Property' remains one of the most useful text-books for acquiring a knowledge of it "

—*Solicitors' Journal.*

WILSHERE'S Analysis of Williams on Real Property. Fifth Edition. 161 pages. Price 7s. 6d. net. 1926

GOODEVE & POTTER'S Modern Law of Real Property. Sixth Edition. By HAROLD POTTER, LL B., Reader in Law at Birmingham University. 665 pages Price £1 7s. 6d net.   1929

"The introductory chapters, including one on the characteristics of the new legislation, are very clearly and pithily written, and to whichever chapter the student turns he will find statements of the law which will engage his attention and often be retained by his memory owing to the freshness, force and significance which characterise this text book "—*Law Times*

"The book contains a very complete, reasoned and helpful exposition of the modern law of real property."—*Law Notes*

RABIN'S Leading Cases and Statutes in Real Property Law. 433 pages. Price 21s net. 1931

167 cases grouped under appropriate headings Preceding each group sections of the Acts bearing on that particular subject are printed A useful companion to all the text books on real property

GARSIA'S Law relating to Real Property in a Nutshell. Fifth Edition. 111 pages Price 4s. 6d. net   1938

"Judiciously used, from the nutshell may emerge the tree of knowledge "—*Justice of the Peace*

PHILLIPS'S Questions and Answers on **Real Property and Conveyancing.** 180 pages. Price 5s net   1932

RECEIVERS.

KERR on the Law and Practice as to Receivers appointed by the High Court of Justice or Out of Court. Tenth Edition 420 pages Price 18s. net.   1935

"What strikes one most on reading the book is the excellent combination of clearness of expression and conciseness"

—*Law Journal*

ROMAN LAW.

☞ A Glossary of Latin words occurring in Roman Law books is printed in **The Concise Law Dictionary.** (See p 14, *ante*)

HARRIS'S Institutes of Gaius and Justinian. With copious References arranged in Parallel Columns, also Chronological and Analytical Tables, Lists of Laws, &c., &c. Primarily designed for the use of Students preparing for Examination at Oxford, Cambridge, and the Inns of Court By F Harris, B C L., M.A , Barrister-at-Law. Third Edition. 223 pages. Price 6s. net.

JACKSON'S Justinian's Digest, Book 20, with an English Translation and an Essay on the Law of Mortgage in the Roman Law. By T. C. Jackson, B.A., LL.B., Barrister-at-Law. 98 pages. Price 7s. 6d net

SALKOWSKI'S Institutes and History of Roman Private Law. With Catena of Texts By Dr Carl Salkowski, Professor of Laws, Konigsberg. Translated and Edited by E E Whitfield, M A Oxon 1076 pages. Price £1 12s. net

HUNTER'S Introduction to the Study of Roman Law and the Institutes of Justinian. New Edition By F H Lawson, Barrister-at-Law 222 pages Price 10s. net.   1934

"Hunter's Introduction has become a student's classic."

— *Law Notes*

"A beginner's book distinguished by its ease, clarity and learning"

GARSIA'S Roman Law in a Nutshell. With a selection of questions set at Bar Examinations. By M Garsia, Barrister-at-Law. Second Edition. 96 pages. Price 4s. net   1931
With this cram book and the small Hunter or Kelke the examinations can be passed

FARRIN'S Questions and Answers on Roman Law. 118 pages   Price 5s net.   1932

SALE OF GOODS.

WILLIS'S Law of Contract of Sale. Contained in a Course of Six Lectures delivered by WILLIAM WILLIS, one of His Majesty's Counsel, at the request of the Council of Legal Education   Third Edition, with the text of the Sale of Goods Act. By W. N. HIBBERT, LL D   176 pages   Price 10s. net   1929
"Those who are familiar with the same author's lectures on Negotiable Securities will find here the same clear grasp of principles and the same luminous explanation of the law"
—*Irish Law Times*

"A careful study of these lectures will greatly facilitate the study of the Act "—*Law Notes*

BALFOUR'S Law of the Sale of Goods in a Nutshell. By J. A. BALFOUR, Barrister-at-Law.   40 pages   Price 2s. 6d net   1934
Including some leading cases on Sale of Goods

STATUTES.

(And see Interpretation)

MAXWELL on the Interpretation of Statutes. By Sir PETER BENSON MAXWELL, late Chief Justice of the Straits Settlements. Eighth Edition   By Sir GILBERT JACKSON, late Puisne Justice of the High Court at Madras. 362 pages   Price £1 12s net. 1937
"This is an admirable book, excellent in its method and arrangement, and clear and thorough in its treatment of the different questions involved "—*Law Magazine*
"The whole book is very readable as well as instructive."
—*Solicitors' Journal*

CRAIES on Statute Law. With Appendices containing the Popular and Short Titles of certain Statutes, and the Interpretation Act, 1889. Fourth

Edition. By WALTER S. SCOTT, K.C , of the Alberta
Bar. 536 pages. Price £1 17s 6d. net.   · 1936
"Both the profession and students will find this work of great
assistance as a guide in that difficult branch of our law, namely
the construction of Statutes "—*Law Times*

TORTS.

**WILSHERE'S Outline of the Law of Contracts and
Torts.** By A. M WILSHERE, Barrister-at-Law.
Fourth Edition   158 pages. Price 7s. 6d. net. 1936
"Of great use to students for revision purposes "—*Law Notes.*

WINFIELD'S Textbook of the Law of Tort. By
P. H WINFIELD, LL.D , Professor of English Law,
Cambridge   709 pages   Price £1 10s net.   1937
"We can confidently predict that it will be recognized by the
Bar and the law teachers as an outstanding legal authority,
perhaps even the bench will be prepared to cite it without
waiting for its author's decease But those who will greet it
most warmly are the students, for Dr Winfield writes with an
infectious enthusiasm which will stir even the dullest of them."
—*Law Quarterly Review*

"The book is fresh and vivid Thought and expression have
each done their part to stimulate students of all ages to renewed
interest in an interesting and extensive subject A perusal of any
of the twenty-eight chapters will show that this is so No chapter
is too long, and each is clear, cogent, and arresting "—*Law Times*

WINFIELD'S Cases on the Law of Tort. By P. H
WINFIELD, LL D., Professor of English Law,
Cambridge 303 pages Price 15s. net   1938
This selection of seventy-seven cases, with notes, while designed
primarily as a companion volume to the author's Textbook,
will be found useful by all students The method adopted is
to set out in a headnote the principle of law involved, followed
by a short summary of the facts, and a verbatim extract from
the judgment
"The work has all the qualities of learning, lucidity and
originality associated with the name of the author "
—*Law Notes*

SALMOND'S Law of Torts. A Treatise on the English
Law of Liability for Civil Injuries.   Ninth
Edition   By W. T. S. STALLYBRASS, Barrister-at-
Law. 669 pages. Price £1 10s net   1936
"It would be difficult to find any book on the subject of Torts
in which the principles are more clearly and accurately expressed
or the case law more usefully referred to "—*Solicitors' Journal*

Torts—*continued.*

BURRELL'S Epitome of Salmond on Torts. By J. G BURRELL, Barrister-at-Law Price 8s net. 1937

"This work has been well done, and the principles and leading cases are set out clearly and accurately "—*Law Notes*

CONYERS' Torts in a Nutshell. With Epitomes of Leading Cases. By A. J CONYERS Second Edition. 113 pages Price 4s. net 1936

PADLEY'S Questions and Answers on Torts. By C. S PADLEY. 108 pages Price 5s net 1936

"The Questions and Answers series are not intended to take the place of the standard text-books, in fact, references to them are given after each answer But as an aid to revision, and as a means of training the Student's mind along the kind of line it will have to follow in examinations, particularly for the Bar, they are invaluable when as competently prepared as this book has been We recommend it without reservation to all Bar students: it need not be despised even by the ambitious and thorough worker to whom cram books are normally anathema "—*Law Notes*

TRUSTEES.

The Trustee's Handbook. Containing his Powers, Duties and Liabilities, the Investment of Trust Funds, and the Powers of a Tenant for Life. Reprinted from Snell's Equity, Williams' Real Property, etc. Third Edition. 113 pages Price 3s 6d. net. 1936

WILLS AND SUCCESSION.

PARRY on Succession, Testate and Intestate. By D. HUGHES PARRY, Barrister-at-Law, Professor of English Law in the University of London. 296 pages. Price 15s. net. 1937

Including Administration of Assets and Death Duties A textbook for the LL B and Solicitors' Final examinations

" As editor of Williams on Executors he is responsible for the leading practitioners' Treatise on Succession, and we forecast that the present work will prove to be the leading students' text-book on that subject '—*Law Quarterly Review*

" He has contrived to make the whole subject full of interest to students He has the late Professor Maitland s priceless faculty of ' making dry bones live' "—*Jl Pub Teachers of Law*

Printed in Great Britain by The Eastern Press, Ltd , London and Reading

5000/1/39

CPSIA information can be obtained at www.ICGtesting.com
Printed in the USA
LVOW101955230412

278799LV00013B/76/P